Mobile Application Development: JavaScript Frameworks

Enhance your JavaScript skills by venturing into the domain of developing mobile applications

A course in three modules

BIRMINGHAM - MUMBAI

Mobile Application Development: JavaScript Frameworks

Published on: September 2016

Production reference: 1200117

Published by Packt Publishing Ltd.
Livery Place
35 Livery Street
Birmingham B3 2PB, UK.

ISBN 978-1-78712-995-5

www.packtpub.com

Credits

Authors

Hazem Saleh

Ethan Holmes

Tom Bray

Sani Yusuf

Reviewers

Raymond, Xie Liming

Ranganadh Paramkusam

Juris Vecvanags

Soliury

Luca Mezzalira

Content Development Editor

Amedh Pohad

Graphics

Kirk D'Penha

Production Coordinator

Shantanu N. Zagade

Module 1: JavaScript Mobile Application Development

Module 2: Getting Started with React Native

Module 3: Ionic Framework By Example

Preface

Mobile development is one of the hottest trends and an essentiality in today's software industry. As you might have noticed, almost every popular website today has its own equivalent mobile application version to allow its current users to access the website's functions from their mobiles and cater to a large number of users who don't have personal computers. Added to this, with the powerful hardware specification and computing capability of today's smart phones, they have become real competitors to personal computers, and many people now prefer to use their smart phones for their daily activities (such as checking the current news, capturing videos and posting them on Facebook and YouTube, and checking e-mails), instead of using their personal computers.

This Learning Path course will help you explore various mobile application development technologies such as jQuery, ReactJS, and Ionic. You'll go through the course at full speed and land into a surprise at the end that will help you counter real-world security threats on mobile applications.

What this learning path covers

*Module 1, JavaScript Mobile Application Development, This module is the learning resource to use when you want to efficiently develop your own mobile applications using Apache Cordova as the platform for your HTML, CSS, and JavaScript. In order to develop good-looking mobile applications, this module also utilizes jQuery Mobile. jQuery Mobile is one of the best available frameworks for developing mobile-friendly web applications. After finishing this module, you should be able to develop your very own mobile application on different mobile platforms using only JavaScript, without having to learn the native programming languages of every mobile platform.

Module 2, Getting Started with React Native, This module will show you all the advantages of true native development that React Native has without the steep learning curve, leveraging the knowledge you already have. We do this by getting you up and running quickly with a sample application. Next, we'll introduce you to the fundamentals of creating components and explain how React Native works under the hood. Once you have established a solid foundation, you will dive headfirst into developing a real-world application from start to finish. Along the way, we will demonstrate how to create multiple screens and navigate between them, use layout and style native UI components, and access native APIs such as local storage and geolocation. Finally, we tackle the advanced topic of Native modules, which demonstrates that there are truly no limits to what you can do with React Native.

Module 3, Ionic Framework By Example, This module shows you how to get started with Ionic framework immediately. But it doesn't just give you instructions and then expect you to follow them. Instead it demonstrates what Ionic is capable of through three practical projects you can follow and build yourself. From a basic to-do list app, a London tourist app, to a complete social media app, all three projects have been designed to help you learn Ionic at its very best. From setting up your project to developing on both the server side and front end, and best practices for testing and debugging your projects, you'll quickly become a better mobile developer, delivering high performance mobile apps that look awesome. Ionic Framework by Example is for people who don't want to learn now, build later – it's for people who want to learn and build at the same time – so they can meet today's mobile development challenges head on and deliver better products than anyone else.

What you need for this learning path
Module 1:

For this module, you should have basic knowledge of the common web technologies (HTML, CSS, and JavaScript). It is also highly recommended that you learn the basics of jQuery and jQuery Mobile in order to be familiar with the code examples. A quick introduction to jQuery and jQuery Mobile can be found at http://www.w3schools.com/jquery/ and http://www.w3schools.com/jquerymobile/, respectively.

Module 2:

The software requirements for this module are as follows:

* Xcode
* Command Line Tools

- npm 2.x
- JDK
- Android SDK

Module 3:

Firstly, you will need a Windows, Linux, or Mac computer to follow the code samples in this module. A beyond basic or intermediate knowledge of JavaScript and HTML5 is certainly essential to understand concepts discussed in this module. A basic understanding of Cordova is expected at the very least. You are expected to also have an idea of how to issue commands in a terminal window. You should also have access to a working Internet connection, and a Google account is necessary for *Chapter 9, Connecting to Firebase.*

Who this learning path is for

This Learning Path is for JavaScript web developers looking to develop mobile applications using various JavaScript descendent technologies. It is for those who want to learn how to build fast, good-looking, native mobile applications using the skills they already have. If you are already using React on the web, then you will be able to quickly get up and running with React Native for iOS and Android. See Ionic in action - and find out how it can transform the way you build mobile apps. If you're a JavaScript web developer, you'll be building great projects in no time.

Reader feedback

Feedback from our readers is always welcome. Let us know what you think about this course—what you liked or disliked. Reader feedback is important for us as it helps us develop titles that you will really get the most out of.

To send us general feedback, simply e-mail feedback@packtpub.com, and mention the course's title in the subject of your message.

If there is a topic that you have expertise in and you are interested in either writing or contributing to a course, see our author guide at www.packtpub.com/authors.

Customer support

Now that you are the proud owner of a Packt course, we have a number of things to help you to get the most from your purchase.

Downloading the example code

You can download the example code files for this course from your account at `http://www.packtpub.com`. If you purchased this course elsewhere, you can visit `http://www.packtpub.com/support` and register to have the files e-mailed directly to you.

You can download the code files by following these steps:

1. Log in or register to our website using your e-mail address and password.
2. Hover the mouse pointer on the **SUPPORT** tab at the top.
3. Click on **Code Downloads & Errata**.
4. Enter the name of the course in the **Search** box.
5. Select the course for which you're looking to download the code files.
6. Choose from the drop-down menu where you purchased this course from.
7. Click on **Code Download**.

You can also download the code files by clicking on the **Code Files** button on the course's webpage at the Packt Publishing website. This page can be accessed by entering the course's name in the **Search** box. Please note that you need to be logged in to your Packt account.

Once the file is downloaded, please make sure that you unzip or extract the folder using the latest version of:

- WinRAR / 7-Zip for Windows
- Zipeg / iZip / UnRarX for Mac
- 7-Zip / PeaZip for Linux

The code bundle for the course is also hosted on GitHub at `https://github.com/PacktPublishing/Mobile-Application-Development-JavaScript-Frameworks`. We also have other code bundles from our rich catalog of books, courses and videos available at `https://github.com/PacktPublishing/`. Check them out!

Errata

Although we have taken every care to ensure the accuracy of our content, mistakes do happen. If you find a mistake in one of our courses—maybe a mistake in the text or the code—we would be grateful if you could report this to us. By doing so, you can save other readers from frustration and help us improve subsequent versions of this course. If you find any errata, please report them by visiting http://www.packtpub.com/submit-errata, selecting your course, clicking on the **Errata Submission Form** link, and entering the details of your errata. Once your errata are verified, your submission will be accepted and the errata will be uploaded to our website or added to any list of existing errata under the Errata section of that title.

To view the previously submitted errata, go to https://www.packtpub.com/books/content/support and enter the name of the course in the search field. The required information will appear under the **Errata** section.

Piracy

Piracy of copyrighted material on the Internet is an ongoing problem across all media. At Packt, we take the protection of our copyright and licenses very seriously. If you come across any illegal copies of our works in any form on the Internet, please provide us with the location address or website name immediately so that we can pursue a remedy.

Please contact us at copyright@packtpub.com with a link to the suspected pirated material.

We appreciate your help in protecting our authors and our ability to bring you valuable content.

Questions

If you have a problem with any aspect of this course, you can contact us at questions@packtpub.com, and we will do our best to address the problem.

Module 1

JavaScript Mobile Application Development

Create neat cross-platform mobile apps using Apache Cordova and jQuery Mobile

1
An Introduction to Apache Cordova

In this chapter, we will discover the world of Apache Cordova and cover the following topics:

- What Apache Cordova is
- The differences between the different mobile development approaches (mobile web, hybrid mobile, and native mobile applications)
- Why you should use Apache Cordova to develop your mobile applications
- The basics of Apache Cordova architecture

Finally, we will have a quick overview of the current APIs of Apache Cordova 3.

What is Apache Cordova?

The Apache Cordova project is an Apache open source project that targets the creation of native mobile applications using common web technologies such as **HyperText Markup Language (HTML)**, **Cascading Style Sheets (CSS)**, and JavaScript. It offers a set of JavaScript APIs, which provide access to a number of natively built core plugins. Cordova offers many core APIs, some of which grant the ability to perform the following:

- Process the device contact lists
- Process files on the device storage
- Capture a photo using the device camera
- Get a photo from the device gallery
- Record voice using the device microphone

- Get device direction using the device compass
- Retrieve the device locale
- Find out the device location
- Get the device motion
- Get the device connection information

Cordova supports a wide variety of different mobile platforms such as:

- Android
- iOS
- Windows platform:
    - Windows Phone 7 (this support will be removed soon in Cordova Version 3.7)
    - Windows Phone 8
    - Windows 8
- BlackBerry
- Tizen
- Web OS
- Firefox OS
- Bada
- Ubuntu

The Apache Cordova official API documentation is at `http://docs.cordova.io`.

You can also refer to the following GitHub repositories to find the source code of Apache Cordova implementations on the different platforms:

- Cordova for Android (`https://github.com/apache/cordova-android`)
- Cordova for iOS (`https://github.com/apache/cordova-ios`)
- Cordova for Windows 8 (`https://github.com/apache/cordova-wp8`)
- Cordova for BlackBerry (`https://github.com/apache/cordova-blackberry`)
- Cordova for Tizen (`https://github.com/apache/cordova-tizen`)
- Cordova for Web OS (`https://github.com/apache/cordova-webos`)

- Cordova for Firefox OS (`https://github.com/apache/cordova-firefoxos`)
- Cordova for Bada (`https://github.com/apache/cordova-bada`)
- Cordova for Ubuntu (`https://github.com/apache/cordova-ubuntu`)

You will find it very useful to know about GitHub, which is a web-based hosting service for software development projects that use the Git revision control system. GitHub offers both paid plans for private repositories and free accounts for open source projects. The site was launched in 2008 by Tom Preston-Werner, Chris Wanstrath, and PJ Hyett.

The differences between mobile web, hybrid mobile, and native mobile applications

It is very important to understand the differences between mobile web, hybrid mobile, and native mobile applications. Mobile web application(s) can be accessed using the web browser and are designed to be responsive. Responsive means that they can adapt their views in order to be displayed properly on different resolutions of mobile and tablet devices. Mobile web applications usually require you to be online in order to use them. They are not real mobile native applications, although they might have the same look and feel as mobile native applications that use the CSS technology. Mobile web applications are, in fact, not uploaded to app stores and do not have the same physical formats of the platform native mobile applications. They use limited native features of the mobile device, such as geolocation and storage features.

Although hybrid and native mobile applications have the same physical formats, they are developed using totally different technologies. Hybrid mobile applications are developed using common web technologies (HTML, CSS, and JavaScript), while native mobile applications are developed using the mobile platform programming language (for example, Java for Android, Objective-C for iOS, and .NET programming language(s) for Windows Phone).

If you are a native mobile application developer, then in order to develop a single native application that can work on the different mobile platforms, you will need to develop your application on one platform and then reimplement its logic on other platforms. Reimplementing the same logic on every platform that you have to support is a pain. This is because you will need to use the mobile platform programming language and handle different types of problems, which you will face on every platform.

Hybrid applications have the great advantage of allowing you to use the same code base (which consists of your HTML, CSS, and JavaScript code) for the different platforms of your application. This means that you write your application code once, and then, you can run it everywhere. Of course, you might need to do specific changes on every platform, but in the end, these changes are mostly minimal. Adding to this advantage, all of your application logic is implemented using a single and neat programming language, which is JavaScript.

The time taken to develop hybrid mobile applications, which run across many mobile platforms, will definitely be shorter. Furthermore, the required resources to implement a hybrid mobile project will be minimized compared to developing native mobile applications. This is because hybrid applications use a unified programming language (JavaScript), while native mobile applications use many non-unified programming languages (such as Objective-C, Java, and C#), which, by definition, require a larger team of developers with different skill sets.

Finally, it is worth mentioning that native mobile applications might be a little bit faster than hybrid applications (assuming that they are implementing the same set of requirements), because native applications are compiled and native code is optimized. However, applying the common best practices in your hybrid applications can definitely increase your application's performance to be as close as the native application. In this module, you will learn how to boost the performance of your hybrid mobile application using Apache Cordova and jQuery Mobile.

If you take a look at the following table, you will find that it summarizes the differences between the three types of mobile applications:

	Mobile web	Hybrid application	Native application
Uploaded to app store	No	Yes	Yes
Used technologies	JavaScript, CSS, and HTML		The native programming language of the platform
Complexity	Normal	Normal	High
Cross-platform mobiles support	Yes	Yes	No
Device native features	Partial	Full (thanks to Hybrid application frameworks such as Apache Cordova).	Full
Performance (assuming following best practices)	Very good		Excellent

This table summarizes the key differences between mobile web, hybrid mobile, and native mobile applications.

 Apache Cordova is currently one of the most popular frameworks for building Hybrid applications.

From the developers' perspective, if you are a web developer, then creating hybrid applications using Apache Cordova is a great option for you as you will not have to spend time learning JavaScript, CSS, and HTML. Using your existing skill set with Apache Cordova allows you to develop cross-platform mobile applications in less time.

If you are a native developer, then spending some time learning the common web technologies will add great value and have an impact on your work. This is because after acquiring these skills along with Apache Cordova, you will be able to develop cross-platform mobile application(s) in less time and effort compared to the time and effort you would spend in order to develop the same application(s) on every platform using native programming languages.

Why you should use Cordova

In order to understand the importance of using Apache Cordova, you first need to understand the current challenges of mobile development, which are summarized as follows:

- Every mobile platform has its own programming philosophy
- Every mobile platform has its own set of unique problems
- Developing, testing, and maintaining native application(s) on different mobile platforms is expensive

One of the biggest challenges of current mobile development is that every mobile platform has its own programming philosophy. There are various programming languages and tools that are required in order to develop mobile applications on the different platforms. For example, if you want to develop a native mobile application on Android, you will need to use Java as the programming language and Eclipse or IntelliJ (or another equivalent Java IDE) as an **Integrated Development Environment (IDE)**. On the other hand, if you want to develop a native mobile application in iOS, you will need to use Objective-C as the programming language and Xcode or JetBrains AppCode as the programming IDE. Finally, if you want to develop a Windows platform mobile application, you will need to use a .NET programming language and Visual Studio as the IDE.

As a result of this previous challenge, developing, testing and maintaining a single application that has different implementations on mobile platforms is really hard and costly. You will have many code bases that are usually inconsistent, because every code base will be written in a different language by developers from different backgrounds. This is because it is really hard to find a single developer who is aware of all of these programming languages and tools.

 Using an IDE to develop mobile applications is not mandatory. However, it is recommended as it speeds up the process of application development and testing.

Adding to these challenges, handling the incompatible behaviors of mobile platforms is a challenge that cannot be ignored. One of the problems that you might face when you develop your native Android application on iOS is that you cannot send SMS messages directly using the platform API without launching the native platform SMS application to the user. On the other hand, in Android, you can send SMS messages using the platform API directly from your application code. This means that you will have the burden of not only implementing your application logic on the different platforms, but you might also need to implement different workarounds using different programming languages in order to have a consistent behavior of your application as much as you can across the mobile platforms.

Using Apache Cordova will reduce the complexity of these challenges. It will give you the ability to use a single programming language (JavaScript) to write your application on the different mobile platforms; you won't need to have a big set of programming languages anymore after using Apache Cordova. Apache Cordova gives you the ability to have a common code base for all of the implementations of your application on the different mobile platforms. This means that the complexity of developing, testing, and maintaining your mobile application will be greatly reduced.

Having a single code base that is developed using JavaScript gives a great flexibility for mobile developers to handle the unique problems of every mobile platform. This puts everything neatly in a centralized place in the code. This makes your application code more readable and maintainable.

Cordova architecture

The following diagram includes the main components of an Apache Cordova application (HTML, CSS, and JavaScript files). It can also contain helper files (such as application's JSON resource bundle files). Here, HTML files include JavaScript and CSS files. In order to access a device's native feature, JavaScript application objects (or functions) call Apache Cordova APIs.

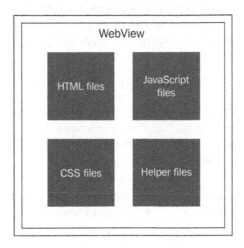

Apache Cordova creates a single screen in the native application; this screen contains only a single WebView that consumes the available space on the device screen. Apache Cordova uses the native application's WebView in order to load the application's HTML and its related JavaScript and CSS files.

It is important to note that WebView is a component that is used to display a web page or content (basically HTML) in the application window. We can simply say that it is an embedded mobile web browser inside your native application that allows you to display the web content.

When the application launches, Apache Cordova loads the application's default startup page (usually `index.html`) in the application's WebView and then passes the control to the WebView, allowing the user to interact with the application. Application users can interact with the application by doing many things such as entering data in input fields, clicking on action buttons, and viewing results in the application's WebView.

Thanks to this technique and because WebView is a native component that provides web content rendering, users feel that they are interacting with a native application screen if the application's CSS is designed to have the mobile platform look and feel.

> WebView has an implementation in all the major mobile platforms. For example, in Android, WebView refers to the `android.webkit.WebView` class. In iOS, however, it refers to the `UIWebView` class that belongs to the `System/Library/Frameworks/UIKit` framework. In the Windows Phone platform, meanwhile, it refers to the `WebView` class that belongs to the `Windows.UI.Xaml.Controls` classes.

In order to allow you to access a mobile's native functions such as audio recording or camera photo capture, Apache Cordova provides a suite of JavaScript APIs that developers can use from their JavaScript code, as shown in the following diagram:

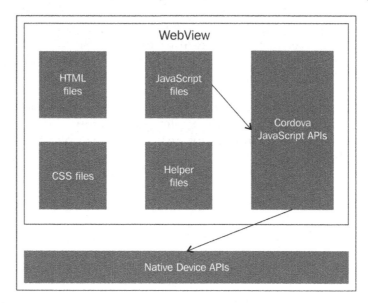

The calls to Apache Cordova JavaScript APIs are translated to the native device API calls using a special bridge layer. In Apache Cordova, the device native APIs are accessed from Apache Cordova plugins.

 You will learn how to develop your own custom Cordova plugin in *Chapter 6, Developing Custom Cordova Plugins*.

The beautiful thing behind this approach is that you can use a unified API interface in order to perform a specific native function (such as camera photo capturing or audio recording) transparently across the various mobile platforms. It is important to note that in order to perform these native functions as a native developer, you will need to call completely different native APIs that are usually implemented using different native programming languages. All of the Cordova JavaScript-unified APIs and their corresponding native code implementations are implemented using plugins. We will illustrate Cordova plugins in much more detail in *Chapter 6, Developing Custom Cordova Plugins*.

If you are interested to know what will happen when a call is performed to a Cordova JavaScript API, then we can take a look at a complete example for a Cordova API call under Android and Windows Phone platforms. In order to get a complete picture, you simply call the following Cordova JavaScript API:

```
navigator.camera.getPicture(onSuccess, onFail, { quality: 50,
    destinationType: Camera.DestinationType.DATA_URL
});

function onSuccess(imageData) {
    var image = document.getElementById('myImage');
    image.src = "data:image/jpeg;base64," + imageData;
}

function onFail(message) {
    alert('Failed because: ' + message);
}
```

As shown in preceding code snippet, a simple call to the `getPicture()` method of the `camera` object is performed with the following three parameters:

- `onSuccesscallback`: This parameter is called if the `getPicture` operation succeeds.

- `onFailcallback`: This parameter is called if the `getPicture` operation fails.

- { quality: 50, destinationType: Camera.DestinationType.
  DATA_URL }: This is a JavaScript object that contains the configuration
  parameters. In our example, only the two parameters, quality, which refers
  to the quality of the output picture (it should be a value from 0 to 100),
  and destinationType, which refers to the format of the return value, are
  specified. It can have one of the three values: DATA_URL, which means that
  the format of the returned image will be Base64-encoded string, FILE_URI,
  which means that the image file URI will be returned, or NATIVE_URI, which
  refers to the image native URI.

As we set destinationType to Camera.DestinationType.DATA_URL, the parameter
of onSuccess will represent the Base-64 encoded string of the captured image.

This simple call to the getPicture() method of the camera object calls the following
Android Java native code. Please note that this code is the actual code for the Apache
Cordova Camera plugin Version 3. If you are a native Android developer, then the
following two code snippets will look very familiar to you:

```
public void takePicture(int returnType, int encodingType) {
    // Code is omitted for simplicity ...

    // Display camera
    Intent intent = new Intent("android.media.action.IMAGE_CAPTURE");

    // Specify file so that large image is captured and returned
    File photo = createCaptureFile(encodingType);

    intent.putExtra(android.provider.MediaStore.EXTRA_OUTPUT, Uri.
fromFile(photo));
    this.imageUri = Uri.fromFile(photo);

    if (this.cordova != null) {
        this.cordova.startActivityForResult((CordovaPlugin) this,
intent, (CAMERA + 1) * 16 + returnType + 1);
    }
}
```

As shown in the previous code, in order to open a camera in an Android device, you need to start the "android.media.action.IMAGE_CAPTURE" intent and receive the result back using the startActivityForResult() API of the Android Activity class. In order to receive the image capture intent result in Android, your Android Activity class needs to implement the onActivityResult() callback, as shown in the following Apache Cordova Android Camera plugin code:

```
public void onActivityResult(int requestCode, int resultCode, Intent
intent) {
    // Get src and dest types from request code
    int srcType = (requestCode / 16) - 1;
    int destType = (requestCode % 16) - 1;
    int rotate = 0;

    // If CAMERA
    if (srcType == CAMERA) {

        // If image available
        if (resultCode == Activity.RESULT_OK) {
            // ... Code is omitted for simplicity ...

            Bitmap bitmap = null;
            Uri uri = null;

            // If sending base64 image back
            if (destType == DATA_URL) {
                bitmap = getScaledBitmap(FileHelper.
stripFileProtocol(imageUri.toString()));

                // ... Code is omitted for simplicity ...

                this.processPicture(bitmap);
            }

            // If sending filename back
            else if (destType == FILE_URI || destType == NATIVE_
URI) {
                if (this.saveToPhotoAlbum) {
                    Uri inputUri = getUriFromMediaStore();
```

```
                                //Just because we have a media URI doesn't
      mean we have a real file, we need to make it
                                uri = Uri.fromFile(new File(FileHelper.
      getRealPath(inputUri, this.cordova)));
                            } else {
                                uri = Uri.fromFile(new File(DirectoryManager.
      getTempDirectoryPath(this.cordova.getActivity()), System.
      currentTimeMillis() + ".jpg"));
                            }

                            if (uri == null) {
                                this.failPicture("Error capturing image - no
      media storage found.");
                            }

                            // ... Code is omitted for simplicity ...
                            // Send Uri back to JavaScript for viewing image
                            this.callbackContext.success(uri.toString());
                        }

                        // ... Code is omitted for simplicity ...
                    } catch (IOException e) {
                        e.printStackTrace();
                        this.failPicture("Error capturing image.");
                    }
                }

                // If cancelled
                else if (resultCode == Activity.RESULT_CANCELED) {
                    this.failPicture("Camera cancelled.");
                }

                // If something else
                else {
                    this.failPicture("Did not complete!");
                }
            }
        }
```

If the camera capture operation succeeds, then `resultCode == Activity.RESULT_OK` will be `true`, and if the user requires the result of the captured image as a Base-64 encoded string, then the captured bitmap image is retrieved and processed in the `processPicture(bitmap)` method. As shown in the following code snippet, `processPicture(bitmap)` compresses the bitmap image and then converts it to a byte array, which is encoded to Base-64 array. This is then finally converted to a string that is returned to the JavaScript Cordova client using `this.callbackContext.success()`. We will illustrate Android `CallbackContext` in more detail later in this module.

If the user requires the result of the captured image as a file or native URI string, then the file URI of the image file is retrieved and sent to the JavaScript Cordova client using `this.callbackContext.success()`.

```
public void processPicture(Bitmap bitmap) {
    ByteArrayOutputStream jpeg_data = new ByteArrayOutputStream();
    try {
        if (bitmap.compress(CompressFormat.JPEG, mQuality, jpeg_data))
    {
            byte[] code = jpeg_data.toByteArray();
            byte[] output = Base64.encode(code, Base64.DEFAULT);
            String js_out = new String(output);
            this.callbackContext.success(js_out);
            js_out = null;
            output = null;
            code = null;
        }
    } catch (Exception e) {
        this.failPicture("Error compressing image.");
    }
    jpeg_data = null;
}
```

In Android native development, an Android `Activity` class is generally a thing that the user can do. The `Activity` class is also responsible for the creation of a window for you in which you can place your **User Interface (UI)** while using the `setContentView()` API. An Android `Intent` is an abstract description of an operation to be performed so that it can be used with `startActivity` or `startActivityForResult` to launch an activity, as shown in the previous example of Camera photo capturing.

If you are using Microsoft Windows Platform 7 or 8, for example, the call to the `getPicture()` method of the `camera` object will call the following Windows Phone C# native code. Please note that this code is the actual code for Apache Cordova Camera Windows Phone plugin. If you are a native Windows Phone developer, the next two code snippets will look very familiar to you:

```
CameraCaptureTask cameraTask;

public void takePicture(string options)
{
    // ... Code is omitted for simplifying things ...

    if (cameraOptions.PictureSourceType == CAMERA)
    {
```

```
        cameraTask = new CameraCaptureTask();
        cameraTask.Completed += onCameraTaskCompleted;
        cameraTask.Show();
    }


    // ... Code is omitted for simplifying things ...
}
```

As shown in the preceding code, in order to open a camera in a Windows Phone device, you need to create an instance of CameraCaptureTask and call the Show() method. In order to receive the image capture result on the Windows Phone platform, you need to define an event handler that will be executed once the camera task completes. In the previous code, onCameraTaskCompleted is the event handler that will be executed once the camera task completes. The following code snippet shows the onCameraTaskCompleted handler code with its helper methods:

```
public void onCameraTaskCompleted(object sender, PhotoResult e)
{
    // ... Code is omitted for simplifying things ...
    switch (e.TaskResult)
    {
        case TaskResult.OK:
            try
            {
                string imagePathOrContent = string.Empty;

                if (cameraOptions.DestinationType == FILE_URI)
                {
                    // Save image in media library
                    if (cameraOptions.SaveToPhotoAlbum)
                    {
                        MediaLibrary library = new MediaLibrary();
                        Picture pict = library.SavePicture(e.
OriginalFileName, e.ChosenPhoto); // to save to photo-roll ...
                    }

                    int orient = ImageExifHelper.
getImageOrientationFromStream(e.ChosenPhoto);
                    int newAngle = 0;

                    // ... Code is omitted for simplifying things ...
```

```
                    Stream rotImageStream = ImageExifHelper.
RotateStream(e.ChosenPhoto, newAngle);

                    // we should return stream position back after
saving stream to media library
                    rotImageStream.Seek(0, SeekOrigin.Begin);

                    WriteableBitmap image = PictureDecoder.
DecodeJpeg(rotImageStream);

                    imagePathOrContent = this.
SaveImageToLocalStorage(image, Path.GetFileName(e.OriginalFileName));
              }
              else if (cameraOptions.DestinationType == DATA_URL)
              {
                    imagePathOrContent = this.GetImageContent(e.
ChosenPhoto);
              }
              else
              {
                    // TODO: shouldn't this happen before we launch
the camera-picker?
                    DispatchCommandResult(new
PluginResult(PluginResult.Status.ERROR, "Incorrect option:
destinationType"));
                    return;
              }

              DispatchCommandResult(new PluginResult(PluginResult.
Status.OK, imagePathOrContent));

        }
        catch (Exception)
        {
              DispatchCommandResult(new PluginResult(PluginResult.
Status.ERROR, "Error retrieving image."));
        }
        break;

        // ... Code is omitted for simplifying things ...
    }
}
```

If the camera capture operation succeeds, then `e.TaskResult == TaskResult.OK` will be `true`, and if the user requires the result of the captured image as a Base-64 encoded string, then the captured image is retrieved and processed in the `GetImageContent(stream)` method. The `GetImageContent(stream)` function, which is shown in the following code snippet, converts the image to a Base-64 encoded string that is returned to the JavaScript Cordova client using the `DispatchCommandResult()` method. We will illustrate the `DispatchCommandResult()` method in more detail later on in this module.

If the user requires the result of the captured image as a file URI string, then the file URI of the image file is retrieved using the `SaveImageToLocalStorage()` method (whose implementation is shown in the following code snippet) and is then sent to the JavaScript Cordova client using `DispatchCommandResult()`:

```
private string GetImageContent(Stream stream)
{
    int streamLength = (int)stream.Length;
    byte[] fileData = new byte[streamLength + 1];
    stream.Read(fileData, 0, streamLength);

    //use photo's actual width & height if user doesn't provide
width & height
    if (cameraOptions.TargetWidth < 0 &&
cameraOptions.TargetHeight < 0)
    {
        stream.Close();
        return Convert.ToBase64String(fileData);
    }
    else
    {
        // resize photo
        byte[] resizedFile = ResizePhoto(stream, fileData);
        stream.Close();
        return Convert.ToBase64String(resizedFile);
    }
}

private string SaveImageToLocalStorage(WriteableBitmap image,
string imageFileName)
{
    // ... Code is omitted for simplifying things ...
```

```
    var isoFile =
IsolatedStorageFile.GetUserStoreForApplication();
    if (!isoFile.DirectoryExists(isoFolder))
    {
        isoFile.CreateDirectory(isoFolder);
    }

    string filePath = System.IO.Path.Combine("///" + isoFolder +
"/", imageFileName);

    using (var stream = isoFile.CreateFile(filePath))
    {
        // resize image if Height and Width defined via options
        if (cameraOptions.TargetHeight > 0 && cameraOptions.
TargetWidth > 0)
        {
            image.SaveJpeg(stream, cameraOptions.TargetWidth,
cameraOptions.TargetHeight, 0, cameraOptions.Quality);
        }
        else
        {
            image.SaveJpeg(stream, image.PixelWidth,
image.PixelHeight, 0, cameraOptions.Quality);
        }
    }

    return new Uri(filePath, UriKind.Relative).ToString();
}
```

As you can see from the examples of Android and Windows Phone Platforms, in order to implement a photo capture using the device camera on two mobile platforms, we had to use two different programming languages and deal with totally different APIs. Thanks to Apache Cordova unified programming JavaScript interface, you don't even need to know how every mobile platform is handling the native stuff behind the scene, and you can only focus on implementing your cross-platform mobile application's business logic with a neat unified code base.

By now, you should have been comfortable with knowing and understanding the Apache Cordova architecture. In the upcoming chapters of this module, however, we will explain the bits of Apache Cordova in more detail, and you will acquire a deeper understanding of the Apache Cordova architecture by creating your own custom Cordova plugin in *Chapter 6, Developing Custom Cordova Plugins*.

Overview of Cordova APIs

Currently, Apache Cordova supports the following mobile native functions APIs:

- `Accelerometer`: This allows you to capture the device motion in all directions (x, y, and z)

- `Camera`: This allows you to use the default camera application in order to capture photos

- `Capture`: This allows you to capture audio using the device's audio recording application, capture images using the device's camera application, and capture video using the device's video recording application

- `Compass`: This allows you to get the direction that the device is pointing to

- `Connection`: This provides you with the information about the device's cellular and Wi-Fi connection

- `Contacts`: This allows you to access the device's contacts database, create new contacts in the contacts list, and query the existing device contacts list

- `Device`: This allows you to get the hardware and software information of the device; for example, it allows you to get the device model, receive the platform and its version, and finally, receive the device name

- `Events`: This allows you to listen and create handlers for Apache Cordova life cycle events. These life cycle events are as follows:
  - `deviceready`: This event fires once Apache Cordova is fully loaded
  - `pause`: This event fires if the application is put into the background
  - `resume`: This event fires if the application is resumed from the background
  - `online`: This event fires if the application becomes connected to the Internet
  - `offline`: This event fires if the application becomes disconnected from the Internet
  - `backbutton`: This event fires if the user clicks the device's back button (some mobile devices have a back button, such as Android and Windows Phone devices)
  - `batterycritical`: This event fires if the device's battery power reaches a critical state (that is, reaches the critical-level threshold)

- ○ `batterylow`: This event fires if the device battery power reaches the low-level threshold

- ○ `batterystatus`: This event fires if there is a change in the battery status

- ○ `menubutton`: This event fires if the user presses the device's menu button (the menu button is popular for Android and BlackBerry devices)

- ○ `searchbutton`: This event fires if the user presses the device's search button (the search button can be found in Android devices)

- ○ `startcallbutton`: This event fires when the user presses the start and end call buttons of the device

- ○ `endcallbutton`: This event fires when the user presses the start and end call buttons of the device

- ○ `volumeupbutton`: This event fires when the user presses the volume up and down buttons of the device

- ○ `volumedownbutton`: This event fires when the user presses the volume up and down buttons of the device

- `File`: This allows you to process files (which is to read, write, and navigate filesystem directories), and it is based on the W3C file APIs

- `Geolocation`: This allows you to receive the device's location using GPS or using network signals, and it is based on W3C geolocation APIs

- `Globalization`: This allows you to get the user's locale and perform locale-specific operations

- `InAppBrowser`: This represents a web browser view that is displayed when any call to `window.open()` or a link whose target is set to `"_blank"` is clicked

- `Media`: This allows for the recording of audio files programmatically, without using the device default recording application, as well as playing audio files

- `Notification`: This allows the display of audible notifications such as beeps, the display of tactile notifications such as vibrations, and displaying visual notifications such as the normal device visual messages to the user

- `Splashscreen`: This allows you to display application splash screen

- `Storage`: Apache Cordova provides the following storage capabilities:

    ○ Using the W3C web storage interface which is about `LocalStorage` and `SessionStorage`. It is important to know that local storage is a permanent storage that exists on your device even if your application is closed, while session storage is a temporary storage that is erased when the user session ends, which is when the application is closed.

    ○ Using the full features of relational databases by supporting Web SQL on almost all the platforms. For Windows Phone and Windows Platform, it supports `IndexedDB`, which is currently a W3C standard.

 Although Web SQL is deprecated, it was and still is a powerful specification for creating and working with relational data.

All of these APIs will be illustrated in far more detail, along with examples, as you read this module. It is important to note that not all of these APIs are supported in all the platforms. You will be able to specifically check which ones are not supported in the following list. Also note that this list applies to Apache Cordova Version 3.4, and it might be changed later. The following table shows the unsupported APIs on the different platforms. Please note that X here means unsupported:

	Firefox OS	Tizen	Windows 8	Blackberry 10
Capture API	X	X	X	
Compass	X			
Connection	X			
Contacts		X	X	
Events	X			
File	X	X		
Globalization	X	X	X	X
InAppBrowser	X	X		
Media	X			
Notification	X			
Splashscreen	X	X		
Storage	X			

Summary

In this chapter, you have been given a powerful introduction to Apache Cordova. You now know what Apache Cordova is, and understand the current challenges of today's mobile development and how it can reduce the complexities of these challenges. You should now understand the differences between mobile web, hybrid mobile, and native mobile applications. You should also know the architecture of Cordova and how it works behind the scenes with an example of a photo capture using a camera. Finally, you have an overview of Apache Cordova APIs and what every API does from a high-level point of view.

In the next chapter, you will start the real work with Apache Cordova by developing your first Apache Cordova application from scratch.

2
Developing Your First Cordova Application

In the previous chapter, you had a powerful introduction to Apache Cordova. In this chapter, you will develop, build, and deploy your first Apache Cordova application from scratch. The application you will develop is a Sound Recorder utility that you can use to record your voice or any sound and play it back. In this chapter, you will learn about the following topics:

- Generating your initial Apache Cordova project artifacts by utilizing the Apache Cordova **Command-line Interface (CLI)**
- Developing and building your mobile application from the initial Cordova generated code
- Deploying your developed mobile application to a real Android mobile device to see your application in action

An introduction to Cordova CLI

In order to create, develop, build, and test a Cordova application, you first need to use the Cordova CLI. Using this, you can create new Apache Cordova project(s), build them on mobile platforms such as iOS, Android, Windows Phone, and so on, and run them on real devices or within emulators. Note that in this chapter, we will focus on deploying our Sound Recorder application in Android devices only.

 In the next chapter, we will learn how to deploy our Sound Recorder application in iOS and Windows Phone devices.

Installing Apache Cordova

Before installing Apache Cordova CLI, you need to make sure that you install the following software:

- **Target platform SDK**: For Android, you can download its SDK from `http://developer.android.com/sdk/index.html` (for other platforms, you need to download and install their corresponding SDKs)

- **Node.js**: This is accessible at `http://nodejs.org` and can be downloaded and installed from `http://nodejs.org/download/`

 If you want to know more about the details of configuring Android, iOS, and Windows Phone environments in your development machine, refer to *Chapter 3, Apache Cordova Development Tools*.

After installing Node.js, you should be able to run Node.js or **node package manager** (**npm**) from the command line. In order to install Apache Cordova using npm, run the following command (you can omit `sudo` if you are working in a Windows environment):

```
> sudo npm install -g cordova
```

It's worth mentioning that npm is the official package manager for Node.js and it is written completely in JavaScript. npm is a tool that allows users to install Node.js modules, which are available in the npm registry.

 The `sudo` command allows a privileged Unix user to execute a command as the super user, or as any other user, according to the `sudoers` file. The `sudo` command, by default, requires you to authenticate with a password. Once you are authenticated, you can use the command without a password, by default, for 5 minutes.

After successfully installing Apache Cordova (Version 3.4.0), you should be able to execute Apache Cordova commands from the command line, for example, the following command will show you the current installed version of Apache Cordova:

```
> cordova -version
```

In order to execute the Cordova commands without any problem, you also need to have Apache Ant installed and configured in your operating system.

You can download Apache Ant from `http://ant.apache.org`. The complete instructions on how to install Ant are mentioned at `https://ant.apache.org/manual/install.html`.

Generating our Sound Recorder's initial code

After installing Apache Cordova, we can start creating our Sound Recorder project by executing the following command:

```
> cordova create soundRecorder com.jsmobile.soundrecorder SoundRecorder
```

After successfully executing this command, you will find a message similar to the following one (note that the location path will be different on your machine):

```
Creating a new cordova project with name "SoundRecorder" and id
"com.jsmobile.soundrecorder" at location "/Users/xyz/projects/
soundRecorder"
```

If we analyze the `cordova create` command, we will find that its first parameter represents the path of your project. In this command, a `soundRecorder` directory will be generated for your project under the directory from which the `cordova create` command is executed. The second and third parameters are optional. The second parameter, `com.jsmobile.soundrecorder`, provides your project's namespace (it should be noted that in Android projects, this namespace will be translated to a Java package with this name), and the last parameter, `SoundRecorder`, provides the application's display text. You can edit both these values in the `config. xml` configuration file later, which will be illustrated soon.

The following screenshot shows our `SoundRecorder` project's generated artifacts:

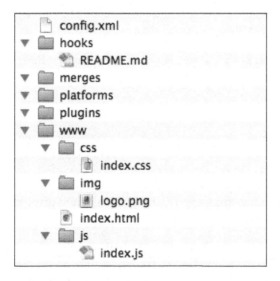

The Sound Recorder's initial structure

As shown in the preceding screenshot, the generated Apache Cordova project contains the following main directories and files:

- www: This directory includes your application's HTML, JavaScript, and CSS code. You will also find the application's starting page (index.html), along with various subdirectories, which are as follows:

    ○ css: This directory includes the default Apache Cordova application's CSS file (index.css)

    ○ js: This directory includes the default Apache Cordova application's JavaScript file (index.js)

    ○ img: This directory includes the default Apache Cordova application's logo file (logo.png)

- config.xml: This file contains the application configuration. The following code snippet shows the initial code of the config.xml file:

```xml
<?xml version='1.0' encoding='utf-8'?>
<widget id="com.jsmobile.soundrecorder" version="0.0.1"
        xmlns="http://www.w3.org/ns/widgets"
        xmlns:cdv="http://cordova.apache.org/ns/1.0">
    <name>SoundRecorder</name>
    <description>
        A sample Apache Cordova application that responds to the
deviceready event.
    </description>
    <author email="dev@cordova.apache.org" href="http://cordova.
io">
        Apache Cordova Team
    </author>
    <content src="index.html" />
    <access origin="*" />
</widget>
```

As shown in the preceding config.xml file, config.xml contains the following elements that are available on all the supported Apache Cordova platforms:

- ○ The <widget> element's id attribute represents the application's namespace identifier as specified in our cordova create command, and the <widget> element's version attribute represents its full version number in the form of major.minor.patch.

- ○ The `<name>` element specifies the application's name.

- ○ The `<description>` and `<author>` elements specify the application's description and author, respectively.

- ○ The `<content>` element (which is optional) specifies the application's starting page that is placed directly under the `www` directory. The default value is `index.html`.

- ○ The `<access>` element(s) defines the set of external domains that the application is allowed to access. The default value is `*`, which means that the application is allowed to access any external server(s).

> Specifying the `<access>` element's origin to `*` is fine during application development, but it is considered a bad practice in production due to security concerns. Note that before moving your application to production, you should review its whitelist and declare its access to specific network domains and subdomains.

There is another element that is not included in the default `config.xml`, and this is the `<preference>` element. The `<preference>` element(s) can be used to set the different preferences of the Cordova application and can work on all or a subset of the Apache Cordova-supported platforms. Take the example of the following code:

```
<preference name="Fullscreen" value="true" />
```

If the `Fullscreen` preference is set to `true`, it means that the application will be in fullscreen mode on all Cordova-supported platforms (by default, this option is set to `false`). It is important to note that not all preferences work on all Cordova-supported platforms. Consider the following example:

```
<preference name="HideKeyboardFormAccessoryBar" value="true"/>
```

If the `HideKeyboardFormAccessoryBar` preference is set to `true`, then the additional helper toolbar, which appears above the device keyboard, will be hidden. This preference works only on iOS and BlackBerry platforms.

- `platforms`: This directory includes the application's supported platforms. After adding a new platform using Apache Cordova CLI, you will find a newly created directory that contains the platform-specific generated code under the `platforms` directory. The `platforms` directory is initially empty because we have not added any platforms yet. We will add support to the Android platform in the next step.

- `plugins`: This directory includes your application's used plugins. If you aren't already aware, a plugin is the mechanism to access the device's native functions in Apache Cordova. After adding a plugin (such as the `Media` plugin) to the project, you will find a newly created directory under the `plugins` directory, which contains the plugin code. Note that we will add three plugins in our Sound Recorder application example.

- `merges`: This directory can be used to override the common resources under the `www` directory. The files placed under the `merges/[platform]` directory will override the matching files (or add new files) under the `www` directory for the specified platform (the `[platform]` value can be iOS, Android, or any other valid supported platform).

- `hooks`: This directory contains scripts that can be used to customize Apache Cordova commands. A hook is a piece of code that executes before and/or after the Apache Cordova command runs.

An insight into the www files

If we look in the `www` directory, we will find that it contains the following three files:

- `index.html`: This file is placed under the application's `www` directory, and it contains the HTML content of the application page

- `index.js`: This file is placed under the `www/js` directory, and it contains a simple JavaScript logic that we will illustrate soon

- `index.css`: This file is placed under the `www/css` directory, and it contains the style classes of the HTML elements

The following code snippet includes the most important part of the `index.html` page:

```
<div class="app">
    <h1>Apache Cordova</h1>
    <div id="deviceready" class="blink">
        <p class="event listening">Connecting to Device</p>
        <p class="event received">Device is Ready</p>
    </div>
</div>
<script type="text/javascript" src="cordova.js"></script>
<script type="text/javascript" src="js/index.js"></script>
<script type="text/javascript">
    app.initialize();
</script>
```

The `index.html` page has a single div `"app"`, which contains a child div `"deviceready"`. The `"deviceready"` div has two paragraph elements, the `"event listening"` and `"event received"` paragraphs. The `"event received"` paragraph is initially hidden as indicated by `index.css`:

```
.event.received {
    background-color:#4B946A;
    display:none;
}
```

In the `index.html` page, there are two main JavaScript-included files, as follows:

- `cordova.js`: This file contains Apache Cordova JavaScript APIs
- `index.js`: This file contains the application's simple logic

Finally, the `index.html` page calls the `initialize()` method of the `app` object. Let's see the details of the `app` object in `index.js`:

```
var app = {
    initialize: function() {
        this.bindEvents();
    },
    bindEvents: function() {
        document.addEventListener('deviceready', this.onDeviceReady,
false);
    },
    onDeviceReady: function() {
        app.receivedEvent('deviceready');
    },
    receivedEvent: function(id) {
        var parentElement = document.getElementById(id);
        var listeningElement = parentElement.querySelector('.
listening');
        var receivedElement =
parentElement.querySelector('.received');

        listeningElement.setAttribute('style', 'display:none;');
        receivedElement.setAttribute('style', 'display:block;');

        console.log('Received Event: ' + id);
    }
};
```

The initialize() method calls the bindEvents() method, which adds an event listener for the 'deviceready' event. When the device is ready, the onDeviceReady() method is called, and this in turn calls the receivedEvent() method of the app object.

In the receivedEvent() method, the "event listening" paragraph is hidden and the "event received" paragraph is shown to the user. This is to display the **Device is Ready** message to the user once Apache Cordova is fully loaded.

 It is important to note that you must not call any Apache Cordova API before the 'deviceready' event fires. This is because the 'deviceready' event fires only once Apache Cordova is fully loaded.

Now you have an Apache Cordova project that has common cross-platform code, so we need to generate a platform-specific code in order to deploy our code on a real device. To generate Android platform code, you need to add the Android platform as follows:

```
> cd soundRecorder
> cordova platform add android
```

In order to add any platform, you need to execute the cordova platform command from the application directory. Note that in order to execute the cordova platform command without problems, you need to perform the following instructions:

- Have Apache Ant installed and configured in your operating system as described in the *Installing Apache Cordova* section
- Make sure that the path to your Android SDK platform tools and the tools directory are added to your operating system's PATH environment variable

After executing the cordova platform add command, you will find a new subdirectory Android added under the soundRecorder/platforms directory. In order to build the project, use the following command:

```
> cordova build
```

Finally, you can run and test the generated Android project in the emulator by executing the following command:

```
> cordova emulate android
```

You might see the **ERROR: No emulator images (avds) found** message flash if no Android AVDs are available in your operating system. So, make sure you create one!

Refer to the *Creating an Android virtual device* section in *Chapter 3, Apache Cordova Development Tools*, to know how to create an Android AVD.

The following screenshot shows our Sound Recorder application's initial screen:

It is recommended that you make your code changes in the root www directory, and not in the platforms/android/assets/www directory (especially if you are targeting multiple platforms) as the platforms directory will be overridden every time you execute the cordova build command, unless you are willing to use Apache Cordova CLI to initialize the project for a single platform only.

Developing Sound Recorder application

After generating the initial application code, it's time to understand what to do next.

Sound Recorder functionality

The following screenshot shows our **Sound Recorder** page:

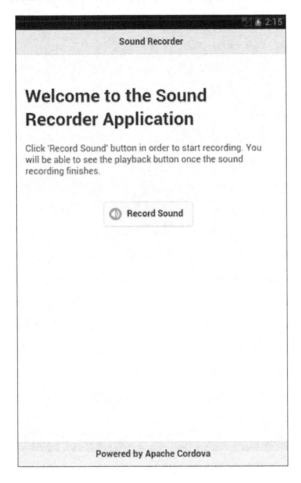

When the user clicks on the **Record Sound** button, they will be able to record their voices; they can stop recording their voices by clicking on the **Stop Recording** button. You can see this in the following screenshot:

As shown in the following screenshot, when the user clicks on the **Playback** button, the recorded voice will be played back:

Sound Recorder preparation

In order to implement this functionality using Apache Cordova, we need to add the following plugins using the indicated commands, which should be executed from the application directory:

- `media`: This plugin is used to record and play back sound files:

  ```
  > cordova plugin add https://git-wip-us.apache.org/repos/asf/
  cordova-plugin-media.git
  ```

- `device`: This plugin is required to access the device information:

  ```
  > cordova plugin add https://git-wip-us.apache.org/repos/asf/
  cordova-plugin-device.git
  ```

- `file`: This plugin is used to access the device's filesystem:

  ```
  > cordova plugin add https://git-wip-us.apache.org/repos/asf/
  cordova-plugin-file.git
  ```

In order to apply these plugins to our Apache Cordova project, we need to run the `cordova build` command again from the `project` directory, as follows:

```
> cordova build
```

Sound Recorder details

Now we are done with the preparation of our Sound Recorder application. Before moving to the code details, let's see the hierarchy of our Sound Recorder application, as shown in the following screenshot:

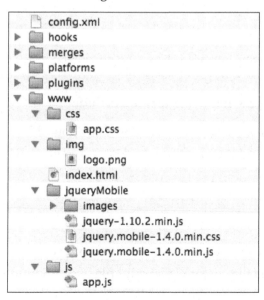

The application's www directory contains the following directories:

- css: This directory contains the custom application CSS file(s)
- img: This directory contains the custom application image file(s)
- js: This directory contains the custom application JavaScript code
- jqueryMobile: This directory (which is a newly added one) contains jQuery Mobile framework files

Finally, the index.html file contains the application's single page whose functionality was illustrated earlier in this section.

 It is important to note that Apache Cordova does not require you to use a JavaScript mobile **User Interface** (**UI**) framework. However, it is recommended that you use a JavaScript mobile UI framework in addition to Apache Cordova. This is in order to facilitate building the application UI and speed up the application development process. The jQuery Mobile framework is one of the best mobile UI frameworks, and as such will be used in all the Apache Cordova applications developed in this module.

Let's see the details of the index.html page of our Sound Recorder application. The following code snippet shows the included files in the page:

```
<link rel="stylesheet" type="text/css" href="css/app.css" />
<link rel="stylesheet" href="jqueryMobile/jquery.mobile-1.4.0.min.
css">
<script src="jqueryMobile/jquery-1.10.2.min.js"></script>
<script src="jqueryMobile/jquery.mobile-1.4.0.min.js"></script>
...
<script type="text/javascript" src="cordova.js"></script>
<script type="text/javascript" src="js/app.js"></script>
```

In the preceding code, the following files are included:

- app.css: This is the custom style file of our Sound Recorder application
- The files required by the jQuery Mobile framework, which are:
    - jquery.mobile-1.4.0.min.css
    - jquery-1.10.2.min.js
    - jquery.mobile-1.4.0.min.js
- cordova.js: This is the Apache Cordova JavaScript API's file
- app.js: This is the custom JavaScript file of our Sound Recorder application

It is important to know that you can download the jQuery Mobile framework files from `http://jquerymobile.com/download/`.

The following code snippet shows the HTML content of our application's single page, whose id is `"main"`:

```
<div data-role="page" id="main">
    <div data-role="header">
        <h1>Sound Recorder</h1>
    </div>
    <div data-role="content">
    <div data-role="fieldcontain">
        <h1>Welcome to the Sound Recorder Application</h1>
        <p>Click 'Record Sound' button in order to start
recording. You will be able to see
            the playback button once the sound recording
finishes.<br/><br/></p>
        <input type="hidden" id="location"/>
        <div class="center-wrapper">
            <input type="button" id="recordSound" data-
icon="audio" value="Record Sound" class="center-button" data-
inline="true"/>
            <input type="button" id="playSound" data-
icon="refresh" value="Playback" class="center-button" data-
inline="true"/><br/>
        </div>

        <div data-role="popup" id="recordSoundDialog" data-
dismissible="false" style="width:250px">
            <div data-role="header">
                <h1>Recording</h1>
            </div>

            <div data-role="content">
                <div class="center-wrapper">
                    <div id="soundDuration"></div>
                    <input type="button" id="stopRecordingSound"
value="Stop Recording"
                                class="center-button" data-
inline="true"/>
                </div>
            </div>
            </div>
        </div>
    </div>
```

```
            <div data-role="footer" data-position="fixed">
                <h1>Powered by Apache Cordova</h1>
            </div>
        </div>
```

Looking at the preceding code, our Sound Recording page ("main") is defined by setting a div's data-role attribute to "page". It has a header defined by setting a div's data-role to "header". It has content defined by setting a div's data-role to "content", which contains the recording and playback buttons.

The content also contains a "recordSoundDialog" pop up, which is defined by setting a div's data-role to "popup". The "recordSoundDialog" pop up has a header and content. The pop-up content displays the recorded audio duration in the "soundDuration" div, and it has a "stopRecordingSound" button that stops recording the sound.

Finally, the page has a footer defined by setting a div's data-role to "footer", which contains a statement about the application.

Now, it's time to learn how we can define event handlers on page HTML elements and use the Apache Cordova API inside our defined event handlers to implement the application's functionality.

The following code snippet shows the page initialization code:

```
(function() {

    $(document).on("pageinit", "#main", function(e) {
            e.preventDefault();

            function onDeviceReady() {
                $("#recordSound").on("tap", function(e) {
                    // Action is defined here ...
                });

                $("#recordSoundDialog").on("popupafterclose",
function(event, ui) {
                    // Action is defined here ...
                });

                $("#stopRecordingSound").on("tap", function(e) {
                    // Action is defined here ...
                });

                $("#playSound").on("tap", function(e) {
                    // Action is defined here ...
```

```
            });
        }

        $(document).on('deviceready', onDeviceReady);

        initPage();
    });

    // Code is omitted here for simplicity

    function initPage() {
        $("#playSound").closest('.ui-btn').hide();
    }
})();
```

In jQuery Mobile, the `"pageinit"` event is called once during page initialization. In this event, the event handlers are defined and the page is initialized. Note that all of the event handlers are defined after the `'deviceready'` event fires. The event handlers are defined for the following:

- Tapping the `"recordSound"` button
- Closing the `"recordSoundDailog"` dialog
- Tapping the `"stopRecordingSound"` button
- Tapping the `"playSound"` button

In `initPage()`, the `"playSound"` button is hidden as no voice has been recorded yet. As you noticed, in order to hide an element in jQuery Mobile, you just need to call its `hide()` method. We can now see the details of each event handler; the next code snippet shows the `"recordSound"` tap event handler:

```
var recInterval;
$("#recordSound").on("tap", function(e) {
    e.preventDefault();

    var recordingCallback = {};

    recordingCallback.recordSuccess = handleRecordSuccess;
    recordingCallback.recordError = handleRecordError;

    startRecordingSound(recordingCallback);

    var recTime = 0;
```

```
        $("#soundDuration").html("Duration: " + recTime + " seconds");

        $("#recordSoundDialog").popup("open");

        recInterval = setInterval(function() {
                                recTime = recTime + 1;
                                $("#soundDuration").html("Duration: "
+ recTime + " seconds");
                                }, 1000);
});
```

The following actions are performed in the `"recordSound"` tap event handler:

1. A call to the `startRecordingSound(recordingCallback)` function is performed. The `startRecordingSound(recordingCallback)` function is a helper function that starts the sound recording process using the Apache Cordova Media API. Its `recordingCallback` parameter represents a JSON object, which has the `recordSuccess` and `recordError` callback attributes. The `recordSuccess` callback will be called if the recording operation is a success, and the `recordError` callback will be called if the recording operation is a failure.

2. Then, the `"recordSoundDialog"` dialog is opened and its `"soundDuration"` div is updated every second with the duration of the recorded sound.

The following code snippet shows the `startRecordingSound(recordingCallba ck)`, `stopRecordingSound()`, and `requestApplicationDirectory(callback)` functions:

```
var BASE_DIRECTORY = "CS_Recorder";
var recordingMedia;

function startRecordingSound(recordingCallback) {
    var recordVoice = function(dirPath) {
        var basePath = "";

        if (dirPath) {
            basePath = dirPath + "/";
        }

        var mediaFilePath = basePath + (new Date()).getTime() +
".wav";

        var recordingSuccess = function() {
```

```
                recordingCallback.recordSuccess(mediaFilePath);
            };
            recordingMedia = new Media(mediaFilePath,
    recordingSuccess, recordingCallback.recordError);

            // Record audio
            recordingMedia.startRecord();
        };

        if (device.platform === "Android") {
            var callback = {};

            callback.requestSuccess = recordVoice;
            callback.requestError = recordingCallback.recordError;

            requestApplicationDirectory(callback);
        } else {

            recordVoice();
        }
    }

    function stopRecordingSound() {
        recordingMedia.stopRecord();
        recordingMedia.release();
    }

    function requestApplicationDirectory(callback) {
        var directoryReady = function (dirEntry) {
            callback.requestSuccess(dirEntry.toURL());
        };

        var fileSystemReady = function(fileSystem) {
            fileSystem.root.getDirectory(BASE_DIRECTORY, {create:
    true}, directoryReady);
        };

        window.requestFileSystem(LocalFileSystem.PERSISTENT, 0,
    fileSystemReady, callback.requestError);
    }
```

The next section illustrates the preceding code snippet.

Recording and playing the audio files back

In order to record the audio files using Apache Cordova, we need to create a `Media` object, as follows:

```
recordingMedia = new Media(src, mediaSuccess, mediaError);
```

The `Media` object constructor has the following parameters:

- `src`: This refers to the URI of the media file
- `mediaSuccess`: This refers to the callback that will be invoked if the media operation (play/record or stop function) succeeds
- `mediaError`: This refers to the callback that will be invoked if the media operation (again a play/record or stop function) fails

In order to start recording an audio file, a call to the `startRecord()` method of the `Media` object must be performed. When the recording is over, a call to `stopRecord()` of the `Media` object method must be performed.

In `startRecordingSound(recordingCallback)`, the function gets the current device platform by using `device.platform`, as follows:

- If the current platform is Android, then a call to `requestApplicationDirectory(callback)` is performed in order to create an application directory (if it is not already created) called `"CS_Recorder"` under the device's SD card root directory using the Apache Cordova File API. If the directory creation operation succeeds, `recordVoice()` will be called by passing the application directory path as a parameter. The `recordVoice()` function starts recording the sound and saves the resulting audio file under the `application` directory. Note that if there is no SD card in your Android device, then the `application` directory will be created under the app's private data directory (`/data/data/[app_directory]`), and the audio file will be saved under it.

- In the `else` block which refers to the other supported platforms (Windows Phone 8 and iOS, which we will add using Cordova CLI in the next chapter), `recordVoice()` is called without creating an application-specific directory. At the time of writing this module, in iOS and Windows Phone 8, every application has a private directory, and applications cannot store their files in any place other than this directory, using the Apache Cordova APIs. In the case of iOS, the audio files will be stored under the `tmp` directory of the application's `sandbox` directory (the application's private directory). In the case of Windows Phone 8, the audio files will be stored under the application's local directory.

Note that using the native Windows Phone 8 API (`Window.Storage`), you can read and write files in an SD card with some restrictions. However, until the moment you cannot do this using Apache Cordova; hopefully this capability will soon be supported by Cordova (http://msdn.microsoft.com/en-us/library/windows/apps/xaml/dn611857.aspx).

- In `recordVoice()`, it starts creating a media file using the `Media` object's `startRecord()` function. After calling the media file's `stopRecord()` function and after the success of the recording operation, `recordingCallback.recordSuccess` will be called by `recordingSuccess`. The `recordingCallback.recordSuccess` function calls `handleRecordSuccess`, passing the audio file's full path `mediaFilePath` as a parameter.

- The following code snippet shows the `handleRecordSuccess` function:

```
function handleRecordSuccess(currentFilePath) {

    $("#location").val(currentFilePath);
    $("#playSound").closest('.ui-btn').show();
}
```

- The `handleRecordSuccess` function stores the recorded audio filepath in the `"location"` hidden field, which is used later by the playback button, and shows the `"playSound"` button.

- In `requestApplicationDirectory(callback)`, which is called in case of Android, it does the following:
    ◦ Calls `window.requestFileSystem` in order to request the device filesystem before performing any file operation(s)
    ◦ Calls `fileSystem.root.getDirectory` when the filesystem is ready in order to create our custom application directory
    ◦ When our custom application directory is created successfully, the path of the created directory, or the existing directory, is passed to `recordVoice()` that was illustrated earlier

- In the other application actions, the following code snippet shows the `"stopRecordingSound"` tapping and `"recordSoundDialog"` closing event handlers:

```
$("#recordSoundDialog").on("popupafterclose", function(event, ui)
{
    clearInterval(recInterval);
    stopRecordingSound();
});
```

```
    $("#stopRecordingSound").on("tap", function(e) {
        $("#recordSoundDialog").popup("close");
    });

    function stopRecordingSound(recordingCallback) {
        recordingMedia.stopRecord();
        recordingMedia.release();
    }
```

In the "stopRecordingSound" tapping event handler, it closes the open "recordSoundDialog" pop up. Generally, if "recordSoundDialog" is closed by the "stopRecordingSound" button's tapping action or by pressing special device keys, such as the back button in Android devices, then the recording timer stops as a result of calling clearInterval(recInterval), and then it calls the stopRecordingSound() function to stop recording the sound.

The stopRecordingSound() function calls the Media object's stopRecord() method, and then releases it by calling the Media object's release() method. The following code snippet shows the "playSound" tap event handler:

```
    var audioMedia;
    var recordingMedia;

    $("#playSound").on("tap", function(e) {
        e.preventDefault();

        var playCallback = {};

        playCallback.playSuccess = handlePlaySuccess;
        playCallback.playError = handlePlayError;

        playSound($("#location").val(), playCallback);
    });

    function playSound(filePath, playCallback) {
        if (filePath) {
            cleanUpResources();

            audioMedia = new Media(filePath, playCallback.playSuccess,
    playCallback.playError);

            // Play audio
            audioMedia.play();
        }
    }
```

```
function cleanUpResources() {
    if (audioMedia) {
        audioMedia.stop();
        audioMedia.release();
        audioMedia = null;
    }

    if (recordingMedia) {
        recordingMedia.stop();
        recordingMedia.release();
        recordingMedia = null;
    }
}
```

In the "playSound" tap event handler, it calls the playSound(filePath, playCallback) function by passing the audio file location, which is stored in the "location" hidden field and playCallback.

The playSound(filePath, playCallback) function uses the Media object's play() method to play back the saved audio file after releasing used Media objects. Note that this is a requirement to avoid running out of system audio resources.

This is all you need to know about our Sound Recorder application. In order to see the complete application's source code, you can download it from the course page or get it from GitHub at https://github.com/hazems/soundRecorder.

Building and running Sound Recorder application

Now, after developing our application code, we can start building our application using the following cordova build command:

```
> cordova build
```

In order to run the application in your Android mobile or tablet, just make sure you enable USB debugging in your Android device. Then, plug your Android device into your development machine and execute the following command from the application directory:

```
> cordova run android
```

Congratulations! After running this command, you will see the Sound Recorder application deployed in your Android device; you can now start testing it on your real device.

In order to learn how to enable USB debugging in your Android device, refer to the *Configuring the Android development environment* section in *Chapter 3, Apache Cordova Development Tools*.

Summary

In this chapter, you developed your first Apache Cordova application. You now know how to use the Apache Cordova Device API at a basic level. You also know how to use the Media and File APIs along with jQuery Mobile to develop the Sound Recorder application. You now understand how to use Apache Cordova CLI in order to manage your Cordova mobile application. In addition, you know how to create a Cordova project, add a new platform (in our case, Android), build your own Cordova mobile application, and deploy your Cordova mobile application to the emulator, and most importantly, to a real device!

In the next chapter, we will show you how to prepare your Android, iOS, and Windows Phone development environments. Along with this, you will see how to make our Sound Recorder application works on Windows Phone 8 and iOS.

3
Apache Cordova Development Tools

In the previous chapter, you developed, built, and deployed your first Apache Cordova application from scratch. In this chapter, you will learn:

- How to configure the Apache Cordova development tools for the most popular mobile platforms (Android, iOS, and Windows Phone 8) on your development machine(s)

- How to build the Sound Recorder application (which we developed in *Chapter 2, Developing Your First Cordova Application*) on these platforms

- How to deploy the Sound Recorder application on real Android, iOS, and Windows Phone 8 devices

- How to handle the common issues that you will face when supporting our Sound Recorder application (which we supported on Android in *Chapter 2, Developing Your First Cordova Application*) on the other mobile platforms (iOS and Windows Phone 8)

Configuring Android development environment

In order to install Android development environment, we first need to install **Java Development Kit (JDK)**. JDK 6 or 7 can work perfectly with Android development tools. In order to get JDK, use the following URLs:

- JDK 7 (`http://www.oracle.com/technetwork/java/javase/downloads/jdk7-downloads-1880260.html`)

- JDK 6 (http://www.oracle.com/technetwork/java/javaee/downloads/java-ee-sdk-6u3-jdk-6u29-downloads-523388.html)

Once the download page appears, accept the license and then download the JDK installer that matches your operating system, as shown in the following screenshot. After downloading the JDK installer, follow the steps of the JDK installer in order to properly install JDK.

Java SE Development Kit 7u55		
You must accept the Oracle Binary Code License Agreement for Java SE to download this software. Thank you for accepting the Oracle Binary Code License Agreement for Java SE; you may now download this software.		
Product / File Description	**File Size**	**Download**
Linux x86	115.67 MB	jdk-7u55-linux-i586.rpm
Linux x86	133 MB	jdk-7u55-linux-i586.tar.gz
Linux x64	116.97 MB	jdk-7u55-linux-x64.rpm
Linux x64	131.82 MB	jdk-7u55-linux-x64.tar.gz
Mac OS X x64	179.56 MB	jdk-7u55-macosx-x64.dmg
Solaris x86 (SVR4 package)	138.86 MB	jdk-7u55-solaris-i586.tar.Z
Solaris x86	95.14 MB	jdk-7u55-solaris-i586.tar.gz
Solaris x64 (SVR4 package)	24.55 MB	jdk-7u55-solaris-x64.tar.Z
Solaris x64	16.25 MB	jdk-7u55-solaris-x64.tar.gz
Solaris SPARC (SVR4 package)	138.23 MB	jdk-7u55-solaris-sparc.tar.Z
Solaris SPARC	98.18 MB	jdk-7u55-solaris-sparc.tar.gz
Solaris SPARC 64-bit (SVR4 package)	24 MB	jdk-7u55-solaris-sparcv9.tar.Z
Solaris SPARC 64-bit	18.34 MB	jdk-7u55-solaris-sparcv9.tar.gz
Windows x86	123.67 MB	jdk-7u55-windows-i586.exe
Windows x64	125.49 MB	jdk-7u55-windows-x64.exe

Downloading JDK 1.7

If you want to have an Android development environment installed quickly on your machine, you can download **Android Developer Tools** (**ADT**) Bundle. The ADT Bundle includes the essential Android SDK components and a version of the Eclipse IDE with a built-in ADT to start developing your Android applications. You can download it from http://developer.android.com/sdk/index.html.

You can start downloading the ADT Bundle by clicking on the **Download the SDK** button, as shown in the following screenshot:

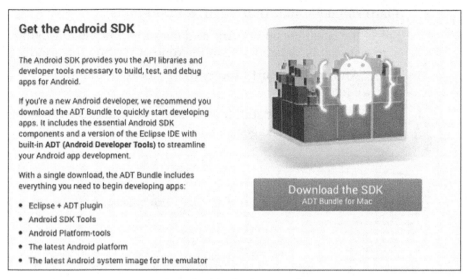

Downloading the ADT Bundle

Extending your existing Eclipse IDE

If you have an existing Eclipse IDE and you would prefer to use it as your Android development IDE, then you will need to configure things by yourself, start the configuration process by downloading the Android SDK tools from http://developer.android.com/sdk/index.html#download.

After downloading the Android SDK tools, and in order to start developing Android applications, you need to download at least one Android platform and the latest SDK platform tools using SDK Manager, as follows:

1. Open SDK Manager. If you use Linux or Mac, you can open a terminal and navigate to the `tools` directory under the Android SDK root directory and execute the following command:

```
> android sdk
```

   If you use Windows, then open the `SDK Manager.exe` file under the Android SDK root directory.

2. After opening SDK Manager, follow these steps:

    1. Select the latest tools packages (**Android SDK Tools**, **Android SDK Platform-tools**, and **Android SDK Build-tools**).

    2. Select the latest version of Android (as shown in the following screenshot, it is Version 4.4.2 at the time of writing this module).

    3. Select **Android Support Library** that is located under the Extras folder.

    4. Finally, click on the **Install** button, and after the process is complete, you will find the packages installed on your machine.

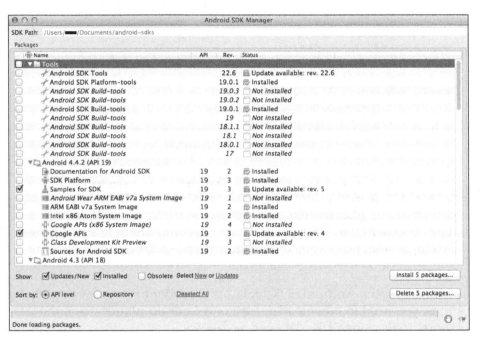

Android SDK Manager

Now, your Android environment is ready to develop your Android applications. However, in order to develop Android applications from your existing Eclipse IDE, Android provides an Eclipse plugin called ADT. This plugin provides a neat and integrated environment that you can use to develop your Android applications. ADT allows you to create new Android projects easily, build your Android application user interface, test and debug your Android applications, and export your application for distribution.

In order to install ADT in your Eclipse IDE, follow these steps:

1. Open Eclipse.

2. Choose **Install New Software** from the **Help** menu.

3. Click on the **Add** button.

4. In the **Add Repository** dialog, enter ADT for the name and the URL `https://dl-ssl.google.com/android/eclipse/` for the location.

5. Click on **OK**.

6. In the **Available Software** dialog, select **Developer Tools** and click on **Next**, as shown in the following screenshot:

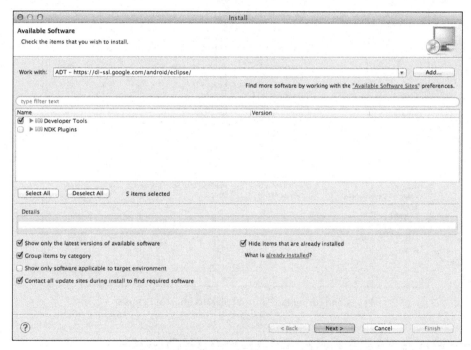

Installing the ADT plugin for Eclipse

7. The tools list to be downloaded will be shown to you. Then, click on **Next**.

8. Accept the license agreements, and finally, click on **Finish**.

 Sometimes, you will see a security warning telling you that you are installing software that contains unsigned content. Just ignore this message and click on **OK**, and then restart your Eclipse when the installation completes.

After restarting Eclipse, you need to specify the Android SDK path for Eclipse. You can do this by:

- Selecting the **Preferences** option from **Window** menu (in Windows or Linux), or by selecting **Preferences** from **Eclipse** menu in Mac

- Selecting the **Android** preference and specifying the SDK location, as shown in the following screenshot:

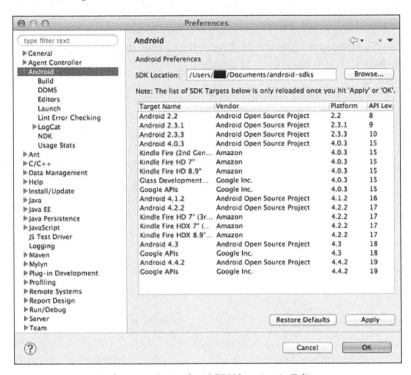

Configuring the Android SDK location in Eclipse

Creating an Android Virtual Device

In order to test your Android application in an emulator, you need to create an **Android Virtual Device (AVD)**. An AVD represents the Android emulator device configuration that allows you to model the different configurations of Android-powered devices. In order to create an AVD easily, you can use the graphical AVD Manager. To start AVD Manager from the command line, you can run the following command from the `tools` directory under the root of the Android SDK directory:

```
> android avd
```

After executing this command, the **Android Virtual Device Manager** window will appear, as shown in the following screenshot:

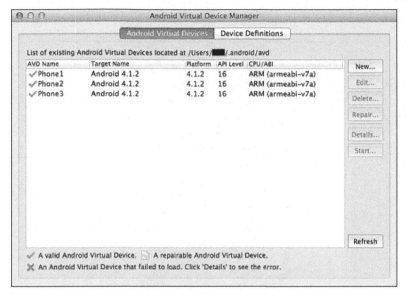

Android Virtual Device Manager

Note that while using Eclipse, you can also start AVD Manager by selecting **Android Virtual Device Manager** from the **Window** menu.

As shown in the preceding screenshot, using the AVD Manager, you can:

- Create a new AVD
- Delete an AVD
- Repair an AVD
- Check the details of an AVD
- Start running an AVD

In order to create a new AVD to test your Android applications, follow these steps:

1. Click on **New**.

2. Enter the details of your AVD, as shown in the following screenshot:

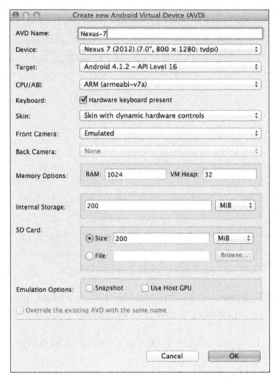

Creating a new Android Virtual Device (AVD)

As shown in the preceding screenshot, the following information is provided:

- **AVD Name**
- **Device**
- **Target**
- **CPU/ABI** (where ABI stands for Application Binary Interface)
- **Skin**

- ° **Front Camera**
- ° **Back Camera**
- ° **Memory Options**
- ° **Internal Storage**
- ° **SD Card**

3.   Then, click on **OK**.

After this, you can start launching your AVD by clicking on the **Start** button; wait until your Android emulator is up and running, as shown in the following screenshot:

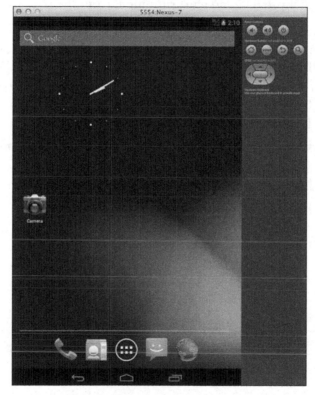

Android emulator start up screen

A best practice is to download the system images for all versions of Android that your application needs to support and test your application on them using the Android emulator. Another thing you need to consider is to select an AVD platform target that is greater than or equal to the API level used to compile your Android application.

Importing the Sound Recorder application in to Eclipse

Now, we have everything in place. We can now import our Sound Recorder Android application in our Eclipse IDE and start running it from the IDE. In order to import our project into Eclipse, follow these steps:

1. Before starting to import the project into your Eclipse IDE, and in order to avoid getting errors after importing the project into your IDE, make sure that our Sound Recorder project directories and subdirectories have **Read and Write** access for your user (that is, not read-only access).

2. Select the **Import** option from the **File** menu.

3. Select **Existing Android Code into workspace** from the **Android** menu.

4. In **Import Projects**, browse to the `${path_to_soundRecorder}/platforms/android` directory in **Root Directory**, as shown in the following screenshot:

Importing the Sound Recorder project into Eclipse

5. Click on **Finish**.

By default, your HTML, CSS, and JavaScript Android resources under ${project_ root}/assets are not shown in Eclipse; this shows your Android web resources.

1. Right-click on the project and then select **Properties**.
2. Select **Resource Filters** from the **Resources** dropdown.
3. Delete all the **Exclude all** rules, as shown in the following screenshot:

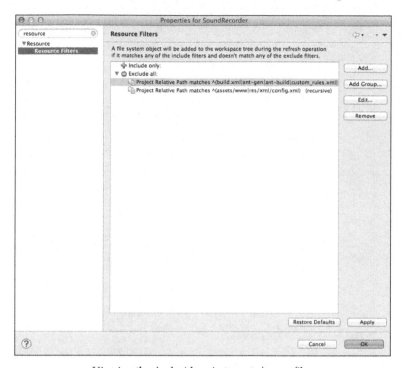

Viewing the Android project assets/www files

Now, you can view all the project assets/www files from the Eclipse workspace.

Do not forget that it is not recommended to edit the files under the platforms directory of your project as the cordova build command can overwrite your changes with the original resources in the root www directory. You can edit files under the platforms directory only if you want to use Apache Cordova to generate the initial artifacts of your project.

Before running our Sound Recorder Android project, make sure that the project is built by selecting **Build All** from **Project** menu (or select your project and choose **Build project** from the **Project** menu, or just select the **Build Automatically** option from the **Project** menu).

Now, you can run our Sound Recorder Android project from Eclipse by selecting the project and then selecting **Android Application** from the **Run as** menu, as shown in the following screenshot:

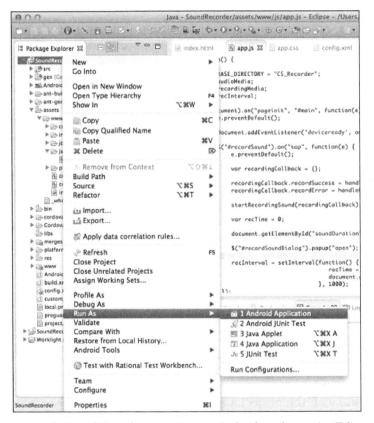

Running the Sound Recorder project in your Android emulator using Eclipse

You will have the option to select the emulator you want to run your project on, as shown in the following screenshot:

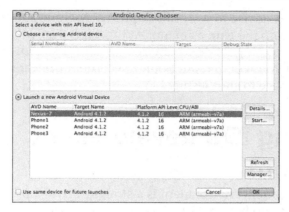

Selecting the Android emulator to run the project on

After selecting the Android emulator and clicking on the **OK** button, your selected Android emulator will be launched and your application will be installed on it for you to start testing.

Running the Sound Recorder application on a real Android device

In order to test your Android application on your Android mobile or tablet using the Eclipse IDE, just make sure that you enable USB debugging on your Android device. You can enable the **USB debugging** option on your device by clicking on **Developer Options** from the device **Settings** and then checking the **USB debugging** option, as shown in the following screenshot:

Enabling USB debugging on your Android device

Plug in your Android device to your development machine and then select **Android Application** again from the **Run as** menu. At this time, you will find your device available under the running Android device option in the **Android Device Chooser** dialog; select it, and you will find our Sound Recorder application deployed and launched in your device to start testing.

Configuring iOS development environment

Creating iOS development environment is a straightforward process if you meet the requirements. In order to have an iOS development environment, you need to:

- Have a Mac machine that runs OS X Mountain Lion (10.8) or higher versions
- Install Xcode on your Mac machine
- Install the iOS SDK on your Mac machine

Xcode is the official Apple IDE that allows you to develop applications for Mac, iPhone, and iPad. Xcode has a lot of great features, some of which are:

- Source code editor
- Assistant editor
- User-interface builder
- iOS simulator
- Static code analyzer
- A powerful built-in open source **low-level virtual machine (LLVM)** compiler for C, C++, and Objective-C
- The Live Issues feature, which highlights the common coding mistakes while coding your application, without the need to build your project
- Complete support for SCM systems (subversion and Git source control)

You can download the latest version of Xcode from the Apple App Store on your Mac machine. You will find the iOS SDK included with Xcode, so there is no need to download anything other than Xcode.

In order to download the latest version of Xcode, follow these steps:

1. Open the App Store application on your Mac machine.

2. In the search field of App Store, type in Xcode and press enter.

3. Download Xcode, and after completing the download, you will find it under your applications directory. The following screenshot shows the Xcode icon:

The Xcode icon

If you have an earlier version of OS X (less than 10.8), you need to upgrade it. In order to download Xcode, you need OS X Version 10.8 (or higher).

Importing the Sound Recorder application into Xcode

Now, it is time to make our Sound Recorder application support iPad and iPhone devices. The following command adds iOS platform support for our Sound Recorder application:

```
> cordova platform add ios
```

Then, build our application in the iOS platform using the following Cordova build command:

```
> cordova build ios
```

Open your Xcode environment, click on **Open other**, and then select the SoundRecorder.xcodeproj file under the platforms/ios directory to open our Sound Recorder iOS project.

You will find our Sound Recorder application open in Xcode. In order to run our project on an iPhone (or iPad) emulator, click on the **Build and run** button after selecting the iPhone emulator, as shown in the following screenshot:

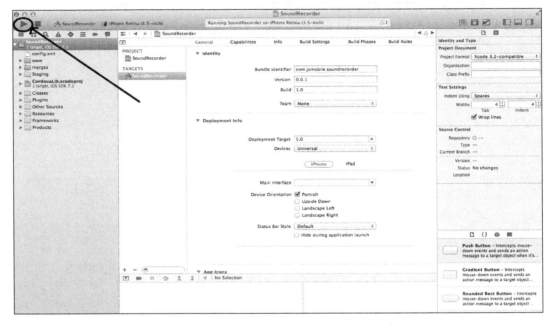

Running the Sound Recorder application in Xcode

After clicking on the **Build and run** button, the iPhone emulator will be launched with our Sound Recorder application and you can start using it.

An important point that you have to be aware of is that if you are deploying your application on iOS 7, and because of a bug in Apache Cordova 3.4, you will find an overlay between your application and the device status bar, as shown in the following screenshot:

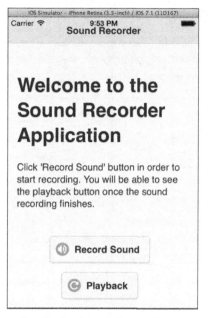

Apache Cordova 3.4 bug with iOS 7

In order to fix this issue (which I hope to be fixed soon in the next releases of Apache Cordova 3.x), one of the possible workarounds is to hide the status bar by adding and setting two properties in our `SoundRecorder-info.plist` file, which is located under the `Resources` directory of our application, as shown in the following screenshot:

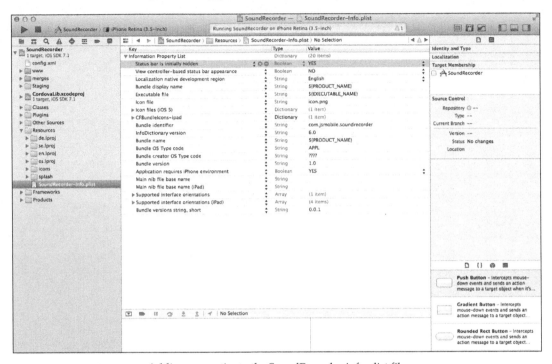

Adding properties to the SoundRecorder-info.plist file

The two properties and values are:

- The **Status bar is initially hidden** property set to the **YES** value
- The **View controller-based status bar appearance** property set to the **NO** value

 In order to add a property to the `*-info.plist` file, you can select the information list property in Xcode and then click on **Add Row**.

After setting these two properties, click on the **Build and run** button again to see the fixed screen in iOS 7, as shown in the following screenshot:

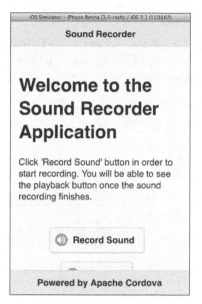

The Sound Recorder application fixed in iOS 7

Running the Sound Recorder application on a real iOS device

In order to deploy our Sound Recorder application on a real iOS device (iPhone or iPad), you will need to follow these 20 steps carefully:

1. Sign up for the iOS developer program at https://developer.apple.com/programs/ios/. There are two available enrollment types:

    ° **Individual**: Select this enrollment type if you are an individual

    ° **Company/Organization**: Select this enrollment type if you represent a company

 Sign up to the **Individual** program if you just want to develop applications in App Store. Note that at the time of writing this module, this will cost you 99 USD per year.

2. Generate a **Certificate Signing Request (CSR)** using the **Keychain Access** application, which you can get from the `/Applications/Utilities` directory. In order to generate the certificate signing request, follow these steps:

1. Navigate to **Keychain Access | Certificate Assistant | Request a Certificate From a Certificate Authority**, as shown in the following screenshot:

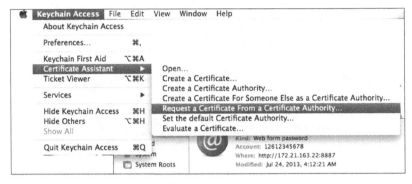

Creating a CSR using Keychain Access

2. In the **Certificate Assistant** window, enter your e-mail address, click on the **Saved to disk** radio button, and check the **Let me specify key pair information** checkbox. Then, click on **Continue**.

3. In the **Key Pair Information** window, choose **2048 bits** as the key size and **RSA** as the algorithm. Then, click on **Continue**.

4. Use the default filename to save the certificate request to your disk, and click on **Save**.

 By default, the generated certificate request file has the filename with the following extension `CertificateSigningRequest.certSigningRequest`.

3. Now, we need to use the iOS member center (`https://developer.apple.com/membercenter/`) in order to create the application ID, register your iOS device, generate a development certificate, and create a provision profile.

4. Click on the **Certificates, Identifiers & Profiles** link, as shown in the following screenshot. You will be introduced to the overview page, where you can click on the **Identifiers** link.

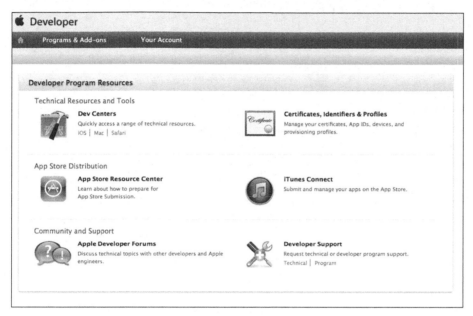

Managing certificates, identifiers, and profiles from the member center

5. Select **App IDs** from **Identifiers**. Register your application ID by entering an application name and the application bundle identifier (you can get the bundle identifier from the `SoundRecorder-info.plist` file), as shown in the following screenshot. Then, click on **Continue**.

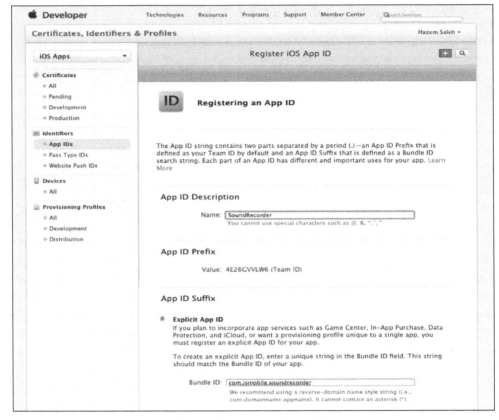

Registering your application ID

6. You will be introduced to the confirmation page. Click on **Submit** to confirm your application ID.

7. Select **All** from **Devices**. Register your iOS device by entering the device name and the device's **Unique Identifier** (UDID), as shown in the following screenshot. Then, click on **Continue**.

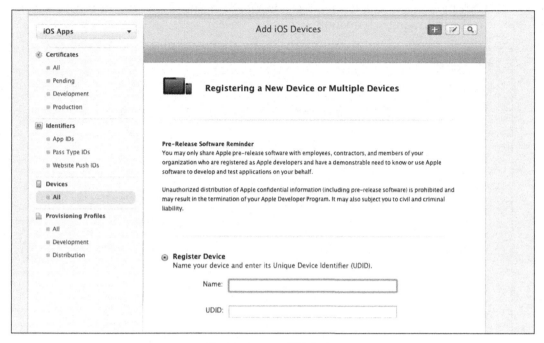

Registering your iOS device

 In order to get your iOS device's UDID, you can get it after connecting your iOS device to iTunes. Select your device from the left-hand side menu of iTunes and then click on **Serial Number**; you will find it changed to **Identifier (UDID)** with the device UDID.

8. You will be introduced to the review page. Click on **Register** to register your device.

9. Select **Development** in **Certificates** to create your development certificate file. Read the introduction page and click on **Continue**.

10. In the second step of the development certificate creation process, choose the CSR file that we created in step 2 and click on the **Generate** button, as shown in the following screenshot:

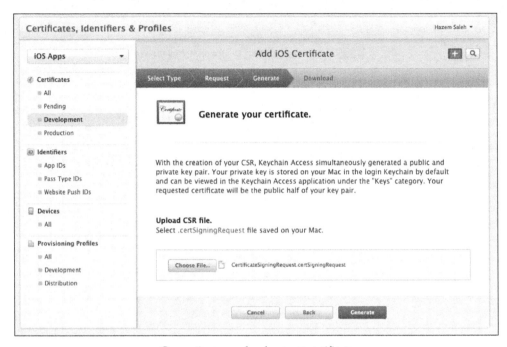

Generating your development certificate

11. In the last step of the development certificate creation process, click on the **Download** button to download the development certificate to your machine.

12. Select **All** from the **Provision Profiles** to create a provision profile, which will be installed on your iOS device. Choose the **iOS App Development** option from **Development**, as shown in the following screenshot, and then click on **Continue**:

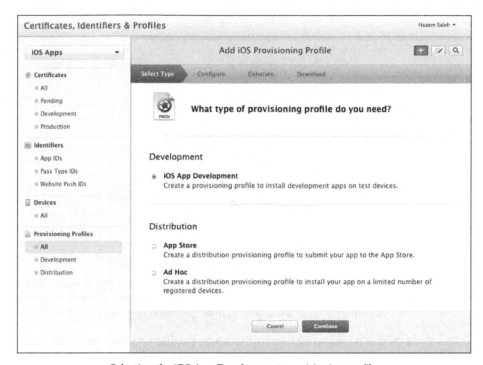

Selecting the iOS App Development provisioning profile

13. In the second step of the development provisioning profile creation process, select **App ID**, which we created in step 5, and then click on the **Continue** button.

14. In step 3 of the development provisioning profile creation process, select the **Development certificate** checkbox that we created in step 10, as shown in the following screenshot, and then click on the **Continue** button:

Selecting the certificate to include in the provisioning profile

15. In step 4 of the development provisioning profile creation process, select your iOS device checkbox, which you registered in step 8, and then click on the **Continue** button.

16. In step 5 of the development provisioning profile creation process, enter your preferred profile name (for example, **SoundRecorderProfile**) and then click on the **Generate** button.

17. In the last step of the development provisioning profile creation process, click on the **Download** button to download the provisioning profile to your machine.

18. Now that we have created and downloaded both the development certificate and the provisioning profile, we need to install them. Double-click on the .cer file that you downloaded in step 11 to install it onto a keychain on your Mac machine. If you are prompted with the **Add Certificates** dialog, click on **OK**.

19. In order to install the downloaded provisioning profile to your iOS device, connect your iOS device to your Mac, open the organizer application from your Xcode by selecting **Organizer** from **Window** menu, and then click on the **Add** button and select the .mobileprovision file. You should find that this profile is a valid one, as shown in the following screenshot:

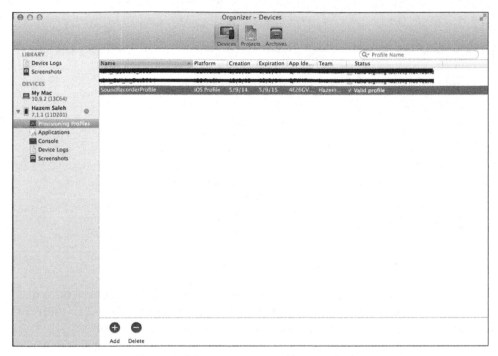

Adding a mobile provisioning profile to an iOS device

20. Finally, you can deploy your application on your iOS device by selecting your iOS device from the active scheme dropdown and clicking on the **Build and run** button, as shown in the following screenshot. After clicking on the button, you will find our Sound Recorder application finally launched on your iOS device.

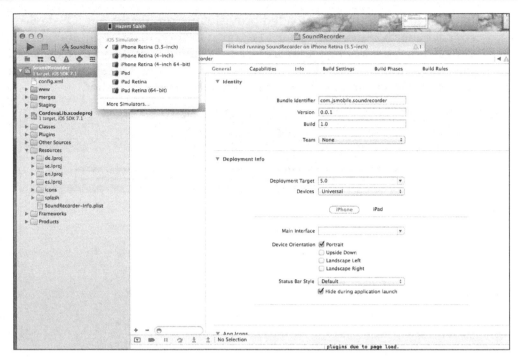

Deploying our Sound Recorder application to a real iOS device

When running your iOS application on a real device for the first time, you will receive the prompt message **codesign wants to sign using key "-----" in your keychain**. If you see this message, click on the **Always allow** button.

Configuring the Windows Phone development environment

In order to configure your Windows Phone 8 development environment, you will need the following:

- Windows 8 operating system or any higher compatible Windows versions.
- Windows Phone SDK 8.0, which includes a standalone Visual Studio Express 2012 for Windows Phone, Windows Phone emulators, and other useful tools to profile Windows Phone applications. The Windows Phone SDK can also work as an add-in to the Visual Studio 2012 Professional, Premium, or Ultimate editions.

In order to download Windows Phone SDK 8.0, go to `http://www.microsoft.com/en-us/download/details.aspx?id=35471`.

Visual Studio for Windows Phone is the official Microsoft IDE for Windows Phone development. It is a complete development environment to create Windows Phone applications and has many features, some of which are as follows:

- Source code editor
- User-interface builder
- Templates for Windows Phone projects
- Testing and debugging features on Windows Phone emulators or real Windows Phone devices
- Simulation, monitoring, and profiling capabilities for Windows Phone applications

After getting the Windows Phone 8.0 SDK, installing it onto your Windows machine is a very straightforward process. Launch the SDK installer and follow these steps:

1. Provide the path in which the SDK will be installed.

2. Check the **I agree to license terms and conditions** option.

3. Click on the **Install** button, and you will see the status of the SDK installation on your Windows machine, as shown in the following screenshot. After installation completes, you might be asked to reboot your operating system.

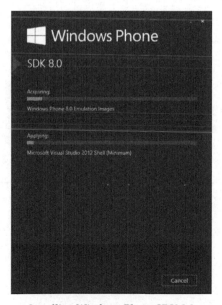

Installing Windows Phone SDK 8.0

Importing the Sound Recorder application into Visual Studio

Now, it is time to make our Sound Recorder application compatible on Windows Phone 8. The following command adds Windows Phone 8 platform support to our Sound Recorder application:

```
> cordova platform add wp8
```

Open your Visual Studio IDE and then follow these steps:

1. Select **Open File** from the **File** menu and then select the `SoundRecorder.sln` file under the `platforms/wp8` directory to open our Sound Recorder Windows Phone 8 project.

2. Select **Build Solution** from the **Build** menu.

3. In order to run your project in the Windows Phone 8 emulator, click on the **Run** button by selecting a target emulator, as shown in the following screenshot:

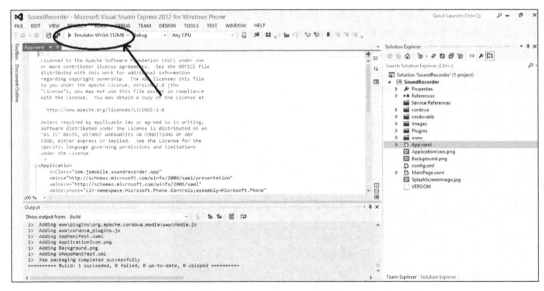

Running a Windows Phone 8 project in the Visual Studio IDE

After clicking on the **Run** button, the Windows Phone 8 emulator will be launched with our Sound Recorder application and you can start working with it, as shown in the following screenshot:

First run of our Sound Recorder application in WP8

If you notice in the preceding screenshot, there are two problems that occur when we run the application in a WP8 emulator:

- The header title is truncated
- The jQuery Mobile application footer is not aligned with the bottom of the page

The first problem appears because jQuery Mobile set the CSS overflow property of its header and title to `hidden`. In order to fix this issue, we need to change this behavior by setting the `overflow` property to visible in the `css/app.css` file, as shown in the following code:

```
.ui-header .ui-title {
    overflow: visible !important;
}
```

In order to fully align the application footer in both portrait and landscape modes of Windows Phone 8, you need to hide the system tray by setting `shell:SystemTray.IsVisible="False"` instead of `shell:SystemTray.IsVisible="True"` in `MainPage.xaml` (which is located under the `platforms/wp8` directory), as shown in the following code snippet:

```
<phone:PhoneApplicationPage
    x:Class="com.jsmobile.soundrecorder.MainPage"
    xmlns="http://schemas.microsoft.com/winfx/2006/xaml/presentation"
    ...
    xmlns:shell="clr-namespace:Microsoft.Phone.
Shell;assembly=Microsoft.Phone"
    shell:SystemTray.IsVisible="False" ...>
    ...
</phone:PhoneApplicationPage>
```

After performing these two fixes, we can rerun our Sound Recorder application; we will find that the screen is now fine, as shown in the following screenshot:

Fixed Sound Recorder application in WP8

Running the Sound Recorder application on a real Windows Phone

Now, it is time to deploy our Sound Recorder application on a real Windows Phone 8 device. In order to do this, you have to unlock your Windows Phone for development using the **Windows Phone Developer Registration** tool. In order to use and run this tool, note the following prerequisites:

- A registered Windows Phone developer account. You can create your registered Windows Phone developer account from `https://dev. windowsphone.com/en-us/join`. Note that creating a Windows Phone developer account is not free and the exact cost that you will pay depends on your country and region.
- A Microsoft account associated with your Windows Phone developer account.
- Connect your Windows Phone to your Windows machine and make sure that:
    ○ The mobile screen is unlocked
    ○ The date and time of your mobile are correct

Now, you can launch the **Windows Phone Developer Registration** tool by switching to Windows' **All Apps view** and select **Windows Phone Developer Registration** under **Windows Phone SDK 8.0**. When the tool starts, follow these steps in order to unlock your Windows Phone for development:

1. Make sure that the tool status displays the **Identified Windows Phone 8 device** message.

2. Click on the **Register** button to unlock your phone for development. If your phone is already registered, you will see an **Unregister** button, as shown in the following screenshot:

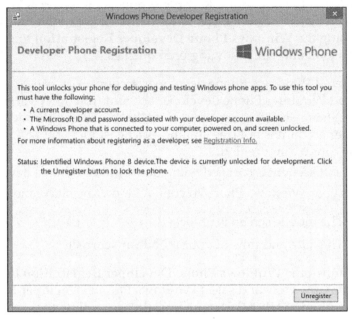

The Windows Phone Developer Registration tool

3. After clicking on the **Register** button, you will be introduced to the **Sign In** dialog box to enter your Microsoft account information (e-mail and password); you can then click on **Sign In**.

4. After clicking on **Sign In**, and assuming that you met all the prerequisites, your Windows Phone will be successfully unlocked for development, and you will be able to deploy your Windows Phone 8 application to it.

Now, in order to deploy our Sound Recorder application to your Windows Phone 8 device, select your Windows Phone8 device from the target device list and click on the **Run** button, as shown in the following screenshot:

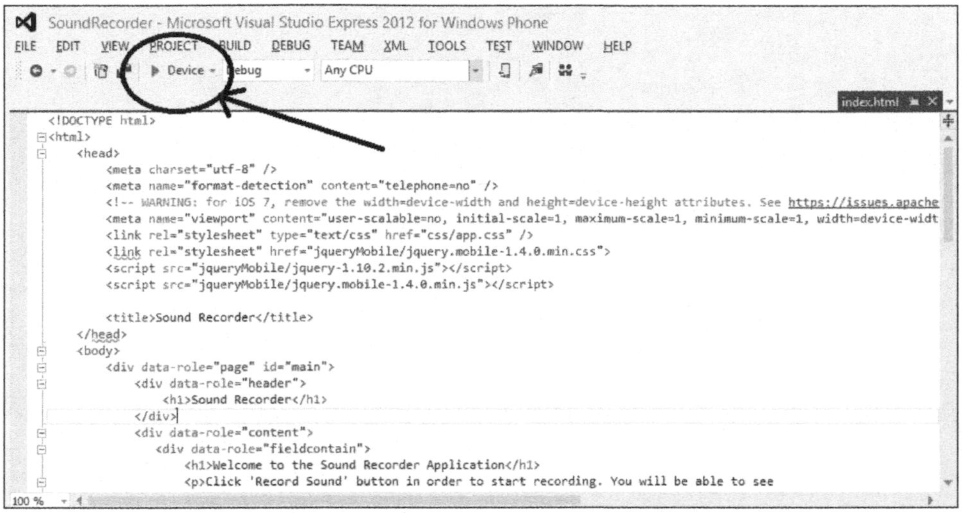

Running the Sound Recorder application in WP8

After clicking on the **Run** button, you can enjoy testing our Sound Recorder application on your Windows Phone 8 device.

Summary

After reading and applying the steps mentioned in this chapter, you will have the three most popular mobile platform development environments (Android, iOS, and Windows Phone 8) installed on your machine(s). You can now build your Apache Cordova applications using these development tools and deploy your applications on their emulators. In this chapter, you learned how to deploy your Apache Cordova application on real devices of all these popular mobile platforms in detail. Finally, you learned the common problems and solutions that occur when you decide to support your Apache Cordova application on iOS and Windows Phone 8. In the next chapter, you will start learning how to use the different APIs provided by Apache Cordova in detail.

4
Cordova API in Action

In this chapter, we will start taking a deep dive in Apache Cordova API and see Apache Cordova API in action. You will learn how to work with the Cordova accelerometer, camera, compass, connection, contacts, device, geolocation, globalization, and the InAppBrowser APIs. This chapter as well as the next one illustrates a Cordova mobile app, Cordova Exhibition (which is developed using Apache Cordova and jQuery Mobile), that explores the main features of the Apache Cordova API in order to give you real-life usage examples of the Apache Cordova API in Android, iOS, and Windows Phone 8.

Exploring the Cordova Exhibition app

The Cordova Exhibition app aims at showing the main features of the Apache Cordova API. The demo shows practical examples of the following Apache Cordova API plugins:

- Accelerometer
- Camera
- Compass
- Connection
- Contacts
- Device
- Geolocation
- Globalization
- InAppBrowser
- Media, file, and capture
- Notification
- Storage

As well as Apache Cordova, the Cordova Exhibition app uses jQuery Mobile in order to create the app's user interface. The Cordova Exhibition app is supported on the following platforms:

- Android
- iOS
- Windows Phone 8

The following screenshot shows the home page of the Cordova Exhibition app. The home page displays a list from which users can choose the feature they want to try.

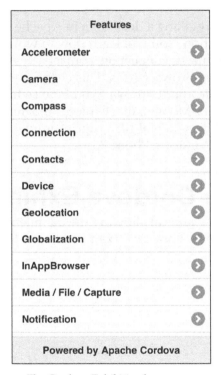

The Cordova Exhibition home page

In this chapter and the next one, we will explore each feature individually in its own section.

The Cordova Exhibition app structure

In order to create the Cordova Exhibition app from the **Command-line Interface** (**CLI**), we run the following `cordova create` command:

```
> cordova create cordova-exhibition com.jsmobile.cordovaexhibition
CordovaExhibition
```

In order to add Android, iOS, and Windows Phone 8 support from the CLI, we run the usual `cordova platform add` commands from the app directory as follows:

```
> cd cordova-exhibition
```

```
> cordova platform add android
```

```
> cordova platform add ios
```

```
> cordova platform add wp8
```

In order to add the different plugins to our Cordova Exhibition app, we use the usual `cordova plugin add` command (we will show the details of every plugin URL in its corresponding section).

To build and run the Cordova Exhibition app in your emulators and devices, you can follow the same steps that we used in *Chapter 3*, *Apache Cordova Development Tools*, to build and run the Sound Recorder application.

> The complete source code of our Cordova Exhibition app with all of the three supported platforms can be downloaded from the course's web page, or you can access the code directly from GitHub at `https://github.com/hazems/cordova-exhibition`.

Now, let's understand the structure of our Cordova Exhibition code. The following screenshot shows our Cordova Exhibition app's hierarchy:

The Cordova Exhibition application's structure

The www directory contains the following files and subdirectories:

- css: This directory contains the custom app's **Cascading Style Sheet (CSS)**.

- img: This directory contains the custom app's images.

- jqueryMobile: This directory contains the files of the jQuery Mobile framework and used plugins (the jQuery Mobile page params plugin and jQuery validation plugin).

- js: This directory contains all the custom app's JavaScript code. It has the following two subdirectories:

    ° api: This directory contains the app managers that interact with the Apache Cordova API in order to decouple the Cordova API from the app event handlers. This gives us the ability to change the implementation of our app API without changing our app event handlers and, at the same time, the ability to keep our app event handlers small.

    ° vc: This directory contains the app view controllers that register and implement the event handlers of every page and their user interface components. Event handlers usually call the app managers (the app API) in order to access the device's native features and, finally, they display the results in the app page.

The js directory also includes common.js file, which has common utilities. Finally, under the www directory, the index.html file contains all the app pages. The index.html file will be illustrated in *Finalizing the Cordova Exhibition app* section in *Chapter 5, Diving Deeper into the Cordova API*.

 It is important to note that not all Cordova features are supported across all platforms. In order to know the unsupported features, check out the last part in the *Overview of Cordova API* section in *Chapter 1, Introduction to Apache Cordova*.

Accelerometer

The accelerometer plugin provides access to the device's accelerometer in order to get the delta in movement relative to the current device's orientation in the x, y, and z axes.

In order to use the accelerometer in our Apache Cordova project, we need to use the following `cordova plugin add` command:

```
> cordova plugin add https://git-wip-us.apache.org/repos/asf/cordova-
plugin-device-motion.git
```

Demo

In order to access the accelerometer demo, you need to click on the accelerometer list item. You will be introduced to the **Accelerometer** page. You can then click on the **Start Watch Acceleration** button in order to start watching the accelerometer. You will then be able to get the acceleration information in the x, y, and z axes, as shown in the following screenshot:

The Accelerometer page in action

You can click on the **Stop Watch Acceleration** button to stop watching the accelerometer at any time.

The HTML page

The following code snippet shows the `"accelerometer"` page:

```
<div data-role="page" id="accelerometer">
    <div data-role="header">
        <h1>Accelerometer</h1>
        <a href="#" data-role="button" data-rel="back" data-
icon="back">Back</a>
    </div>
    <div data-role="content">
        <h1>Welcome to the Accelerometer Gallery</h1>
        <p>Click 'Start Watch Acceleration' button below to start
watch acceleration.</p>
        <input type="button" id="startWatchAcceleration"
value="Start Watch Acceleration"/>
        <input type="button" id="stopWatchAcceleration"
value="Stop Watch Acceleration"/>
        <div id="acceleration">
        </div>
    </div>
</div>
```

As shown in the preceding `"accelerometer"` page code snippet, it contains the following:

- A page header that includes a back button
- Page content that includes the following main elements:
  - `"startWatchAcceleration"`: This button is used to start watching acceleration
  - `"stopWatchAcceleration"`: This button is used to stop watching acceleration
  - `"acceleration"`: This div is used to display the acceleration result

View controller

The following code snippet shows the page view controller JavaScript object, which includes the event handlers of the page (`accelerometer.js`):

```
(function() {
    var accelerometerManager = AccelerometerManager.getInstance();
    var watchID;

    $(document).on("pageinit", "#accelerometer", function(e) {
        e.preventDefault();

        $("#startWatchAcceleration").on("tap", function(e) {
            e.preventDefault();

            enableStartWatchAccelerationButton(false);

            var callback = {};

            callback.onSuccess = onSuccess;
            callback.onError = onError;

            watchID = accelerometerManager.
startWatchAcceleration(callback);
        });

        $("#stopWatchAcceleration").on("tap", function(e) {
            e.preventDefault();

            enableStartWatchAccelerationButton(true);

            accelerometerManager.stopWatchAcceleration(watchID);
        });

        initPage();
    });

    $(document).on("pagebeforehide", "#accelerometer", function(e) {
        accelerometerManager.stopWatchAcceleration(watchID);
        enableStartWatchAccelerationButton(true);
    });

    function initPage() {
        $("#stopWatchAcceleration").closest('.ui-btn').hide();
    }
```

```
function onSuccess(acceleration) {
    $("#acceleration").html("Acceleration X: " + acceleration.x +
"<br/>" +
        "Acceleration Y: " + acceleration.y + "<br/>" +
        "Acceleration Z: " + acceleration.z + "<br/>" +
        "Timestamp: "      + acceleration.timestamp + "<br/>");
}

function onError() {
    $("#acceleration").html("An error occurs during watching
acceleration.");
}

function enableStartWatchAccelerationButton(enable) {
    if (enable) {
        $("#startWatchAcceleration").button("enable");
        $("#stopWatchAcceleration").closest('.ui-btn').hide();
    } else {
        $("#startWatchAcceleration").button("disable");
        $("#stopWatchAcceleration").closest('.ui-btn').show();
    }

    $("#startWatchAcceleration").button("refresh");
}

})();
```

The "pageinit" event handler, which is called once in the page initialization, registers the "startWatchAcceleration" tap event handler. The "startWatchAcceleration" tap event handler does the following:

- It disables the "startWatchAcceleration" button and shows the "stopWatchAcceleration" button by calling enableStartWatchAccelerat ionButton(false)

- It starts watching the acceleration by calling accelerometerManager.star tWatchAcceleration(callback), specifying a callback object that contains the following:

    ○ The onSuccess callback that will be called if the operation succeeds

    ○ The onError callback that will be called if the operation fails

The `accelerometerManager.startWatchAcceleration(callback)` function returns `watchID`, which will be used in order to stop watching the acceleration.

The `"pageinit"` event handler, which is called once in the page initialization, registers the `"stopWatchAcceleration"` tap event handler. The `"stopWatchAcceleration"` tap event handler does the following:

- It hides the `"stopWatchAcceleration"` button and enables the `"startWatchAcceleration"` button by calling `enableStartWatchAccelerationButton(true)`

- It stops watching the acceleration by calling `accelerometerManager.stopWatchAcceleration(watchID)` and specifying `watchID`, which we get from the `accelerometerManager.startWatchAcceleration(callback)` call

The `"pageinit"` event handler also calls `initPage()` in order to hide the `"stopWatchAcceleration"` button at the beginning. In `onSuccess(acceleration)`, which will be called if `accelerometerManager.startWatchAcceleration(callback)` succeeds, the x, y, and z acceleration is shown with the current timestamp. In `onError()`, which will be called if `accelerometerManager.startWatchAcceleration(callback)` fails, an error message is displayed.

Finally, in order to stop watching acceleration before leaving the page, `accelerometerManager.stopWatchAcceleration()` is called in the `"pagebeforehide"` event, which will be called every time we transition away from the page.

API

The following code snippet shows the accelerometer manager JavaScript object that interacts with the Apache Cordova Accelerometer API (`AccelerometerManager.js`). Note that the manager files are always included in the `index.html` file before the view controller files so that the manager objects can be used by view controller objects:

```
var AccelerometerManager = (function () {
  var instance;

  function createObject() {
      return {
          startWatchAcceleration: function (callback) {
              return navigator.accelerometer.
watchAcceleration(callback.onSuccess,
callback.onError,
```

```
{frequency: 2000});
        },
        stopWatchAcceleration: function (watchID) {
            if (watchID) {
                navigator.accelerometer.clearWatch(watchID);
            }
        }
    };
};

return {
  getInstance: function () {
    if (!instance) {
        instance = createObject();
    }

    return instance;
  }
};
})();
```

As you can see, `AccelerometerManager` is a singleton object that has the following two methods, as highlighted in the preceding code:

- `startWatchAcceleration(callback)`: This uses the Cordova `navigator.accelerometer.watchAcceleration()` method to watch acceleration. The `navigator.accelerometer.watchAcceleration(accelerometerSuccess, accelerometerError, [accelerometerOptions])` method has the following parameters:

    - `accelerometerSuccess`: This will be called if the operation succeeds with an object that contains the current acceleration along the x, y, and z axes and the timestamp. In `AccelerometerManager`, `accelerometerSuccess` is set to `callback.onSuccess`.

    - `accelerometerError`: This will be called if the operation fails. In `AccelerometerManager`, `accelerometerError` is set to `callback.onError`.

    - `accelerometerOptions`: This is an optional parameter that holds the accelerometer's configuration. It has a `frequency` attribute to specify how often to retrieve acceleration in milliseconds. In `AccelerometerManager`, the `frequency` parameter is set to `2000` milliseconds (note that this parameter is `10000` milliseconds by default).

- stopWatchAcceleration(watchID): This uses the Cordova `navigator.accelerometer.clearWatch()` method to remove watching acceleration. `navigator.accelerometer.clearWatch(watchID)` has the following parameter:

  ○ watchID: This represents the ID returned by `navigator.accelerometer.watchAcceleration()`.

We are now done with the `Accelerometer` functionality in our Cordova Exhibition app. However, before exploring the `Camera` functionality, note that the `navigator.accelerometer` object has also the method shown in the following table:

Method name	Description
navigator.accelerometer.getCurrentAcceleration (accelerometerSuccess, accelerometerError)	This method retrieves the current acceleration along the x, y, and z axes. Acceleration values are returned to the accelerometerSuccess callback function.

Camera

The camera plugin provides access to the device's camera in order to take pictures. This plugin also allows you to pick images from the device's image library.

In order to use the camera in our Apache Cordova project, we need to use the following `cordova plugin add` command:

```
> cordova plugin add https://git-wip-us.apache.org/repos/asf/cordova-plugin-camera.git
```

Demo

In order to access the camera demo, you need to click on the camera list item. You will be introduced to the **Camera** page. You can click on the **Get Picture** button in order to select whether to get a picture from the device's gallery or the device's camera. If you choose the **Camera** menu item, the default camera application of the device will be launched for you to capture a picture. If you choose the **Gallery** menu item, the device's gallery will be opened for you to pick an image. After getting the image from the camera or the gallery, you will be able to view the image on the **Camera** page, as shown in the following screenshot:

A selected image is shown on the camera page

The HTML page

The following code snippet shows the `"camera"` page:

```
<div data-role="page" id="camera">
    <div data-role="header">
        <h1>Camera</h1>
        <a href="#" data-role="button" data-rel="back" data-
icon="back">Back</a>
    </div>
    <div data-role="content">
        <h1>Welcome to the Camera Gallery</h1>
        <p>Click 'Get Picture' button below</p>
        <div class="center-wrapper">
            <input type="button" id="getPicture" data-
icon="camera" value="Get Picture"
```

```
                    class="center-button" data-inline="true"/>
        </div>
        <br/>

        <div style="width: 100%;">
            <img id="imageView" style="width: 100%;"></img>
        </div>

        <div data-role="popup" id="pictureTypeSelection">
            <ul data-role="listview" data-inset="true" style="min-
width:210px;">
                <li data-role="divider" data-theme="a">Get Picture
From</li>
                <li><a id="pictureFromGallery"
href="#">Gallery</a></li>
                <li><a id="pictureFromCamera"
href="#">Camera</a></li>
            </ul>
        </div>
    </div>
</div>
```

As shown in the preceding `"camera"` page code snippet, it contains the following:

- A page header that includes a back button
- Page content that includes the following main elements:
    - `"getPicture"`: This button is used to get a picture
    - `"imageView"`: This is used in order to display the selected or captured image
    - `"pictureTypeSelection"`: This div element is a pop up that will be displayed to allow the user to select whether to get a picture from the camera or from the gallery

View controller

The following code snippet shows the page view controller JavaScript object that includes the action handlers of the page (`camera.js`):

```
(function() {
    var cameraManager = CameraManager.getInstance();

    $(document).on("pageinit", "#camera", function(e) {
        e.preventDefault();
```

```
        $("#imageView").hide();

        $("#getPicture").on("tap", function(e) {
            e.preventDefault();

            $("#pictureTypeSelection").popup("open");
        });

        $("#pictureFromGallery").on("tap", function(e) {
            e.preventDefault();
            $("#pictureTypeSelection").popup("close");

            getPhoto(true);
        });

        $("#pictureFromCamera").on("tap", function(e) {
            e.preventDefault();
            $("#pictureTypeSelection").popup("close");

            getPhoto(false);
        });
    });

    function getPhoto(fromGallery) {
        var callback = {};

        callback.onSuccess = onSuccess;
        callback.onError = onError;

        cameraManager.getPicture(callback, fromGallery);
    }

    function onSuccess(fileURI) {
        $("#imageView").show();
        $("#imageView").attr("src", fileURI);
    }

    function onError(message) {
        console.log("Camera capture error");
    }
})();
```

The `"pageinit"` event handler registers the following event handlers:

- `"getPicture"` tap event handler: This opens the `"pictureTypeSelection"` pop up to allow the user to select the way to get a picture

- `"pictureFromGallery"` tap event handler: This closes the currently opened `"pictureTypeSelection"` pop up and calls `getPhoto(true)` to pick a photo from the device's gallery

- `"pictureFromCamera"` tap event handler: This closes the currently opened `"pictureTypeSelection"` pop up and calls `getPhoto(false)` to capture a photo using the device's camera

The `getPhoto(fromGallery)` method can get a photo (from the gallery or using the camera) by calling `cameraManager.getPicture(callback, fromGallery)` and specifying the following parameters:

- The `callback` object that contains the following attributes:
  - `onSuccess`: This callback will be called if the operation succeeds. It receives the `fileURI` of the picked image as a parameter, this allows the callback to display the picked image in `"imageView"`.
  - `onError`: This callback will be called if the operation fails.

- The `fromGallery` parameter informs `cameraManager.getPicture()` to get the photo from the device's gallery if it is set to `true`, and if `fromGallery` is set to `false`, then it informs `cameraManager.getPicture()` to get the photo using the device's camera

API

The following code snippet shows the camera manager JavaScript object that interacts with the Apache Cordova Camera API (`CameraManager.js`):

```
var CameraManager = (function () {
  var instance;

  function createObject() {
      var fileManager = FileManager.getInstance();

      return {
          getPicture: function (callback, fromGallery) {
              var source = Camera.PictureSourceType.CAMERA;
```

```
        if (fromGallery) {
            source = Camera.PictureSourceType.PHOTOLIBRARY;
        }

        navigator.camera.getPicture(callback.onSuccess,
                                    callback.onError,
                                    {
                                        quality: 80,
                                        destinationType:
Camera.DestinationType.FILE_URI,

                                        sourceType: source,
                                        correctOrientation: true
                                    });

        }
    };
};

return {
    getInstance: function () {
        if (!instance) {
            instance = createObject();
        }

        return instance;
    }
};
})();
```

As you can see, `CameraManager` is a singleton object that has a single method as highlighted in the preceding code. The `getPicture(callback, fromGallery)` function uses the Cordova `navigator.camera.getPicture()` method to get a picture.

The `navigator.camera.getPicture(cameraSuccess, cameraError, [cameraOptions])` function has the following parameters:

- `cameraSuccess`: This callback will be called if the operation succeeds. It receives a parameter that represents a file URI, or a native URI, or a Base-64 encoded string based on the specified `cameraOptions` parameter. In `CameraManager`, `cameraSuccess` is set to `callback.onSuccess`.

- `cameraError`: This parameter will be called if the operation fails. In `CameraManager`, `cameraError` is set to `callback.onError`. Note that `CameraError` receives a string that represents the error description.

- `cameraOptions`: This is an optional parameter that holds the camera's configuration.

The `cameraOptions` parameter has many attributes. The attributes in the following table are used by our `CameraManager` object:

Attribute name	Description
`quality`	This represents the quality of the saved image. It is expressed in a range of 0-100, where 100 is typically the full resolution with no loss due to file compression. In our `CameraManager` object, the quality is set to `80`. As per the Cordova documentation, setting the quality below 50 is recommended to avoid memory errors on some iOS devices. Setting the quality to `80` has always given me a good picture quality and has worked fine with me in my Cordova projects; however, if you find any memory errors because of the `navigator.camera.getPicture()` method, then please set the quality below 50 and rebuild/rerun the project again in your iOS device.
`destinationType`	This represents the type of the operation's returned value. It can have one of the following values: • `Camera.DestinationType.DATA_URL`: This means that the returned value will be a Base64-encoded string that represents the image • `Camera.DestinationType.FILE_URI`: This means that the returned value will be a file URI of the image • `Camera.DestinationType.NATIVE_URI`: This means that the returned value will be a native URI of the image In our `CameraManager` object, `destinationType` is set to `Camera.DestinationType.FILE_URI`, which means that the success callback of the `navigator.camera.getPicture()` method will receive the image file URI.
`sourceType`	This represents the source of the picture. It can have one of the following values: • `Camera.PictureSourceType.PHOTOLIBRARY` • `Camera.PictureSourceType.CAMERA` • `Camera.PictureSourceType.SAVEDPHOTOALBUM` In our `CameraManager` object, `sourceType` is set to `Camera.PictureSourceType.PHOTOLIBRARY` if `fromGallery` is set to `true`. If `fromGallery` is set to `false`, then `sourceType` is set to `Camera.PictureSourceType.CAMERA`.
`correctOrientation`	If this is set to `true`, then it will rotate the image to correct it for the orientation of the device during capture.

We are now done with the `Camera` functionality in our Cordova Exhibition app. However, before exploring the compass functionality, note that the `navigator.camera.getPicture()` function's `CameraOptions` parameter has also the attributes shown in the following table:

Attribute name	Description
`allowEdit`	If set to `true`, this will allow the user to edit an image before selection.
`cameraDirection`	This represents the type of camera to use (front facing or back facing). It can have one of the following values: • `Camera.Direction.BACK` • `Camera.Direction.FRONT`
`encodingType`	This represents the returned image file's encoding; it can have one of the following values: • `Camera.EncodingType.JPEG` • `Camera.EncodingType.PNG`
`mediaType`	This represents the type of media to select from. It only works when `PictureSourceType` is set to `PHOTOLIBRARY` or `SAVEDPHOTOALBUM`. It can have one of the following values: • `Camera.MediaType.PICTURE`: This allows the selection of only pictures • `Camera.MediaType.VIDEO`: This allows the selection of only videos • `Camera.MediaType.ALLMEDIA`: This allows the selection of all media types
`popoverOptions`	This represents the popover location in iPad. It works only for iOS.
`saveToPhotoAlbum`	If set to `true`, then this will save the image to the photo album on the device after capture.
`targetWidth`	This represents the width in pixels to scale image. It must be used with `targetHeight`.
`targetHeight`	This represents the height in pixels to scale image. It must be used with `targetWidth`.

The `navigator.camera` object has also the method shown in the following table:

Method name	Description

`navigator.camera.`
`cleanup(cameraSuccess,`
`cameraError)`
	This forces the removal of the intermediate image files that are kept in temporary storage after calling the `camera.getPicture()` method. This API applies only when the value of `Camera.sourceType` is `Camera.PictureSourceType.CAMERA` and the value of `Camera.destinationType` is `Camera.DestinationType.FILE_URI`. This works only on iOS.
	
	In iOS, the temporary images in `/tmp` might be deleted when exiting the application. Using this API will force an instant cleanup of the temporary images.

Compass

The compass plugin provides access to the device's compass in order to detect the direction (heading) that the device is pointed to (the compass measures the heading in degrees from 0 to 359.99, where 0 represents north). In order to use the compass in our Apache Cordova project, we need to use the following `cordova plugin add` command:

```
>cordova plugin add https://git-wip-us.apache.org/repos/asf/cordova-
plugin-device-orientation.git
```

Demo

In order to access the compass demo, you need to click on the **Compass** list item. You will be introduced to the **Compass** page. Then, you can click on the **Start Watch Heading** button in order to start watching the compass heading. You will be able to get the heading value, as shown in the following screenshot:

The Compass page in action

You can click on the **Stop Watch Heading** button to stop watching the compass heading at any time.

The HTML page

The following code snippet shows the "compass" page:

```
<div data-role="page" id="compass">
    <div data-role="header">
        <h1>Compass</h1>
        <a href="#" data-role="button" data-rel="back" data-
icon="back">Back</a>
    </div>
    <div data-role="content">
        <h1>Welcome to the Compass Gallery</h1>
        <p>Click 'Start Watch Heading' button below to start watch
heading using your device's compass.</p>
        <input type="button" id="startWatchHeading" value="Start
Watch Heading"/>
        <input type="button" id="stopWatchHeading" value="Stop
Watch Heading"/><br/>

        <div id="compassHeading">
        </div>
    </div>
</div>
```

As shown in the preceding "compass" page code snippet, it contains the following:

- A page header that includes a back button
- Page content that includes the following main elements:

    ○ "startWatchHeading": This button is used to start watching the compass heading

    ○ "stopWatchHeading": This button is used to stop watching the compass heading

    ○ "compassHeading": This div is used to display the compass heading result

View controller

The following code snippet shows the page view controller JavaScript object that includes the event handlers of the page (compass.js):

```
(function() {
    var compassManager = CompassManager.getInstance();
    var watchID;

    $(document).on("pageinit", "#compass", function(e) {
        e.preventDefault();

        $("#startWatchHeading").on("tap", function(e) {
            e.preventDefault();

            enableStartWatchHeadingButton(false);

            var callback = {};

            callback.onSuccess = onSuccess;
            callback.onError = onError;

            watchID = compassManager.startWatchHeading(callback);
        });

        $("#stopWatchHeading").on("tap", function(e) {
            e.preventDefault();

            enableStartWatchHeadingButton(true);

            compassManager.stopWatchHeading(watchID);
        });

        initPage();
    });
```

```
    $(document).on("pagebeforehide", "#compass", function(e) {
        compassManager.stopWatchHeading(watchID);
        enableStartWatchHeadingButton(true);
    });

    function initPage() {
        $("#stopWatchHeading").closest('.ui-btn').hide();
    }

    function onSuccess(heading) {
        $("#compassHeading").html("Heading: " +
heading.magneticHeading);
    }

    function onError(error) {
        $("#compassHeading").html("An error occurs during watch
heading: " + error.code);
    }

    function enableStartWatchHeadingButton(enable) {

        if (enable) {
            $("#startWatchHeading").button("enable");
            $("#stopWatchHeading").closest('.ui-btn').hide();
        } else {
            $("#startWatchHeading").button("disable");
            $("#stopWatchHeading").closest('.ui-btn').show();
        }

        $("#startWatchHeading").button("refresh");
    }

})();
```

The "pageinit" event handler registers the "startWatchHeading" tap event
handler. The "startWatchHeading" tap event handler does the following:

- It disables the "startWatchHeading" button and
  shows the "stopWatchHeading" button by calling
  enableStartWatchHeadingButton(false)

- It starts to watch the heading by calling `compassManager.startWatchHeading(callback)` and specifying the `callback` object parameter, which contains the following attributes:

  ○ `onSuccess`: This callback will be called if the operation succeeds

  ○ `onError`: This callback will be called if the operation fails

The `compassManager.startWatchHeading(callback)` function returns `watchID` that we will be using in order to stop watching the compass heading.

The `"pageinit"` event handler also registers the `"stopWatchHeading"` tap event handler. The `"stopWatchHeading"` tap event handler does the following:

- It hides the `"stopWatchHeading"` button and enables the `"startWatchHeading"` button by calling `enableStartWatchHeadingButton(true)`

- It stops watching the heading by calling `compassManager.stopWatchHeading(watchID)` and specifying `watchID` parameter, which we get from the `compassManager.startWatchHeading(callback)` call

The `"pageinit"` event handler also calls `initPage()` in order to hide the `"stopWatchHeading"` button at the beginning.

In `onSuccess(heading)`, which will be called if `compassManager.startWatchHeading(callback)` succeeds, `heading.magneticHeading` (which represents the heading in degrees) is displayed in the `"compassHeading"` div. In `onError()`, which will be called if `compassManager.startWatchHeading(callback)` fails, an error message is displayed in the `"compassHeading"` div. Finally, in order to make sure to stop watching the heading before leaving the page, `compassManager.stopWatchHeading()` is called in the `"pagebeforehide"` event.

API

The following code snippet shows the compass manager JavaScript object that interacts with the Apache Cordova Compass API (`CompassManager.js`):

```
var CompassManager = (function () {
  var instance;

  function createObject() {
    return {
```

```
        startWatchHeading: function (callback) {
            return navigator.compass.watchHeading(callback.
onSuccess,
                                        callback.onError,
                                        {frequency:
2000});
        },
        stopWatchHeading: function (watchID) {
            if (watchID) {
                navigator.compass.clearWatch(watchID);
            }
        }
    };
};

return {
    getInstance: function () {
        if (!instance) {
            instance = createObject();
        }

        return instance;
    }
};
})();
```

As you can see in the preceding code, `CompassManager` is a singleton object that has the following two methods, as highlighted in the code:

- `startWatchHeading(callback)`: This uses the Cordova `navigator. compass.watchHeading()` method to watch the compass heading. The `navigator.compass.watchHeading(compassSuccess, compassError, [compassOptions])` method has the following parameters:

    ○ `compassSuccess(heading)`: This callback will be called if the operation succeeds. It receives an object (`heading`) that contains the current heading's information as a parameter. In `CompassManager`, `compassSuccess` is set to `callback.onSuccess`.

    ○ `compassError`: This callback will be called if the operation fails. In `CompassManager`, `compassError` is set to `callback.onError`.

- ° compassOptions: This is an optional parameter that holds the compass' configuration. It has a frequency attribute to specify how often to retrieve the compass heading in milliseconds. In CompassManager, the frequency parameter is set to 2000 milliseconds (note that this parameter is 100 milliseconds by default).

- stopWatchHeading(watchID): This uses the Cordova navigator.compass. clearWatch() method to remove the compass heading. The navigator. compass.clearWatch(watchID) method has the following parameter:

  - ° watchID: This represents the ID returned by navigator.compass. watchHeading().

This compassOptions object (which is passed as the last parameter to navigator. compass.watchHeading method) has the attributes shown in the following table:

Attribute name	Description
frequency	This represents the frequency of compass heading retrieval in milliseconds. By default, it is 100 milliseconds.
filter	This represents the change in degrees that is required in order to initiate a watchHeading success callback. It is not supported in Android, Windows Phone 7 and 8, Tizen, Firefox OS, and Amazon Fire OS.

The heading object (which is passed as a parameter to the compassSuccess callback) has the attributes shown in the following table:

Attribute name	Description
magneticHeading	This represents the heading in degrees from 0 to 359.99 at a single point of time.
trueHeading	This represents the heading relative to the geographic North Pole in degrees from 0 to 359.99 at a single point of time. A negative value indicates that the true heading cannot be determined.
headingAccuracy	This is the deviation in degrees between the reported heading and the true heading.
timestamp	This is the time in which the compass heading was retrieved.

We are now done with the `Compass` functionality in our Cordova Exhibition app. However, before exploring the `Connection` functionality, note that the `navigator.compass` object has also the method shown in the following table:

Method name	Description
`navigator.compass.getCurrentHeading (compassSuccess, compassError, compassOptions)`	This retrieves the information of the current compass heading. When the operation succeeds, the heading information is passed to the `compassSuccess` callback as a parameter.

Connection

The connection plugin provides information about the connection type of the device. In order to use the connection plugin in our Apache Cordova project, we need to use the following `cordova plugin add` command:

```
> cordova plugin add https://git-wip-us.apache.org/repos/asf/cordova-
plugin-network-information.git
```

Demo

In order to access the connection demo, you can click on the **Connection** list item. You will be introduced to the **Connection** page. You can click on the **Get Connection Type** button in order to know the current connection type of your device, as shown in the following screenshot:

Getting the device's connection type

The HTML page

The following code snippet shows the `"connection"` page:

```
<div data-role="page" id="connection">
    <div data-role="header">
        <h1>Connection</h1>
        <a href="#" data-role="button" data-rel="back" data-
icon="back">Back</a>
    </div>
    <div data-role="content">
        <h1>Welcome to the Connection Gallery</h1>
        <p>Click 'Get Connection Type' button below to know the
connection type.</p>
        <input type="button" id="getConnectionType" value="Get
Connection Type"/><br/>
        <div id="connectionType">
        </div>
    </div>
</div>
```

As shown in the preceding `"connection"` page code snippet, it contains the following:

- A page header that includes a back button
- Page content that includes only one button, `"getConnectionType"`, and one div, `"connectionType"`, to display the connection type

View controller

The following code snippet shows the page view controller JavaScript object that includes the action handlers of the page (`connection.js`):

```
(function() {
    var connectionManager = ConnectionManager.getInstance();
    $(document).on("pageinit", "#connection", function(e) {
        e.preventDefault();

        $("#getConnectionType").on("tap", function(e) {
            e.preventDefault();

            $("#connectionType").html("Current Connection: " +
connectionManager.getCurrentConnection());
        });
    });
})();
```

The "pageinit" event handler registers the "getConnectionType" tap event handler. In the "getConnectionType" tap event handler, it displays the current connection of the device, which is retrieved by calling the connectionManager.getCurrentConnection() method.

API

The following code snippet shows the connection manager JavaScript object that interacts with the Apache Cordova Connection API (ConnectionManager.js):

```
var ConnectionManager = (function () {
  var instance;

  function createObject() {
      return {
          getCurrentConnection: function () {
              var connectionType = navigator.connection.type;

              switch(connectionType) {
                  case Connection.UNKNOWN:
                      return "Unknown connection";
                  case Connection.ETHERNET:
                      return "Ethernet connection";
                  case Connection.WIFI:
                      return "WiFi connection";
                  case Connection.CELL_2G:
                      return "Cell 2G connection";
                  case Connection.CELL_3G:
                      return "Cell 3G connection";
                  case Connection.CELL_4G:
                      return "Cell 4G connection";
                  case Connection.CELL:
                      return "Cell generic connection";
                  case Connection.NONE:
```

```
                    return "No network connection";
                default:
                    return "Un-recognized connection";
                }
            }
        };
    };
    return {
      getInstance: function () {
        if (!instance) {
            instance = createObject();
        }

        return instance;
      }
    };
})();
```

As you can see, `ConnectionManager` is a singleton object that has a single method as highlighted in the code. The `getCurrentConnection()` method uses the Cordova `navigator.connection.type` property in order to get the currently active network connection (Ethernet, Wi-Fi, cell 2G, cell 3G, and so on).

Contacts

The contacts plugin provides access to the device's contacts database in order to find and create contacts. In order to use the contacts plugin in our Apache Cordova project, we need to use the following `cordova plugin add` command:

```
> cordova plugin add https://git-wip-us.apache.org/repos/asf/cordova-
plugin-contacts.git
```

Demo

In order to access the contacts demo, you can click on the **Contacts** list item. You will be introduced to the **Contacts** page. You can search for contacts by typing in the search field (you have to type at least three characters), as shown in the following screenshot:

Searching for contacts

You can click on any of the filtered contacts, and you will be introduced to the **Contact Details** page in order to check the contact details, as shown in the following screenshot:

Viewing contact details

The HTML page

The following code snippet shows the `"contacts"` page:

```
<div data-role="page" id="contacts">
    <div data-role="header">
        <h1>Contacts</h1>
        <a href="#" data-role="button" data-rel="back" data-
icon="back">Back</a>
    </div>
    <div data-role="content">
        <ul data-role="listview" id="contactList" data-
filter="true" data-filter-placeholder="Enter 3+ chars to search
...">
        </ul>
    </div>
</div>
```

As shown in the preceding `"contacts"` page code snippet, it contains the following:

- A page header that includes a back button.
- Page content that includes a jQuery Mobile list view element (`"contactList"`) that is defined by setting the `data-role` attribute to `"listview"`. Setting the `data-filter` attribute to `true` tells jQuery Mobile to provide a search field for our list view. Finally, the `placeholder` attribute informs the user to enter at least three characters in order to search for contacts.

When the user clicks on any of the filtered contacts, the user will be introduced to the `"contactDetails"` page. The following code snippet shows the `"contactDetails"` page:

```
<div data-role="page" id="contactDetails">
    <div data-role="header">
        <h1>Contact Details</h1>
        <a href="#" data-role="button" data-rel="back" data-
icon="back">Back</a>
    </div>
    <div data-role="content">
        <div id="contactInfo"></div>
    </div>
</div>
```

As shown in the preceding `"contact details"` page code snippet, it contains the following:

- A page header that includes a back button
- Page content that includes a `"contactInfo"` div to display information on contact details

View controller

The following code snippet shows the contacts page view controller JavaScript object that includes the event handlers of the page (`contacts.js`):

```
(function() {
    var contactsManager = ContactsManager.getInstance();

    $(document).on("pageinit", "#contacts", function(e) {
        e.preventDefault();

        $("#contactList").on("filterablebeforefilter", function
(e, data) {
            e.preventDefault();
```

```
                    var filterText = data.input.val();

                    if (filterText && filterText.length > 2) {
                        var callback = {};

                        callback.onSuccess = function (contacts) {
                            updateContactsList(contacts);
                        };

                        callback.onError = function (error) {
                            $("#contactList").empty();
                            $("<li>Error displaying contacts</li>").
appendTo("#contactList");
                        };

                        contactsManager.getAllContacts(callback,
filterText);
                    }
                });
            });

        function updateContactsList(contacts) {
            $("#contactList").empty();

            if (jQuery.isEmptyObject(contacts)) {
                $("<li>No Contacts Available</li>").
appendTo("#contactList");
            } else {
                var i;

                //Display the top 50 elements
                for (i = 0; i < contacts.length || i < 50; ++i) {
                    if (contacts[i]) {
                        $("<li><a href='#contactDetails?contact=" +
encodeURIComponent(JSON.stringify(contacts[i])) + "'>" +
                            contacts[i].name.formatted +
"</a></li>").appendTo("#contactList");
                    }
                }
            }

            $("#contactList").listview('refresh');
        }
    })();
```

As highlighted in the preceding code snippet, the `"pageinit"` event handler registers the `"filterablebeforefilter"` event handler on the `"contactList"` list view in order to create our custom contacts filter. In the `"filterablebeforefilter"` event handler, the current filter text entered by the user is retrieved by calling `data.input.val()`. In order to minimize the search space, the filter text has to be at least three characters. If the filter text's length exceeds two characters, then a call to the `contactsManager.getAllContacts(callback, filterText)` method is performed in order to get all the contacts that match the entered filter text.

In order to call the `contactsManager.getAllContacts(callback, filterText)` method, we specified a callback object that contains two attributes: the `onSuccess` attribute (which represents a success callback) and the `onError` attribute (which represents a failure callback). The `onSuccess` callback receives the filtered contacts list and then calls the `updateContactsList()` method in order to update the current contacts list view with the new filtered contacts list. The `onError` callback just displays an error message to the user. The second parameter `filterText` represents the input filter text.

The `updateContactsList(contacts)` method clears the `"contactList"` list view, and if the contacts list (`contacts`) is not empty, contacts are appended to the `"contactList"` list view, and finally, the `"contactList"` list view is refreshed with new updates.

You might notice that every contact item in the list view is linked to the `"contactDetails"` page and passes the item's contact object as a parameter (after converting the contact object to an encoded JSON string).

Thanks to the jQuery Mobile page parameters plugin (which can be downloaded from `https://github.com/jblas/jquery-mobile-plugins/tree/master/page-params`) and its inclusion in the `index.html` file, we can pass parameters between pages easily using `"#pageID?param1=value1&param2=value2 ...etc`.

However, in our application, in the `js/common.js` file (which contains common utilities across all of the app pages and is included after the plugin, that is, the `jqm.page.params.js` file), we added a small utility over the plugin in order to retrieve page parameters at any event of the `"to"` page. In order to implement this, we create an event handler for the `"pagebeforechange"` event in order to get the passed parameter(s), as shown in the following code snippet:

```
$(document).bind("pagebeforechange", function(event, data) {
    $.mobile.pageData = (data && data.options &&
data.options.pageData)
                        ? data.options.pageData : null;
});
```

By checking `data.options.pageData`, we can determine whether there are any passed parameters from the `"from"` page to the `"to"` page, thanks to the page parameters plugin. After getting the passed parameters, we set them in `$.mobile.pageData`, which can be accessible from any event in the `"to"` page. If there are no passed parameters, then `$.mobile.pageData` will be set to `null`.

The following code snippet shows `contactDetails.js`, which is the view controller of the `"contactDetails"` page:

```
(function() {
    $(document).on("pageshow", "#contactDetails", function(e) {
        e.preventDefault();

        var contactDetailsParam = $.mobile.pageData.contact ||
null;
        var contactDetails = JSON.parse(decodeURIComponent(contactDet
ailsParam));
        var i;
        var numbers = "";

        if (contactDetails.phoneNumbers) {
            for (i = 0; i < contactDetails.phoneNumbers.length; ++i)
{
                numbers = "<a href='tel:" + contactDetails.
phoneNumbers[i].value + "'>" +
                        contactDetails.phoneNumbers[i].value +
"</a><br/>";
            }
        } else {
            numbers = "NA<br/>";
        }

        $("#contactInfo").html("<p>" +
                "Name: <strong>" + contactDetails.name.formatted +
"</strong><br/><br/>" +
                "Phone(s): " + "<br/>" +
                numbers +
                "</p>");
    });
})();
```

In the "pageshow" event handler of the "contactDetails" page, contactDetails is retrieved using $.mobile.pageData.contact and then decoded and parsed to be converted to a JavaScript object. Finally, the contact names and numbers are acquired from contactDetails using contactDetails.name.formatted and contactDetails.phoneNumbers and are displayed in the "contactInfo" div.

 The jQuery Mobile "pageshow" event is triggered on the "to" page after the transition completes.

API

The following code snippet shows the contacts manager JavaScript object that wraps the Apache Cordova Contacts API (ContactsManager.js):

```
var ContactsManager = (function () {
    var instance;

    function createObject() {
        return {
            getAllContacts: function (callback, filterText) {
                var options = new ContactFindOptions();

                options.filter = filterText || "";
                options.multiple = true;

                var fields = ["id", "name", "phoneNumbers"];

                navigator.contacts.find(callback.onSuccess, callback.
onError, fields, options);
            }
        };
    };

    return {
        getInstance: function () {
            if (!instance) {
                instance = createObject();
            }

            return instance;
        }
    };
})();
```

As you can see, `ContactsManager` is a singleton object that has a single method as highlighted in the preceding code. The `getAllContacts(callback, filterText)` method uses the Cordova `navigator.contacts.find()` method to retrieve contacts.

The `navigator.contacts.find(contactSuccess, contactError, contactFields, contactFindOptions)` method has the following parameters:

- `contactSuccess`: This callback will be called if the operation succeeds. It receives the retrieved contacts array as a parameter. In `ContactsManager`, `contactSuccess` is set to `callback.onSuccess`.

- `contactError`: This callback will be called if the operation fails. In `ContactsManager`, `contactError` is set to `callback.onError`.

- `contactFields`: This object specifies the fields of every contact object in the returned result of `navigator.contacts.find()`. In `ContactsManager`, we specified the `["id", "name", "phoneNumbers"]` contact fields.

- `contactFindOptions`: This is an optional parameter that is used to filter contacts.

The `contactFindOptions` parameter has the attributes shown in the following table:

Attribute name	Description
`filter`	This represents the search string used to filter contacts. In `ContactsManager`, the value is set to `filterText`.
`multiple`	This specifies whether the `find` operation returns multiple contacts. By default, it is `false`. In our `ContactsManager`, it is set to `true`.

We are now done with the `Contacts` functionality in the Cordova Exhibition app. However, before exploring the device's API functionality, note that the `navigator.contacts.find()` method's `contactFields` parameter can have one or more attribute(s) from the `Contact` object, whose attributes are specified in the following table:

Attribute name	Description
`id`	This represents a globally unique identifier for the contact. It is used in our contacts example.
`displayName`	This represents the name of this contact.
`name`	This represents a `ContactName` object that contains all the components of a name, which will be illustrated later. It is used in our contacts example.
`nickname`	This represents the contact's nickname.

Attribute name	Description
phoneNumbers	This represents a ContactField array of all the contacts' phone numbers. It is used in our contacts example. The ContactField object will be illustrated later.
Emails	This represents a ContactField array of all the contacts' e-mail addresses.
addresses	This represents a ContactAddress array of all the contacts' addresses. It will be illustrated later.
ims	This represents a ContactField array of all the contacts' IM addresses.
organizations	This represents a ContactOrganization array of all the contacts' organizations. It will be illustrated later.
birthday	This represents the contact's birthday.
note	This represents a note about the contact.
photos	This represents a ContactField array of the contacts' photos.
categories	This represents a ContactField array of all the user-defined categories associated with the contact.
urls	This represents a ContactField array of web pages associated with the contact.

The ContactName object has the attributes shown in the following table:

Attribute name	Description
formatted	This represents the complete name of the contact.
familyName	This represents the contact's family name.
givenName	This represents the contact's given name.
middleName	This represents the contact's middle name.
honorificPrefix	This represents the contact's prefix (such as Mr or Mrs).
honorificSuffix	This represents the contact's suffix.

The ContactField object has the attributes shown in the following table:

Attribute name	Description
type	This represents a string that indicates what type of field it is.
value	This represents the value of the field, for example, a phone number.
pref	If this is set to true, it means that this ContactField object contains the user's preferred value.

The ContactAddress object has the attributes shown in the following table:

Attribute name	Description
type	This represents a string that indicates what type of field it is.
pref	If this is set to true, it means that this ContactAddress object contains the user's preferred value.
formatted	This represents the formatted full address for display.
streetAddress	This represents the full street address.
locality	This represents the city or locality.
region	This represents the state or region.
postalCode	This represents the zip code or postal code.
country	This represents the country name.

The ContactOrganization object has the attributes shown in the following table:

Attribute name	Description
type	This represents a string that indicates what type of field it is, for example, "home".
pref	If this is set to true, it means that this ContactOrganization contains the user's preferred value.
name	This represents the contact's organization name.
department	This represents the contact's department name inside the organization.
title	This represent the contact's title in the organization.

The navigator.contacts object has also the method shown in the following table:

Method name	Description
navigator.contacts.create(properties)	This is used to return a Contact object that you can use, for example, to save a contact in the device contacts database by calling the save() method of the Contact object.

Device

The device plugin defines a global device object that describes the device's hardware and software. It is very important to note that the device object is available after the `"deviceready"` event occurs. In order to use the device plugin in our Apache Cordova project, we need to use the following `cordova plugin add` command:

```
> cordova plugin add https://git-wip-us.apache.org/repos/asf/cordova-
plugin-device.git
```

Demo

In order to access the device demo, you can click on the **Device** list item. You will be introduced to the **Device** page. You can click on the **Get Device Info** button in order to get your device information, as shown in the following screenshot:

Getting device information

The HTML page

The following code snippet shows the `"device"` page:

```
<div data-role="page" id="device">
    <div data-role="header">
        <h1>Device</h1>
        <a href="#" data-role="button" data-rel="back" data-
icon="back">Back</a>
    </div>
    <div data-role="content">
        <h1>Welcome to the Device Gallery</h1>
        <p>Click 'Get Device Info' button below to get the device
information.</p>
        <input type="button" id="getDeviceInfo" value="Get Device
Info"/><br/>

        <div id="deviceInfo">
        </div>
    </div>
</div>
```

As shown in the preceding `"device"` page code snippet, it contains the following:

- A page header that includes a back button
- Page content that includes a `"getDeviceInfo"` button to get the device information and a `"deviceInfo"` div in order to display device information

View controller

The following code snippet shows the `"device"` page view controller JavaScript object that includes the event handlers of the page (`device.js`):

```
(function() {
    var deviceManager = DeviceManager.getInstance();

    $(document).on("pageinit", "#device", function(e) {
        e.preventDefault();

        $("#getDeviceInfo").on("tap", function(e) {
            e.preventDefault();

            $("#deviceInfo").html(deviceManager.getDeviceInfo());
        });
    });
})();
```

As shown in the preceding code snippet, the `"pageinit"` event handler registers the `"tap"` event handler on the `"getDeviceInfo"` button. In the `"tap"` event handler of the `"getDeviceInfo"` button, the device information is displayed in the `"deviceInfo"` div and retrieved by calling the `deviceManager.getDeviceInfo()` method.

API

The following code snippet shows the device manager JavaScript object that uses the Apache Cordova device object (`DeviceManager.js`):

```
var DeviceManager = (function () {
    var instance;

    function createObject() {
        return {
            getDeviceInfo: function () {
                return "Device Model: "     + device.model     + "<br
/>" +
                       "Device Cordova: "   + device.cordova   + "<br
/>" +
                       "Device Platform: "  + device.platform  + "<br
/>" +
                       "Device UUID: "      + device.uuid      + "<br
/>" +
                       "Device Version: "   + device.version   + "<br
/>";
            }
        };
    };

    return {
        getInstance: function () {
            if (!instance) {
                instance = createObject();
            }
```

```
            return instance;
        }
    };
})();
```

The `DeviceManager` object is a singleton object that has a single method as highlighted in the preceding code. The `getDeviceInfo()` function uses the Cordova device object to retrieve the device information.

The `DeviceManager` object uses the attributes of the device object, as shown in the following table:

Attribute name	Description
model	This represents the device's model name.
cordova	This represents the version of Apache Cordova that runs on this device.
platform	This represents the device's operating system name.
uuid	This represents the device's **Universally Unique Identifier (UUID)**.
version	This represents the device's operating system version.

Geolocation

The geolocation plugin provides information about the device's current location that can be retrieved via **Global Positioning System (GPS)**, network signals, and GSM/CDMA cell IDs. Note that there is no guarantee that the API returns the device's actual location.

In order to use the geolocation plugin in our Apache Cordova project, we need to use the following `cordova plugin add` command:

```
> cordova plugin add https://git-wip-us.apache.org/repos/asf/cordova-
plugin-geolocation.git
```

Demo

In order to access the geolocation demo, you can click on the **Geolocation** list item. You will be introduced to the **Geolocation** page. You can click on the **Get Current Position** button in order to get your device's current position, as shown in the following screenshot:

Getting the device's position

The HTML page

The following code snippet shows the `"geolocation"` page:

```
<div data-role="page" id="geolocation">
    <div data-role="header">
        <h1>Geolocation</h1>
        <a href="#" data-role="button" data-rel="back" data-
icon="back">Back</a>
    </div>
    <div data-role="content">
        <h1>Welcome to the Geolocation Gallery</h1>
        <p>Click 'Get Current Position' button below to know where
you are.</p>
        <input type="button" id="getCurrentPosition" value="Get
Current Position"/><br/>

        <div id="position">
        </div>
    </div>
</div>
```

As shown in the preceding `"geolocation"` page code snippet, it contains the following:

- A page header that includes a back button
- Page content that includes a `"getCurrentPosition"` button to get the device's current position and a `"position"` div in order to display it

View controller

The following code snippet shows the `"geolocation"` page view controller JavaScript object that includes the event handlers of the page (`geolocation.js`):

```
(function() {
    var geolocationManager = GeolocationManager.getInstance();

    $(document).on("pageinit", "#geolocation", function(e) {
        e.preventDefault();

        $("#getCurrentPosition").on("tap", function(e) {
            e.preventDefault();

            var callback = {};
```

```
            callback.onSuccess = onSuccess;
            callback.onError = onError;

            geolocationManager.getCurrentPosition(callback);
        });
    });

    function onSuccess(position) {
        console.log("position is retrieved successfully");

        $("#position").html("Latitude: "  +
position.coords.latitude + "<br />" +
                            "Longitude: " +
position.coords.longitude);
    }

    function onError(error) {
        $("#position").html("Error code: " + error.code + ",
message: " + error.message);
    }
})();
```

As shown in the preceding code snippet, the `"pageinit"` event handler registers the `"tap"` event handler on the `"getCurrentPosition"` button. In the `"tap"` event handler of the `"getCurrentPosition"` button, the device's current position is retrieved by calling the `geolocationManager.getCurrentPosition()` method.

The `geolocationManager.getCurrentPosition(callback)` method takes a `callback` object as a parameter that contains two attributes (`onSuccess` and `onError`) that refer to the following callbacks:

- `onSuccess(position)`: This callback will be called if the operation succeeds. It receives a position object (which represents the device's current position) as a parameter. Inside the success callback, the position's longitude and latitude information are displayed in the `"position"` div.

- `onError(error)`: This callback will be called if the operation fails. It receives an `error` object that contains the error information (error code and error message) as a parameter.

API

The following code snippet shows the geolocation manager JavaScript object that interacts with the Apache Cordova geolocation API (GeolocationManager.js):

```
var GeolocationManager = (function () {
    var instance;

    function createObject() {
        return {
            getCurrentPosition: function (callback) {
                navigator.geolocation.getCurrentPosition(callback.
onSuccess,
callback.onError,

                                                        {
timeout: 15000,
enableHighAccuracy: true

                                                        });
            }
        };
    };

    return {
        getInstance: function () {
            if (!instance) {
                instance = createObject();
            }

            return instance;
        }
    };
})();
```

As shown, GeolocationManager is a singleton object that has a single method, getCurrentPosition(callback), as highlighted in the preceding code. This method uses the Cordova navigator.geolocation.getCurrentPosition() method in order to retrieve the device's current position.

The `navigator.geolocation.getCurrentPosition(geolocationSuccess, [geolocationError], [geolocationOptions])` method has the following parameters:

- `geolocationSuccess`: This represents the successful callback that will be called when the operation succeeds. It receives a `Position` object that holds the current position information as a parameter. In `GeolocationManager`, `geolocationSuccess` is set to `callback.onSuccess`.

- `geolocationError`: This is an optional parameter that represents the error callback that will be called when the operation fails. It receives a `PositionError` object that holds the error information (the code that represents the error code and the message that represents the error message) as a parameter. In `GeolocationManager`, `geolocationError` is set to `callback.onError`.

- `geolocationOptions`: This is an optional parameter that represents the geolocation options.

The `geolocationOptions` object has the attributes shown in the following table:

Attribute name	Description
enableHighAccuracy	If this attribute is set to `true`, it informs the plugin to use more accurate methods in order to get the current position, such as satellite positioning. In `GeolocationManager.getCurrentPosition()`, `enableHighAccuracy` is set to `true`.
timeout	This represents the time in milliseconds after which the operation times out. In `GeolocationManager.getCurrentPosition()`, `timeout` is set to `15000`.
maximumAge	This is the maximum time in milliseconds for cached position.

The `Position` object has the attributes shown in the following table:

Attribute name	Description
coords	This represents a `Coordinates` object that represents coordinates of the position.
timestamp	This represents the creation timestamp of `coords`.

The `Coordinates` object has the attributes shown in the following table:

Attribute name	Description
`latitude`	This represents the position's latitude. It is used in our geolocation example.
`longitude`	This represents the position's longitude. It is used in our geolocation example.
`altitude`	This represents the height of the position in meters above the ellipsoid.
`accuracy`	This represents the accuracy level of the latitude and longitude coordinates in meters.
`altitudeAccuracy`	This represents the accuracy level of the altitude coordinate in meters.
`heading`	This represents the direction of travel, specified in degrees, counting clockwise relative to true north.
`speed`	This represents the current ground speed of the device, specified in meters per second.

Note that `navigator.geolocation` has the following two more methods:

- `watchPosition(geolocationSuccess, [geolocationError], [geolocationOptions])`: This can watch for changes in the device's current position. It returns a watch ID that should be used with `clearWatch()` to stop watching for changes in position.
- `clearWatch(watchID)`: This can stop watching the changes to the device's position referenced by the `watchID` parameter.

We are now done with the geolocation functionality in the Cordova Exhibition app.

Globalization

The globalization plugin can be used in order to get the user locale and language and to perform operations specific to the user's locale and time zone.

In order to use the globalization plugin in our Apache Cordova project, we need to use the following `cordova plugin add` command:

```
> cordova plugin add https://git-wip-us.apache.org/repos/asf/cordova-
plugin-globalization.git
```

Demo

In order to access the globalization demo, you can click on the **Globalization** list item. You will be introduced to the **Globalization** page. You can click on the **Get Locale Name** button in order to get the user's locale name or the **Get Preferred Language** button in order to get the user's preferred language, as shown in the following screenshot:

Getting the user's locale and preferred language

The HTML page

The following code snippet shows the "globalization" page:

```
<div data-role="page" id="globalization">
    <div data-role="header">
        <h1>Globalization</h1>
        <a href="#" data-role="button" data-rel="back" data-
icon="back">Back</a>
    </div>
    <div data-role="content">
        <h1>Welcome to the Globalization Gallery</h1>
        <p>Click the buttons below to explore globalization.</p>
        <input type="button" id="getLocaleName" value="Get Locale
Name"/>
        <input type="button" id="getPreferredLanguage" value="Get
Preferred Language"/><br/>

        <div id="globInfo">
        </div>
    </div>
</div>
```

As shown in the preceding "globalization" page code snippet, it contains the following:

- A page header that includes a back button
- Page content that includes a "getLocaleName" button to get the user locale, a "getPreferredLanguage" button to get the user preferred language, and a "globInfo" div in order to display the results

View controller

The following code snippet shows the "globalization" page view controller JavaScript object that includes the event handlers of the page (globalization.js):

```
(function() {
    var globalizationManager = GlobalizationManager.getInstance();

    $(document).on("pageinit", "#globalization", function(e) {
        e.preventDefault();
```

```
        $("#getLocaleName").on("tap", function(e) {
            e.preventDefault();

            var callback = {};

            callback.onSuccess = handleLocaleSuccess;
            callback.onError = handleLocaleError;

            globalizationManager.getLocaleName(callback);
        });

        $("#getPreferredLanguage").on("tap", function(e) {
            e.preventDefault();

            var callback = {};

            callback.onSuccess = handleLangSuccess;
            callback.onError = handleLangError;

            globalizationManager.getPreferredLanguage(callback);
        });
    });

    function handleLocaleSuccess(locale) {
        $("#globInfo").html("Locale Name: " + locale.value +
"<br/>");
    }

    function handleLocaleError() {
        $("#globInfo").html("Unable to get Locale name<br/>");
    }

    function handleLangSuccess(language) {
        $("#globInfo").html("Preferred language name: " +
language.value + "<br/");
    }

    function handleLangError() {
        $("#globInfo").html("Unable to get preferred language
name<br/>");
    }
})();
```

As shown in the preceding code snippet, the `"pageinit"` event handler registers the `"tap"` event handler on the `"getLocaleName"` button. In the `"tap"` event handler of the `"getLocaleName"` button, the user locale is retrieved by calling the `globalizationManager.getLocaleName()` method.

The `globalizationManager.getLocaleName(callback)` method takes a callback object as a parameter that contains two attributes (`onSuccess` and `onError`) that refer to the following callbacks in order:

- `handleLocaleSuccess(locale)`: This callback will be called if the operation succeeds; it receives a locale object that represents the user's current locale as a parameter. In the success callback, the locale value is displayed in the `"globInfo"` div.

- `handleLocaleError()`: This callback will be called if the operation fails.

The `"pageinit"` event handler also registers the `"tap"` event handler on the `"getPreferredLanguage"` button. In the `"tap"` event handler of the `"getPreferredLanguage"` button, the user's preferred language is retrieved by calling the `globalizationManager.getPreferredLanguage()` method.

The `globalizationManager.getPreferredLanguage(callback)` method takes a callback object as a parameter that contains two attributes (`onSuccess` and `onError`) that refer to the following callbacks in order:

- `handleLangSuccess(language)`: This callback will be called if the operation succeeds; it receives a language object that represents the user's preferred language as a parameter. In the success callback, the preferred language value is displayed in the `"globInfo"` div.

- `handleLangError()`: This callback will be called if the operation fails.

API

The following code snippet shows the globalization manager JavaScript object that interacts with the Apache Cordova Globalization API (`GlobalizationManager.js`):

```
var GlobalizationManager = (function () {
    var instance;

    function createObject() {
        return {
            getLocaleName: function (callback) {
                navigator.globalization.getLocaleName(callback.
onSuccess, callback.onError);
            },
```

```
                getPreferredLanguage: function (callback) {
                    navigator.globalization.getPreferredLanguage(callback.
    onSuccess,
    callback.onError);
                }
            };
        };

        return {
            getInstance: function () {
                if (!instance) {
                    instance = createObject();
                }

                return instance;
            }
        };
    })();
```

As shown, `GlobalizationManager` is a singleton object that has two methods as highlighted in the preceding code. The first one is `getLocaleName(callback)`, which uses the Cordova `navigator.globalization.getLocaleName()` method in order to retrieve the user's current locale.

The `navigator.globalization.getLocaleName(successCallback, errorCallback)` method has the following parameters:

- `successCallback`: This represents the successful callback that will be called when the operation succeeds. It receives a locale object that holds the current locale information as a parameter. In `GlobalizationManager`, `sucessCallback` is set to `callback.onSuccess`.

- `errorCallback`: This represents the error callback that will be called when the operation fails. It receives a `GlobalizationError` object that holds the error information (the code that represents the error code and the message that represents the error message) as a parameter. In `GlobalizationManager`, `errorCallback` is set to `callback.onError`.

The second method is `getPreferredLanguage(callback)` that uses the Cordova `navigator.globalization.getPreferredLanguage()` method in order to retrieve the user's preferred language.

The `navigator.globalization.getPreferredLanguage(successCallback, errorCallback)` method has the following parameters:

- `successCallback`: This represents the successful callback that will be called when the operation succeeds. It receives a `language` object that holds the user's preferred language information as a parameter. In `GlobalizationManager`, `sucessCallback` is set to `callback.onSuccess`.

- `errorCallback`: This represents the error callback that will be called when the operation fails. It receives a `GlobalizationError` object that holds the error information (the code that represents the error code and the message that represents the error message). In `GlobalizationManager`, `errorCallback` is set to `callback.onError`.

 The `navigator.globalization` object has more methods that you can check out in the Apache Cordova documentation at `https://github.com/apache/cordova-plugin-globalization/blob/master/doc/index.md`.

We are now done with the globalization functionality in the Cordova Exhibition app.

InAppBrowser

The InAppBrowser plugin can provide a web browser view that is displayed when calling the `window.open()` function or when opening a link formed as `<a target="_blank">`.

In order to use the `InAppBrowser` plugin in our Apache Cordova project, we need to use the following `cordova plugin add` command:

```
> cordova plugin add https://git-wip-us.apache.org/repos/asf/cordova-plugin-inappbrowser.git
```

Demo

In order to access the `InAppBrowser` demo, you can click on the InAppBrowser list item. You will be introduced to the **InAppBrowser** page. As shown in the following screenshot, you can click on the **Open and Close web page** button in order to open the `http://www.google.com/` web page using InAppBrowser. Note that the opened web page will be closed after 10 seconds.

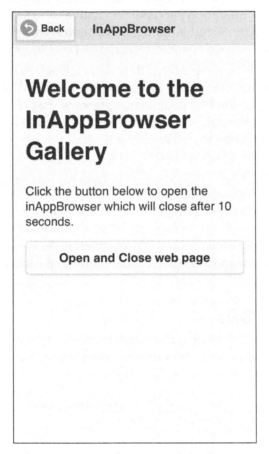

Opening an external page using InAppBrowser

The HTML page

The following code snippet shows the `"inAppBrowser"` page:

```
<div data-role="page" id="inAppBrowser">
    <div data-role="header">
        <h1>InAppBrowser</h1>
        <a href="#" data-role="button" data-rel="back" data-
icon="back">Back</a>
    </div>
    <div data-role="content">
        <h1>Welcome to the InAppBrowser Gallery</h1>
        <p>Click the button below to open the inAppBrowser which
will close after 10 seconds.</p>

        <input type="button" id="openGoogleSearchPage" value="Open
and Close web page"/>
    </div>
</div>
```

As shown in the preceding `"inAppBrowser"` page code snippet, it contains the following:

- A page header that includes a back button
- Page content that includes a `"openGoogleSearchPage"` button to open a web page (http://www.google.com/) and close it after 10 seconds

View controller

The following code snippet shows the InAppBrowser page view controller JavaScript object that includes the event handlers of the page (inAppBrowser.js):

```
(function() {
    var inAppBrowserManager = InAppBrowserManager.getInstance();

    $(document).on("pageinit", "#inAppBrowser", function(e) {
        e.preventDefault();

        $("#openGoogleSearchPage").on("tap", function(e) {
            e.preventDefault();

            var windowRef = inAppBrowserManager.openWindow("http://
www.google.com");
```

```
        //Close the window after 10 seconds...
        window.setTimeout(function() {
            console.log("It is over. Time to close the
window...");
            inAppBrowserManager.closeWindow(windowRef);
        }, 10000);
    });
  });
})();
```

As shown in the preceding code snippet, the `"pageinit"` event handler registers the `"tap"` event handler on the `"openGoogleSearchPage"` button. In the `"tap"` event handler of the `"openGoogleSearchPage"` button, a new window is opened by calling the `inAppBrowserManager.openWindow()` method that specifies the URL to open `"http://www.google.com/"`.

When the `window.setTimeout()` function is executed after 10 seconds using `windowRef`, which is returned from the `inAppBrowserManager.openWindow()` method, the opened window is closed by calling `inAppBrowserManager.closeWindow(windowRef)`.

API

The following code snippet shows `InAppBrowserManager.js`:

```
var InAppBrowserManager = (function () {
    var instance;

    function createObject() {
        return {
            openWindow: function (url) {
                var windowRef = window.open(url, '_blank',
'location=no');

                return windowRef;
            },
            closeWindow: function (windowRef) {
                if (windowRef) {
                    windowRef.close();
                }
            }
        };
    };
```

```
    return {
        getInstance: function () {
            if (!instance) {
                instance = createObject();
            }

            return instance;
        }
    };
})();
```

As shown in the preceding code, `InAppBrowserManager` is a singleton object that has two simple methods, as highlighted in the preceding code:

- `openWindow(url)`: This is used to open a new window by calling the `window.open()` method. The `window.open(url, target, options)` method has the following parameters:

    ○ `url`: This represents the URL to be loaded.

    ○ `target`: This represents the target in which to load the URL. It can be `_self` (default value), which means that the URL opens in the Cordova WebView if it is in the white list; otherwise, it opens in `InAppBrowser` or `_blank` (a specified value by `InAppBrowserManager`). This `_blank` means that the URL opens in `InAppBrowser` or `_system`, which means that the URL opens in the web browser of the system.

    ○ `options`: This represents the options for the `InAppBrowser`. It is a string that must not have any empty spaces, and it consists of key/value pairs, where key represents a feature's name and value represents a feature's value. The separator between any two features in the `options` string must be a comma. A `location` string is one of the available features that can be used in the `options` string. It specifies whether the location bar will be shown or not. In `InAppBrowserManager`, the `location` feature is set to `no` to hide the location bar, as it is by default set to `yes`.

`window.open()` returns a reference to the **InAppBrowser** window. This can be used to close the opened window later.

- `closeWindow(windowRef)`: This is used to close an opened window by calling the `close()` method of the reference to the **InAppBrowser** window (the `windowRef` object).

 InAppBrowser has more methods that you can check out in the Apache Cordova documentation at `https://github.com/apache/cordova-plugin-inappbrowser/blob/master/doc/index.md`.

We are now done with the InAppBrowser functionality in the Cordova Exhibition app.

Summary

In this chapter, we covered a lot of information regarding the Apache Cordova API. You saw the Apache Cordova API in action by exploring some features of the Cordova Exhibition app. You learned how to work with the Cordova accelerometer, camera, compass, connection, contacts, device, geolocation, globalization, and InAppBrowser APIs. In the next chapter, we will continue our look at the Apache Cordova API by exploring the remaining features of the Cordova Exhibition app.

5
Diving Deeper into the Cordova API

In this chapter, we will continue our journey in the Apache Cordova API by exploring the remaining main features of the Cordova Exhibition app. You will learn how to work with Cordova's media, file, capture, notification, and storage APIs. You will also learn how to utilize the Apache Cordova events in your Cordova mobile app.

Media, file, and capture

The media plugin provides the ability to record and play back audio files on a device.

In order to use the media plugin in our Apache Cordova project, we need to use the following `cordova plugin add` command:

```
> cordova plugin add https://git-wip-us.apache.org/repos/asf/cordova-
plugin-media.git
```

The capture plugin provides access to the device's audio, image, and video capture capabilities. In order to use the capture plugin in our Apache Cordova project, we need to use the following `cordova plugin add` command:

```
> cordova plugin add https://git-wip-us.apache.org/repos/asf/cordova-
plugin-media-capture.git
```

The file plugin provides access to the device's filesystem. In order to use the file plugin in our Apache Cordova project, we need to use the following `cordova plugin add` command:

```
> cordova plugin add https://git-wip-us.apache.org/repos/asf/cordova-
plugin-file.git
```

Demo

In order to access the media, file, and capture demo, you can click on the **Media**, **File**, and **Capture** list item, respectively. You will then be introduced to the **Media / File / Capture** page. You can click on the **Record Sound** button in order to start recording. Once you complete recording, you can click on the **Stop Recording** button, as shown in the following screenshot, and you will be able to play back your recorded sound by clicking on the **Playback** button:

Record your voice

You also have the option to click on **Record Sound Externally**, which will open your device's default recording application in order to perform recording. Once you are done, you will return to the page, and then, you can use the **Playback** button to play back your recorded sound again.

The HTML page

The following code snippet shows the media page ("mediaFC"):

```
<div data-role="page" id="mediaFC">
    <div data-role="header">
        <h1>Media / Capture</h1>
        <a href="#" data-role="button" data-rel="back" data-
icon="back">Back</a>
    </div>
    <div data-role="content">
        <h1>Welcome to the Media / Capture Gallery</h1>
        <p>Click 'Record Sound' or 'Record Sound Externally'
button below to start recording your voice.</p>
        <input type="hidden" id="location"/>
        <div class="center-wrapper">
            <input type="button" id="recordSound" data-
icon="audio" value="Record Sound"/>
            <input type="button" id="recordSoundExt" data-
icon="audio" value="Record Sound Externally"/>
            <input type="button" id="playSound" data-
icon="refresh" value="Playback"/><br/>
        </div>

        <div data-role="popup" id="recordSoundDialog" data-
dismissible="false" style="width:250px">
            <div data-role="header">
                <h1>Recording</h1>
            </div>

            <div data-role="content">
                <div class="center-wrapper">
                    <div id="soundDuration"></div>
                    <input type="button" id="stopRecordingSound"
value="Stop Recording"
                                class="center-button" data-
inline="true"/>
                </div>
            </div>
        </div>
    </div>
</div>
```

As shown in the preceding `"mediaFC"` page, it contains the following:

- A page header that includes a back button
- Page content that includes the following elements:
  - `"recordSound"`: This button is used to record sound using our app interface. Clicking on this button will show the `"recordSoundDialog"` pop up to allow the user to stop the recording when the operation is finished.
  - `"recordSoundExt"`: This button is used to record sound externally using the device's default recording app.
  - `"playSound"`: This button is used to play the recorded sound.
  - `"recordSoundDialog"`: This is a custom pop up that will be shown when the user clicks on the `"recordSound"` button. It contains the `"stopRecordingSound"` button, which is used to stop recording sound when the recording is finished.

View controller

The following code snippet shows the first main part of the `"mediaFC"` page view controller JavaScript object:

```
(function() {
    var mediaManager = MediaManager.getInstance(), recInterval;

    $(document).on("pageinit", "#mediaFC", function(e) {
        e.preventDefault();

        $("#recordSound").on("tap", function(e) {
            e.preventDefault();

            disableActionButtons();

            var callback = {};

            callback.onSuccess = handleRecordSuccess;
            callback.onError = handleRecordError;

            mediaManager.startRecording(callback);

            var recTime = 0;
```

```
    $("#soundDuration").html("Duration: " + recTime + "
seconds");

        $("#recordSoundDialog").popup("open");

        recInterval = setInterval(function() {
                        recTime = recTime + 1;
                        $("#soundDuration").html("Duration:
" + recTime + " seconds");
                    }, 1000);
    });

    $("#recordSoundExt").on("tap", function(e) {
        e.preventDefault();

        disableActionButtons();

        var callback = {};

        callback.onSuccess = handleRecordSuccess;
        callback.onError = handleRecordError;

        mediaManager.recordVoiceExternally(callback);
    });

    $("#recordSoundDialog").on("popupafterclose", function(e,
ui) {
        e.preventDefault();

        clearInterval(recInterval);
        mediaManager.stopRecording();
    });

    $("#stopRecordingSound").on("tap", function(e) {
        e.preventDefault();

        $("#recordSoundDialog").popup("close");
    });

    $("#playSound").on("tap", function(e) {
        e.preventDefault();

        disableActionButtons();
```

```
                      var callback = {};

                      callback.onSuccess = handlePlaySuccess;
                      callback.onError = handlePlayError;

                      mediaManager.playVoice($("#location").val(),
          callback);
                  });

              initPage();
          });

          $(document).on("pagebeforehide", "#mediaFC", function(e) {
              mediaManager.cleanUpResources();
              enableActionButtons();
          });

          // code is omitted for simplicity ...
      })();
```

The `"pageinit"` event handler registers the `"tap"` event handler on the `"recordSound"`, `"recordSoundExt"`, `"playSound"`, and `"stopRecordingSound"` buttons.

In the `"tap"` event handler of the `"recordSound"` button:

- Sound recording and playing buttons are disabled by calling the `disableActionButtons()` method
- In order to start recording sound:
    - A call to `mediaManager.startRecording(callback)` is performed specifying a callback parameter with the success and error callbacks
    - The `"recordSoundDialog"` pop up is shown, and its `"soundDuration"` div is updated every second with the current recording duration using the `window's setInterval()` method

In the `"tap"` event handler of the `"recordSoundExt"` button:

- Sound recording and playing buttons are disabled by calling the `disableActionButtons()` method
- In order to start recording sound externally, a call to `mediaManager.recordVoiceExternally(callback)` is performed specifying a callback parameter with the success and error callbacks

In the "tap" event handler of the "stopRecordingSound" button, it closes the "recordSoundDialog" pop up in order to trigger the "popupafterclose" event of the "recordSoundDialog" pop up in the "popupafterclose" event handler of the "recordSoundDialog" pop up:

- The recording timer is stopped using the window's clearInterval() method
- In order to stop recording sound, a call to mediaManager.stopRecording() is performed

In the "tap" event handler of the "playSound" button:

- Sound recording and playing buttons are disabled by calling the disableActionButtons() method
- In order to start playing the recorded sound, a call to mediaManager. playVoice(filePath, callback) is performed specifying a filePath parameter with the media file location to play (media file location is stored in the "location" hidden field when the recording operation succeeds) and a callback parameter with the success and error callbacks

The "pageinit" event handler also calls initPage(), whose code will be shown in the following code snippet. Finally, in the "pagebeforehide" event handler, which will be called every time, we are transitioning away from the page. A call to mediaManager.cleanUpResources() is performed in order to stop any playing sounds and clean up any used media resources when the media page is left.

The following code snippet shows the second main part of the "mediaFC" page view controller, which mainly includes the callback handlers and the initPage() method:

```
(function() {
    // code is omitted here for simplicity

    function initPage() {
        $("#playSound").closest('.ui-btn').hide();
    }

    function handleRecordSuccess(filePath) {
        $("#location").val(filePath);
        enableActionButtons();
        $("#playSound").closest('.ui-btn').show();
    }

    function handleRecordError(error) {
        console.log("An error occurs during recording: " +
error.code);
```

```
            enableActionButtons();
        }

        function handlePlaySuccess() {
            console.log("Sound file is played successfully ...");
            enableActionButtons();
        }

        function handlePlayError(error) {
            if (error.code) {
                console.log("An error happens when playing sound file
...");

                enableActionButtons();
            }
        }

        // Code is omitted here for simplicity ...
    })();
```

As shown in the preceding code, we have the following methods:

- `initPage()`: This is called in the `"pageinit"` event. It initially hides the `"playSound"` button.

- `handleRecordSuccess(filePath)`: This represents the success callback of `mediaManager.startRecording(callback)` and `mediaManager.recordVoiceExternally(callback)`. It does the following:

  - It receives `filePath` of the recorded file as a parameter and saves it in the `"location"` hidden field in order to be used by the playback operation
  - It enables the sound recording (`"recordSound"` and `"recordSoundExt"`) and playback (`"playsound"`) buttons
  - It shows the `"playSound"` button

- `handleRecordError(error)`: This represents the error callback of `mediaManager.startRecording(callback)` and `mediaManager.recordVoiceExternally(callback)`. It does the following:

  - It receives an `error` object as a parameter and the error code is logged in the console
  - It enables the sound recording and playback buttons

- handlePlaySuccess(): This represents the success callback of mediaManager.playVoice(filePath, callback). It does the following:
    ° It logs a successful message in the console
    ° It enables the sound recording and playing buttons

- handlePlayError(error): This represents the error callback of mediaManager.playVoice(filePath, callback). It does the following:
    ° It logs an error message in the console
    ° It enables the sound recording and playing buttons

API

The following code snippet shows the first part of MediaManager.js that interacts with the Cordova media and capture APIs:

```
var MediaManager = (function () {
    var instance;

    function createObject() {
        var fileManager = FileManager.getInstance();
        var recordingMedia;
        var audioMedia;

        return {
            startRecording : function (callback) {
                var recordVoice = function(dirEntry) {
                    var basePath = "";

                    if (dirEntry) {
                        basePath = dirEntry.toURL() + "/";
                    }

                    var mediaFilePath = basePath + (new Date()).
getTime() + ".wav";

                    var recordingSuccess = function() {
                        callback.onSuccess(mediaFilePath);
                    };

                    recordingMedia = new Media(mediaFilePath,
recordingSuccess, callback.onError);
```

```
                    // Record audio
                    recordingMedia.startRecord();
                };

                if (device.platform === "Android") {
                    var cb = {};

                    cb.requestSuccess = recordVoice;
                    cb.requestError = callback.onError;

                    fileManager.requestApplicationDirectory(cb);
                } else {
                    recordVoice();
                }
            },
            stopRecording : function () {
                if (recordingMedia) {
                    recordingMedia.stopRecord();
                    recordingMedia.release();

                    recordingMedia = null;
                }
            },
            playVoice : function (filePath, callback) {
                if (filePath) {
                    this.cleanUpResources();

                    audioMedia = new Media(filePath,
callback.onSuccess, callback.onError);

                    // Play audio
                    audioMedia.play();
                }
            },
            recordVoiceExternally: function (callback) {
                // code is omitted for simplicity ...
            },
            cleanUpResources : function () {
                // code is omitted for simplicity ...
            }
        };
    };
```

```
        return {
            getInstance: function () {
                if (!instance) {
                    instance = createObject();
                }

                return instance;
            }
        };
    }) ();
```

As you can see in the preceding highlighted code, `MediaManager` is a singleton object that has five methods. In order to record audio files using Apache Cordova, we can create a `Media` object as follows:

```
recordingMedia = new Media(src, [mediaSuccess], [mediaError],
[mediaStatus]);
```

The `Media` object constructor has the following parameters in order:

- `src`: This refers to the URI of the media file
- `mediaSuccess`: This is an optional parameter that refers to the callback, which will be called if the media operation (play/record or stop function) succeeds
- `mediaError`: This is an optional parameter that refers to the callback, which will be called if the media operation (play/record or stop function) fails
- `mediaStatus`: This is an optional parameter that executes to indicate status changes

In order to start recording an audio file, a call to the `startRecord()` method of the `Media` object must be performed. When the recording is finished, a call to `stopRecord()` method of the `Media` object must be performed. Now, let's check out the details of the `MediaManager` methods:

- `startRecording(callback)`: This starts the audio recording by doing the following:
  - Getting the current device platform by calling `device.platform`.

- ° If the current platform is Android, then a call to `fileManager.requestApplicationDirectory(cb)` is performed in order to create an application directory (if it hasn't already been created) under the device SD card's root directory using the `fileManager` object. If the directory creation operation succeeds, then `cb.requestSuccess` will be called, in this case, and the application directory path will be passed as a parameter. The `recordVoice()` method starts recording the sound and saves the result audio file under the application directory. Note that if there is no SD card in your Android device, then the application directory will be created under the app's private data directory (`/data/data/[app_directory]`), and the audio file will be saved under it.

- ° In the `else` block, which refers to the other supported platforms (Windows Phone 8 and iOS), `recordVoice()` is called without creating an application-specific directory. As you know from *Chapter 2, Developing Your First Cordova Application*, in iOS and Windows Phone 8, every application has a private directory, and applications cannot store their files in any place other than this directory using Apache Cordova APIs. In the case of iOS, the application audio files will be stored under the `tmp` directory of the application `sandbox` directory (the application private directory). In the case of Windows Phone 8, the audio files will be stored under the application's local directory. As you know from *Chapter 2, Developing Your First Cordova Application*, using the Windows Phone 8 native API (`Window.Storage`), you can read and write files in an SD card with some restrictions; however, until this moment, you cannot do this using the Apache Cordova API.

- ° In `recordVoice()`, `startRecording(callback)` starts creating a media file using the `Media` object's (`recordingMedia`) `startRecord()` method. After calling the `recordingMedia` object's `stopRecord()` method and if the recording operation succeeds, then `callback.onSuccess` will be called and the audio file's full path, `mediaFilePath` will be passed as a parameter. If the recording operation fails, then `callback.onError` will be called.

- `stopRecording()`: This stops the audio recording by doing the following:
  - ° Calling `stopRecord()` of `recordingMedia` in order to stop recording
  - ° Calling `release()` of `recordingMedia` in order to release the underlying operating system's audio resources

- `playVoice(filePath, callback)`: This plays an audio file by doing the following:
    - ° Cleaning up resources before playing the audio file by calling the `cleanUpResources()` method, which will be shown in the following code snippet
    - ° Creating a `Media` object (`audioMedia`) specifying `filePath` as the media source, `callback.onSuccess` as the media success callback, and `callback.onError` as the media error callback
    - ° Calling the `play()` method of the `audioMedia` object

The following code snippet shows the second part of `MediaManager.js`:

```javascript
var MediaManager = (function () {
    var instance;

    function createObject() {
        // ...
        return {
            // ...
            recordVoiceExternally: function (callback) {
                var onSuccess = function (mediaFiles) {
                    if (mediaFiles && mediaFiles[0]) {
                        var currentFilePath =
mediaFiles[0].fullPath;

                        if (device.platform === "Android") {
                            var fileCopyCallback = {};

                            fileCopyCallback.copySuccess =
function(filePath) {
                                callback.onSuccess(filePath);
                            };

                            fileCopyCallback.copyError =
callback.onError;

                            fileManager.copyFileToAppDirectory(current
FilePath, fileCopyCallback);
                        } else {
                            callback.onSuccess(currentFilePath);
                        }
                    }
                };
```

```
                    navigator.device.capture.captureAudio(onSuccess,
        callback.onError, {limit: 1});
                },
                cleanUpResources : function () {
                    if (audioMedia) {
                        audioMedia.stop();
                        audioMedia.release();
                        audioMedia = null;
                    }

                    if (recordingMedia) {
                        recordingMedia.stop();
                        recordingMedia.release();
                        recordingMedia = null;
                    }
                }
            };
        };
        // ...
    })();
```

In order to record the audio files using the device's default audio recording app, we can use the `captureAudio` method of Cordova's `capture` object as follows:

```
navigator.device.capture.captureAudio(captureSuccess,
captureError, [options])
```

The `captureAudio()` method has the following parameters:

- `captureSuccess`: This will be called when the audio capture operation is performed successfully. It receives an array of `MediaFile` as a parameter. As shown in the following table, these are the attributes of `MediaFile`:

Attribute name	Description
name	This is the name of the file
fullPath	This is the full path of the file, including the name
type	This is the file's mime type
lastModifiedDate	This is the date and time when the file was last modified
size	This is the file size in bytes

- `captureError`: This will be called when the audio capture operation fails. It receives a `CaptureError` object as a parameter. The `CaptureError` object has a `code` attribute, which represents the error code.

- `options`: This represents the options of capture configuration. The following table shows the `options` attributes:

Attribute name	Description
`limit`	This is the maximum number of audio clips that the device user can record in a single capture operation. The value must be greater than or equal to 1 (defaults to 1).
`duration`	This is the maximum duration in seconds of an audio sound clip.

The preceding code snippet shows the other methods of the `MediaManager` object as follows:

- `recordVoiceExternally`(`callback`): This starts audio recording using the device's default recording app by doing the following:

    ○ In order to start audio recording using the device's default recording app, `navigator.device.capture.captureAudio(onSuccess, callback.onError, {limit: 1})` is called. This means that `onSuccess` is set as the success callback, `callback.onError` is set as the error callback, and finally, `options` is set to `{limit: 1}` in order to limit the maximum number of audio clips that the device user can record in a single capture to 1.

    ○ In the `onSuccess` callback, if the current platform is Android, then a call to `fileManager.copyFileToAppDirectory(currentFilePath, fileCopyCallback)` is performed in order to copy the recorded file to the `app` directory using the `fileManager` object. If the copy operation succeeds, then the original `recordVoiceExternally()` method's `callback.onSuccess(filePath)` will be called in this case and the new copied file path under the `app` directory (`filePath`) will be passed as a parameter.

    ○ If the current platform is not Android (in our case, Windows Phone 8 and iOS), `callback.onSuccess(currentFilePath)` will be called and the current filepath (`currentFilePath`) will be passed as a parameter.

- `cleanUpResources()`: This makes sure that all resources are cleaned up by calling `stop()` and `release()` methods of all the `Media` objects.

As the current implementation of the media plugin does not adhere to the W3C specification for media capture, a future implementation is considered for compliance with the W3C specification, and the current APIs might be deprecated.

Before going into the details of the `FileManager.js` file, note that the `Media` object has more methods that you can check out in the Apache Cordova Documentation at `https://github.com/apache/cordova-plugin-media/blob/master/doc/index.md`.

Cordova Capture also has more objects and methods that you can look at in the Apache Cordova Documentation at `https://github.com/apache/cordova-plugin-media-capture/blob/master/doc/index.md`.

The following code snippet shows the first part of `FileManager.js`, which is used by `MediaManager.js`:

```
var FileManager = (function () {
    var instance;

    function createObject() {
        var BASE_DIRECTORY = "CExhibition";
        var FILE_BASE = "file:///";

        return {
            copyFileToAppDirectory: function (filePath, cb) {
                var callback = {};

                callback.requestSuccess = function (dirEntry) {
                    if (filePath.indexOf(FILE_BASE) != 0) {
                        filePath = filePath.replace("file:/",
FILE_BASE);
                    }

                    window.resolveLocalFileSystemURL(filePath,
function(file) {
                        var filename = filePath.replace(/^.*[\\\/]/,
'');

                        var copyToSuccess = function (fileEntry) {
                            console.log("file is copied to: " +
fileEntry.toURL());
                            cb.copySuccess(fileEntry.toURL());
                        };
```

```
                              file.copyTo(dirEntry, filename,
copyToSuccess, cb.copyError);
                    }, cb.copyError);
            };

            callback.requestError = function (error) {
                console.log(error);
            };

            this.requestApplicationDirectory(callback);
        },
        requestApplicationDirectory: function (callback) {
            var fileSystemReady = function(fileSystem) {
                fileSystem.root.getDirectory(BASE_DIRECTORY,
{create: true}, callback.requestSuccess);
            };

            window.requestFileSystem(LocalFileSystem.PERSISTENT,
0,
fileSystemReady, callback.requestError);
            }
        };
    };

    return {
        getInstance: function () {
            if (!instance) {
                instance = createObject();
            }

            return instance;
        }
    };
})();
```

As you can see in the preceding highlighted code, `FileManager` is a singleton object that has two methods. In order to work with directories or files using Apache Cordova, we first need to request a filesystem using the `requestFileSystem()` method as `window.requestFileSystem(type, size, successCallback, errorCallback)`.

The `window.requestFileSystem` method has the following parameters in order:

- `type`: This refers to the local filesystem type
- `size`: This indicates how much storage space, in bytes, the application expects to need
- `successCallback`: This will be called if the operation succeeds, and it will receive a `FileSystem` object as a parameter
- `errorCallback`: This will be called if an operation error occurs

In order to create a directory after getting the `FileSystem` object, we can use the `getDirectory()` method of the `DirectoryEntry` object as `fileSystem.root.getDirectory(path, options, successCallback, errorCallback)`.

The `directoryEntry.getDirectory` method takes the following parameters:

- `path`: This is either a relative or absolute path of the directory in which we can look up or create a directory
- `options`: This refers to an `options` JSON object that specifies the `create` directory using `{create: true}` or exclusively creates the directory using `{create: true, exclusive: true}`
- `successCallback`: This will be called if the operation succeeds, and it receives the new or existing `DirectoryEntry` as a parameter
- `errorCallback`: This will be called if an operation error occurs

If you look at the first method `requestApplicationDirectory(callback)` of the `FileManager` object, you will find that it creates a directory called `"CExhibition"` if it has not already been created (in the case of an Android device with an SD card, `"CExhibition"` will be created under the SD card root).

In order to get an `Entry` object of a specific URI to perform a file or directory operation, we need to use `resolveLocalFileSystemURL()` as `window.resolveLocalFileSystemURL(uri, successCallback, errorCallback)`.

The `window.resolveLocalFileSystemURL` method takes the following parameters:

- `uri`: This is a URI that refers to a local file or directory
- `successCallback`: This will be called if the operation succeeds, and it will receive an `Entry` object that corresponds to the specified URI (it can be `DirectoryEntry` or `FileEntry`) as a parameter
- `errorCallback`: This will be called if an operation error occurs

In order to copy a file, we need to use the `copyTo()` method of the `Entry` object as `fileEntry.copyTo(parent, newName, successCallback, errorCallback)` the `Entry` object.

The `fileEntry.copyTo` method takes the following parameters:

- `parent`: This represents the directory to which the entry will be copied
- `newName`: This represents the new name of the copied file, and it defaults to the current name
- `successCallback`: This will be called if the operation succeeds, and it will receive the new entry object as a parameter
- `errorCallback`: This will be called if an operation error occurs

If you look at the second method `copyFileToAppDirectory (filePath, cb)` of the `FileManager` object, you will find that it creates an `app` directory called `"CExhibition"` if it has not already been created. Then, it copies the file specified in `filePath` under the `app` directory using the `copyTo()` method of the `fileEntry` object. Finally, if the copy operation succeeds, then the `cb.copySuccess()` callback will be called and the new copied file path will be passed as a parameter.

> The Cordova file has more objects and methods that you can have a look at in the Apache Cordova Documentation at `https://github.com/apache/cordova-plugin-file/blob/master/doc/index.md`.

Now, we are done with the media, file, and capture functionalities in the Cordova Exhibition app.

Notification

The notification plugin provides the ability to create visual, audible, and tactile device notifications. In order to use the notification plugin in our Apache Cordova project, we need to use the following `cordova plugin add` command:

```
> cordova plugin add https://git-wip-us.apache.org/repos/asf/cordova-plugin-vibration.git
```

```
> cordova plugin add https://git-wip-us.apache.org/repos/asf/cordova-plugin-dialogs.git
```

Demo

In order to access the notification demo, you can click on the **Notification** list item. You will be introduced to the **Notification** page. You can click on one of the available buttons to see, hear, and feel the different available notifications. The following screenshot shows the result of clicking on the **Show Prompt** button, which shows a prompt dialog to have the user input:

The notification prompt

You also have the option to show an alert message and confirmation dialog. You can vibrate the device by clicking on the **Vibrate** button, and finally, you can make the device beep by clicking on the **Beep** button.

The HTML page

The following code snippet shows the `"notification"` page:

```
<div data-role="page" id="notification">
    <div data-role="header">
        <h1>Notification</h1>
        <a href="#" data-role="button" data-rel="back" data-
icon="back">Back</a>
    </div>
    <div data-role="content">
        <h1>Welcome to the Notification Gallery</h1>
        <p>Click the buttons below to check notifications.</p>
        <input type="button" id="showAlert" value="Show Alert"/>
        <input type="button" id="showConfirm" value="Show
Confirm"/>
        <input type="button" id="showPrompt" value="Show Prompt"/>
        <input type="button" id="vibrate" value="Vibrate"/>
        <input type="button" id="beep" value="Beep"/>

        <div id="notificationResult">
        </div>
    </div>
</div>
```

The preceding `"notification"` page contains the following:

- A page header that includes a back button.

- Page content that includes five buttons: `"showAlert"` to show an alert, `"showConfirm"` to show a confirmation dialog, `"showPrompt"` to show a prompt dialog, `"vibrate"` to vibrate the device, and finally, `"beep"` to make the device beep. It also has a `"notificationResult"` div to display the notification result.

View controller

The following code snippet shows the `"notification"` page view controller JavaScript object, which includes the event handlers of the page (`notification.js`):

```
(function() {
    var notificationManager = NotificationManager.getInstance();

    $(document).on("pageinit", "#notification", function(e) {
        e.preventDefault();
```

```
    $("#showAlert").on("tap", function(e) {
        e.preventDefault();

        notificationManager.showAlert("This is an Alert",
onOk, "Iam an Alert", "Ok");
    });

    $("#showConfirm").on("tap", function(e) {
        e.preventDefault();

        notificationManager.showConfirm("This is a
confirmation", onConfirm, "Iam a confirmation", "Ok,Cancel");
    });

    $("#showPrompt").on("tap", function(e) {
        e.preventDefault();

        notificationManager.showPrompt("What is your favorite
food?", onPrompt, "Iam a prompt", ["Ok", "Cancel"], "Pizza");
    });

    $("#vibrate").on("tap", function(e) {
        e.preventDefault();

        notificationManager.vibrate(2000);
    });

    $("#beep").on("tap", function(e) {
        e.preventDefault();

        notificationManager.beep(3);
    });

});

function onOk() {
    $("#notificationResult").html("You clicked Ok<br/>");
}

function onConfirm(index) {
    $("#notificationResult").html("You clicked " + ((index ==
1) ? "Ok":"Cancel") + "<br/>");
}
```

```
    function onPrompt(result) {
        if (result.buttonIndex == 1) {
            $("#notificationResult").html("You entered: " +
result.input1);
        }
    }
})();
```

As shown in the preceding code snippet, the `"pageinit"` event handler registers the `"tap"` event handlers on the `"showAlert"`, `"showConfirm"`, `"showPrompt"`, `"vibrate"`, and `"beep"` buttons.

In the `"tap"` event handler of the `"showAlert"` button, an alert is shown by calling the `notificationManager.showAlert(message, callback, title, buttonName)` method specifying the message to display (`"This is an Alert"`), the callback to be called when the dialog is dismissed (`onOk`), the dialog title (`"I am an Alert"`), and finally, the button name (`Ok`). In `onOk`, the `"You clicked Ok"` message is displayed in the `"notificationResult"` div.

In the `"tap"` event handler of the `"showConfirm"` button, a confirmation dialog is shown by calling the `notificationManager.showConfirm(message, callback, title, buttonLabels)` method specifying the message to display (`"This is a confirmation"`), the callback to be called when the dialog is dismissed or if any of the confirmation dialog buttons is clicked (`onConfirm`), the dialog title (`"I am a confirmation"`), and finally, the button labels, which are represented using a comma-separated string that specify button labels (`"Ok,Cancel"`). In `onConfirm(index)`, the clicked button is displayed in the `notificationResult` div using the received `index` callback parameter, which represents the index of the pressed button. Note that `index` uses one-based indexing, which means that the `"Ok"` button has the index 1 and the `"Cancel"` button has the index 2.

In the `"tap"` event handler of the `"showPrompt"` button, a confirmation dialog is shown by calling the `notificationManager.showPrompt(message, callback, title, buttonLabels, defaultText)` method specifying the message to display (`"What is your favorite food?"`), the callback to be called when any of the prompt dialog buttons is clicked (`onPrompt`), the dialog title (`"I am a prompt"`), the button labels, which are represented as an array of strings that specify button labels (`["Ok", "Cancel"]`), and finally, the default input text (`"Pizza"`). In `onPrompt(result)`, `result.buttonIndex` represents the button index (which is one-based indexing) that is clicked. If the `"Ok"` button (which has the index 1) is clicked, then the user input is obtained using `result.input1`.

In the `"tap"` event handler of the `"vibrate"` button, the device is vibrated by calling the `notificationManager.vibrate(milliseconds)` method specifying milliseconds to vibrate the device (2,000 milliseconds).

In the `"tap"` event handler of the `"beep"` button, the device is made to beep by calling the `notificationManager.beep(times)` method specifying the times to repeat the beep (three times).

API

The following code snippet shows `NotificationManager.js`:

```
var NotificationManager = (function () {
    var instance;

    function createObject() {
        return {
            showAlert: function (message, callback, title,
buttonName) {
                navigator.notification.alert(message, callback,
title, buttonName);
            },
            showConfirm: function (message, callback, title,
buttonLabels) {
                navigator.notification.confirm(message, callback,
title, buttonLabels);
            },
            showPrompt: function (message, callback, title,
buttonLabels, defaultText) {
                navigator.notification.prompt(message, callback,
title, buttonLabels, defaultText);
            },
            beep: function (times) {
                navigator.notification.beep(times);
            },
            vibrate: function (milliseconds) {
                navigator.notification.vibrate(milliseconds);
            }
        };
    };

    return {
        getInstance: function () {
            if (!instance) {
```

```
                instance = createObject();
        }

        return instance;
    }
  };
})();
```

As shown, `NotificationManager` is a singleton object that does a simple wrapping for the Cordova Notification API. It has the following methods:

- `showAlert(message, callback, title, buttonName)`: This shows an alert by calling the `navigator.notification.alert()` method. The `navigator.notification.alert(message, callback, [title], [buttonName])` method has the following parameters:

  ○ `message`: This represents the alert message

  ○ `Callback`: This represents the callback to be called when the alert is dismissed

  ○ `Title`: This is an optional parameter that represents the alert title (the default value is `"Alert"`)

  ○ `buttonName`: This represents the button name (the default value is `"Ok"`)

- `showConfirm(message, callback, title, buttonLabels)`: This shows a confirmation dialog by calling the `navigator.notification.confirm()` method. The `navigator.notification.confirm(message, callback, [title], [buttonLabels])` method has the following parameters:

  ○ `message`: This represents the dialog message.

  ○ `callback(index)`: This represents the callback to be called when the user presses one of the buttons in the confirmation dialog. It receives an `index` parameter that represents the pressed button's index, which starts from 1.

  ○ `title`: This is an optional parameter that represents the dialog title (the default value is `"Confirm"`).

  ○ `buttonLabels`: This is an optional parameter that represents a comma-separated string that specifies button labels (the default value is `"Ok", Cancel"`).

- `showPrompt(message, callback, title, buttonLabels, defaultText)`: This shows a prompt dialog by calling the `navigator.notification.prompt()` method. The `navigator.notification.prompt(message, promptCallback, [title], [buttonLabels], [defaultText])` method has the following parameters:
    - `Message`: This represents the dialog message.
    - `promptCallback(results)`: This represents the callback to be called when the user presses one of the buttons in the prompt dialog. It receives a `results` parameter that has the following attributes: `buttonIndex`, which represents the pressed button's index, which starts from 1 and `input1`, which represents the text entered by the user in the prompt dialog box.
    - `title`: This is an optional parameter that represents the dialog title (the default value is `"Prompt"`).
    - `buttonLabels`: This is an optional parameter that represents a string array, which specifies button labels (the default value is `["OK","Cancel"]`).
    - `defaultText`: This is an optional parameter that represents the default text input value of the prompt dialog (the default value is an empty string).
- `beep(times)`: This makes the device beeps by calling the `navigator.notification.beep()` method. The `navigator.notification.beep(times)` method has the following parameter:
    - `times`: This represents the number of times to repeat the beep.
- `vibrate(milliseconds)`: This vibrates the device by calling the `navigator.notification.vibrate()` method. The `navigator.notification.vibrate(milliseconds)` method has the following parameter:
    - `milliseconds`: This represents the milliseconds to vibrate the device.

Now, we are done with the notification functionality in the Cordova Exhibition app.

Storage

The Cordova Storage API provides the ability to access the device storage options based on three popular W3C specifications:

- Web Storage API Specification, which allows you to access data using simple key/value pairs (which we will demonstrate in our "Storage" demo).

- Web SQL Database Specification, which offers full-featured database tables, which can be accessed using SQL. Note that this option is only available in Android, iOS, BlackBerry 10, and Tizen and not supported on other platforms.

- IndexedDB Specification is an API for the client-side storage and high performance. It searches on the stored data using indexes. Note that this option is available in Windows Phone 8 and BlackBerry 10.

Demo

In order to use the Storage API, there is no need for a CLI command to run, as it is built in Cordova. In order to access the **Storage** demo, you can do it by clicking on the **Storage** list item. You will be introduced to the **Storage** page. On the **Storage** page, the users can enter their names and valid e-mails and then click on the **Save** button in order to save the information, as shown in the following screenshot:

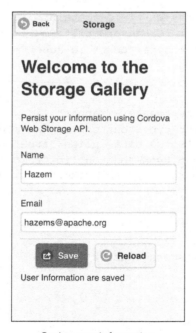

Saving user information

You can exit the app and then open the **Storage** page again; you will find that your saved information is reflected in the **Name** and **Email** fields. At any point, you can click on the **Reload** button in order to reload input fields with your saved data.

The HTML page

The following code snippet shows the `"storage"` page:

```
<div data-role="page" id="storage">
    <div data-role="header">
        <h1>Storage</h1>
        <a href="#" data-role="button" data-rel="back" data-
icon="back">Back</a>
    </div>
    <div data-role="content">
        <h1>Welcome to the Storage Gallery</h1>
        <p>Persist your information using Cordova Web Storage
API.</p>
        <form id="storageForm">
            <div class="ui-field-contain">
                <label for="userName">Name</label>
                <input type="text" id="userName" name="userName"></
input>
            </div>
            <div class="ui-field-contain">
                <label for="userEmail">Email</label>
                <input type="text" id="userEmail" name="userEmail"></
input>
            </div>

            <div class="center-wrapper">
                <input type="button" id="saveInfo" data-
icon="action" value="Save" data-inline="true"/>
                <input type="button" id="reloadInfo" data-
icon="refresh" value="Reload" data-inline="true"/>
            </div>

            <ul id="storageMessageBox"></ul>

            <div id="storageResult">
            </div>
        </form>
    </div>
</div>
```

The preceding `"storage"` page contains the following:

- A page header that includes a back button
- Page content that includes the `"storageForm"` form, which includes the following elements:
    - `"userName"`: This is the user's name text field
    - `"userEmail"`: This is the user's email text field
    - `"saveInfo"`: This button is used to persist user information
    - `"reloadInfo"`: This button is used to reload saved user information in the `"userName"` and `"userEmail"` fields
    - `"messageBox"`: This is an unordered list that displays form validation errors
    - `"storageResult"`: This is a div that displays the storage operation result

View controller

The following code snippet shows the `"storage"` page view controller JavaScript object that includes the event handlers of the page (`storage.js`):

```
(function() {
    var storageManager = StorageManager.getInstance();
    var INFO_KEY = "cordovaExhibition.userInfo";

    $(document).on("pageinit", "#storage", function(e) {
        e.preventDefault();

        $("#saveInfo").on("tap", function(e) {
            e.preventDefault();


            if (! $("#storageForm").valid()) {
                return;
            }

            storageManager.set(INFO_KEY, JSON.stringify({
                                                userName:
$("#userName").val(),

                                                userEmail:
$("#userEmail").val()
                                        })
```

```
                    );

                    $("#storageResult").html("User Information are saved");
              });

              $("#reloadInfo").on("tap", function(e) {
                    e.preventDefault();

                    reloadUserInfo();

                    $("#storageResult").html("Reloading completes");
              });
        });

        $(document).on("pageshow", "#storage", function(e) {
              e.preventDefault();

              $("#storageForm").validate({
                    errorLabelContainer: "#storageMessageBox",
                    wrapper: "li",
                    rules: {
                         userName: "required",
                         userEmail: {
                              required: true,
                              email: true
                         }
                    },
                    messages: {
                         userName: "Please specify user name",
                         userEmail: {
                              required: "Please specify email",
                              email: "Please enter valid email"
                         }
                    }
              });

              reloadUserInfo();
        });

        function reloadUserInfo() {
              var userInfo = JSON.parse(storageManager.get(INFO_KEY));

              populateFormFields(userInfo);
        }
```

```
function populateFormFields(userInfo) {
    if (userInfo) {
        $("#userName").val(userInfo.userName);
        $("#userEmail").val(userInfo.userEmail);
    }
}
})();
```

As shown in the preceding highlighted code snippet, the `"pageinit"` event handler registers the `"tap"` event handlers on the `"saveInfo"` and `"reloadInfo"` buttons.

> In order to validate our `"storage"` form, we use the jQuery validation plugin, which can be found at `http://jqueryvalidation.org`. In order to use the plugin, all we need to do is include the `jquery.validate.min.js` file below the `jquery.js` file that will be shown in the `index.html` file in *Finalizing the Cordova Exhibition App* section. After including the jQuery validation plugin JS file, we can simply use the plugin by defining the validation rules on the form fields using the form's `validate()` method and then validate the form using the form's `valid()` method, as shown in the `"storage"` page view controller code.

In the `"tap"` event handler of the `"saveInfo"` button:

- The `"storageForm"` is validated using the `$("#storageForm").valid()` method.

- If the form is valid, then both the `"userName"` and `"userEmail"` valid input text values are set as attributes in a JSON object, which is converted to a string using `JSON.stringify()`. Finally, the `stringified` JSON object is persisted in the device storage by calling the `storageManager.set(key, value)` specifying key to be `INFO_KEY` and the value to be the `stringified` JSON object.

In the `"tap"` event handler of the `"reloadInfo"` button:

- The user information is retrieved by calling `reloadUserInfo()`. The `reloadUserInfo()` method calls `storageManager.get(INFO_KEY)` in order to get the stored `stringified` JSON object and then use `JSON.parse()` in order to convert the `stringified` JSON object to a JSON object (`userInfo`).

- Using `populateFormFields(userInfo)`, `userInfo` is populated to both `"userName"` and `"userEmail"` input text elements.

In the `"pageshow"` event of the `"storage"` page, our `"storageForm"` form validation is constructed by specifying the `options` parameter of the form's `validate()` method as follows:

- `errorLabelContainer`: This is set to `"storageMessageBox"` to display the validation errors
- `wrapper`: This is set to `"li"` to wrap the error messages in list items
- `rules` object is set as follows:
    - `userName`: This is set to required
    - `userEmail`: This is set to be an e-mail and required

- `messages` object specifies `userName` and `userEmail` validation error messages

Finally, in the `"pageshow"` event of the `"storage"` page, `reloadUserInfo()` is called to reload the user information in the `"userName"` and `"userEmail"` input text elements.

API

The following code snippet shows `StorageManager.js` that does a simple wrapping for two `localStorage` methods:

```
var StorageManager = (function () {
    var instance;

    function createObject() {
        return {
            set: function (key, value) {
                window.localStorage.setItem(key, value);
            },
            get: function (key) {
                return window.localStorage.getItem(key);
            }
        };
    };

    return {
        getInstance: function () {
            if (!instance) {
                instance = createObject();
            }
```

```
              return instance;
          }
      };
})();
```

As you can see in the preceding highlighted code, `StorageManager` is a singleton object that has the following methods:

- `set(key, value)`: This persists the key/value pair in the local storage by calling the `window.localStorage.setItem(key, value)` method

- `get(key)`: This gets the stored value using the passed key parameter by calling the `window.localStorage.getItem(key)` method

> The complete W3C Web Storage specification is available at
> `http://www.w3.org/TR/webstorage/`, and you can also look at
> the W3C Web SQL Database specification at `http://dev.w3.org/`
> `html5/webdatabase/`. Finally, you can look at the W3C IndexedDB
> specification at `http://www.w3.org/TR/IndexedDB/`.

Now, we are done with the storage functionality in the Cordova Exhibition app.

Finalizing the Cordova Exhibition app

The last part we need to check is `index.html`; the following code snippet shows this part, which is the most important, of the `index.html` page:

```html
<!DOCTYPE html>
<html>
    <head>
        <!-- omitted code ... -->
        <link rel="stylesheet" type="text/css" href="css/app.css"
/>
        <link rel="stylesheet" href="jqueryMobile/jquery.mobile-
1.4.0.min.css">

        <script src="jqueryMobile/jquery-1.10.2.min.js"></script>
        <script src="jqueryMobile/jquery.mobile-
1.4.0.min.js"></script>

        <script>
            var deviceReadyDeferred = $.Deferred();
            var jqmReadyDeferred = $.Deferred();
```

```
            $(document).ready(function() {
                document.addEventListener("deviceready", function() {
                    deviceReadyDeferred.resolve();
                }, false);
            });

            $(document).on("mobileinit", function () {
                jqmReadyDeferred.resolve();
            });

            $.when(deviceReadyDeferred, jqmReadyDeferred).
then(function () {

                //Now everything loads fine, you can safely go to the
app home ...
                $.mobile.changePage("#features");
            });
        </script>

        <script src="jqueryMobile/jqm.page.params.js"></script>
        <script src="jqueryMobile/jquery.validate.min.js"></script>
        <script src="js/common.js"></script>

        <title>Cordova Exhibition</title>
    </head>
    <body>
        <div id="loading" data-role="page">
            <div class="center-screen">Please wait ...</div>
        </div>

        <!-- Other pages are placed here ... -->

        <script type="text/javascript" src="cordova.js"></script>

        <!-- API JS files -->
        <script type="text/javascript" src="js/api/
AccelerometerManager.js"></script>
        <script type="text/javascript" src="js/api/FileManager.js"></
script>
        <script type="text/javascript" src="js/api/CameraManager.
js"></script>
        <script type="text/javascript" src="js/api/CompassManager.
js"></script>
        <script type="text/javascript" src="js/api/ConnectionManager.
js"></script>
```

```
        <script type="text/javascript" src="js/api/ContactsManager.
js"></script>
        <script type="text/javascript" src="js/api/DeviceManager.
js"></script>
        <script type="text/javascript" src="js/api/GeolocationManager.
js"></script>
        <script type="text/javascript" src="js/api/
GlobalizationManager.js"></script>
        <script type="text/javascript" src="js/api/
InAppBrowserManager.js"></script>
        <script type="text/javascript" src="js/api/MediaManager.js"></
script>
        <script type="text/javascript" src="js/api/
NotificationManager.js"></script>
        <script type="text/javascript" src="js/api/StorageManager.
js"></script>

        <!-- View controller files -->
        <script type="text/javascript" src="js/vc/accelerometer.js"></
script>
        <script type="text/javascript" src="js/vc/camera.js"></script>
        <script type="text/javascript" src="js/vc/compass.js"></
script>
        <script type="text/javascript" src="js/vc/connection.js"></
script>
        <script type="text/javascript" src="js/vc/contacts.js"></
script>
        <script type="text/javascript" src="js/vc/contactDetails.
js"></script>
        <script type="text/javascript" src="js/vc/device.js"></script>
        <script type="text/javascript" src="js/vc/geolocation.js"></
script>
        <script type="text/javascript" src="js/vc/globalization.js"></
script>
        <script type="text/javascript" src="js/vc/inAppBrowser.js"></
script>
        <script type="text/javascript" src="js/vc/media.js"></script>
        <script type="text/javascript" src="js/vc/notification.js"></
script>
        <script type="text/javascript" src="js/vc/storage.js"></
script>
    </body>
</html>
```

As shown in the preceding code, `index.html` includes the following:

- App custom CSS file (`app.css`)
- jQuery Mobile library files
- A jQuery Page Params plugin file (`jqm.page.params.js`)
- A jQuery Validation plugin file (`jquery.validate.min.js`)
- A Common JS (`common.js`) file, app manager JS files, and finally, app view controller JS files

The preceding highlighted code shows you how to make sure that Apache Cordova and jQuery Mobile are loaded correctly (using the jQuery Deferred object) before proceeding to the app pages. Doing this step is important to make sure that our app's code will not access any API that is not ready yet to avoid any unexpected errors. If Apache Cordova and jQuery Mobile are loaded correctly, then the user will leave the `"loading"` page and will be forwarded to the app's home page (the `"features"` page) to start exploring the Cordova features.

To learn the jQuery Deferred object by example, check out `http://learn.jquery.com/code-organization/deferreds/examples/`.

It's worth mentioning that in order to boost the performance of jQuery Mobile 1.4 with Apache Cordova, it is recommended that you disable transition effects. The `common.js` file applies this tip in the Cordova Exhibition app as follows:

```
$.mobile.defaultPageTransition   = 'none';
$.mobile.defaultDialogTransition = 'none';
$.mobile.buttonMarkup.hoverDelay = 0;
```

Finally, in order to exit the application when the user clicks on the back button (which exists in the Android and Windows Phone 8 devices) on the app's home page, `common.js` also implements this behavior, as shown in the following code snippet:

```
var homePage = "features";

//Handle back buttons decently for Android and Windows Phone 8 ...
function onDeviceReady() {
    document.addEventListener("backbutton", function(e){

        if ($.mobile.activePage.is('#' + homePage)){
            e.preventDefault();
            navigator.app.exitApp();
```

```
      } else {
          history.back();
      }
   }, false);
}

$(document).ready(function() {
    document.addEventListener("deviceready", onDeviceReady,
false);
});
```

We create an event listener on the device's `"backbutton"` after Cordova is loaded. If the user clicks on the back button, we check whether the user is on the home page using `$.mobile.activePage.is()`. If the user is on the home page, then the app exits using `navigator.app.exitApp()`; otherwise, we simply use `history.back()` to forward the user to the previous page.

 The complete source code of our Cordova Exhibition app with all the three supported platforms can be downloaded from the course's web page, or you can access the code directly from GitHub at `https://github.com/hazems/cordova-exhibition`.

Cordova events

Cordova allows listening and creating handlers for its life cycle events. The following table shows the description of these events:

Event name	Description
Deviceready	This fires once Apache Cordova is fully loaded. Once this event fires, you can safely make calls to the Cordova API.
Pause	This fires if the application is put into the background.
Resume	This fires if the application is resumed from the background.
Online	This fires if the application becomes connected to the Internet.
offline	This fires if the application becomes disconnected from the Internet.
backbutton	This fires if the user clicks on the device's back button (some devices such as Android and Windows Phone devices have a back button).

Event name	Description
batterycritical	This fires if the device's battery power reaches a critical state (that is, reached the critical-level threshold).
batterylow	This fires if the device's battery power reaches the low-level threshold.
batterystatus	This fires if there is a change in the battery status.
menubutton	This fires if the user presses the device's menu button (the menu button is popular in Android and BlackBerry devices).
searchbutton	This fires if the user presses the device's search button (the search button can be found in Android devices).
startcallbutton	This fires when the user presses the start call button of the device.
endcallbutton	This fires when the user presses the end call button of the device.
volumeupbutton	This fires when the user presses the volume up button of the device.
volumedownbutton	This fires when the user presses the volume down button of the device.

Access to all of the events, which are not related to the battery status, are enabled by default. In order to use the events related to the battery status, use the following CLI `cordova plugin add` command:

```
> cordova plugin add https://git-wip-us.apache.org/repos/
asf/cordova-plugin-battery-status.git
```

We can create our Cordova event listener using the `document.addEventListener()` method once DOM is loaded as follows:

```
document.addEventListener("eventName", eventHandler, false)
```

Let's see an example; let's assume that we have the following div element in our HTML page, which displays the log of our Cordova app pause and resume events:

```
<div id="results"></div>
```

In our JavaScript code, once the DOM is loaded, we can define our Cordova event listeners for the `"pause"` and `"resume"` events once the `"deviceready"` event is triggered, as follows:

```
function onPause() {
    document.getElementById("results").innerHTML += "App is paused
...<br/>";
};

function onResume() {
    document.getElementById("results").innerHTML += "App is
resumed ...<br/>";
};

function onDeviceReady() {
    document.addEventListener("pause", onPause, false);
    document.addEventListener("resume", onResume, false);
};

$(document).ready(function() {
    document.addEventListener("deviceready", onDeviceReady,
false);
});
```

Summary

In this chapter, you learned how to utilize the most important features in Apache Cordova API by understanding the Cordova Exhibition app. You learned how to work with Cordova media, file, capture, notification, and storage APIs. You also learned how to utilize the Apache Cordova events in your mobile app. In the next chapter, you will learn the advanced part of Apache Cordova, which is building your own custom Cordova plugin on the different mobile platforms (Android, iOS, and Windows Phone 8).

6

Developing Custom Cordova Plugins

In this chapter, we will continue to deep dive into Apache Cordova. You will learn how to create your own custom Cordova plugin on the three most popular mobile platforms: Android (using the Java programming language), iOS (using the Objective-C programming language), and Windows Phone 8 (using the C# programming language).

Developing a custom Cordova plugin

Before going into the details of the plugin, it is important to note that developing custom Cordova plugins is not a common scenario if you are developing Apache Cordova apps. This is because the Apache Cordova core and community custom plugins already cover many of the use cases that are needed to access device's native functions. So, make sure of two things:

- You are not developing a custom plugin that already exists in the Apache Cordova core plugins, which were illustrated in the previous two chapters.

- You are not developing a custom plugin whose functionality already exists in other good Apache Cordova custom plugin(s) that have been developed by the Apache Cordova development community. Building plugins from scratch can consume precious time from your project; otherwise, you can save time by reusing one of the available good custom plugins.

Another thing to note is that developing custom Cordova plugins is an advanced topic. It requires you to be aware of the native programming languages of the mobile platforms, so make sure you have an overview of Java, Objective-C, and C# (or at least one of them) before reading this chapter. This will be helpful in understanding all the plugin development steps (plugin structuring, JavaScript interface definition, and native plugin implementation).

Now, let's start developing our custom Cordova plugin. It can be used in order to send SMS messages from one of the three most popular mobile platforms (Android, iOS, and Windows Phone 8). Before we start creating our plugin, we need to define its API. The following code listing shows you how to call the `sms.sendMessage` method of our plugin, which will be used in order to send an SMS across platforms:

```
var messageInfo = {
    phoneNumber: "xxxxxxxxxx",
    textMessage: "This is a test message"
};

sms.sendMessage(messageInfo, function(message) {
    console.log("success: " + message);
}, function(error) {
    console.log("code: " + error.code + ", message: " +
error.message);
});
```

The `sms.sendMessage` method has the following parameters:

- `messageInfo`: This is a JSON object that contains two main attributes: `phoneNumber`, which represents the phone number that will receive the SMS message, and `textMessage`, which represents the text message to be sent.

- `successCallback`: This is a callback that will be called if the message is sent successfully.

- `errorCallback`: This is a callback that will be called if the message is not sent successfully. This callback receives an `error` object as a parameter. The error object has `code` (the error code) and `message` (the error message) attributes.

Using plugman

In addition to the Apache Cordova CLI utility, you can use the `plugman` utility in order to add or remove plugin(s) to/from your Apache Cordova projects. However, it's worth mentioning that `plugman` is a lower-level tool that you can use if your Apache Cordova application follows a **platform-centered workflow** and not a **cross-platform workflow**. If your application follows a **cross-platform workflow**, then Apache Cordova CLI should be your choice.

If you want your application to run on different mobile platforms (which is a common use case if you want to use Apache Cordova), it's recommend that you follow a **cross-platform workflow**. Use a **platform-centered workflow** if you want to develop your Apache Cordova application on a single platform and modify your application using the platform-specific SDK.

Besides adding and removing plugins to/from a **platform-centered workflow**, the Cordova projects `plugman` can also be used:

- To create basic scaffolding for your custom Cordova plugin
- To add and remove a platform to/from your custom Cordova plugin
- To add user(s) to the Cordova plugin registry (a repository that hosts the different Apache Cordova core and custom plugins)
- To publish your custom Cordova plugin(s) to the Cordova plugin registry
- To unpublish your custom plugin(s) from the Cordova plugin registry
- To search for plugin(s) in the Cordova plugin registry

In this section, we will use the `plugman` utility to create the basic scaffolding of our custom SMS plugin. In order to install `plugman`, you need to make sure that Node.js is installed on your operating system. Then, to install `plugman`, execute the following command:

```
> npm install -g plugman
```

After installing `plugman`, we can start generating our initial custom plugin artifacts using the `plugman create` command as follows:

```
> plugman create --name sms --plugin_id  com.jsmobile.plugins.sms --
plugin_version 0.0.1
```

It is important to note the following parameters:

- `--name`: This specifies the plugin name (in our case, `sms`)
- `--plugin_id`: This specifies an ID for the plugin (in our case, `com.jsmobile.plugins.sms`)
- `--plugin_version`: This specifies the plugin version (in our case, 0.0.1)

The following are two parameters that the `plugman create` command can accept as well:

- `--path`: This specifies the directory path of the plugin
- `--variable`: This can specify extra variables such as author or description

After executing the previous command, we will have initial artifacts for our custom plugin. As we will be supporting multiple platforms, we can use the `plugman platform add` command. The following two commands add the Android and iOS platforms to our custom plugin:

```
> plugman platform add --platform_name android
> plugman platform add --platform_name ios
```

In order to run the `plugman platform add` command, we need to run it from the `plugin` directory. Unfortunately, for Windows Phone 8 platform support, we need to add it manually later to our plugin.

Now, let's check the initial scaffolding of our custom plugin code. The following screenshot shows the hierarchy of our initial plugin code:

Hierarchy of our initial plugin code

As shown in the preceding screenshot, there is one file and two parent directories. They are as follows:

- `plugin.xml` file: This contains the plugin definition.

- `src` directory: This contains the plugin native implementation code for each platform. For now, it contains two subdirectories: `android` and `ios`. The `android` subdirectory contains `sms.java`. This represents the initial implementation of the plugin in `Android`. `ios` subdirectory contains `sms.m`, which represents the initial implementation of the plugin in iOS.

- `www` directory: This mainly contains the JavaScript interface of the plugin. It contains `sms.js`, which represents the initial implementation of the plugin's JavaScript API.

We will need to edit these generated files (and maybe, refactor and add new implementation files) in order to implement our custom SMS plugin. The details of our SMS plugin definition, JavaScript interface, and native implementations will be illustrated in detail in the upcoming sections.

Plugin definition

First of all, we need to define our plugin structure. In order to do so, we need to define our plugin in the plugin.xml file. The following code listing shows our plugin.xml code:

```xml
<?xml version='1.0' encoding='utf-8'?>
<plugin id="com.jsmobile.plugins.sms" version="0.0.1"
    xmlns="http://apache.org/cordova/ns/plugins/1.0"
    xmlns:android="http://schemas.android.com/apk/res/android">

    <name>sms</name>
    <description>A plugin for sending sms messages</description>
    <license>Apache 2.0</license>
    <keywords>cordova,plugins,sms</keywords>

    <js-module name="sms" src="www/sms.js">
        <clobbers target="window.sms" />
    </js-module>

    <platform name="android">
        <config-file parent="/*" target="res/xml/config.xml">
            <feature name="Sms">
                <param name="android-package" value="com.jsmobile.
plugins.sms.Sms" />
            </feature>
        </config-file>

        <config-file target="AndroidManifest.xml" parent="/manifest">
            <uses-permission android:name="android.permission.SEND_
SMS" />
        </config-file>

        <source-file src="src/android/Sms.java"
                     target-dir="src/com/jsmobile/plugins/sms" />
    </platform>

    <platform name="ios">
        <config-file parent="/*" target="config.xml">
```

```
            <feature name="Sms">
                <param name="ios-package" value="Sms" />
            </feature>
        </config-file>

        <source-file src="src/ios/Sms.h" />
        <source-file src="src/ios/Sms.m" />

        <framework src="MessageUI.framework" weak="true" />
    </platform>

    <platform name="wp8">
        <config-file target="config.xml" parent="/*">
            <feature name="Sms">
                <param name="wp-package" value="Sms" />
            </feature>
        </config-file>

        <source-file src="src/wp8/Sms.cs" />
    </platform>

</plugin>
```

The `plugin.xml` file defines the plugin structure and contains a top-level element `<plugin>`, which contains the following attributes:

- `xmlns`: This attribute represents the plugin namespace which is `http://apache.org/cordova/ns/plugins/1.0`
- `id`: This attribute represents the plugin ID; in our case, it is `com.jsmobile.plugins.sms`
- `version`: This attribute represents the plugin version number, 0.0.1

The `<plugin>` element contains the following subelements:

- `<name>`: This element represents the plugin name; in our case, it is `sms`.
- `<description>`: This element represents the plugin description; in our case, it is `"A plugin for sending sms messages"`.
- `<licence>`: This element represents the plugin license; in our case, it is Apache 2.0.
- `<keywords>`: This element represents the keywords of the plugin; in our case, it is `cordova,plugins,sms`.

- `<js-module>`: This element represents the plugin JavaScript module, and it corresponds to a JavaScript file. It has a `name` attribute that represents the JavaScript module name (in our case, `"sms"`). It also has an `src` attribute that represents the JavaScript module file. The `src` attribute references a JavaScript file in the `plugin` directory that is relative to the `plugin.xml` file (in our case, `"www/sms.js"`). The `<clobbers>` element is a subelement of `<js-module>`. It has a `target` attribute, whose value, in our case, is `"window.sms"`. The `<clobbers target="window.sms" />` element mainly inserts the `smsExport` JavaScript object that is defined in the `www/sms.js` file and exported using `module.exports` (the `smsExport` object will be illustrated in the *Defining the plugin's JavaScript interface* section) into the `window` object as `window.sms`. This means that our plugin users will be able to access our plugin's API using the `window.sms` object (this will be shown in detail in the *Testing our Cordova plugin* section).

A `<plugin>` element can contain one or more `<platform>` element(s). A `<platform>` element specifies a platform-specific plugin's configuration. It has mainly one attribute name that specifies the platform name (`android`, `ios`, `wp8`, `bb10`, `wp7`, and so on). The `<platform>` element can have the following sub-elements:

- `<source-file>`: This element represents the native platform source code that will be installed and executed in the plugin-client project. The `<source-file>` element has the following two main attributes:

    ○ `src`: This attribute represents the location of the source file relative to `plugin.xml`.

    ○ `target-dir`: This attribute represents the `target` directory (that is relative to the project root) in which the source file will be placed when the plugin is installed in the client project. This attribute is mainly needed in Java platform (Android), because a file under the `x.y.z` package must be placed under `x/y/z` directories. For iOS and Windows platforms, this parameter should be ignored.

- `<config-file>`: This element represents the configuration file that will be modified. This is required for many cases; for example, in Android, in order to send an SMS from your Android application, you need to modify the Android configuration file for asking to have the permission to send an SMS from the device. The `<config-file>` element has two main attributes:

    ○ `target`: This attribute represents the file to be modified and the path relative to the project root.

    ○ `parent`: This attribute represents an XPath selector that references the parent of the elements to be added to the configuration file.

- `<framework>`: This element specifies a platform-specific framework that the plugin depends on. It mainly has the `src` attribute to specify the framework `name` and `weak` attributes to indicate whether the specified framework should be weakly linked.

Given this explanation for the `<platform>` element and getting back to our `plugin.xml` file, you will notice that we have the following three `<platform>` elements:

- Android (`<platform name="android">`) performs the following operations:
  - It creates a `<feature>` element for our SMS plugin under the root element of the `res/xml/config.xml` file to register our plugin in the Android project. In Android, the `<feature>` element's `name` attribute represents the service name, and its `"android-package"` parameter represents the fully qualified name of the Java plugin class:

    ```
    <feature name="Sms">
        <param name="android-package"
    value="com.jsmobile.plugins.sms.Sms" />
    </feature>
    ```

  - It modifies the `AndroidManifest.xml` file to add the `<uses-permission android:name="android.permission.SEND_SMS" />` element (to have permission to send an SMS in Android platform) under the `<manifest>` element.
  - Finally, it specifies the plugin's implementation source file, `"src/android/Sms.java"`, and its `target` directory, `"src/com/jsmobile/plugins/sms"` (we will explore the contents of this file in the *Developing Android code* section).

- iOS (`<platform name="ios">`) performs the following operations:
  - It creates a `<feature>` element for our SMS plugin under the root element of the `config.xml` file to register our plugin in the iOS project. In iOS, the `<feature>` element's `name` attribute represents the service name, and its `"ios-package"` parameter represents the Objective-C plugin class name:

    ```
    <feature name="Sms">
        <param name="ios-package" value="Sms" />
    </feature>
    ```

  - It specifies the plugin implementation source files: `Sms.h` (the header file) and `Sms.m` (the methods file). We will explore the contents of these files in the *Developing iOS code* section.

- It adds `"MessageUI.framework"` as a weakly linked dependency for our iOS plugin.

- Windows Phone 8 (`<platform name="wp8">`) performs the following operations:

  - It creates a `<feature>` element for our SMS plugin under the root element of the `config.xml` file to register our plugin in the Windows Phone 8 project. The `<feature>` element's `name` attribute represents the service name, and its `"wp-package"` parameter represents the C# service class name:

    ```
    <feature name="Sms">
            <param name="wp-package" value="Sms" />
    </feature>
    ```

  - It specifies the plugin implementation source file, `"src/wp8/Sms.cs"` (we will explore the contents of this file in the *Developing Windows Phone 8 code* section).

This is all we need to know in order to understand the structure of our custom plugin; however, there are many more attributes and elements that are not mentioned here, as we didn't use them in our example. In order to get the complete list of attributes and elements of `plugin.xml`, you can check out the plugin specification page in the Apache Cordova documentation at `http://cordova.apache.org/docs/en/3.4.0/plugin_ref_spec.md.html#Plugin%20Specification`.

Defining the plugin's JavaScript interface

As indicated in the plugin definition file (`plugin.xml`), our plugin's JavaScript interface is defined in `sms.js`, which is located under the `www` directory. The following code snippet shows the `sms.js` file content:

```
var smsExport = {};

smsExport.sendMessage = function(messageInfo, successCallback,
errorCallback) {
    if (messageInfo == null || typeof messageInfo !== 'object') {
        if (errorCallback) {
            errorCallback({
                code: "INVALID_INPUT",
```

```
                    message: "Invalid Input"
            });
        }

        return;
    }

    var phoneNumber = messageInfo.phoneNumber;
    var textMessage = messageInfo.textMessage || "Default Text
from SMS plugin";

    if (! phoneNumber) {
        console.log("Missing Phone Number");

        if (errorCallback) {
            errorCallback({
                code: "MISSING_PHONE_NUMBER",
                message: "Missing Phone number"
            });
        }

        return;
    }

    cordova.exec(successCallback, errorCallback, "Sms",
"sendMessage", [phoneNumber, textMessage]);
};

module.exports = smsExport;
```

The `smsExport` object contains a single method, `sendMessage(messageInfo, successCallback, errorCallback)`. In the `sendMessage` method, `phoneNumber` and `textMessage` are extracted from the `messageInfo` object. If a phone number is not specified by the user, then `errorCallback` will be called with a JSON error object, which has a `code` attribute set to `"MISSING_PHONE_NUMBER"` and a `message` attribute set to `"Missing Phone number"`. After passing this validation, a call is performed to the `cordova.exec()` API in order to call the native code (whether it is Android, iOS, Windows Phone 8, or any other supported platform) from Apache Cordova JavaScript.

It is important to note that the cordova.exec(successCallback, errorCallback, "service", "action", [args]) API has the following parameters:

- successCallback: This represents the success callback function that will be called (with any specified parameter(s)) if the Cordova exec call completes successfully

- errorCallback: This represents the error callback function that will be called (with any specified error parameter(s)) if the Cordova exec call does not complete successfully

- "service": This represents the native service name that is mapped to a native class using the <feature> element (in sms.js, the native service name is "Sms")

- "action": This represents the action name to be executed, and an action is mapped to a class method in some platforms (in sms.js, the action name is "sendMessage")

- [args]: This is an array that represents the action arguments (in sms.js, the action arguments are [phoneNumber, textMessage])

> It is very important to note that in cordova.exec(successCallback, errorCallback, "service", "action", [args]), the "service" parameter must match the name of the <feature> element, which we set in our plugin.xml file in order to call the mapped native plugin class correctly.

Finally, the smsExport object is exported using module.exports. Do not forget that our JavaScript module is mapped to window.sms using the <clobbers target="window.sms" /> element inside <js-module src="www/sms.js"> element, which we discussed in the plugin.xml file. This means that in order to call the sendMessage method of the smsExport object from our plugin-client application, we use the sms.sendMessage() method.

In the upcoming sections, we will explore the implementation of our custom Cordova plugin in Android, iOS, and Windows Phone 8 platforms.

Developing Android code

As specified in our `plugin.xml` file's platform section for Android, the implementation of our plugin in Android is located at `src/android/Sms.java`. The following code snippet shows the first part of the `Sms.java` file:

```java
package com.jsmobile.plugins.sms;

import org.apache.cordova.CordovaPlugin;
import org.apache.cordova.CallbackContext;
import org.apache.cordova.PluginResult;
import org.apache.cordova.PluginResult.Status;
import org.json.JSONArray;
import org.json.JSONException;
import org.json.JSONObject;

import android.app.Activity;
import android.app.PendingIntent;
import android.content.BroadcastReceiver;
import android.content.Context;
import android.content.Intent;
import android.content.IntentFilter;
import android.content.pm.PackageManager;
import android.telephony.SmsManager;

public class Sms extends CordovaPlugin {
    private static final String SMS_GENERAL_ERROR =
"SMS_GENERAL_ERROR";
    private static final String NO_SMS_SERVICE_AVAILABLE =
"NO_SMS_SERVICE_AVAILABLE";
    private static final String SMS_FEATURE_NOT_SUPPORTED =
"SMS_FEATURE_NOT_SUPPORTED";
    private static final String SENDING_SMS_ID = "SENDING_SMS";

    @Override
    public boolean execute(String action, JSONArray args,
CallbackContext callbackContext) throws JSONException {
        if (action.equals("sendMessage")) {
            String phoneNumber = args.getString(0);
            String message = args.getString(1);

            boolean isSupported = getActivity().getPackageManager().ha
sSystemFeature(PackageManager.
FEATURE_TELEPHONY);
```

```
            if (! isSupported) {
                JSONObject errorObject = new JSONObject();

                errorObject.put("code", SMS_FEATURE_NOT_SUPPORTED);
                errorObject.put("message", "SMS feature is not
supported on this device");

                callbackContext.sendPluginResult(new
PluginResult(Status.ERROR, errorObject));
                return false;
            }

            this.sendSMS(phoneNumber, message, callbackContext);

            return true;
        }

        return false;
    }

    // Code is omitted here for simplicity ...

    private Activity getActivity() {
        return this.cordova.getActivity();
    }
}
```

In order to create our Cordova Android plugin class, our Android plugin class must extend the CordovaPlugin class and must override one of the execute() methods of CordovaPlugin. In our Sms Java class, the execute(String action, JSONArray args, CallbackContext callbackContext) execute method, which has the following parameters, is overridden:

- String action: This represents the action to be performed, and it matches the specified action parameter in the cordova.exec() JavaScript API

- JSONArray args: This represents the action arguments, and it matches the [args] parameter in the cordova.exec() JavaScript API

- CallbackContext callbackContext: This represents the callback context used when calling back into JavaScript

In the execute() method of our Sms class, the phoneNumber and message parameters are retrieved from the args parameter. Using getActivity(). getPackageManager().hasSystemFeature(PackageManager.FEATURE_TELEPHONY), we can check whether the device has a telephony radio with data communication support. If the device does not have this feature, this API returns false, so we create errorObject of the JSONObject type that contains an error code attribute ("code") and an error message attribute ("message") that inform the plugin user that the SMS feature is not supported on this device. The plugin tells the JavaScript caller that the operation failed by calling callbackContext.sendPluginResult() and specifying a PluginResult object as a parameter (the PluginResult object's status is set to Status.ERROR, and message is set to errorObject).

As indicated in our Android implementation, in order to send a plugin result to JavaScript from Android, we use the callbackContext. sendPluginResult() method specifying the PluginResult status and message. Other platforms (iOS and Windows Phone 8) have much a similar way, as we will see in the upcoming sections.

If an Android device supports sending SMS messages, then a call to the sendSMS() private method is performed. The following code snippet shows the sendSMS() method:

```
private void sendSMS(String phoneNumber, String message, final
CallbackContext callbackContext) throws JSONException {
    PendingIntent sentPI =
PendingIntent.getBroadcast(getActivity(), 0, new
Intent(SENDING_SMS_ID), 0);

    getActivity().registerReceiver(new BroadcastReceiver() {
        @Override
        public void onReceive(Context context, Intent intent) {
            switch (getResultCode()) {
            case Activity.RESULT_OK:
                callbackContext.sendPluginResult(new
PluginResult(Status.OK, "SMS message is sent successfully"));
                break;
            case SmsManager.RESULT_ERROR_NO_SERVICE:
                try {
                    JSONObject errorObject = new JSONObject();
```

```
                errorObject.put("code", NO_SMS_SERVICE_AVAILABLE);
                errorObject.put("message", "SMS is not sent
because no service is available");

                callbackContext.sendPluginResult(new
PluginResult(Status.ERROR, errorObject));
            } catch (JSONException exception) {
                exception.printStackTrace();
            }
            break;
        default:
            try {
                JSONObject errorObject = new JSONObject();

                errorObject.put("code", SMS_GENERAL_ERROR);
                errorObject.put("message", "SMS general error");

                callbackContext.sendPluginResult(new
PluginResult(Status.ERROR, errorObject));
            } catch (JSONException exception) {
                exception.printStackTrace();
            }

            break;
        }
    }
    }, new IntentFilter(SENDING_SMS_ID));

    SmsManager sms = SmsManager.getDefault();

    sms.sendTextMessage(phoneNumber, null, message, sentPI, null);
}
```

In order to understand the `sendSMS()` method, let's look into the method's last
two lines:

```
SmsManager sms = SmsManager.getDefault();
sms.sendTextMessage(phoneNumber, null, message, sentPI, null);
```

`SmsManager` is an Android class that provides an API to send text messages. Using
`SmsManager.getDefault()` returns an object of `SmsManager`. In order to send a
text-based message, a call to `sms.sendTextMessage()` should be performed.

The `sms.sendTextMessage` (`String destinationAddress`, `String scAddress`, `String text`, `PendingIntent sentIntent`, `PendingIntent deliveryIntent`) method has the following parameters:

- `destinationAddress`: This represents the address (phone number) to send the message to.
- `scAddress`: This represents the service center address. It can be set to `null` to use the current default SMS center.
- `text`: This represents the text message to be sent.
- `sentIntent`: This represents a `PendingIntent`, which broadcasts when the message is successfully sent or failed. It can be set to `null`.
- `deliveryIntent`: This represents a `PendingIntent`, which broadcasts when the message is delivered to the recipient. It can be set to `null`.

As shown in the preceding code snippet, we specified a destination address (`phoneNumber`), a text message (`message`), and finally, a pending intent (`sendPI`) in order to listen to the message-sending status.

If you return to the `sendSMS()` code and look at it from the beginning, you will notice that `sentPI` is initialized by calling `PendingIntent.getBroadcast()`, and in order to receive the SMS-sending broadcast, a `BroadcastReceiver` is registered.

When the SMS message is sent successfully or fails, the `onReceive()` method of `BroadcastReceiver` will be called, and the result code can be retrieved using `getResultCode()`. The result code can indicate:

- Success when `getResultCode()` is equal to `Activity.RESULT_OK`. In this case, a `PluginResult` object is constructed with `status = Status.OK` and `message = "SMS message is sent successfully"`, and it is sent to the client using `callbackContext.sendPluginResult()`.
- Failure when `getResultCode()` is not equal to `Activity.RESULT_OK`. In this case, a `PluginResult` object is constructed with `status = Status.ERROR` and `message = errorObject` (which contains the error code and error message), and it is sent to the client using `callbackContext.sendPluginResult()`.

These are the details of our SMS plugin implementation in Android platform. Now, let's move to the iOS implementation of our plugin.

Developing iOS code

As specified in our `plugin.xml` file's platform section for iOS, the implementation of our plugin in iOS is located at the `src/ios/Sms.h` and `src/ios/Sms.m` Objective-C files. The following code snippet shows the `Sms.h` file (the header file):

```
#import <Cordova/CDV.h>
#import <MessageUI/MFMessageComposeViewController.h>

@interface Sms : CDVPlugin <MFMessageComposeViewControllerDelegate> {
}

@property(strong) NSString* callbackID;
- (void)sendMessage:(CDVInvokedUrlCommand*)command;
@end
```

The preceding code declares an `Sms` class that extends `CDVPlugin`. It is important to note that in order to create a Cordova iOS plugin class, our Objective-C plugin class must extend the `CDVPlugin` class. In our `Sms` class declaration, there is a declared `callbackID` property of the `NSString` type and a declared `sendMessage` method, which returns `void` and takes `CDVInvokedUrlCommand` as a parameter. Now, let's move on to the `Sms` class implementation. The following code snippet shows the first part of the `Sms.m` file:

```
#import "Sms.h"

@implementation Sms

- (void)sendMessage:(CDVInvokedUrlCommand*)command
{
    CDVPluginResult* pluginResult = nil;
    NSString* phoneNumber = [command.arguments objectAtIndex:0];
    NSString* textMessage = [command.arguments objectAtIndex:1];

    self.callbackID = command.callbackId;

    if (![MFMessageComposeViewController canSendText]) {
        NSMutableDictionary* returnInfo = [NSMutableDictionary
dictionaryWithCapacity:2];

        [returnInfo setObject:@"SMS_FEATURE_NOT_SUPPORTED"
forKey:@"code"];
        [returnInfo setObject:@"SMS feature is not supported on
this device" forKey:@"message"];
```

```
            pluginResult = [CDVPluginResult
    resultWithStatus:CDVCommandStatus_ERROR
    messageAsDictionary:returnInfo];

            [self.commandDelegate sendPluginResult:pluginResult
    callbackId:command.callbackId];

            return;
    }

        MFMessageComposeViewController *composeViewController =
    [[MFMessageComposeViewController alloc] init];
        composeViewController.messageComposeDelegate = self;

        NSMutableArray *recipients = [[NSMutableArray alloc] init];

        [recipients addObject:phoneNumber];

        [composeViewController setBody:textMessage];
        [composeViewController setRecipients:recipients];

        [self.viewController presentViewController:composeViewController
    animated:YES
    completion:nil];
    }
    // Code is omitted from here for simplicity
    @end
```

In our Sms class implementation, we have the Objective-C instance method, - (void)sendMessage:(CDVInvokedUrlCommand*)command, which maps to the action parameter in the cordova.exec() JavaScript API.

In the sendMessage() method of our Sms class, the phoneNumber and message parameters are retrieved from the command.arguments parameter (phoneNumber is located at index 0 and message is located at index 1).

The MFMessageComposeViewController class provides a standard system user interface to compose text messages. Unlike Android, we cannot send SMS messages directly in iOS devices from our plugin code without using the default device's (iPhone or iPad) SMS application. In iOS, all we can do from our plugin code is use the MFMessageComposeViewController class to launch the SMS application with the SMS recipient and SMS message and listen for the user actions to know if the user sent or, cancelled, or failed to send the message. However, before interacting with the MFMessageComposeViewController class, we need to check whether the current iOS device is capable of sending text messages. This can be done using the canSendText method of MFMessageComposeViewController as [MFMessageComposeViewController canSendText].

If the iOS device does not have the feature to send text messages (which means that
[MFMessageComposeViewController canSendText] returns NO), we will create a
returnInfo object (that is of the NSMutableDictionary type), which contains two
entries: one for the error code and the other one for the error message that tells the
plugin user that the SMS feature is not supported on this device. Our plugin tells the
JavaScript caller that the operation failed by calling the sendPluginResult method
(of self.commandDelegate), which has the following signature:

```
- (void)sendPluginResult:(CDVPluginResult*)result
callbackId:(NSString*)callbackId;
```

To this method, we pass a CDVPluginResult object (whose status is
CDVCommandStatus_ERROR, and message is returnInfo) and callbackId, which is
set to command.callbackId.

If your iOS device supports sending SMS messages, then a composeViewController
object (of the MFMessageComposeViewController type) is created and
initialized with recipients as the message recipients and textMessage as the
message body. Then, we present composeViewController modally using the
presentModalViewController method of self.viewController. It is important to
highlight this line:

```
composeViewController.messageComposeDelegate = self;
```

This line tells composeViewController to send the message-related notifications
to our Sms class. In order to receive these notifications, our Sms class needs
to implement the messageComposeViewController method that has the following
signature:

```
- (void)messageComposeViewController:
(MFMessageComposeViewController *)controller
didFinishWithResult:(MessageComposeResult)result
```

The messageComposeViewController class has the following parameters:

- Controller: This represents the message composition view controller that
  returns the result

- Result: This represents a result code that indicates how the user chose
  to complete the message composition (cancels or sends successfully or fails
  to send)

The following code snippet shows the implementation of
`messageComposeViewController` in our `Sms` class:

```
- (void)messageComposeViewController:(MFMessageComposeViewController
*)controller didFinishWithResult:(MessageComposeResult)result {
    BOOL succeeded = NO;
    NSString* errorCode = @"";
    NSString* message = @"";

    switch(result) {
        case MessageComposeResultSent:
            succeeded = YES;
            message = @"Message sent";
            break;
        case MessageComposeResultCancelled:
            message = @"Message cancelled";
            errorCode = @"SMS_MESSAGE_CANCELLED";
            break;
        case MessageComposeResultFailed:
            message = @"Message Compose Result failed";
            errorCode = @"SMS_MESSAGE_COMPOSE_FAILED";
            break;
        default:
            message = @"Sms General error";
            errorCode = @"SMS_GENERAL_ERROR";
            break;
    }

    [self.viewController dismissViewControllerAnimated:YES
completion:nil];

    if (succeeded == YES) {
        [super writeJavascript:[[CDVPluginResult
resultWithStatus:CDVCommandStatus_OK messageAsString:message]
                            toSuccessCallbackString:self.
callbackID]];
    } else {
        NSMutableDictionary* returnInfo = [NSMutableDictionary
dictionaryWithCapacity:2];

        [returnInfo setObject:errorCode forKey:@"code"];
        [returnInfo setObject:message forKey:@"message"];
```

```
        [super writeJavascript:[[CDVPluginResult
resultWithStatus:CDVCommandStatus_ERROR
messageAsDictionary:returnInfo]
                                 toErrorCallbackString:self.
callbackID]];
    }
}
```

The `messageComposeViewController` method is called when the user taps on one of the buttons to dismiss the message composition interface. In the implementation of the `messageComposeViewController` method, the following two actions are performed:

- Dismiss the view controller by calling the `dismissViewControllerAnimated` method of `self.viewController`.

- Check whether the `result` parameter is equal to `MessageComposeResultSent` (which means that the user sent the message successfully) in order to send a `CDVPluginResult` with `status` = `CDVCommandStatus_OK` and `message` = `"Message sent"` to the plugin client. If the result is not equal to `MessageComposeResultSent`, then a `CDVPluginResult` is sent with `status` = `CDVCommandStatus_ERROR` and `message` = `returnInfo` (which contains two entries: one entry for the error code and the other one for the error message that contains the error details such as `"Message cancelled"` or `"Message Compose Result failed"`) to the plugin client.

These are the details of our SMS plugin implementation in iOS platform. Next, let's move to the Windows Phone 8 implementation of our plugin.

Developing Windows Phone 8 code

As specified in our `plugin.xml` file's platform section for Windows Phone 8 (wp8), the implementation of our plugin in wp8 is located at `src/wp8/Sms.cs`. The following code snippet shows `Sms.cs` code:

```
using System;
using Microsoft.Phone.Tasks;
using WPCordovaClassLib.Cordova;
using WPCordovaClassLib.Cordova.Commands;
using WPCordovaClassLib.Cordova.JSON;

namespace WPCordovaClassLib.Cordova.Commands
{
  public class Sms : BaseCommand
  {
```

```
    public void sendMessage(string options)
    {
      string[] optValues = JsonHelper.Deserialize<string[]>(options);
      String number = optValues[0];
      String message = optValues[1];

      SmsComposeTask sms = new SmsComposeTask();

      sms.To = number;
      sms.Body = message;

      sms.Show();

      /*Since there is no way to track SMS application events in
WP8, always send Ok status.*/
      DispatchCommandResult(new PluginResult(PluginResult.Status.OK,
"Success"));
    }
  }
}
```

In order to create our Cordova wp8 C# plugin class, our wp8 plugin C# class (Sms) must extend the `BaseCommand` class. In our `Sms` class, we have the C# method, `public void sendMessage(string options)`, which maps to the action parameter in the `cordova.exec()` JavaScript API. The `sendMessage()` action method must follow these rules:

- The method must be `public`
- The method must return `void`
- Its argument is a string (not an array as you might expect as the `cordova.exec()` method's `args` parameter is originally an array)

In the `sendMessage()` method of our `Sms` class, in order to get the original arguments' array, we need to use the `JsonHelper.Deserialize()` method to deserialize the string parameter to an array. After performing this deserialization, the `number` and `message` parameters are retrieved from the result array (`optValues`).

After getting the `number` and `message` parameters, all we can do is create an `sms` object from `SmsComposeTask` and then set the (`To` and `Body`) attributes to the (`number` and `message`) parameters. After that, we call the `Show()` method of the `sms` object, which will show the wp8 SMS application.

Unfortunately in wp8, you cannot send an SMS message directly using the wp8 API. In order to send an SMS message in wp8, you have to use the default SMS application using `SmsComposeTask`, which does not give you any ability to know what the user did (this means that you will not know whether the user sent an SMS successfully or not or even whether the user cancels sending the SMS).

> The wp8 API is more restrictive than iOS API in SMS sending. In iOS, you cannot send an SMS directly using the iOS API, but the iOS API gives us the ability to know what the user did. This gives us the ability to send successful or failing plugin results to the plugin client in the case of our iOS implementation.

Finally, and because our plugin is now blind once the `Show()` method of `SmsComposeTask` is called, our plugin assumes that sending SMS is completed successfully and sends a `PluginResult` object, whose status = `PluginResult.Status.OK` and message = `"Success"`, to the plugin client in order to have a consistent behavior across the different platforms. Consistent behavior here means that when the users call our API from JavaScript in any supported platform, our API has to always respond to their calls with either successful or failed responses.

These are the details of our SMS plugin implementation on Windows Phone 8 platform. Now, let's publish our plugin to the Cordova Registry to be used by the Apache Cordova community.

Publishing our plugin to Cordova Registry

After completing our plugin implementation, we can publish our SMS plugin to the Apache Cordova Registry. Before publishing our custom SMS plugin, let's revise our final SMS plugin structure. The following screenshot shows the final structure of our custom SMS plugin:

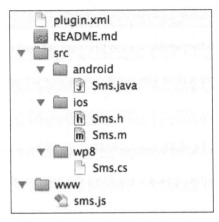

Hierarchy of our final plugin structure

As shown in the preceding screenshot, the final structure has the following main additions:

- A new wp8 directory under the src directory; it has our wp8 plugin implementation

- A markdown README.md file that explains the purpose of the plugin and an example of its usage

Now, after understanding the final structure of our custom SMS plugin, we can now publish our plugin to the Apache Cordova Registry. In order to do this, just execute the following plugman publish command specifying our SMS plugin directory:

```
> plugman publish sms
```

After executing this command successfully, you will be notified that our com.jsmobile.plugins.sms@0.0.1 plugin has been published successfully.

By uploading our custom plugin to the Apache Cordova Registry, the Apache Cordova community can now use our plugin by just using the normal Cordova CLI's `plugin add` command as follows:

```
> cordova plugin add com.jsmobile.plugins.sms
```

In order to make the source code of our plugin accessible, we published its source code on GitHub, and it can be downloaded from https://github.com/hazems/cordova-sms-plugin.

Publishing our custom plugin to GitHub gives our plugin consumers the ability to add our custom plugin to their projects by specifying the plugin GitHub URL as follows:

```
> cordova plugin add https://github.com/hazems/cordova-sms-plugin.git
```

In the next section, we will create our test Cordova application, which will test the functionality of our plugin across the different platforms (Android, iOS, and wp8).

Testing our Cordova plugin

Now, it is time to create our test Cordova application, `"SmsApp"`. In order to create our test Cordova application, we can execute the following `cordova create` command:

```
> cordova create smsApp com.jsmobile.sms.app SmsApp
```

Then, we can add Android, iOS, and wp8 from the application directory as follows:

```
> cordova platform add android
> cordova platform add ios
> cordova platform add wp8
```

The following code snippet shows the jQuery Mobile page (`index.html`), which allows the user to enter a phone number and message. The user can then click on the **Send** button to send an SMS.

```html
<html>
<head>
    <!-- meta data and jQuery mobile includes are omitted for
saving space -->
    <script src="jqueryMobile/jquery.validate.min.js"></script>
    <title>SMS App</title>
</head>
<body>
```

```
    <div data-role="page" id="sms">
        <div data-role="header">
            <h1>Send SMS</h1>
        </div>
        <div data-role="content">
            <h1>Send SMS now</h1>
            <p>Enter mobile number and mobile message and click
"send" button.</p>

            <form id="smsForm">
                <div class="ui-field-contain">
                    <label for="phoneNo">Phone Number</label>
                    <input type="text" id="phoneNo"
name="phoneNo"></input>
                </div>
                <div class="ui-field-contain">
                    <label for="textMessage">Message</label>
                    <input type="text" id="textMessage"
name="textMessage"></input>
                </div>
                <input type="submit" id="sendSMS" data-icon="action"
value="Send"></input>
                <ul id="messageBox"></ul>
                <div id="result">
                </div>
            </form>
        </div>
    </div>

    <script type="text/javascript" src="cordova.js"></script>
    <script type="text/javascript" src="js/sms.js"></script>
</body>
</html>
```

As shown in the preceding highlighted code, we are utilizing the jQuery validation plugin. This is why we included the `jquery.validate.min.js` file. The `"smsForm"` form element contains the following elements:

- `"phoneNo"`: It includes a label and an input text to enter phone number
- `"textMessage"`: It includes a label and an input text to enter text message.
- `"sendSMS"`: It is a button to send an SMS message
- `"messageBox"`: This is an unordered list used to display validation errors
- `"result"`: This div is used to display the SMS operation result

Finally, we included `sms.js`. The `sms.js` file includes the implementation for the event handlers of `"smsForm"`. The following code snippet shows the `sms.js` file's code:

```
(function() {
    $(document).on("pageinit", "#sms", function(e) {
        e.preventDefault();

        function onDeviceReady() {
            console.log("Apache Cordova is loaded ...");

            $("#sendSMS").on("tap", function(e) {
                e.preventDefault();

                if (! $("#smsForm").valid()) {
                    return;
                }

                var messageInfo = {
                    phoneNumber: $("#phoneNo").val(),
                    textMessage: $("#textMessage").val()
                };

                sms.sendMessage(messageInfo, function() {
                    $("#result").html("Message is sent successfully
...");
                }, function(error) {
                    $("#result").html("Error code: " + error.code +
", Error message: " + error.message);
                });
            });
        }

        document.addEventListener("deviceready", onDeviceReady,
false);
    });

    $(document).on("pageshow", "#sms", function(e) {
        e.preventDefault();

        $("#smsForm").validate({
            errorLabelContainer: "#messageBox",
            wrapper: "li",
            rules: {
                textMessage: "required",
```

```
                               phoneNo: {
                                   required: true,
                                   number: true
                               }
                          },
                          messages: {
                              textMessage: "Please specify text message",
                              phoneNo: {
                                  required: "Please specify Phone number",
                                  number: "Phone number is numeric only"
                              }
                          }
                   });
              });
         }) ();
```

As shown in the preceding code, in the `"pageinit"` event of the `"sms"` page, the `"tap"` event handler of the `"sendSMS"` button is registered after Apache Cordova is loaded. In the implementation of the `"sendSMS"` button's tap event handler:

- The `"smsForm"` is validated using `$("#smsForm").valid()`.

- If the form is valid, then, as shown in the preceding highlighted code, the `messageInfo` object is constructed using the `phoneNumber` and `textMessage` attributes. The `phoneNumber` and `textMessage` attributes are initialized with the `"phoneNo"` and `"textMessage"` input text values.

- A call to `sms.sendMessage(messageInfo, successCallback, errorCallback)` is performed with the following parameters in order:

  - The `messageInfo` object.
  - The `success` callback function that will be called when an SMS is successfully sent. The `success` callback function displays the `"Message is sent successfully ..."` message inside the `"result"` div.
  - The `error` callback function that will be called when sending SMS fails. The `failure` callback function displays both the error code and error message inside the `"result"` div.

In the `"pageshow"` event of the `"sms"` page, our form validation is specified as follows:

- `errorLabelContainer`: This is set to `"messageBox"` to display the validation errors inside

- `wrapper`: This is set to `"li"` to wrap the error messages in list items

- `rules`: This is set as follows:

    ○ `textMessage` is set to `required`

    ○ `phoneNumber` is set to `number` and `required`

- `messages`: This is set to `textMessage` and `phoneNumber` validation errors messages

Now, let's build and run our SMS app in order to observe how our custom SMS plugin will behave across the different platforms (Android, iOS, and Windows Phone 8). When the user enters a valid phone number and a text message and then clicks on the **Send** button, the following will happen:

- In Android, an SMS will be sent directly from our Android SMS app without any intervention from the platform's default SMS app.

- In iOS, the user will be forwarded to the default iOS SMS app initialized with the phone number and text message from our custom SMS plugin. Once the user clicks on the **Send** or even **Cancel** button, the user will get back to our SMS app with the correct result displayed.

- In Windows Phone 8, the user will be forwarded to the default Windows Phone 8 SMS app initialized with the phone number and text message from our custom SMS plugin. Unfortunately, due to wp8 API limitations, when the user clicks on the **Send** or even **Cancel** button, we will not be able to detect what happens. This is why when you click on your wp8 device's back button to get back to our SMS app, you will find our SMS application always displaying the success message, which is not always correct due to the current wp8 API limitations.

 The complete source code of `"SmsApp"` can be downloaded from the course's web page or from GitHub (`https://github.com/hazems/cordova-sms-plugin-test`).

Summary

This chapter showed you how to design and develop your own custom Apache Cordova plugin using JavaScript and Java for Android, Objective-C for iOS, and finally, C# for Windows Phone 8. In the next chapter, you will learn how to develop JavaScript tests for your Cordova app's logic using Jasmine. You will also learn how to automate the Jasmine tests that you will develop, using Karma and Jenkins CI.

7
Unit Testing the Cordova App's Logic

In this chapter, you will learn how to develop JavaScript unit tests for your Cordova app logic. In this chapter, you will:

- Learn the basics of the Jasmine JavaScript unit testing framework
- Use Jasmine in order to test both synchronous and asynchronous JavaScript code
- Utilize Karma as a powerful JavaScript test runner in order to automate the running of your developed Jasmine tests
- Generate test and code coverage reports from your developed tests
- Automate your JavaScript tests by integrating your developed tests with **Continuous Integration (CI)** tools

What is Jasmine

Jasmine is a powerful JavaScript unit testing framework. It provides a clean mechanism to test synchronous and asynchronous JavaScript code. It is a behavior-driven development framework that provides descriptive test cases, which focus on business value more than on technical details. As it is written in a simple, natural language, Jasmine tests can be read by nonprogrammers and provide a clear description when a single test succeeds or fails and the reason behind its failure.

> **Behavior-driven development (BDD)** is an agile software development technique introduced by Dan North; it focuses on writing descriptive tests from a business perspective. BDD extends TDD by writing test cases that test the software behavior (requirements) in a natural language that anyone (does not necessarily have to be a programmer) can read and understand. The names of the unit tests are complete sentences that usually start with the word "should," and they are written in the order of their business value.

Configuring Jasmine

In order to configure Jasmine, the first step is to download the framework from `https://github.com/pivotal/jasmine/tree/master/dist`. In this download link, you will find the latest releases of the framework.

> At the time of writing this module, the latest release is v2.0 that we will use in this chapter.

After unpacking `jasmine-standalone-2.0.0.zip`, you will find the following directories and files, as shown in the following screenshot:

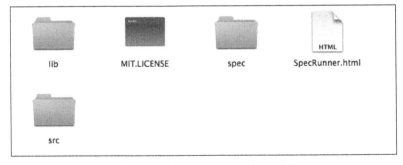

Jasmine Standalone 2.0 directories and files

The `src` directory contains the JavaScript source files that you want to test. The `spec` directory contains the JavaScript test files, while the `SpecRunner.html` file is the test cases' runner HTML file. The `lib` directory contains the framework files.

In order to make sure that everything is running okay, click on the `SpecRunner.html` file; you should see specs passing, as shown in the following screenshot:

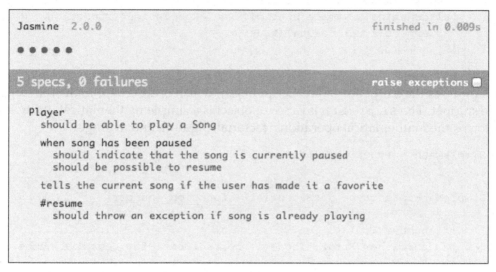

Jasmine specs passing

Note that this structure is not rigid; we can modify it to serve the organization of our app, as we will see in the *Jasmine in action – developing Cordova app tests* section.

Writing your first Jasmine test

Before writing our first Jasmine test, we need to understand the difference between a suite and a spec (test specification) in Jasmine. Jasmine suite is a group of test cases that can be used to test a specific behavior of the JavaScript code. In Jasmine, the test suite begins with a call to the `describe` Jasmine global function that has two parameters. The first parameter represents the title of the test suite, while the second parameter represents a function that implements the test suite.

A Jasmine spec represents a test case inside the test suite. In Jasmine, the test case begins with a call to the Jasmine global function `it` that has two parameters. The first parameter represents the title of the spec and the second parameter represents a function that implements the test case.

A Jasmine spec contains one or more expectations. Every expectation represents an assertion that can be either `true` or `false`. In order to pass the specs, all of the expectations inside the spec have to be `true`. If one or more expectations inside a spec is `false`, then the spec fails. The following code listing shows an example of a Jasmine test suite and a spec with an expectation:

```
describe("A sample suite", function() {
    it("contains a sample spec with an expectation", function() {
        expect(true).toEqual(true);
    });
});
```

Let's move to the `SimpleMath` JavaScript object, which is described in the following code snippet. The `SimpleMath` JavaScript object is a simple mathematical utility that performs the mathematical operations: factorial, Signum, and average:

```
SimpleMath = function() {
};

SimpleMath.prototype.getFactorial = function (number) {

    if (number < 0) {
        throw new Error("There is no factorial for negative numbers");
    }
    else if (number == 1 || number == 0) {

        // If number <= 1 then number! = 1.
        return 1;
    } else {

        // If number > 1 then number! = number * (number-1)!
        return number * this.getFactorial(number-1);
    }
}

SimpleMath.prototype.signum = function (number) {
    if (number > 0)  {
        return 1;
    } else if (number == 0) {
        return 0;
    } else {
        return -1;
    }
}
```

```
SimpleMath.prototype.average = function (number1, number2) {
    return (number1 + number2) / 2;
}
```

The `SimpleMath` object is used to calculate the factorial of numbers. In mathematics, the factorial of a non-negative integer *n*, denoted by *n!*, is the product of all the positive integers less than or equal to *n*, for example, *4! = 4 x 3 x 2 x 1 = 24*.

The `SimpleMath` object calculates the factorial number using the `getFactorial` recursive function. It throws an error when the parameter passed to the `getFactorial` method is a negative number, because there is no factorial value for negative numbers.

Adding to calculating factorial, `SimpleMath` can get the Signum of any number using the `signum` method. In mathematics, the Signum function is a mathematical function that extracts the sign of a real number.

Finally, `SimpleMath` can calculate the average of two numbers using the average method. The average value of two numbers can be calculated by dividing the sum of the two numbers by 2.

Now, let's start writing the specs using Jasmine. First of all, in order to test the `getFactorial` method, let's look at the following three test scenarios. We will calculate the factorial of:

- A positive number
- Zero
- A negative number

The following code snippet shows how to calculate the factorial of a positive number `3`, `zero`, and a negative number `-10`:

```
describe("SimpleMath", function() {
    var simpleMath;

    beforeEach(function() {
        simpleMath = new SimpleMath();
    });

    describe("when SimpleMath is used to find factorial",
function() {
        it("should be able to find factorial for positive number",
function() {
            expect(simpleMath.getFactorial(3)).toEqual(6);
        });
```

```
        it("should be able to find factorial for zero", function()
{
            expect(simpleMath.getFactorial(0)).toEqual(1);
        });

        it("should be able to throw an exception when the number
is negative", function() {
            expect(
                function() {
                    simpleMath.getFactorial(-10)
                }).toThrow();
        });
    });
    //...
});
```

The describe keyword declares a new test suite called "SimpleMath". beforeEach is used for initialization of the specs inside the suite, that is, beforeEach is called once before the run of each spec in describe. beforeEach, simpleMath object is created using new SimpleMath().

In Jasmine, it is also possible to execute the JavaScript code after running each spec in describe using the afterEach global function. Having beforeEach and afterEach in Jasmine allows the developer not to repeat the set up and finalization code for each spec.

After initializing the simpleMath object, you can either create a direct spec using the "it" keyword or create a child test suite using the describe keyword. For the purpose of organizing the example, we create a new describe function for each group of tests with similar functionalities. This is why we create an independent "describe" function to test the functionality of getFactorial provided by the SimpleMath object.

In the first test scenario of the getFactorial test suite, the spec title is "should be able to find factorial for positive number", and the expect() function calls simpleMath.getFactorial(3) and expects it to be equal to 6. If simpleMath.getFactorial(3) returns a value other than 6, then the test fails.

We have many other options (matchers) to use instead of toEqual; we will show them in the *Jasmine Matchers* section.

In the second test scenario of the getFactorial test suite, the expect() function calls simpleMath.getFactorial(0) and expects it to be equal to 1. In the final test scenario of the getFactorial test suite, the expect() function calls simpleMath. getFactorial(-10) and expects it to throw an exception using the toThrow matcher. The toThrow matcher succeeds if the function of the expect() function throws an exception when executed.

After finalizing the getFactorial suite test, we come to a new test suite that tests the functionality of the signum method provided by the SimpleMath object, as shown in the following code snippet:

```
describe("when SimpleMath is used to find signum", function() {
    it("should be able to find the signum for a positive number",
function() {
        expect(simpleMath.signum(3)).toEqual(1);
    });

    it("should be able to find the signum for zero", function() {
        expect(simpleMath.signum(0)).toEqual(0);
    });

    it("should be able to find the signum for a negative number",
function() {
        expect(simpleMath.signum(-1000)).toEqual(-1);
    });
});
```

We have three test scenarios for the signum method. The first test scenario is getting the Signum of a positive number, the second test scenario is getting the Signum of zero, and the last test scenario is getting the Signum of a negative number. As validated by the specs, the signum method has to return 1 for a positive number (3), 0 for zero, and finally, -1 for a negative number (-1000). The following code snippet shows the average test suite:

```
describe("when SimpleMath is used to find the average of two
values", function() {
    it("should be able to find the average of two values",
function() {
        expect(simpleMath.average(3, 6)).toEqual(4.5);
    });
});
```

In the average spec, the test ensures that the average is calculated correctly by trying to calculate the average of two numbers, 3 and 6, and expecting the result to be 4.5.

Now, after writing the suites and specs, it is time to run our JavaScript tests. In order to run the tests, follow these steps:

1. Place the `simpleMath.js` file in the `src` folder.

2. Place the `simpleMathSpec.js` file in the `spec` folder.

3. Edit the `SpecRunner.html` file, as shown by the highlighted code in the following code snippet:

```html
<!DOCTYPE HTML>
<html>
    <head>
        <meta http-equiv="Content-Type" content="text/html;
charset=UTF-8">
        <title>Jasmine Spec Runner v2.0.0</title>

        <link rel="shortcut icon" type="image/png"
href="lib/jasmine-2.0.0/jasmine_favicon.png">
        <link rel="stylesheet" type="text/css"
href="lib/jasmine-2.0.0/jasmine.css">

        <script type="text/javascript" src="lib/jasmine-
2.0.0/jasmine.js"></script>
        <script type="text/javascript" src="lib/jasmine-
2.0.0/jasmine-html.js"></script>
        <script type="text/javascript" src="lib/jasmine-
2.0.0/boot.js"></script>

        <!-- include source files here... -->
        <script type="text/javascript" src="src/simpleMath.js"></
script>

        <!-- include spec files here... -->
        <script type="text/javascript" src="spec/simpleMathSpec.
js"></script>
    </head>
    <body>
    </body>
</html>
```

As shown in the highlighted lines, `<script type="text/javascript" src="spec/simpleMathSpec.js"></script>` is added under the `include spec files` omment , while `<script type="text/javascript" src="src/simpleMath.js"></script>` is added under the `include source files` comment. After clicking on the `SpecRunner.html` file, you will see our developed JavaScript tests succeed.

Jasmine Matchers

In the first Jasmine example, we used the `toEqual` and `toThrow` Jasmine Matchers. In the following table, some of the other built-in matchers provided by Jasmine are explained briefly:

Matcher	Description
`expect(x).toBe(y)`	The `toBe` matcher passes if x is of the same type and value of y. The `toBe` matcher uses `===` to perform this comparison.
`expect(x).toBeDefined()`	The `toBeDefined` matcher is used to ensure that x is defined.
`expect(x).toBeUndefined()`	The `toBeUndefined` matcher is used to ensure that x is undefined.
`expect(x).toBeNull()`	The `toBeNull` matcher is used to ensure that x is null.
`expect(x).toBeTruthy()`	The `toBeTruthy` matcher is used to ensure that x is *truthy*.
`expect(x).toBeFalsy()`	The `toBeFalsy` matcher is used to ensure that x is *falsy*.
`expect(x).toContain(y)`	The `toContain` matcher is used to check whether the x string or array value contains y. A valid y value can be a substring of x or an item of x.
`expect(x).toBeLessThan(y)`	The `toBeLessThan` matcher is used to ensure that x is less than y.
`expect(x).toBeGreaterThan(y)`	The `toBeGreaterThan` matcher is used to ensure that x is greater than y.
`expect(x).toMatch(y)`	The `toMatch` matcher is used to check whether x matches a string or regular expression (y).

 Adding to built-in matchers, you can create your own Jasmine custom matcher. To create your own Jasmine custom matcher, check the Jasmine 2.0 custom matcher documentation page at `http://jasmine.github.io/2.0/custom_matcher.html`.

Jasmine in action – developing Cordova app tests

Now, let's see Jasmine in action. In the following sections, we will illustrate a Cordova mobile app (weather application), which we will develop its tests using Jasmine. We will see how to test both the synchronous and asynchronous JavaScript code of the app, automate running our developed Jasmine tests using Karma, run our tests on the mobile device browser, generate test and code coverage reports, and finally, fully automate our tests by integrating our developed tests with CI tools.

An overview of the weather application

The main purpose of the weather application is to allow its users to know the current weather information of a specified place. It has two main views; the first view represents **First Time login**, which appears to the users for their first login time, as shown in the following screenshot:

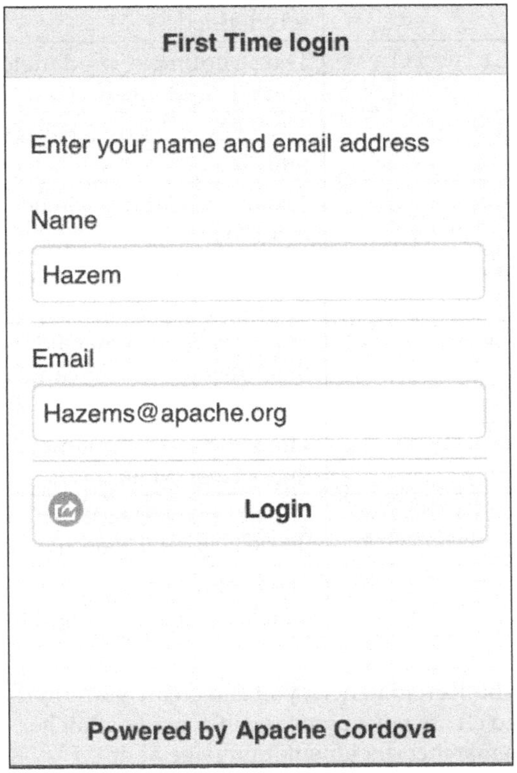

Weather application's first time login

After entering the valid information and clicking on the **Login** button, the user will be forwarded to the weather information page. On the weather information page, the user can enter the place information and then click on the **Weather Info** button to get the current weather information, as shown in the following screenshot:

Again, pretty obvious

After entering valid information on the **First Time login** page and clicking on the **Login** button, if the user exits the app and opens it again, the user will automatically be forwarded to the weather information page with his/her name displayed in the welcome message.

In order to create weather application from CLI, we run the following `cordova create` command:

```
> cordova create weather com.jsmobile.weather Weather
```

We run the usual `cordova platform add` commands from the `app` directory to add the platforms we want to support as follows:

```
> cd weather
> cordova platform add ios
```

Finally, we can build our app using the `cordova build` command as follows:

```
> cordova build
```

Now, let's examine the structure of our weather application code. The following screenshot shows our weather application hierarchy:

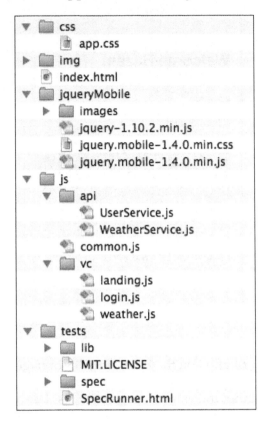

The www directory contains the following files and subdirectories:

- css: This directory contains the custom application's **Cascading Style Sheet (CSS)**.

- jqueryMobile: This directory contains the jQuery Mobile framework files.

- js: This directory contains all the application JavaScript code. It has two subdirectories:
    - api: This directory contains the app services.

- ° vc: This directory contains the app view controllers, which register and implement the event handlers of every page and its user interface components. An event handler usually calls one or more app services in order to perform an action and optionally display the returned results on an app page.

- tests: This directory contains the tests of app services, which are implemented using Jasmine.

The js directory also includes common.js file, which includes the common app utilities. Under the www directory, the index.html file contains all of the app pages, and finally, the img directory can contain any app's custom images.

The index.html file contains the following pages:

- "landing": This page displays a loading message to the user in the app startup and forwards the user to either the **First Time login** page if the user has not logged in to the app before or to the weather information page if the user is already registered.

- "login": This page displays a form that includes the username and e-mail input fields and a **Login** button. The "login" page allows the users to enter their information while they are accessing the app for the first time. If the users enter valid information on the "login" page and clicks on the **Login** button, the users will not be introduced to this page during their next visit.

- "weather": This page allows the user to enter information about a place and then click on the **Weather Info** button to find out the current weather information of the place entered.

The following code snippet shows the "login" page:

```
<div data-role="page" id="login">
    <div data-role="header" data-position="fixed">
        <h1>First Time login</h1>
    </div>
    <div data-role="content">
        <p>Enter your name and email address</p>
        <form id="loginForm">
            <div class="ui-field-contain">
                <label for="userName">Name</label>
                <input type="text" id="userName"></input>
            </div>
            <div class="ui-field-contain">
                <label for="userEmail">Email</label>
```

```
                    <input type="text" id="userEmail"></input>
            </div>

            <input type="button" id="loginUser" data-icon="action"
value="Login"/>

            <div id="loginFormMessages" class="error"></div>
        </form>
    </div>
    <div data-role="footer" data-position="fixed">
        <h1>Powered by Apache Cordova</h1>
    </div>
</div>
```

As shown in the preceding `"login"` page, it contains the following:

- A page header and page footer
- Page content that includes the following main elements:
    - `"userName"`: This input field is used to enter the username
    - `"userEmail"`: This input field is used to enter the user's e-mail
    - `"loginUser"`: This button is used to save the user information and then go to the weather information page
    - `"loginFormMessages"`: This div is used to display the error messages on the login page

The following code snippet shows the `"login"` page view controller JavaScript object that includes the event handlers of the page (`login.js`):

```
(function() {
    var userService = UserService.getInstance();

    $(document).on("pageinit", "#login", function(e) {
        e.preventDefault();

        $("#loginUser").on("tap", function(e) {
            e.preventDefault();

            try {
                userService.saveUser({
                    'name': $("#userName").val(),
                    'email': $("#userEmail").val(),
                });
```

```
                            $.mobile.changePage("#weather");
                    } catch (exception) {
                        $("#loginFormMessages").html(exception.message);
                    }
                });
            });
        })();
```

The `"pageinit"` event handler that is called once in the initialization of the page
registers the `"loginUser"` tap event handler, which:

- Saves the entered user information by calling the `saveUser()` method of
  the `userService` object, specifying the user object with the `name` and `email`
  attributes. The `name` and `email` attributes are populated with the `"userName"`
  and `"userEmail"` input field values, respectively.

- Forwards the user to the `"weather"` page.

If an exception occurs while saving the user information, the `"loginFormMessages"`
div is populated with the exception message.

The following code snippet shows the `UserService` JavaScript object, which
interacts with the Web Storage API to save and retrieve the user information
(`UserService.js`):

```
var UserValidationException = function(code, message) {
    this.code = code;
    this.message = message;
}

var UserService = (function () {
    var instance;
    var USER_KEY = "WEATHER_USER";

    function isValidEmail(email) {
        var regex = /^([a-zA-Z0-9_.+-])+\@(([a-zA-Z0-9-])+\.)+([a-zA-Z0-9]{2,4})+$/;

        return regex.test(email);
    }

    function createObject() {
        return {
            saveUser: function (user) {
```

```
                        if (!user.name || !user.email || user.name.trim().
length == 0 || user.email.trim().length == 0) {
                        console.log("You need to specify both user name
and email!");

                        throw new UserValidationException("EMPTY_FIELDS",
"You need to specify both user name and email!");
                    }

                    if (user.name.trim().length > 6) {
                        console.log("User name must not exceed 6
characters!");

                        throw new UserValidationException("MAX_LENGTH_
EXCEEDED", "User name must not
exceed 6 characters!");
                    }

                    if (! isValidEmail(user.email)) {
                        console.log("Email is invalid!");

                        throw new UserValidationException("INVALID_
FORMAT", "Email is invalid!");
                    }

                    window.localStorage.setItem(USER_KEY,
JSON.stringify(user));
                },
                getUser:function() {
                    var user = window.localStorage.getItem(USER_KEY);

                    if (user) {
                        user = JSON.parse(user);
                    }

                    return user;
                }
            };
        };

        return {
            getInstance: function () {
                if (!instance) {
                    instance = createObject();
                }
```

```
                    return instance;
            }
        };
    })();
```

As you can see, `UserService` is a singleton object that has two methods, as highlighted in the preceding code:

- `saveUser(user)`: This uses the `window.localStorage.setItem()` method to save the user information in the Local Storage:

    ○ `window.localStorage.setItem(USER_KEY, JSON.stringify(user))`: This has the two parameters in order: `USER_KEY`, which is a string that represents the Local Storage item name, and `JSON.stringify(user)`, which returns the user object JSON string. This parameter represents the Local Storage item value.

    ○ If any of the user object information is invalid, then an exception of the `UserValidationException` type is thrown.

- `getUser()`: This uses the `window.localStorage.getItem()` method to get the user information string from the Local Storage and then parses it as a JSON object using `JSON.parse()`.

We are now done with the `"login"` page; let's check out the `"weather"` page. The following code snippet shows the `"weather"` page:

```html
<div data-role="page" id="weather">
    <div data-role="header" data-position="fixed">
        <h1>Weather Info</h1>
    </div>
    <div data-role="content">
        <h2>Welcome <span id="user"></span>,</h2>
        <form id="weatherForm">
            <div class="ui-field-contain">
                <label for="location">Location</label>
                <input type="text" id="location"></input>
            </div>
            <input type="button" id="getWeatherInfo" data-
icon="action" value="Weather Info"/>

            <div id="weatherResult">
            </div>
        </form>
    </div>
</div>
```

As shown in the preceding "weather" page, it contains the following:

- A page header
- Page content that includes the following main elements:
    - "user": This span is used to display the username
    - "location": This input field is used to enter the location information
    - "getWeatherInfo": This button is used to get the current weather information of the location entered in the "location" input field
    - "weatherResult": This div is used to display the current weather information

The following code snippet shows the page view controller JavaScript object, which includes the event handlers of the page (weather.js):

```
(function() {
    var weatherService = WeatherService.getInstance();
    var userService = UserService.getInstance();

    $(document).on("pageinit", "#weather", function(e) {
        e.preventDefault();

        $("#getWeatherInfo").on("tap", function(e) {
            e.preventDefault();

            $("#location").blur(); //Hide keyboard

            $.mobile.loading('show');

            var successCallback = function(result) {
                $.mobile.loading('hide');
                $("#weatherResult").removeClass("error");

                var result = "<img class='center' src='" +
result.icon + "'><br/>"
                            + "Temperature: " + result.temperature
+ "<br/>"
                            + "Humidity: " + result.humidity +
"<br/>"
                            + "Description: " + result.description
+ "<br/>";

                $("#weatherResult").html(result);
            };
```

```
                  var errorCallback = function(errorMessage) {
                      $.mobile.loading('hide');
                      $("#weatherResult").addClass("error");
                      $("#weatherResult").html(errorMessage);
                  };

                  weatherService.getWeatherInfo($("#location").val(),
        successCallback, errorCallback);
              });
          });

          $(document).on("pageshow", "#weather", function(e) {
              $("#user").html(userService.getUser().name || "");
          });

      })();
```

The `"pageinit"` event handler registers the `"getWeatherInfo"` tap event handler.
The `"getWeatherInfo"` tap event handler gets the current weather information
by calling the `getWeatherInfo()` method of the `weatherService` object with the
following parameters in order:

- `$("#location").val()`: This is the user's location entered in the
  `"location"` input text
- `successCallback`: This is the successful callback that will be called if the
  weather information query operation succeeds
- `errorCallback`: This is the error callback that will be called if the weather
  information query operation fails

In `successCallback`, the `result` object, which holds the current weather
information, is received as a parameter, and its main information is displayed
in the `"weatherResult"` div.

In `errorCallback`, `errorMessage` is displayed in the `"weatherResult"` div.

> In our weather page, we use $.mobile.loading to show and hide the
> jQuery Mobile loading dialog. The jQuery Mobile loading dialog can be
> used to give the user the impression that there is an operation in progress.

The `"pageshow"` event handler displays the username (which is retrieved using
`userService.getUser().name`) in the `"user"` span.

The following code snippet shows the `WeatherService` JavaScript object, which interacts with the weather API provided by `OpenWeatherMap` (http://openweathermap.org) to get the current weather information for a specified location (`WeatherService.js`):

```
var WeatherService = (function () {
    var instance;
    var BASE_ICON_URL = "http://openweathermap.org/img/w/";

    function createObject() {
        return {
            getWeatherInfo: function (locationText, successCallback,
errorCallback) {
                if (!location || locationText.trim().length == 0) {
                    errorCallback("You have to specify a location!");
                }

                $.ajax({
                    url: "http://api.openweathermap.org/data/2.5/
weather?q=" +
escape(locationText),
                    success: function(response) {
                        console.log(response);

                        // If response code != 200 then this is an
error
                        if (response.cod != 200) {
                            errorCallback(response.message);
                            return;
                        }

                        successCallback({
                            'temperature': (response.main.temp -
273.15).toFixed(1) + " °C",
                            'pressure': response.main.pressure,
                            'humidity': response.main.humidity + "%",
                            'description': (response.weather[0]) ?
(response.weather[0].description) : "NA",
                            'icon': (response.weather[0]) ?
BASE_ICON_URL+ (response.weather[0].icon) + ".png" : ""
                        });
                    }
                });
            }
        };
```

```
        };

        return {
            getInstance: function () {
                if (!instance) {
                    instance = createObject();
                }

                return instance;
            }
        };
    })();
```

As you can see, `WeatherService` is a singleton object that has a single method, as highlighted in the preceding code. The `getWeatherInfo(locationText, successCallback, errorCallback)` method which makes an Ajax call using `$.ajax` to `http://api.openweathermap.org/data/2.5/weather`, specifying `q` (the query parameter) with `locationText`. If the operation response code (`response.cod`) is not equal to `200` (this means that the operation was not performed successfully), then `errorCallback` is called with the response message specified by `response.message`. If the operation response code (`response.cod`) is equal to `200` (this means that the operation was performed successfully), then `successCallback` is called with a resulting JSON object that contains temperature, pressure, humidity, description, and icon information.

Finally, let's check the code of the `"landing"` page, which is used to decide the weather application initial page. The following code snippet shows the `"landing"` page HTML content:

```html
<div id="landing" data-role="page">
    <div class="center-screen">Please wait ...</div>
</div>
```

The following code snippet shows the page view controller JavaScript object of the `"landing"` page, which is located in `landing.js`:

```javascript
(function() {
    var userService = UserService.getInstance();

    $(document).on("pageinit", "#landing", function(e) {
        e.preventDefault();

        function onDeviceReady () {
            console.log("Apache Cordova is loaded");
```

```
            var home = '#login';

            if (userService.getUser()) {
                home = '#weather';
            }

            $.mobile.changePage(home);
        }

        document.addEventListener("deviceready", onDeviceReady,
    false);
        });
}) ();
```

The "pageinit" event handler of the landing page tries to get the user information using the getUser() method of userService once Cordova is loaded. If there is an object that is not returned as null from the getUser() method, then the initial page is chosen to be the "weather" page; else, the initial page is chosen to be the "login" page.

After exploring the weather application code, let's see how we can develop Jasmine tests for weather app services.

Developing synchronous code tests

It is the time to develop Jasmine tests for the synchronous JavaScript code (UserService) in our weather app services. First of all, in order to test the UserService object, let's basically consider the following four test scenarios:

- Test that UserService will not save a user with an empty user name
- Test that UserService will not save a user with an invalid e-mail
- Test that UserService will not save a user with a username of more than six characters
- Test that UserService will save a user with a valid username and e-mail, and load the saved user properly when requested

The following code snippet shows UserServiceSpec.js, which includes the test scenarios mentioned earlier:

```
describe("UserService", function() {
    var userService;

    beforeEach(function() {
        userService = UserService.getInstance();
```

```
    });

    it("should NOT be able to save a user with an empty user
name", function() {
        var user = {
            'name': ' ',
            'email': 'hazems@apache.org'
        };

        expect(function() {
            userService.saveUser(user);
        }).toThrow();
    });

    it("should NOT be able to save a user with invalid email",
function() {
        var user = {
            'name': 'Hazem',
            'email': 'Invalid_Email'
        };

        expect(function() {
            userService.saveUser(user);
        }).toThrow();
    });

    it("should NOT be able to save a user with a user name more
than 6 characters", function() {
        var user = {
            'name': 'LengthyUserName',
            'email': 'hazems@apache.org'
        };

        expect(function() {
            userService.saveUser(user);
        }).toThrow();
    });

    it("should be able to save and load a valid user", function()
{
        var originalUser = {
            'name': 'Hazem',
            'email': 'hazems@apache.org'
        };
```

```
        userService.saveUser(originalUser);

        var user = userService.getUser();

        expect(user).toEqual(originalUser);
    });
});
```

We have a test suite called `"UserService"`, which has fours specs. In `beforeEach`, the `userService` object is created using `UserService.getInstance()`.

In the first test scenario of the `"UserService"` test suite, the spec title is `"should NOT be able to save a user with an empty user name"`. The spec creates a `user` object with an empty username and then passes the created `user` object to `userService.saveUser()`. Finally, the spec expects `userService.saveUser()` to throw an exception using the `toThrow` matcher.

In the second test scenario of the `"UserService"` test suite, the spec title is `"should NOT be able to save a user with invalid email"`. The spec creates a `user` object specifying an invalid e-mail (`'Invalid_Email'`) and then passes the created `user` object to `userService.saveUser()`. Finally, the spec expects `userService.saveUser()` to throw an exception using the `toThrow` matcher.

In the third test scenario of the `"UserService"` test suite, the spec title is `"should NOT be able to save a user with a user name more than 6 characters"`. The spec creates a `user` object specifying a username whose length is more than six characters (`'LengthyUserName'`) and then passes the created `user` object to `userService.saveUser()`. Finally, the spec expects `userService.saveUser()` to throw an exception using the `toThrow` matcher.

In the final test scenario of the `"UserService"` test suite, the spec title is `"should be able to save and load a valid user"`. The spec creates a `user` object (`originalUser`) with a valid username and e-mail. The spec then passes the `originalUser` object to `userService.saveUser()` to save the user. After saving `originalUser`, the spec then retrieves the saved `user` object by calling `userService.getUser()`. Finally, the spec makes sure that the retrieved `user` object is identical to `originalUser` using the `toEqual` matcher.

Developing asynchronous code tests

Before developing Jasmine tests for the asynchronous JavaScript code in our weather app services, you need to understand how we can test asynchronous operations in Jasmine.

Since Jasmine 2.0, testing asynchronous JavaScript code in Jasmine is a very simple task. In order to develop asynchronous operation Jasmine tests, you need to know that:

- Jasmine provides an optional single parameter (usually named `done`) for specs (and also for `beforeEach` and `afterEach`).

- A spec will not complete until `done` is called. This means that if `done` is included as a parameter of a spec, then `done` has to be called when the asynchronous operation completes in all cases (whether the operation succeeds or fails). Note that if `done` is included as a parameter in `beforeEach`, then the spec after `beforeEach` will not start until `done` is called in `beforeEach`.

- If `done` is not called for 5 seconds by default, then the test will fail; however, you can change this default timeout interval by setting the `jasmine.DEFAULT_TIMEOUT_INTERVAL` variable.

Now, let's develop Jasmine tests for the asynchronous JavaScript code (`WeatherService`) in our weather application services to see how to develop Jasmine tests for asynchronous JavaScript code in action. In order to test the `WeatherService` object, let's basically consider the following two test scenarios:

- Test that `WeatherService` will be able to get the weather information for a valid place

- Test that `WeatherService` will not be able to get the weather information for an invalid place

The following code snippet shows `WeatherServiceSpec.js`, which covers the test scenarios mentioned earlier:

```
describe("WeatherService", function() {
    var weatherService;
    var originalTimeout;

    beforeEach(function() {
        weatherService = WeatherService.getInstance();
        originalTimeout = jasmine.DEFAULT_TIMEOUT_INTERVAL;
        jasmine.DEFAULT_TIMEOUT_INTERVAL = 8000;
    });

    it("should be able to get weather information for a valid place",
function(done) {
        var successCallback = function(result) {
            expect(result.temperature).not.toBeNull();
            done();
        };
```

```
                var errorCallback = function() {
                    expect(true).toBe(false); // force failing test manually
                    done();
                };

                weatherService.getWeatherInfo("Paris, France",
            successCallback, errorCallback);
            });

            it("should NOT be able to get weather information for an invalid
        place", function(done) {
                var successCallback = function(result) {
                    expect(true).toBe(false); // force failing test manually
                    done();
                };

                var errorCallback = function(message) {
                    expect(message).not.toBeNull();
                    done();
                };

                weatherService.getWeatherInfo("Invalid Place",
            successCallback, errorCallback);
            });

        afterEach(function() {
            jasmine.DEFAULT_TIMEOUT_INTERVAL = originalTimeout;
        });
    });
```

We have a test suite called `"WeatherService"`, which has two specs. In `beforeEach`, the `weatherService` object is created using `WeatherService.getInstance()`, and `jasmine.DEFAULT_TIMEOUT_INTERVAL` is set to 8000 to change the default timeout interval to 8 seconds instead of 5 seconds. In `afterEach`, the `jasmine.DEFAULT_TIMEOUT_INTERVAL` is set to its default timeout value again.

As shown in the preceding highlighted code, in the first test scenario of the `"WeatherService"` test suite, the spec title is `"should be able to get weather information for a valid place"`. The spec calls the `weatherService.getWeatherInfo(locationText, successCallback, errorCallback)` method, specifying the following parameters in order:

- `locationText`: This is set to a valid place, that is, `"Paris, France"`.

- successCallback: This is set to a successful callback function that takes result as a parameter. In successCallback(result), the result returned is validated to have a valid temperature value, and finally, the done parameter is called.

- errorCallback: This is set to an error callback function. In errorCallback(), the test is forced to fail as this callback should never be called if weatherService.getWeatherInfo executes successfully. Finally, the done parameter is called.

In the second test scenario of the "WeatherService" test suite, the spec title is "should NOT be able to get weather information for an invalid place". The spec calls the weatherService.getWeatherInfo(locationText, successCallback, errorCallback) method, specifying the following parameters in order:

- locationText: This is set to an invalid place, that is, "Invalid Place".

- successCallback: This is set to a successful callback function that takes result as a parameter. In successCallback(result), the test is forced to fail. This is because this successful callback should never be called if weatherService.getWeatherInfo behaves correctly, as it does not make sense to get the weather information successfully for an invalid place. Finally, the done parameter is called.

- errorCallback: This is set to an error callback function that takes message as a parameter. In errorCallback(message), the returned message is validated to be a non-null value, which means that weatherService.getWeatherInfo behaves correctly, as it produces an error message when asked to get the weather information for an invalid place. Finally, the (done) parameter is called.

It is important to note that JavaScript unit testing can be implemented using many frameworks and has many details that cannot be covered completely by a single small chapter. To get more information about Jasmine (such as mocking asynchronous operations using Spies and loading HTML fixtures using jasmine-jquery) and other popular JavaScript Unit testing frameworks such as YUI Test and QUnit, we recommend that you read *JavaScript Unit Testing, Hazem Saleh, Packt Publishing*.

Manually executing tests

After developing Jasmine tests for both the weather application's synchronous and asynchronous JavaScript code, it is the time to run the developed Jasmine tests from the `SpecRunner.html` file. The following code snippet shows the important contents of the `SpecRunner.html` file:

```html
<!DOCTYPE HTML>
<html>
    <head>
        <meta http-equiv="Content-Type" content="text/html;
charset=UTF-8">
        <title>Jasmine Spec Runner v2.0.0</title>

        <script src="../jqueryMobile/jquery-1.10.2.min.js"></script>

        <!-- ... Jasmine files are included here .. -->

        <!-- include source files here... -->
        <script type="text/javascript" src="../js/api/UserService.
js"></script>
        <script type="text/javascript" src="../js/api/WeatherService.
js"></script>

        <!-- include spec files here... -->
        <script type="text/javascript" src="spec/UserServiceSpec.
js"></script>
        <script type="text/javascript" src="spec/WeatherServiceSpec.
js"></script>
    </head>

    <body>
    </body>
</html>
```

As shown in the preceding highlighted code, besides the Jasmine framework files, `SpecRunner.html` also includes the following files:

- `jquery-1.10.2.min.js`, as it is required by `WeatherService`
- JavaScript source files (`UserService.js` and `WeatherService.js`)
- JavaScript test files (`UserServiceSpec.js` and `WeatherServiceSpec.js`)

We can check the results of our developed tests by clicking on the `SpecRunner.html` file, and then we will see the tests passing.

Automating tests using Karma

Running Jasmine tests manually by running `SpecRunner.html` on every browser can be a time-consuming process; this is why automating Jasmine tests is important. In order to automate Jasmine tests, we can use Karma (`http://karma-runner.github.io`).

Karma is one of the best modern JavaScript test runners that can be used to automate JavaScript tests. Karma is based on Node.js and is distributed as a node package. Karma provides an easy-to-use command-line interface that we will illustrate in detail in the following sections.

Karma includes a web server that can capture one or more browser(s), execute JavaScript tests on the captured browsers, and finally, report the test results of every browser in the command-line interface. In order to capture a browser in Karma, you can execute one of the following two methods:

- Make the browser(s) that you want to capture visiting Karma server URL (usually, it is `http://${karma_server_ip}:9876/`).
- In the configuration file, you can specify the browser(s) to launch automatically when the Karma server starts (check the *Karma Configuration* section). Doing this configuration will save a lot of time spent on executing your JavaScript tests manually on the different browsers.

The following sections will show you how we will use Karma with Jasmine in detail.

Installing Karma

In order to work with Karma, you need to make sure that you have Node.js installed in your operating system. In order to install Node.js in Windows and Mac, you can download their installers from `http://nodejs.org/download/`; for Linux, you can use the **Node Version Manager (NVM)** from `https://github.com/creationix/nvm`. Currently, Karma works perfectly with the latest stable versions of Node.js (0.8.x and 0.10.x).

It is recommended that you install Karma and all of its plugins that our project needs in the `project` directory. In order to install Karma in our project, execute the following command directly under the www directory of our weather project:

```
> npm install karma --save-dev
```

Then, we can install karma-Jasmine 2.0 (to run the Jasmine 2.0 code over Karma) and karma-chrome-launcher (to launch the Chrome browser automatically when requested by the Karma configuration) plugins from the command-line interface as follows:

```
> npm install karma-jasmine@2_0  karma-chrome-launcher --save-dev
```

In order to avoid typing the full path of Karma every time you execute a `karma` command, it is recommended that you install Karma CLI globally by executing the following command:

```
> npm install -g karma-cli
```

Karma configuration

We can generate the initial Karma configuration using CLI by executing the following command and answering the Karma configuration questions:

```
> karma init config.js
Which testing framework do you want to use?
Press tab to list possible options. Enter to move to the next
question.
> jasmine

Do you want to use Require.js?
This will add Require.js plugin.
Press tab to list possible options. Enter to move to the next
question.
> no

Do you want to capture any browsers automatically?
Press tab to list possible options. Enter empty string to move to the
next question.
> Chrome
>

What is the location of your source and test files?
You can use glob patterns, eg. "js/*.js" or "test/**/*Spec.js".
Enter empty string to move to the next question.
>jqueryMobile/jquery-1.10.2.min.js
>js/api/*.js
> tests/spec/*.js
>
```

Should any of the files included by the previous patterns be excluded
?
You can use glob patterns, eg. "**/*.swp".
Enter empty string to move to the next question.
>

Do you want Karma to watch all the files and run the tests on change ?
Press tab to list possible options.
> **yes**
Config file generated at "${somePath}/config.js".

The following code snippet shows the generated Karma `config.js` file:

```
module.exports = function(config) {
    config.set({
        basePath: '',
        frameworks: ['jasmine'],
        files: [
            'jqueryMobile/jquery-1.10.2.min.js',
            'js/api/*.js',
            'tests/spec/*.js'
        ],
        exclude: [
        ],
        preprocessors: {
        },
        reporters: ['progress'],
        port: 9876,
        colors: true,
        logLevel: config.LOG_INFO,
        autoWatch: true,
        browsers: ['Chrome'],
        singleRun: false
    });
};
```

The following table explains the meaning of the generated configuration attributes briefly:

Attribute	Description
basePath	This specifies the base path that will be used to resolve all patterns in files, exclude attributes. In our case, we specified ' ', which means that the current configuration file path is the base path.
frameworks	This specifies the frameworks to use. You can use many frameworks, other than Jasmine, with Karma, such as QUnit and mocha. In our case, we specified 'jasmine'.
files	This specifies the list of files (or file patterns) to load in the browser. In our case, we specified the jQuery JavaScript file, 'jqueryMobile/jquery-1.10.2.min.js' (as a dependency needed by the source files), the source files, 'js/api/*.js', and finally, the test files, 'tests/spec/*.js'.
exclude	This specifies the list of files to exclude.
preprocessors	This specifies the files that should be preprocessed before serving them to the browser. We will use this attribute in the code coverage section.
reporters	This specifies the test result reporter to use. In our case, we specified the 'progress' reporter to show the detailed test progress (in every browser) in the console. You can specify the 'dots' reporter to ignore these details and replace them with dots for simplification.
port	This specifies the Karma server port.
colors	This specifies whether to enable or disable colors in the output.
logLevel	This specifies the level of logging. It can have one of the possible values: config.LOG_DISABLE, config.LOG_ERROR, config.LOG_WARN, config.LOG_INFO, and config.LOG_DEBUG. In our case, we specified config.LOG_INFO.
autoWatch	If this attribute is set to true, then Karma will watch the files and execute tests whenever any file changes.
browsers	This specifies the browser(s) to launch and capture when the Karma server starts. In our case, we specify 'Chrome'; we can also specify the Safari, Firefox, Opera, PhantomJS, and IE browsers.
singleRun	Setting this attribute to true means that Karma will start the specified browser(s), run the tests, and finally exit. Setting this attribute to true is suitable for a Continuous Integration mode (check the *Integrating tests with Build and CI tools* section). In our case, we set it to false to declare that it is not a single run.

Running tests (on mobile devices)

In order to start running our developed Jasmine test using Karma, we can start the Karma server specifying our configuration file as a parameter as follows:

```
> karma start config.js
```

This will automatically start a Chrome browser instance and execute our developed Jasmine tests on it. Finally, you will find output results like the following in the console:

```
INFO [karma]: Karma v0.12.19 server started at http://localhost:9876/
INFO [launcher]: Starting browser Chrome
INFO [Chrome 36.0.1985 (Mac OS X 10.9.2)]: Connected on socket
PF7lhJWBohNMJqOlUdnP with id 78567722
... Some test results information here...
Executed 6 of 6 SUCCESS (1.575 secs / 1.57 secs)
```

If we want Karma to test our Jasmine code on more browsers, we can simply:

- Specify more browsers in the `browsers` attribute of the configuration file
- Install the browser launcher plugin in our `app` directory

For example, if we want to test our Jasmine code in Firefox, we will do the following:

1. In the `config.js` file, add `'Firefox'` to the browser's attribute as follows:

   browsers: ['Chrome', 'Firefox']

2. Install the Firefox launcher plugin in our `app` directory as follows:

   ```
   > npm install karma-firefox-launcher --save-dev
   ```

3. Run the `karma start config.js` command again to see the test results in the CLI for both Chrome and Firefox.

In order to run our tests on a mobile browser, we can make the mobile browser visit the URL of the Karma server. The following screenshot shows the tests run on an Android mobile browser.

Running the tests on an Android mobile browser

The following are the test results in the Android browser that are displayed in the console:

```
INFO [Android 4.1.2 (Android 4.1.2)]: Connected on socket
Rv85bR0dfNpt5S8ecBnc with id manual-7523
... Some test results information here ...
Android 4.1.2 (Android 4.1.2): Executed 6 of 6 SUCCESS (1.094 secs /
1.02 secs)
```

Generating XML JUnit and code coverage reports

Karma, by default, outputs test results in the console. In order to output the test results in an XML JUnit report, we need to use the Karma JUnit reporter plugin (https://github.com/karma-runner/karma-junit-reporter).

In order to install Karma JUnit reporter plugin, execute the following command:

```
> npm install karma-junit-reporter --save-dev
```

Then, we need to add the plugin configuration in our `config.js` file, as highlighted in the following code snippet:

```
module.exports = function(config) {
    config.set({
        reporters: ['progress', 'junit'],

        // The default configuration
        junitReporter: {
            outputFile: 'test-results.xml',
            suite: ''
        }
    });
};
```

This means that the JUnit reporter will output the test results in the `'test-results.xml'` file. In order to see the XML JUnit report, execute `karma start config.js` again, and you will find the XML JUnit report, as shown in the following code:

```
<?xml version="1.0"?>
<testsuites>
    ...
    <testsuite name="Chrome 36.0.1985 (Mac OS X 10.9.2)" package=""
timestamp="2014-08-11T10:42:53" id="0" hostname="IBMs-
MacBook-Pro-2.local" tests="6" errors="0" failures="0" time="1.017">
        <properties>
            <property name="browser.fullName" value="Mozilla/5.0
(Macintosh; Intel Mac OS X 10_9_2) AppleWebKit/537.36 (KHTML, like
Gecko) Chrome/36.0.1985.125 Safari/537.36"/>
        </properties>
        <testcase name="should NOT be able to save a user with an
empty user name" time="0.004" classname="Chrome 36.0.1985 (Mac OS
X 10.9.2).UserService"/>
        <testcase name="should NOT be able to save a user with
invalid email" time="0.001" classname="Chrome 36.0.1985 (Mac OS X
10.9.2).UserService"/>
        <testcase name="should NOT be able to save a user with a
user name more than 6 characters" time="0" classname="Chrome
36.0.1985 (Mac OS X 10.9.2).UserService"/>
```

```
        <testcase name="should be able to save and load a valid
user" time="0.002" classname="Chrome 36.0.1985 (Mac OS X
10.9.2).UserService"/>
        <testcase name="should be able to get weather information
for a valid place" time="0.419" classname="Chrome 36.0.1985 (Mac
OS X 10.9.2).WeatherService"/>
        <testcase name="should NOT be able to get weather
information for an invalid place" time="0.591" classname="Chrome
36.0.1985 (Mac OS X 10.9.2).WeatherService"/>
        <system-out> ... </system-out>
        <system-err/>
    </testsuite>
</testsuites>
```

Adding to JUnit XML reports, Karma can generate code coverage reports. In order to generate code coverage using Karma, we can use the Karma coverage plugin (`https://github.com/karma-runner/karma-coverage`).

In order to install the Karma coverage plugin, execute the following command:

```
> npm install karma-coverage --save-dev
```

Then, we need to add the plugin configuration in our `config.js` file, as highlighted in the following code snippet:

```
module.exports = function(config) {
    config.set({
        // ...
        reporters: ['progress', 'coverage'],
        preprocessors: {
            'js/api/*.js': ['coverage']
        },
        coverageReporter: {
            type : 'html',
            dir : 'coverage/'
        }
    });
};
```

This previous configuration means that the Karma code coverage plugin will generate code coverage report(s) for our JavaScript source files, `'js/api/*.js'`, and output the code coverage results under the `'coverage'` directory in an HTML format. Note that every browser will have its own directory under the `'coverage'` directory, including its code coverage report. The following screenshot shows the code coverage report for the Chrome browser:

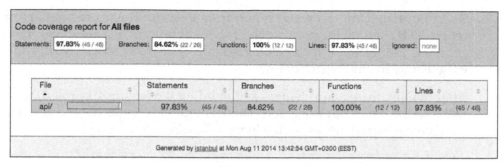

Code coverage report

As shown in the preceding screenshot, the code coverage is generated for code statements, branches, and functions.

Integrating tests with the CI tools

Having the ability to execute Karma tests from the command-line interface allows us to fully automate running Karma tests using CI tools. In order to integrate Karma tests with Jenkins (a popular CI tool), we need to perform the following steps in the Jenkins project configuration:

1. Select **Execute Shell** from **Add build step** (or **Execute Windows batch command** if you are using Windows), then specify the location of the shell file that starts the Karma server and run the tests. The shell file can have the following commands:

    ```
    #!/bin/bash
    cd weather/www
    export PATH=$PATH:/usr/local/bin
    karma start config.js --single-run --browsers PhantomJS
    ```

    The previous shell script code starts the Karma server in a single run mode and specifies PhantomJS (`http://phantomjs.org`) as the browser that will execute JS tests. PhantomJS is a very light-weight, headless browser that can be a good choice for CI environments. In order to work with PhantomJS in Karma, we have to install its launcher plugin from CLI as follows:

    ```
    > npm install karma-phantomjs-launcher --save-dev
    ```

2. Select **Publish JUnit test result report** from **Post-build Actions**, and in **test report XML**, specify the path of the XML JUnit report, `'weather/www/test-results.xml'`. Jenkins fortunately recognizes the JUnit XML format, which we generate in our JavaScript tests.

After making these main changes and building the Jenkins CI project, we will find the JavaScript test results shown in the project dashboard after some builds have been done, as shown in the following screenshot:

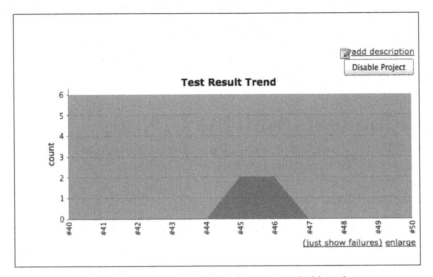

JavaScript test results in the Jenkins project dashboard

You can get the complete source code of the weather application with its JavaScript tests from the course page or from GitHub using `https://github.com/hazems/cordova-js-unit-testing`.

Summary

In this chapter, you understood how to develop JavaScript tests for both synchronous and asynchronous JavaScript code of your Cordova app logic using Jasmine. You learned how to utilize Karma in order to automate running your JavaScript tests. You know how to generate test and code coverage reports from your JavaScript tests. Finally, you learned how to fully automate your JavaScript tests by integrating your tests with Jenkins as an example of the CI tools. In the next chapter, you will learn how to design and develop a complete app (Mega App) using Apache Cordova and the jQuery Mobile API on the three popular mobile platforms (Android, iOS, and Windows Phone 8).

8
Applying it All – the Mega App

In this chapter, you will learn how to design and develop a complete app (the Mega App) using Apache Cordova and jQuery Mobile APIs. Mega App is a memo utility that allows users to create, save, and view audible and visual memos on the three most popular mobile platforms (Android, iOS, and Windows Phone 8). In order to create this utility, Mega App uses jQuery Mobile to build the user interface and Apache Cordova to access the device information, camera, audio (microphone and speaker), and filesystem. In this chapter, you will learn how to create a portable app that respects the philosophy differences between Android, iOS, and Windows Phone 8.

Mega App specification/wireframes

Mega App is a Cordova App that uses some of the Cordova plugins and jQuery Mobile in order to build a memo utility. It allows you to create your audible memos (such as talks, lectures, reminders, business meetings, and kids' voices) and also visual memos using an easy-to-use and responsive user interface. It also allows you to manage all your memos from a single unified listing. Mega App works on the Android, iOS, and Windows Phone 8 platforms. The following screenshot shows the home page of Mega App; it displays a list of the user's audio and visual memos:

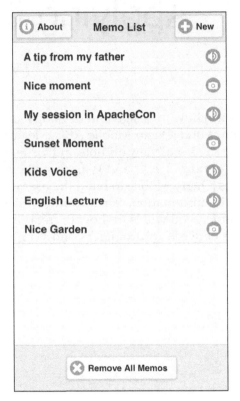

Mega App home page

In order to create a new memo, click on the **New** button on the page header, and you can select to create either "**Voice memo**" or "**Photo memo**". When you select creating a new "**Voice memo**", you will be introduced to the voice memo page in which you can enter the voice memo details in the **Title** and **Details** fields and click on the **Record** button to start recording audio, as shown in the following screenshot:

Creating a new voice memo

Once you are done, click on the **Stop Recording** button to finish recording. You can then listen to the recorded voice by clicking on the **Playback** button. After entering all the voice-recording information, you can finally click on the **Save Memo** button to save your voice memo. After clicking on the **Save Memo** button, you will be forwarded to the app's home page to view your saved voice memo in the memo list (a voice memo is marked with an audio icon at the end of the voice memo item).

In order to create a new photo memo, click on the **New** button on the page header and then select the **Photo Memo** option; you will be introduced to the photo memo page in which you can enter the photo memo details in the **Title** and **Details** fields and click on the **Get Photo** button to get a photo either by capturing it using the camera or by getting it from the device's gallery.

If you choose to get a photo from **Gallery**, you will be forwarded to the device's gallery to pick a picture from there, and if you choose to get a photo from **Camera**, then the device's camera app will be launched to allow you to capture a photo. Once you are done with getting the photo, you can view the photo in the photo memo page, as shown in the following screenshot:

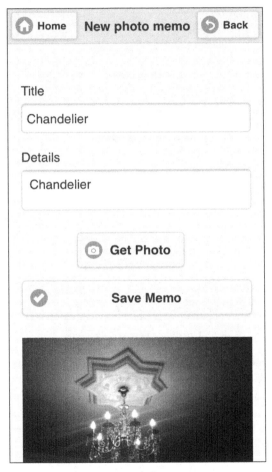

Creating a new photo memo

After entering all the photo memo information, you can click on the **Save Memo** button to save your photo memo. After clicking on the **Save Memo** button, you will be forwarded to the app's home page to view your saved photo memo in the memo list (a photo memo is marked with a camera icon at the end of the photo memo item).

It is important to note that at any point in time, you can click on any listing item (in the app's home page listing), which represents either a voice or a photo memo, to get its details. The following screenshot shows a detailed saved voice memo:

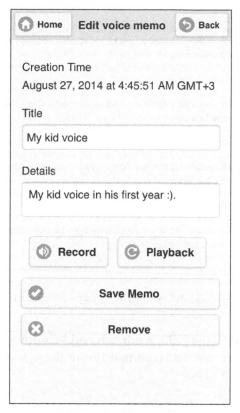

Editing voice memo details

In the memo details page, you can view and edit the memo information and can also delete the created memo by clicking on the **Remove** button.

Finally, in the home page, you have the option to delete all of the created memos by clicking on the **Remove All Memos** button and confirming the deletion of memo items.

Preparing for the Mega App

In order to create our Mega App's initial files from the Cordova CLI, we run the `cordova create` command as follows:

```
> cordova create megaapp com.jsmobile.megaapp MegaApp
```

Then, we will add the following Cordova plugins to our project using the `cordova plugin add` command:

- Camera plugin:

  ```
  > cordova plugin add https://git-wip-us.apache.org/repos/asf/
  cordova-plugin-camera.git
  ```

- Media plugin:

  ```
  > cordova plugin add https://git-wip-us.apache.org/repos/asf/
  cordova-plugin-media.git
  ```

- File plugin:

  ```
  > cordova plugin add https://git-wip-us.apache.org/repos/asf/
  cordova-plugin-file.git
  ```

- Device plugin:

  ```
  > cordova plugin add https://git-wip-us.apache.org/repos/asf/
  cordova-plugin-device.git
  ```

- Dialogs plugin:

  ```
  > cordova plugin add https://git-wip-us.apache.org/repos/asf/
  cordova-plugin-dialogs.git
  ```

As we support three platforms (iOS, Android, and Windows Phone 8), we run the following `cordova platform add` command from the `app` directory to add the platforms that we want to support:

```
> cd megaapp
> cordova platform add ios
> cordova platform add android
> cordova platform add wp8
```

Finally, we can build our app on all the platforms using the following `cordova build` command:

```
> cordova build
```

Do not forget to apply the general Cordova 3.4 app fixes for iOS 7 and Windows Phone 8, which were illustrated in detail in *Chapter 3, Apache Cordova Development Tools.*

The Mega App architecture

As Mega App needs to store audio and image files in the device's storage so that users can access them later, we need to be aware of the nature of every platform's filesystem to properly store our app's audio and image files.

In Android, we do not have any restrictions on storing our app files under the device's SD card root if the SD card is available, so we can save our audio and picture files in our app's directory under the device's SD card root without any issues.

 As a matter of fact, not all Android devices have SD cards. This is why if your Android device does not have an SD card, then the Mega App's audio files will be stored under the app's private data directory, /data/data/[app_directory].

At the time of writing this module, storing app files outside the app directory is not possible in iOS. iOS places each app (including its preferences and data) in a Sandbox at the time of installation for security reasons. As part of the Sandboxing process, the system installs each app in its own Sandbox directory, which acts as the home for the app and its data. The following screenshot shows the subdirectories for an iOS app's Sandbox directory:

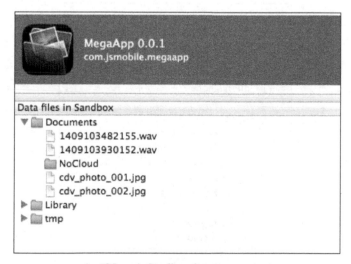

An iOS app's Sandbox directory content

As shown in the preceding screenshot, an iOS app's Sandbox directory mainly contains the following subdirectories:

- `Documents`: This directory can be used to store the user's documents and app's data files.
- `Library`: This is a directory for the files that are not user data files.
- `tmp`: This directory can be used to store temporary files that you don't need to persist between launches of your app. Note that iOS might purge files from this directory when your app is not running.

We will store our app's voice and picture files under the `Documents` directory of our iOS app's Sandbox directory.

 Besides the shown Sandbox directory content, an iOS app's Sandbox directory also includes `<<AppName>>.app`, which represents the bundle directory that contains the app.

Finally, in Windows Phone 8, we will save our audio and picture files under the `app` local directory. Note that using the native Windows Phone 8 API (`Window.Storage`), you can read and write files in an SD card with some restrictions, check: `http://msdn.microsoft.com/en-us/library/windows/apps/xaml/dn611857.aspx`. However, at this moment, you cannot do this using Apache Cordova; hopefully, this capability will be supported soon by Cordova.

Now, let's check the Mega App structure. The following screenshot shows the structure of our Mega App:

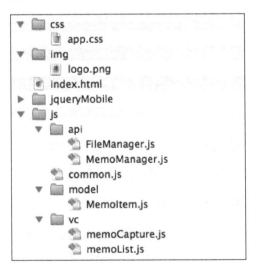

Mega App structure

The www directory contains the following files and subdirectories:

- css: This directory contains the custom app's Cascading Style Sheets.
- jqueryMobile: This directory contains the jQuery Mobile framework files.
- js: This directory contains all the app JavaScript code. It has three subdirectories:
  - ° api: This directory contains the app's services (managers).
  - ° model: This directory contains the app's model.
  - ° vc: This directory contains the app's view controllers, which register and implement the event handlers of every page and its user interface elements. An event handler usually calls one or more of the app's services (specifying a model object or more if needed) in order to perform an action and optionally display the returned results on an app page.

This js directory also includes common.js file, which includes the common app utilities. Under the www directory, the index.html file contains all the app pages, and finally, the img directory can contain any app custom images.

The details of the most important app files will be illustrated in the next sections of the chapter.

The Mega App model and API

The Mega App model contains only one JavaScript object that represents the voice and photo memo data, as shown in the following code snippet:

```
var MemoItem = function(memoItem) {
    this.id = memoItem.id || "Memo_" + (new Date()).getTime();
    this.title = memoItem.title || "";
    this.desc = memoItem.desc || "";
    this.type = memoItem.type || "voice";
    this.location = memoItem.location || "";
    this.mtime = memoItem.mtime || "";
};
```

The MemoItem object contains the following attributes:

- id: This represents the memo ID (its default value is unique as it includes a numeric value of the current time in milliseconds)
- title: This represents the memo title

- desc: This represents the memo description
- type: This represents the memo type, and it can be "voice" or "photo" (its default value is "voice")
- location: This represents the location of the media (audio or photo) file in the device's filesystem
- mtime: This represents the time when the memo was created

We mainly have one service (MemoManager) that is used by the app view controllers. The MemoManager object contains the API needed to:

- Save a memo
- Update a memo
- Remove a memo
- Remove all memos
- Get memo details
- Get all memos
- Record and play a voice
- Get a photo from the camera or gallery

The MemoManager object uses FileManager in order to perform the required file operations, which will be illustrated later.

The following code snippet shows the first part of the MemoManager object:

```
var MemoManager = (function () {
    var instance;

    function createObject() {
        var MEMOS_KEY = "memos";
        var APP_BASE_DIRECTORY = "Mega";
        var audioMedia;
        var recordingMedia;
        var mediaFileName;

        return {
            getMemos: function () {
                var items = window.localStorage.getItem(MEMOS_KEY);

                if (items) {
```

```
                memoMap = JSON.parse(items);
            } else {
                memoMap = {};
            }

            return memoMap;
        },
        getMemoDetails: function (memoID) {
            var memoMap = this.getMemos();

            return memoMap[memoID];
        },
        saveMemo: function (memoItem) {
            var memoMap = this.getMemos();

            memoMap[memoItem.id] = memoItem;

            window.localStorage.setItem(MEMOS_KEY, JSON.
stringify(memoMap));
        },
        removeMemo: function(memoID) {
            var memoMap = this.getMemos();

            if (memoMap[memoID]) {
                delete memoMap[memoID];
            }

            window.localStorage.setItem(MEMOS_KEY, JSON.
stringify(memoMap));
        },
        removeAllMemos: function() {
            window.localStorage.removeItem(MEMOS_KEY);
        }

        // code is omitted for simplicity ...
    };
};

return {
    getInstance: function () {
        if (!instance) {
            instance = createObject();
        }
```

```
            return instance;
        }
    };
})();
```

As shown in the preceding code, the first part of `MemoManager` is straightforward. It has the following methods, which are used to save, update, delete, and retrieve memos:

- `saveMemo(memoItem)`: This uses the `window.localStorage.setItem()` method to save or update a memo item in the device's Local Storage by adding (updating) it to the `memoMap` object. The `memoMap` object is a JSON map whose key represents the memo item ID and value represents the memo item object.

- `removeMemo(memoID)`: This removes the memo, whose ID is `memoID`, from `memoMap` and finally saves the updated `memoMap` object in the device's local storage using the `window.localStorage.setItem()` method.

- `removeAllMemos()`: This uses the `window.localStorage.removeItem()` method to remove `memoMap` from the device's local storage.

- `getMemoDetails(memoID)`: This gets the memo details from `memoMap` using `memoID`.

- `getMemos()`: This gets all the app's memos by returning the stored `memoMap` object. The stored `memoMap` object is retrieved from the device's local storage using the `window.localStorage.getItem()` method.

The following code snippet shows the voice recording and playback parts of `MemoManager`:

```
startRecordingVoice: function (recordingCallback) {
    var recordVoice = function(dirPath) {
        var basePath = "";

        if (dirPath) {
            basePath = dirPath;
        }

        mediaFileName = (new Date()).getTime() + ".wav";

        var mediaFilePath = basePath + mediaFileName;

        var recordingSuccess = function() {
            recordingCallback.recordSuccess(mediaFilePath);
        };
```

```
                recordingMedia = new Media(mediaFilePath, recordingSuccess,
    recordingCallback.recordError);

            // Record audio
            recordingMedia.startRecord();
        };

        if (device.platform === "Android") {

            // For Android, store the recording in the app directory
    under the SD Card root if available ...
            var callback = {};

            callback.requestSuccess = recordVoice;
            callback.requestError = recordingCallback.recordError;

            fileManager.requestDirectory(APP_BASE_DIRECTORY, callback);
        } else if (device.platform === "iOS") {

            // For iOS, store recording in app documents directory ...
            recordVoice("documents://");
        } else {

            // Else for Windows Phone 8, store recording under the app
    directory
            recordVoice();
        }
    },
    stopRecordingVoice: function () {
        recordingMedia.stopRecord();
        recordingMedia.release();
    },
    playVoice: function (filePath, playCallback) {
        if (filePath) {
            this.cleanUpResources();

            audioMedia = new Media(filePath, playCallback.playSuccess,
    playCallback.playError);

            // Play audio
            audioMedia.play();
        }
    },
```

```
cleanUpResources: function() {
    if (audioMedia) {
        audioMedia.stop();
        audioMedia.release();
        audioMedia = null;
    }

    if (recordingMedia) {
        recordingMedia.stop();
        recordingMedia.release();
        recordingMedia = null;
    }
}
```

The `startRecordingVoice(recordingCallback)` method, starts the voice recording action, checks the current device's platform in order to save the audio file properly:

- If the current platform is Android, then it requests the `app` directory path (**"Mega"**) in order to save the recorded media file under it. In order to do this, a call to `fileManager.requestDirectory(APP_BASE_DIRECTORY, callback)` is performed in order to get the `app` directory path and optionally create it if it does not exist under the device's SD card root using the Apache Cordova file API (or create it under the app's private data directory, (`/data/data/[app_directory]`, if the SD card is not available). If the `app` directory request operation succeeds, then `recordVoice(dirPath)` will be called, in this case, and the `app` directory path (`dirPath`) will be passed as a parameter. The `recordVoice()` function starts recording the voice using the `Media` object's `startRecord()` method. In order to create a `Media` object, the following parameters are specified in the `Media` object constructor:

  - The complete path of the media file (`mediaFilePath`).

  - `recordingSuccess` which refers to the callback that will be invoked if the media operation succeeds. `recordingSuccess` calls the original `recordingCallback.recordSuccess` method specifying `mediaFilePath` as a parameter.

  - `recordingCallback.recordError` which refers to the callback that will be invoked if the media operation fails.

- In iOS, `recordVoice()` is called with `"documents://"` as the directory path (`dirPath`) in order to save our app's media audio file under the `Documents` directory of the app's Sandbox directory.

> In iOS, if we just specify the audio filename without any path in the `Media` object constructor:
>
> ```
> var recordingMedia = new Media("test.wav" ...);
> ```
>
> Then `"test.wav"` will be saved under the `tmp` directory of our iOS app's Sandbox directory (if you do this, then your app users will be surprised to find, maybe after a while, that their saved audio files have been deleted as the `tmp` directory can be cleaned automatically by iOS, so be aware of this).
>
> Specifying the `"documents://"` prefix before the media filename in the `Media` object constructor will enforce the `Media` object to save the `"test.wav"` file under the app's `Documents` directory:
>
> ```
> var recordingMedia = new Media("documents://test.wav"
> ...);
> ```

- In the final `else` block that represents the Windows Phone 8 case, `recordVoice()` is called without specifying any parameters that tell the `Media` object to save the audio file under the `app` local directory.

As you can see, we have to respect the nature of every supported platform in order to get the expected results.

The `stopRecordingVoice()` method simply stops recording the voice by calling the `stopRecord()` method of the `Media` object and finally releases the used media resource by calling the `release()` method of the `Media` object.

The `playVoice(filePath, playCallback)` method creates a `Media` object that points to the file specified in `filePath`, and then plays the file using the `play()` method of the `Media` object. The `cleanUpResources()` method makes sure that all of the used media resources are cleaned up.

The following code snippet shows the photo capturing and picking part of `MemoManager`:

```
getPhoto: function (capturingCallback, fromGallery) {
    var source = Camera.PictureSourceType.CAMERA;

    if (fromGallery) {
        source = Camera.PictureSourceType.PHOTOLIBRARY;
    }

    var captureSuccess = function(filePath) {
```

```
        //Copy the captured image from tmp to app directory ...
        var fileCallback = {};

        fileCallback.copySuccess = function(newFilePath) {
            capturingCallback.captureSuccess(newFilePath);
        };

        fileCallback.copyError = capturingCallback.captureError;

        if (device.platform === "Android") {

            //If it is Android then copy image file to App
directory under SD Card root if available ...
            fileManager.copyFileToDirectory(APP_BASE_DIRECTORY,
filePath, true, fileCallback);
        } else if (device.platform === "iOS") {

            //If it is iOS then copy image file to Documents
directory of the iOS app.
            fileManager.copyFileToDirectory("", filePath, true,
fileCallback);
        } else {

            //Else for Windows Phone 8, store the image file in
the application's isolated store ...
            capturingCallback.captureSuccess(filePath);
        }
    };
    navigator.camera.getPicture(captureSuccess,
        capturingCallback.captureError,
        {
            quality: 30,
            destinationType: Camera.DestinationType.FILE_URI,
            sourceType: source,
            correctOrientation: true
        });
}
```

The getPhoto(capturingCallback, fromGallery) method, is used to get the photo by picking it from the device's gallery or by capturing it using the device's camera, it checks the fromGallery parameter and if it is set to true, then the picture source type is set to Camera.PictureSourceType.PHOTOLIBRARY, and if it is set to false, the picture source type will be Camera.PictureSourceType.CAMERA.

A photo is obtained by calling the `navigator.camera.getPicture()` method specifying the following parameters in order:

- `captureSuccess`: This refers to the callback that will be invoked if the `getPicture()` operation succeeds

- `capturingCallback.captureError`: This refers to the callback that will be invoked if the `getPicture()` operation fails

- In the last parameter, the camera options are set (`destinationType` is set to `Camera.DestinationType.FILE_URI` to get the image file URI, `sourceType` is set to the picture source type, quality is set to `30`, and finally, `correctOrientation` is set to `true`)

`captureSuccess` checks the current device's platform to properly save the picture file:

- If the current platform is Android, then it copies the picture file to the `app` directory. In order to do this, a call to the `fileManager.copyFileToDirectory(APP_BASE_DIRECTORY, filePath, true, fileCallback)` method is performed. The `fileManager.copyFileToDirectory(dirPath, filePath, enforceUniqueName, fileCallback)` method has the following parameters placed in order:

    ○ `dirPath`: This represents the full path of the destination directory to which the file will be copied.

    ○ `filePath`: This represents the full path of the file to be copied.

    ○ `enforceUniqueName`: If this parameter is set to `true`, this will enforce the copied file to have a new name in the destination directory.

    ○ `fileCallback`: This represents a callback object that includes the two callback attributes (`copySuccess`, which will be called if the copy file operation succeeds, and `copyError`, which will be called if the copy file operation fails).

    If the file-copy operation succeeds, then `fileCallback.copySuccess` will be called. In this case, `fileCallback.copySuccess` calls `capturingCallback.captureSuccess(newFilePath)`, specifying the new copied file path (`newFilePath`) as a parameter.

- In iOS, the image file is copied to the app's `Documents` directory. In order to do this, a call to `fileManager.copyFileToDirectory("", filePath, true, fileCallback)` is performed.

> In iOS, when any photo is captured using the device camera or picked from the device gallery using `navigator.camera.getPicture()`, it is placed under the `tmp` directory of the iOS app's Sandbox directory. If you want to access the captured image later, make sure to copy or move the captured image to the app's `Documents` directory as shown earlier.

- Finally, in the final `else` block that represents the Windows Phone 8 case, there is no need to do any file copy, as the image file (captured using the camera or picked from the device gallery) is automatically placed under the `app` local directory.

`FileManager` is very similar to the `FileManager` object discussed in *Chapter 5, Diving Deeper into the Cordova API* (refer to this chapter if you feel uncomfortable with the highlighted code in the following code snippet):

```
var FileManager = (function () {
    var instance;

    function createObject() {
        var FILE_BASE = "file:///";

        return {
            copyFileToDirectory: function (dirPath, filePath,
enforceUniqueName, fileCallback) {
                var directoryReady = function (dirEntry) {
                    if (filePath.indexOf(FILE_BASE) != 0) {
                        filePath = filePath.replace("file:/", FILE_
BASE);
                    }

                    window.resolveLocalFileSystemURL(filePath,
function(file) {
                        var filename = filePath.replace(/^.*[\\\/]/,
'');

                        if (enforceUniqueName) {
                            console.log("file name before: " +
filename);
                            filename = (new Date()).getTime() +
filename;
                            console.log("file name after: " +
filename);
                        }
```

```
                              file.copyTo(dirEntry, filename,
function(fileEntry) {
                                      fileCallback.copySuccess(dirEntry.toURL()
+ filename);
                              }, fileCallback.copyError);
                    }, fileCallback.copyError);
                };

                var fileSystemReady = function(fileSystem) {
                      fileSystem.root.getDirectory(dirPath, {create:
true}, directoryReady);
                };

                window.requestFileSystem(LocalFileSystem.PERSISTENT,
0, fileSystemReady, fileCallback.copyError);
            },
            requestDirectory: function (dirPath, callback) {
                var directoryReady = function (dirEntry) {
                    callback.requestSuccess(dirEntry.toURL());
                };

                var fileSystemReady = function(fileSystem) {
                      fileSystem.root.getDirectory(dirPath, {create:
true}, directoryReady);
                };

                window.requestFileSystem(LocalFileSystem.PERSISTENT,
0, fileSystemReady, callback.requestError);
            }
        };
    };

    return {
        getInstance: function () {
            if (!instance) {
                instance = createObject();
            }

            return instance;
        }
    };
})();
```

Now that we are done with the model and API code of our Mega App, the next section will illustrate the Mega App's pages and view controllers.

The Mega App user interface

In Mega App, we have three main pages:

- "memoList": This page is the app's home page. It displays the different types of the user memos

- "memoCapture": This page is used to create, view, and edit a memo

- "about": This page is a simple app about page

The following code snippet shows the "memoList" page:

```
<div data-role="page" id="memoList">
    <div data-role="header" data-position="fixed" data-tap-
toggle="false">
        <a href="#about" data-role="button" data-icon="info" data-
mini="true">About</a>
        <h1>Memo List</h1>
        <a id="newMemo" data-role="button" data-
icon="plus">New</a>
    </div>
    <div data-role="content">
        <ul data-role="listview" id="memoListView">
        </ul>
        <div data-role="popup" id="memoTypeSelection">
            <ul data-role="listview" data-inset="true"
class="selectionMenu">
                <li data-role="divider">Memo Type</li>
                <li><a href="#memoCapture?newMemo=voice">Voice
Memo</a></li>
                <li><a href="#memoCapture?newMemo=photo">Photo
Memo</a></li>
            </ul>
        </div>
    </div>
    <div data-role="footer" data-position="fixed" data-tap-
toggle="false">
        <h1>
            <a href="#" data-role="button" data-icon="delete"
id="removeAllMemos">Remove All Memos</a>
        </h1>
    </div>
</div>
```

As shown in the preceding code, the "memoList" page contains the following:

- A page header that includes two buttons: the "newMemo" button to create a new memo and the "About" button to display the about page.
- Page content that includes:
  - "memoListView": This is used to display the different user's saved memos.
  - "memoTypeSelection": This pop up contains a list view that allows the user to select the memo type that the user wants to create. You might notice that every selection item in the list view forwards to the "memoCapture" page with a newMemo parameter that specifies whether the new memo's type is "voice" or "photo".
- A page footer that includes:
  - "removeAllMemos": This button is used to remove all the memos.

The following code snippet shows the "memoList" page's view controller in memoList.js:

```
(function() {
    var memoManager = MemoManager.getInstance();

    $(document).on("pageinit", "#memoList", function(e) {
        $("#removeAllMemos").on("tap", function(e) {
            e.preventDefault();
            memoManager.showConfirmationMessage("Are you sure you
want to remove all the memos?", deleteAllMemos);
        });

        $("#newMemo").on("tap", function(e) {
            e.preventDefault();
            $("#memoTypeSelection").popup("open");
        });

    });

    $(document).on("pageshow", "#memoList", function(e) {
        e.preventDefault();
        updateMemoList();
    });
```

```
        function deleteAllMemos() {
            memoManager.removeAllMemos();
            updateMemoList();
        }

        function updateMemoList() {
            var memos = memoManager.getMemos(), memo;
            var type = "";

            $("#memoListView").empty();

            if (jQuery.isEmptyObject(memos)) {
                $("<li>No Memos Available</li>").
    appendTo("#memoListView");
            } else {
                for (memo in memos) {
                    if (memos[memo].type == "voice") {
                        type = "audio";
                    } else if (memos[memo].type == "photo") {
                        type = "camera";
                    }

                    $("<li data-icon='" + type + "'><a
    href='#memoCapture?memoID=" + memos[memo].id + "'>" +
                        memos[memo].title + "</a></li>").
    appendTo("#memoListView");
                }
            }

            $("#memoListView").listview('refresh');
        }
    })();
```

As shown in the preceding highlighted code snippet, the `"pageinit"` event handler registers the `"tap"` event handlers of the `"removeAllMemos"` and `"newMemo"` buttons.

In the `"tap"` event handler of the `"removeAllMemos"` button, a confirmation message is shown to the user, and if the user confirms, then a call to the `deleteAllMemos()` function is performed. The `deleteAllMemos()` function calls the `removeAllMemos()` method of `MemoManager` in order to remove all the app memos, and then, it calls the `updateMemoList()` method, which updates the memo list view with the saved memos.

The `updateMemoList()` method simply gets all the saved memos by calling the `memoManager.getMemos()` method and then renders every memo item as a list view item. Every list view item has an icon that is rendered based on its associated memo's type (`"voice"` or `"photo"`). When any list view item is clicked, it forwards to the `"memoCapture"` page, passing a `memoID` parameter in order to allow us to view and update the current memo details in the `"memoCapture"` page.

In the `"tap"` event handler of the `"newMemo"` button, the `"memoTypeSelection"` pop up is opened for the user to select either creating a voice memo or a photo memo. When a selection item of the `"memoTypeSelection"` list view is clicked, it forwards to the `"memoCapture"` page, passing a `newMemo` parameter in order to tell the `"memoCapture"` page whether the new memo's type is `"voice"` or `"photo"`.

In the `"pageshow"` event handler, `updateMemoList()` is called in order to display all of the saved memos in the page list view.

The following code snippet shows the `"memoCapture"` page:

```
<div data-role="page" id="memoCapture">
    <div data-role="header">
        <a href="#memoList" data-role="button" data-icon="home">Home</a>
        <h1 id="memoCaptureTitle">Your Memo</h1>
        <a href="#" data-role="button" data-rel="back" data-icon="back">Back</a>
    </div>
    <div data-role="content">
        <input type="hidden" id="mid"/>
        <input type="hidden" id="mtype"/>
        <input type="hidden" id="location"/>

        <div data-role="ui-field-contain">
            <label for="mtime" id="mtime_label">Creation Time</label>
            <div name="mtime" id="mtime"></div>
        </div>

        <div data-role="ui-field-contain">
            <label for="title">Title</label>
            <input type="text" name="title" id="title"></input>
        </div>

        <div data-role="ui-field-contain">
            <label for="desc">Details</label>
```

```
            <textarea name="desc" id="desc"></textarea>
        </div>

        <div class="center-wrapper">
            <input type="button" id="getPhoto" data-icon="camera"
value="Get Photo" class="center-button" data-inline="true"/>
            <input type="button" id="recordVoice" data-
icon="audio" value="Record" class="center-button" data-
inline="true"/>
            <input type="button" id="playVoice" data-
icon="refresh" value="Playback" class="center-button" data-
inline="true"/><br/>
        </div>

        <input type="button" value="Save Memo" data-icon="check"
id="saveMemo"/>
        <input type="button" id="removeMemo" data-icon="delete"
value="Remove"/> <br/>

        <div class="memoPhoto">
            <img id="imageView" class="memoPhoto"></img>
        </div>

        <div data-role="popup" id="photoTypeSelection">
            <ul data-role="listview" data-inset="true"
class="selectionMenu">
                <li data-role="divider">Get Photo From</li>
                <li><a id="photoFromGallery" href="#">Gallery</a></li>
                <li><a id="photoFromCamera" href="#">Camera</a></li>
            </ul>
        </div>

        <div data-role="popup" id="recordVoiceDialog" data-
dismissible="false" class="recordVoicePopup">
            <div data-role="header">
                <h1>Recording</h1>
            </div>

            <div data-role="content">
                <div class="center-wrapper">
                    <div id="voiceDuration"></div>
                    <input type="button" id="stopRecordingVoice"
value="Stop Recording" class="center-button" data-inline="true"/>
                </div>
            </div>
```

```
      </div>
    </div>
  </div>
```

As shown in the preceding code, the `"memoCapture"` page contains the following:

- A page header.
- Page content that mainly includes:
    - `"title"`: This is the input field to enter the memo title (it should be empty when the user creates a new memo and should display the current memo title when the user opens an existing memo to view or update it).
    - `"desc"`: This is the text area field to enter the memo description (it should be empty when the user creates a new memo and should display the current memo description when the user opens an existing memo to view or update it).
    - `"mtime"`: This is the div that displays the time when the memo was created; this field will be displayed only when the user opens an existing memo to view or update it.
    - `"mid"`: This is the hidden field to store the memo ID.
    - `"mtype"`: This is the hidden field to store the memo type.
    - `"location"`: This is the hidden field to store the memo location.
    - `"getPhoto"`: This button is displayed if the memo type is `"photo"`, and it opens a `"photoTypeSelection"` pop up to allow the user to select a photo source.
    - `"photoTypeSelection"`: This pop up includes a list view to allow the user to select a photo source (`"Camera"` or `"Gallery"`). The `"photoTypeSelection"` pop up includes two list item links: `"photoFromGallery"`, which opens the device's gallery for the user to pick a photo from, and `"photoFromCamera"`, which launches the camera app for the user to capture a photo.
    - `"imageView"`: This image displays the captured camera image or the picked gallery image. `"imageView"` is displayed only if the memo type is `"photo"` and there is an available captured or picked image.
    - `"recordVoice"`: This button is displayed if the memo type is `"voice"`, and it opens the `"recordVoiceDialog"` dialog to allow the user to record a voice.

- ○ "recordVoiceDialog": This dialog includes a "voiceDuration" div to display the voice-recording duration progress and a "stopRecordingVoice" button to stop recording the voice.

- ○ "playVoice": This button plays a voice; it is displayed if the memo type is "voice" and there is a recorded voice to play.

- ○ "saveMemo": This button saves or updates the voice or photo memo.

- ○ "removeMemo": This button removes a saved memo. Note that this button will be shown only if the user opens an existing memo to view or update it.

The following code snippet shows the first part of the "memoCapture" page's view controller in memoCapture.js:

```
(function() {

    var memoManager = MemoManager.getInstance();
    var recInterval;

    $(document).on("pageinit", "#memoCapture", function(e) {
        e.preventDefault();

        $("#saveMemo").on("tap", function(e) {
            e.preventDefault();

            var memoItem = new MemoItem({
                "type": $("#mtype").val(),
                "title": $("#title").val() || "Untitled",
                "desc": $("#desc").val() || "",
                "location": $("#location").val() || "",
                "mtime":  $("#mtime").html() || new Date().
toLocaleString(),
                "id": $("#mid").val() || null
            });

            memoManager.saveMemo(memoItem);

            $.mobile.changePage("#memoList");
        });

        $("#removeMemo").on("tap", function(e) {
            e.preventDefault();
```

```
                    memoManager.showConfirmationMessage("Are you sure you
want to remove this memo?", removeCurrentMemo);
          });

        $("#recordVoice").on("tap", function(e) {
            e.preventDefault();

            var recordingCallback = {};

            recordingCallback.recordSuccess = handleRecordSuccess;
            recordingCallback.recordError = handleRecordError;

            memoManager.startRecordingVoice(recordingCallback);

            var recTime = 0;

            $("#voiceDuration").html("Duration: " + recTime + "
seconds");

            $("#recordVoiceDialog").popup("open");

            recInterval = setInterval(function() {
                                        recTime = recTime + 1;
                                        $("#voiceDuration").
html("Duration: " + recTime + " seconds");
                                    }, 1000);
          });

        $("#recordVoiceDialog").on("popupafterclose", function(event,
ui) {
            clearInterval(recInterval);
            memoManager.stopRecordingVoice();
        });

        $("#stopRecordingVoice").on("tap", function(e) {
            e.preventDefault();
            $("#recordVoiceDialog").popup("close");
        });

        $("#playVoice").on("tap", function(e) {
            e.preventDefault();

            var playCallback = {};
```

```
            playCallback.playSuccess = handlePlaySuccess;
            playCallback.playError = handlePlayError;

            memoManager.playVoice($("#location").val(),
    playCallback);
        });

        $("#getPhoto").on("tap", function(e) {
            e.preventDefault();
            $("#photoTypeSelection").popup("open");
        });

        $("#photoFromGallery").on("tap", function(e) {
            e.preventDefault();
            $("#photoTypeSelection").popup("close");

            getPhoto(true);
        });

        $("#photoFromCamera").on("tap", function(e) {
            e.preventDefault();
            $("#photoTypeSelection").popup("close");

            getPhoto(false);
        });
    });

    function removeCurrentMemo() {
        memoManager.removeMemo($("#mid").val());
        $.mobile.changePage("#memoList");
    }

    function handleRecordSuccess(currentFilePath) {
        $("#location").val(currentFilePath);
        $("#playVoice").closest('.ui-btn').show();
    }
```

```
function handleRecordError(error) {
    //log error in the console ...
}

function handlePlaySuccess() {
    console.log("Voice file is played successfully ...");
}

function handlePlayError(error) {
    //log error in the console ...
}

function getPhoto(fromGallery) {
    var capturingCallback = {};

    capturingCallback.captureSuccess = handleCaptureSuccess;
    capturingCallback.captureError = handleCaptureError;

    memoManager.getPhoto(capturingCallback, fromGallery);
}

function handleCaptureSuccess(currentFilePath) {
    $("#imageView").attr("src", currentFilePath);
    $("#imageView").show();
    $("#location").val(currentFilePath);
}

function handleCaptureError(message) {
    //log error in the console ...
}

// code is omitted for simplicity ...
})();
```

As shown in the preceding highlighted code snippet, the "pageinit" event handler registers the "tap" event handlers of "saveMemo", "removeMemo", "recordVoice", "stopRecordingVoice", "playVoice", "getPhoto", "photoFromGallery", and "photoFromCamera". It also registers the "popupafterclose" event handler of "recordVoiceDialog".

The following table illustrates the `"tap"` event handlers of all of the previous mentioned UI elements:

UI element	Tap event handler description
The `"saveMemo"` button	1. An object of the `MemoItem` type is created and initialized with the UI input values of `"mtype"`, `"title"`, `"desc"`, `"location"`, `"mtime"`, and `"mid"`. 2. A call to `memoManager.saveMemo()` is performed; specifying `memoItem` as a parameter to save the memo. 3. The user is forwarded to the `"memoList"` page.
The `"removeMemo"` button	1. A confirmation message pops up for the user to confirm whether the memo needs to be removed. 2. If the user confirms, `removeCurrentMemo()` is called. 3. In `removeCurrentMemo()`, a call to `memoManager.removeMemo()` is performed; specifying `$("#mid").val()` as a parameter that represents the memo ID to be deleted. 4. The user is forwarded to the `"memoList"` page.

UI element	Tap event handler description
The `"recordVoice"` button	1. In order to start recording a voice, a call to `memoManager.startRecordingVoice()` is performed; specifying `recordingCallback` as a parameter. The `recordingCallback` parameter is an object that has a successful callback and error callback attributes (`recordSuccess`, which is set to `handleRecordSuccess`, and `recordError`, which is set to `handleRecordError`, respectively).
	2. The `"recordVoiceDialog"` pop up is opened and updated with the recording duration in seconds using a timer.
	3. When `memoManager.startRecordingVoice()` succeeds, `handleRecordSuccess` is called with the `currentFilePath` parameter (which represents the path of the audio file). In `handleRecordSuccess`, `currentFilePath` is saved in the `"location"` hidden field, and the `"playVoice"` button is shown.
	4. When `memoManager.startRecordingVoice()` fails, `handleRecordError` is called with an `error` parameter (which represents the operation error object). In `handleRecordError`, the error is simply logged.

UI element	Tap event handler description
The "stopRecordingVoice" button	This closes the "recordVoiceDialog" pop up. Closing the "recordVoiceDialog" pop up triggers the "popupafterclose" event of "recordVoiceDialog". This will execute the "popupafterclose" event handler of "recordVoiceDialog", which does the following: • Clears the recording duration timer. • Calls memoManager.stopRecordingVoice() to stop recording the audio.

The "playVoice" button	1. In order to play a recorded voice, a call to memoManager.playVoice() is performed; specifying the following parameters:
	
	    ◦ $("#location").val(): This function call gets the location of the audio file to be played.
	
	    ◦ playCallback: This is an object that has a success callback and error callback attributes (playSuccess, which is set to handlePlaySuccess, and playError, which is set to handlePlayError, respectively).
	
	2. In handlePlaySuccess and handlePlayError, the operations are simply logged in the console.

The "getPhoto" button	This opens the "photoTypeSelection" pop up to allow the user to choose the picture source: "Camera" or "Gallery".

UI element	Tap event handler description

The "photoFromGallery" and "photoFromCamera" anchors	1. This calls getPhoto() specifying the fromGallery parameter with true in case of "photoFromGallery" and with false in case of "photoFromCamera".
	
	 2. In order to get a photo using a camera or from the device gallery, a call to memoManager.getPhoto() is performed; specifying the following parameters in order:
	
	   ◦ capturingCallback: This is an object that has a success callback and error callback attributes (captureSuccess, which is set to handleCaptureSuccess, and captureError, which is set to handleCaptureError, respectively).
	
	   ◦ fromGallery: This determines whether to get the photo from gallery (if it is set to true) or using camera (if it is set to false).
	
	 3. When memoManager.getPhoto() succeeds, handleCaptureSuccess is called with the currentFilePath parameter (which represents the path of the photo file). In handleCaptureSuccess, currentFilePath is saved in the "location" hidden field, and "imageView" shows the current photo file.
	
	 4. When memoManager.getPhoto() fails, handleCaptureError is called with a message error parameter. In handleCaptureError, the error is simply logged.

The following code snippet shows the second part of the `"memoCapture"` page view controller:

```
(function() {
    var memoManager = MemoManager.getInstance();

    // ...

    $(document).on("pageshow", "#memoCapture", function(e) {
        e.preventDefault();

        var memoID = ($.mobile.pageData && $.mobile.pageData.memoID)
    ? $.mobile.pageData.memoID : null;
        var memoType = ($.mobile.pageData && $.mobile.pageData.
    newMemo) ? $.mobile.pageData.newMemo : null;
        var memoItem = null;
        var isNew = true;

        if (memoID) {

            //Update Memo
            memoItem = memoManager.getMemoDetails(memoID);
            isNew = false;

            //Change title
            $("#memoCaptureTitle").html("Edit " + (memoItem.type ?
    memoItem.type : "") + " memo");
        } else {

            //Create a new Memo
            memoItem = new MemoItem({"type": memoType});

            //Change title
            $("#memoCaptureTitle").html("New " + (memoType ? memoType
    : "") + " memo");
        }

        initFields(memoItem, isNew);
    });

    $(document).on("pagebeforehide", "#memoCapture", function(e) {
        memoManager.cleanUpResources();
    });
```

```
function initFields(memoItem, isNew) {
    $("#mid").val(memoItem.id);
    $("#mtype").val(memoItem.type);
    $("#title").val(memoItem.title);
    $("#desc").val(memoItem.desc);
    $("#location").val(memoItem.location);
    $("#mtime").html(memoItem.mtime);

    $("#recordVoice").closest('.ui-btn').hide();
    $("#getPhoto").closest('.ui-btn').hide();
    $("#playVoice").closest('.ui-btn').hide();
    $("#removeMemo").closest('.ui-btn').hide();
    $("#imageView").hide();
    $("#imageView").attr("src", "");

    if (! isNew) {
        $("#removeMemo").closest('.ui-btn').show();
        $("#mtime").show();
        $("#mtime_label").show();
    } else {
        $("#mtime").hide();
        $("#mtime_label").hide();
    }

    if (memoItem.type == "voice") {
        $("#recordVoice").closest('.ui-btn').show();

        if (memoItem.location && memoItem.location.length > 0)
{
            $("#playVoice").closest('.ui-btn').show();
        }
    } else if (memoItem.type == "photo") {
        $("#getPhoto").closest('.ui-btn').show();

        if (memoItem.location && memoItem.location.length > 0)
{
            $("#imageView").show();
            $("#imageView").attr("src", memoItem.location);
        }
    }
}

// ...
})();
```

It is important to know that the `"memoCapture"` page works in the following two modes:

- **Creating a new memo mode**: In this case, a `newMemo` parameter is sent to the page from the caller. The `newMemo` parameter holds the type of new memo that the caller wants to create.

- **Editing an existing memo mode**: In this case, a `memoID` parameter is sent to the page from the caller. The `memoID` parameter refers to the existing memo identifier.

As shown in the preceding highlighted code snippet, in the `"pageshow"` event handler, both `memoID` and `memoType` are retrieved, thanks to the jQuery Mobile page parameters plugin (for more information about this plugin, refer to *Chapter 4, Cordova API in Action*).

If `memoID` is available, this means that the `"memoCapture"` page is required to work in the edit mode, which implies that `"memoCapture"` needs to:

- Get the existing memo details by calling `memoManager.getMemoDetails(memoID)`

- Change the page title to `"Edit xxx"` (for example, `"Edit photo memo"`)

If `memoID` is not available, this means that the `"memoCapture"` page is in the **create new memo** mode, which implies that `"memoCapture"` needs to:

- Create a new `MemoItem` object by setting the type to `memoType` (`"voice"` or `"photo"`)

- Change the page title to `"New xxx"` (for example, `"New voice memo"`)

The fields are then populated with data and are shown based on the current page mode using the `initFields()` method.

Finally, the `"pagebeforehide"` event handler ensures that all the media resources are cleaned up (before transitioning away from the `"memoCapture"` page) by calling `memoManager.cleanUpResources()`.

Finalizing Mega App

The last part that we need to check in Mega App is `index.html`; the following code snippet shows the most important part of the `index.html` page:

```
<html>
    <head>
        <meta charset="utf-8" />
        <meta name="format-detection" content="telephone=no" />
```

```
        <meta name="viewport" content="user-scalable=no, initial-
scale=1, maximum-scale=1, minimum-scale=1, width=device-width,
height=device-height, target-densitydpi=device-dpi" />
        <link rel="stylesheet" type="text/css" href="css/app.css"
/>
        <link rel="stylesheet" href="jqueryMobile/jquery.mobile-
1.4.0.min.css">

        <script src="jqueryMobile/jquery-1.10.2.min.js"></script>

        <script>
            var deviceReadyDeferred = $.Deferred();
            var jqmReadyDeferred = $.Deferred();

            $(document).ready(function() {
                document.addEventListener("deviceready", function() {
                    deviceReadyDeferred.resolve();
                }, false);
            });

            $(document).on("mobileinit", function () {
                jqmReadyDeferred.resolve();
            });

            $.when(deviceReadyDeferred, jqmReadyDeferred).
then(function () {

                //Now everything loads fine, you can safely go to the
app home ...
                $.mobile.changePage("#memoList");
            });
        </script>

        <script src="jqueryMobile/jquery.mobile-1.4.0.min.js"></
script>
        <script src="jqueryMobile/jqm.page.params.js"></script>

        <title>Mega</title>
    </head>
    <body>
        <div id="loading" data-role="page">
            <div class="center-screen">Please wait ...</div>
        </div>
```

```
        <!-- App pages omitted here for simplicity ... --->

        <script type="text/javascript" src="cordova.js"></script>

        <!-- Application JS files -->
        <script type="text/javascript" src="js/common.js"></script>
        <script type="text/javascript" src="js/api/FileManager.js"></
    script>
        <script type="text/javascript" src="js/api/MemoManager.js"></
    script>

        <script type="text/javascript" src="js/model/MemoItem.js"></
    script>

        <script type="text/javascript" src="js/vc/memoList.js"></
    script>
        <script type="text/javascript" src="js/vc/memoCapture.js"></
    script>
    </body>
</html>
```

As shown in the preceding code, `index.html` includes the following:

- App custom CSS file (`app.css`)
- jQuery Mobile library files
- A jQuery Mobile page params plugin file (`jqm.page.params.js`)
- A CommonJS (`common.js`) file, app managers, and app view controllers' JS files

The preceding highlighted code makes sure that Apache Cordova and jQuery Mobile are loaded correctly (using the jQuery `Deferred` object) before proceeding to the app pages. If Apache Cordova and jQuery Mobile are loaded correctly, then the user will leave the `"loading"` page and be forwarded to the app's home page (the `"memoList"` page) to start using the app.

As you know from *Chapter 5, Diving Deeper into the Cordova API*, in order to boost the performance of jQuery Mobile 1.4 with Cordova, it is recommended that you disable the transition effects. The `common.js` file applies this tip in Mega App, as shown in the following code snippet:

```
$.mobile.defaultPageTransition   = 'none';
$.mobile.defaultDialogTransition = 'none';
$.mobile.buttonMarkup.hoverDelay = 0;
```

In order to exit the application when the user presses the back button (which exists on Android and Windows Phone 8 devices) on the app's home page, common.js also implements this behavior. It uses the same technique used in the *Finalizing the Cordova Exhibition app* section in *Chapter 5, Diving Deeper into the Cordova API*.

Deploying and running Mega App

Now, we can deploy our Mega App to our Android, iOS, and Windows Phone 8 devices to see the app in action. All of the screenshots that illustrated the Mega App functionality in the *Mega App specification/wireframes* section were captured from a real iPhone 5 device.

The following screenshot shows the deployed Mega App on a real Android Samsung Galaxy Tab 3 device:

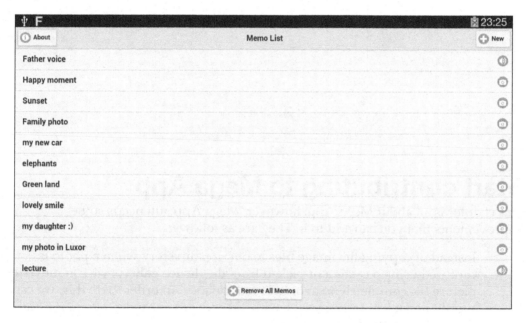

The following screenshot shows the deployed Mega App on a real Windows Phone 8 device:

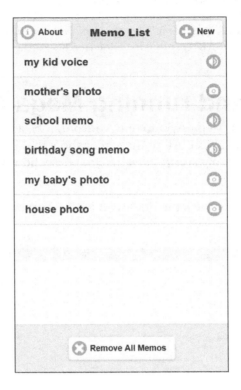

Start contributing to Mega App

This chapter is all about Mega App; however, Mega App still needs some improvements that you can add to it. They are as follows:

- Instead of copying the image files to our `app` directory when a photo is captured using a camera or picked from the device gallery, we can move the picture file completely to avoid file redundancy. In order to do this, we can simply replace `file.copyTo()` with `file.moveTo()` in `FileManager` and change the method name to `moveFileToDirectory`.

- Instead of only deleting the file reference in the Local Storage when removing a memo (or memos) as requested by the `removeMemo()` or `removeAllMemos()` methods of `MemoManager`, we can delete the physical files as well using the `remove()` method of the `FileEntry` Cordova object and adding this to a new method (`deleteFile`) of `FileManager`. The `deleteFile()` method will be called by the `removeMemo()` and `removeAllMemos()` methods to make sure that the memo files are completely removed from the device's filesystem.

This is a good chance for you to improve Mega App by making these updates. Let's go and download the App source code from GitHub at `https://github.com/hazems/cordova-mega-app` and start playing with it. You can also download the source code of this chapter from the course page on the Packt Publishing website.

Summary

This chapter showed you how to utilize Apache Cordova and jQuery Mobile in order to design and develop a useful mobile app that respects the nature of different mobile platforms (iOS, Android, and Windows Phone 8).

Module 2

Getting Started with React Native

Learn to build modern native iOS and Android applications using JavaScript and the incredible power of React

1
Exploring the Sample Application

React Native is beginning to change the game in the mobile development world. Using the skills you already have, as a web developer, you can get a set of familiar methods to build user interfaces for mobile devices. In this module, we'll walk you through many React Natives features while developing a *note-taking* application, which we call **React Notes**. While building the essential features, such as creating notes, saving notes to the device, viewing a list of saved notes, and navigating between screens, you'll learn the fundamental skills you need to develop an app of your own. You'll also have the opportunity to go beyond the basics by adding the ability to store images and geolocation data with notes. Functionality is only a part of what makes a great app — it has to be great looking as well, so we've made sure to equip you with a thorough understanding of layout and styles. By the end of the module, you will have developed a fully featured application from start to finish and have all the skills you need to share your React Native applications with the world!

In this chapter, we'll introduce you to React Notes, the sample application that you'll learn how to build. We'll even point you in the right direction if you're anxious to start tinkering with the sample app to see what happens.

This chapter will focus on the following:

- Installing Xcode on Mac OS X
- Running the sample application in the iOS simulator
- Taking a look at the sample application features
- Modifying the sample application

Installing Xcode

Getting the tools to run the sample application is simple in OS X. The easiest way to install Xcode is through the App Store. In the top right-hand bar, search for the term **Xcode**, and from the list of results navigate to the Xcode store page, as shown in the following screenshot:

Install or update to the latest version of Xcode by clicking on the button.

 You will need to register for an Apple ID in order to download Xcode from the App Store.

You also require the **command-line tools** (CLT) for Xcode. A prompt will display when they need to be installed. You can also download the command-line tools directly from the **Downloads** for Apple developers at `https://developer.apple.com/downloads/`.

Running the sample application

The source code contains the completed application that we will build throughout the module. We are going to start with running the application. The source code is already configured to run in the iOS simulator:

1. Open the `ReactNotes.xcodeproj` in the `ios/` folder in Xcode or from the command line:

    ```
    ReactNotes$ open ios/ReactNotes.xcodeproj/
    ```

2. This module targets iPhone 6 for development; although it does work on other iOS versions, we recommend using this one. Make sure that the iPhone 6 is selected in the iOS simulator device drop-down menu. If you own an iPhone 6, you may select an **iOS Device**:

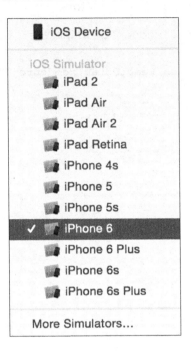

3. Press the **Run** button (*F5*) to launch the iOS simulator:

A sneak peek at the sample application

The goal of this module is to introduce you to how quickly React Native can get you up and running to create user interfaces. No matter what type of mobile application you build, there are certain features that you're very likely to have. Your UI will probably have multiple screens, so you'll need the ability to navigate between them. In *Chapter 3, Beginning with the Example Application* we will start laying the foundation for navigation and the note screen:

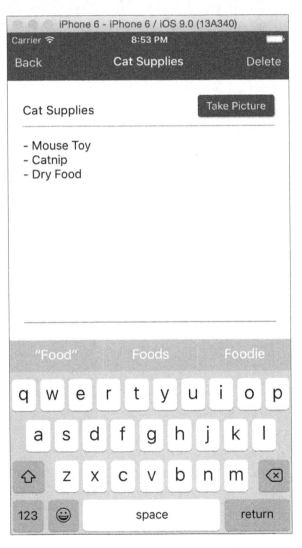

Not long after you have seen a bare-bones application, you'll want to start making it look good. Let us dive deep into styles and layout in *Chapter 4, Working with Styles and Layout*, and carry those lessons throughout the rest of the module.

It's hard to imagine an application that doesn't have lists of data, and React Notes is no exception. We'll cover working with lists in *Chapter 5, Displaying and Saving Data*:

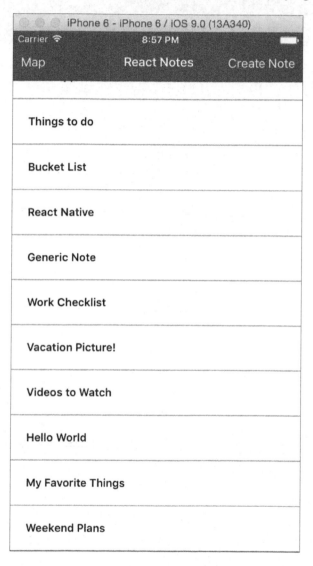

One of the capabilities that sets mobile applications apart from web applications is the ability to access GPS data. We present capturing geolocation data using maps in *Chapter 6, Working with Geolocation and Maps*:

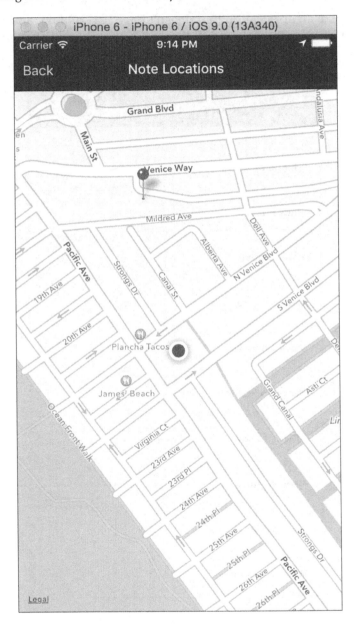

It is very common to capture photos on mobile devices. The camera screen will allow users to attach photos to their notes and save them for viewing later. You will learn how to add camera support to your applications in *Chapter 7, Using Native Modules*:

 Note that the camera screen will be black in the iOS simulator. This is also explained later in *Chapter 7, Using Native Modules*.

Experimenting with the sample application

If you are the adventurous type, then feel free to start playing around and modifying the sample application code. There are two steps to switch the iOS application into development mode:

1. Open the `AppDelegate.m` file in Xcode and uncomment the `jsCodeLocation` assignment from OPTION 1 and comment out the statement in OPTION 2:

    ```
    NSURL *jsCodeLocation;

    /**
     * Loading JavaScript code - uncomment the one you want.
     *
     * OPTION 1
     * Load from development server. Start the server from the
     repository root:
     *
     * $ npm start
     *
     * To run on device, change `localhost` to the IP address of your
     computer
     * (you can get this by typing `ifconfig` into the terminal and
     selecting the
     * `inet` value under `en0:`) and make sure your computer and iOS
     device are
     * on the same Wi-Fi network.
     */

    jsCodeLocation = [NSURL URLWithString:@"http://localhost:8081/
    index.ios.bundle?platform=ios"];

    /**
     * OPTION 2
     * Load from pre-bundled file on disk. To re-generate the static
     bundle
     * from the root of your project directory, run
     *
     * $ react-native bundle --minify
     *
    ```

```
 * see http://facebook.github.io/react-native/docs/runningondevice.
html
 */

//jsCodeLocation = [[NSBundle mainBundle] URLForResource:@"main"
withExtension:@"jsbundle"];
```

2. Then, navigate to **Product | Scheme | Edit Scheme...**. Select **Run**, and under the **Info** tab change **Build Configuration** from **Release** to **Debug**, as shown:

3. **Run** (*F5*) from Xcode to start the application in development mode. Using the Shake gesture from the iOS simulator (**Hardware | Shake | Gesture**) will show the development menu. It may be necessary to run react-native start from the command line to load the JavaScript bundle.

That's it! From here you can freely modify any of the source code in index.ios.js or in the Components folder. Later we will explain how to quickly reload your code in the simulator without having to recompile from Xcode.

Summary

This chapter gave us a brief overview of the type of functionality and user interface we will introduce throughout the rest of the module. We will cover features such as navigation, lists, user inputs, and so on in depth. With Xcode already set up, you will be able to jump right in to iOS development, and for Android developers we begin the setup in *Chapter 3, Beginning with the Example Application*. Next, we will demonstrate the value that React Native offers in rapid mobile development using the skills you have learned as a web developer.

Let's get started!

2
Understanding React Native Fundamentals

You might not be familiar with how React for Web works, so we are going to cover the fundamentals in this chapter. We will also explain the core principles of how React for Web works under the hood. Once you have a solid understanding of the basics, we will dive into how React for Web works and the subtle differences between mobile and web. By the end of this chapter, you will have the necessary skills to start building the example application.

In this chapter we will cover the following topics:

- The Virtual DOM
- Introducing components and JSX
- Writing our first component
- Props and state of components

The Virtual DOM

Do you know how to write a JavaScript function? If you do, that's great! You're well on your way to understand how React and React Native work under the hood. What do we mean exactly? Well, when you research how React works, you'll eventually encounter someone explaining it in the following manner:

```
UI = f(data)
```

You may say, *Nerd alert! How is this helpful?* Well, it's saying that your UI is a function of your data. To put it in more familiar terms, let's say that:

```
var todos = function(data) { return data.join( " -- " ) }
```

You can call the `function` with an array of data, such as:

```
var ui = todos( ["wake up", "get out of bed", "drag a comb across my
head"] );
console.log(ui);
```

This is not a particularly earth-shattering code; however, you're now rendering some content, in this case to the console.

What if, all your UI rendering code could be this predictable? It can be! Let's start getting a little more advanced. What if, in addition to our `todos()` function, we had a function called `todoItem()`, such as:

```
var todoItem = function(data) { return "<strong>" + data + "</strong>"
}
```

That looks a lot like our original `UI` function, doesn't it?:

```
UI = f(data)
```

What if we start composing our `todos()` and `todoItems()`, such as:

```
var ui = todos( [todoItem("wake up"), todoItem("get out of bed")] );
```

You can start to get the picture that we can start to render more and more complex outputs by composing simple functions.

What if we want to start rendering our content to the browser? I'm sure you can imagine changing our `todoItem()` to add elements to the DOM using jQuery; however, in this case we will start repeating ourselves a lot with many instances of `appendChild()` calls and jQuery selectors. If we are really smart, we might write a framework to abstract away the DOM manipulations so that we can write the code that matters to our application, not just the code that matters to the browser.

OK, so now let's say that we've magically got a framework that lets us represent our UI as a `data` function and we don't have to think about how our content will get rendered to the DOM. We can start changing our data over and over and watch the DOM update! That sounds great in theory, but when we have dozens of `div` elements in a deeply nested hierarchy, the underlying DOM manipulations become complex and inefficient.

What if our magic framework had an intermediate representation of the DOM? Let's call it Virtual DOM and let's say that instead of making every little change to the DOM, we batch the changes together. We can even compare the before and after states of the Virtual DOM. Figure out the differences and reduce the number of real DOM manipulations that we need to perform. Now we're really on to something!

So we can now express our UI as a function of our data. We don't have to think about the underlying DOM manipulation code and our UI is nice and snappy because the underlying framework is really smart and reduces the number of DOM manipulations it needs to perform. It will be pretty great to have a framework that could do that for us, but you know what will be really cool? What if the DOM didn't have to be a browser DOM? What if that same abstraction that allows us to write the code that matters to our app could be used to, say, update native mobile components? Enter React Native.

Components

Now here is an interesting problem; we have come across this great framework for making fast differences between the Virtual DOM and its native components. How do we tell React Native what UI to represent or when to change it? A React Native component is a simple, reusable, function-like object that enables us to describe the native mobile components we want to render. They will always contain properties, state, and a render method. Let's start really simple by creating our own component.

Creating your first component

Creating a new component in React Native will look similar to the following:

```
import React, {
  Text,
  View
  } from 'react-native';
class HelloComponent extends React.Component {
  render () {
    return (
    <View>
      <Text>Hello React</Text>
    <View>
  );
  }
}
```

Remember to import the React Native module. Here, we are using the ES6 import statement; it is similar to how the node require module works.

Wait a second... What are these weird XML elements doing in my JavaScript code? Facebook has created its own syntactic extension over JavaScript to describe React components. Here is the exact same code, but written in ordinary JavaScript:

```
var HelloComponent = React.createClass({displayName:
  "HelloComponent"}, render: function () {
  return (
    React.createElement(View, null,
      React.createElement(Text, null, "Hello React")
    )
));
```

While it is possible to write React Native applications only in JavaScript, the previous syntax includes many added benefits for the developer.

JSX

JavaScript XML (JSX) is an XML-like extension to the ECMAScript specification. It combines the component logic (JavaScript) and markup (DOM or Native UI) into a single file.

A JSX Element will take the following form:

```
var element = (
  <JSXElement>
    <SubJSXElement />
    <SubJSXElement />
    <SubJSXElement />
  <JSXElement />
);
```

The JSX specification also defines the following:

- The JSX Elements can be either self-opening `<JSXElement></JSXElement>` or self-closing `<JSXElement />`.
- Accept attributes as an expression `{}` or string `""` `<Component attr="attribute">`. Expressions are JavaScript snippets.
- The children elements can be text, expressions, or elements.

What if you have more than one component or a list of components?
There can only be a single root element; it means that if you have multiple components, you must wrap them in a parent component.

This is cool! We have gone from a deeply nested and imperative JavaScript code to a declarative format that describes the exact elements that we want to see in our components. There is no separation of concerns since our logic is coupled with our markup, making the components easier to debug and test. Since you can always include the same component in multiple other components, there is no need to duplicate the code anyway.

Note that JSX is only meant to be used as a preprocessor and it is not recommended to transpile in your production build. More information on JSX can be found in the official React documentation `https://facebook.github.io/react/docs/jsx-in-depth.html` or in the official JSX Specification `https://facebook.github.io/jsx/`.

Back to our first component

There are a few things that we have overlooked in our component. **View** and **Text** are two of the many components provided by React Native to build a UI. These are not regular components that render in the JavaScript layer, they can map directly to their native container parts! The View component maps to `UIView` in IOS and `android.view` in Android, while Text is the generic component to display text on each platform respectively. **View** and **Text** support various functions, such as layouts, styling, and touch handling.

Displaying the same static text over and over is not very exciting. Let's extend this simple component and add some more functionalities.

Props and states

At this point, you may be wondering how React Native deals with component manipulation and communication as the number of components grows into a component hierarchy. A component hierarchy, similar to a tree, starts with a root component and can contain many children. React Native provides two methods of data passing; one for data-flow down the component hierarchy and another for maintaining internal state.

Props

How do the components in the same component hierarchy communicate with each other? Data is passed down through properties commonly known as **props**. Props are considered to be immutable by convention and should never be modified directly. To pass a prop into a component, just add a camel-cased attribute to the component:

```
<HelloComponent text="Hello React" />
```

Props can be accessed internally in the component through `this.props`:

```
import React, {
  Text,
  View
} from 'react-native';

class HelloComponent extends React.Component {
  render () {
    return (
      <View>
        <Text>{this.props.text}</Text>
      View>
    );
  }
}
```

What if I want to pass down a lot of props?

It is possible to pass an array of props to a component using the ES7 spread operator `<HelloComponent {...props} />`.

It is not always necessary to include props with a component, but if you require a default value for your props, you can assign the `defaultProps` object to the component's class constructor.

```
HelloComponent.defaultProps = {text: "Default Text!"};
```

Validating props

If you are planning to expose your component to the public, it makes sense to constrain the ways developers can use it. To enforce that your components are being used correctly, the **PropTypes** module can be used to validate any props passed in. In the event that a prop does not pass the `propType` validation, a warning is shown to the developer in the console. The `PropTypes` cover a wide range of JavaScript types and primitives, including nested objects. You can define `propTypes` on a component's class constructor:

```
HelloComponent.propTypes = {text: React.PropTypes.string};
```

For more information on `propTypes`, visit the Prop Validation section of React Docs `https://facebook.github.io/react/docs/reusable-components.html`.

State

So now we can pass in the data, but what if the data changes, then how can we display these changes to the user? Components can optionally contain state, a mutable and private set of data. State is a great way to keep track of user input, asynchronous requests, and events. Let's update our component with additional text when the user interacts with it:

```
import React, {
  Text,
  View,
  Component
  } from 'react-native';
class HelloComponent extends React.Component{
  constructor (props) {
    super(props);
    this.state = {  // Set Initial State
    appendText: ''
    };
  }
  render () {
    return (
      <View>
        <Text onPress={() => setState({text: ' Native!'})}>{this.
props.text + this.state.appendText}</Text>
        <View>
    );
  }
}
```

Touching the `Text` component will trigger the function in its `onPress` prop. We are taking advantage of the ES6 arrow syntax to include our functionality in line with the text component.

 Using the ES6 arrow syntax will automatically bind this to a function. For any non-arrow function, if you need access to this then you need to bind the value to the function in the props expression `<Text onPress={this.myFunction.bind(this)}>`.

The `setState` function will merge the object you pass into the first argument with the current state of the component. Calling `setState` will trigger a new render where, instead of being empty, `this.state.appendText` will append **Native!** to the value of text, which we originally passed in from props. The final result is `"Hello React" + " Native!"` to produce `"Hello React Native!"`.

Never try and modify the value of this state on your own. Directly changing the state could result in data loss during the next `setState` call and it will not trigger another re-render.

Summary

Now hopefully, you understand the radical new direction React has taken in achieving performance. The Virtual DOM handles all of the DOM manipulations for us behind the scenes. At the same time, it uses efficient diffing algorithms to minimize the number of calls to the DOM. We have also seen how JSX allows us to express our components declaratively and combine our application logic into a single file. By using props and state, we can pass the data through components and update them dynamically.

I hope you can now take the information you learned in this chapter and convince your boss to start using React Native right away!

3
Beginning with the Example Application

Now that you have an idea about how React Native works and how to create components, let's create your first React Native application. Throughout this module, we will be developing a note-taking application which we'll call **ReactNotes**. By the end of the module, you'll have a fully featured application that allows you to create notes, save them to a device, view the list of the notes you've saved, take pictures with the device and attach them to your notes, and much more.

In this chapter, we'll build the skeleton of the application, create a `HomeScreen` and `NoteScreen`. We'll also add navigation that allows you to switch between the screens, and along the way you'll learn about creating your own components and handling events.

The topics that we will cover in this chapter are:

- How to generate iOS and Android project files
- Examining the React Native starter template
- Creating the first component, `SimpleButton`
- Debugging with Chrome Developer Tools
- Exploring navigation and transitioning between screens
- Developing the UI to create notes

Generating the projects

To start building our note taking application for iOS, we are going to need a couple of command-line tools.

- React Native 0.14.2 requires **Node.js v4+**, we are going to use v5.0.0; visit `https://nodejs.org` for more information (we recommend managing different node versions with NVM `https://github.com/creationix/nvm`)

- Install the latest version of NPM from `https://www.npmjs.com/`

Great, now that we have these tools we can install the `react-native-cli`. The `react-native-cli` exposes an interface that does all the work of setting up a new React Native project for us:

1. To install `react-native-cli`, use the `npm` command:

   ```
   npm install -g react-native-cli
   ```

2. Next, we are going to generate a new React Native project called `ReactNotes` using the `cli` and the `react-native init` command. The output of the command looks similar to the following:

   ```
   $ react-native init ReactNotes
   ```

   This will walk you through the creation of a new React Native project in `/Users/ethanholmes/ReactNotes`.

3. Set up a new React Native app in `/Users/ethanholmes/ReactNotes`:

   ```
   create .flowconfig
   create .gitignore
   create .watchmanconfig
   create index.ios.js
   create index.android.js
   create ios/main.jsbundle
   create ios/ReactNotes/AppDelegate.h
   create ios/ReactNotes/AppDelegate.m
   create ios/ReactNotes/Base.lproj/LaunchScreen.xib
   create ios/ReactNotes/Images.xcassets/AppIcon.
     appiconset/Contents json
   create ios/ReactNotes/Info.plist
   create ios/ReactNotes/main.m
   create ios/ReactNotesTests/ReactNotesTests.m
   create ios/ReactNotesTests/Info.plist
   create ios/ReactNotes.xcodeproj/project.pbxproj
   create ios/ReactNotes.xcodeproj/xcshareddata/xcschemes/
     ReactNotes.xcscheme
   create android/app/build.gradle
   create android/app/proguard-rules.pro
   ```

```
create android/app/src/main/AndroidManifest.xml
create android/app/src/main/res/values/strings.xml
create android/app/src/main/res/values/styles.xml
create android/build.gradle
create android/gradle.properties
create android/settings.gradle
create android/app/src/main/res/mipmap-
  hdpi/ic_launcher.png
create android/app/src/main/res/mipmap-
  mdpi/ic_launcher.png
create android/app/src/main/res/mipmap-
  xhdpi/ic_launcher.png
create android/app/src/main/res/mipmap-
  xxhdpi/ic_launcher.png
create android/gradle/wrapper/gradle-wrapper.jar
create android/gradle/wrapper/gradle-wrapper.properties
create android/gradlew
create android/gradlew.bat
create android/app/src/main/java/com/reactnotes/
  MainActivity.java
```

To run your app on iOS:

```
Open /Users/ethanholmes/ReactNotes/ios/ReactNotes.xcodeproj in
Xcode
  Hit Run button
```

To run your app on Android:

```
Have an Android emulator running, or a device connected
cd /Users/ethanholmes/ReactNotes
react-native run-android
```

The root directory of the Xcode project is generated in the ReactNotes folder, with the same name as we gave react-native-cli when we ran the command. Follow the steps at the end of the React Native set up to see what it produces.

> IOS 7+ requires a launch image. Here's the documentation on how to add it to the Info.plist in the apple developer docs:
>
> https://developer.apple.com/library/ios/documentation/
> iPhone/Conceptual/iPhoneOSProgrammingGuide/
> ExpectedAppBehaviors/ExpectedAppBehaviors.html#//
> apple_ref/doc/uid/TP40007072-CH3-SW3

Xcode and the iOS simulator

We are going to start by running the starter template in the iOS simulator through Xcode:

1. In Xcode, select `File | Open` and navigate to the `ReactNotes` folder.

2. Open the `ReactNotes.xcodeproj` file, as shown in the following figure:

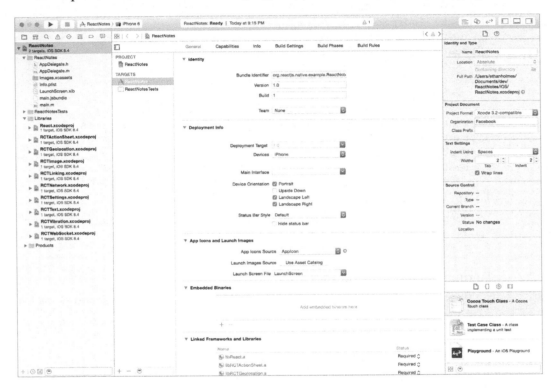

3. Click on **Run** (or *Cmd + R*) to run the application in the iOS simulator, the following screenshot will be shown:

Just like that, we already have the React Native template up and running on the iOS simulator!

The Android SDK and emulator

Facebook has a detailed step by step guide set up on Android SDK and emulator. You can access the React Native Docs at `https://facebook.github.io/react-native/docs/android-setup.html`. In this section, we will only cover the basics of running the application on the Android emulator.

When running the project in the iOS simulator, we can run it from the Xcode IDE. Android, on the other hand, doesn't require any particular IDE and can be launched directly from the command line.

To install the `android apk` to the emulator, use the following command:

```
$ react-native run-android
```

The following screenshot will be generated:

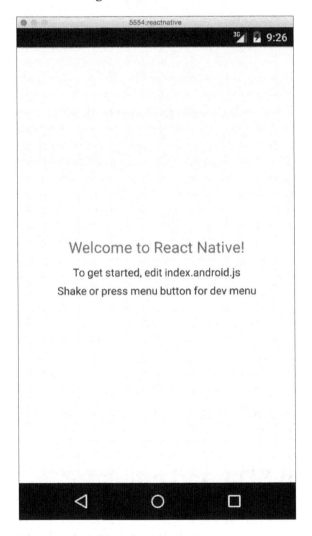

Let's start by modifying the contents of the starter template and display a different message.

Modifying the React Native starter template

Open `index.ios.js`, located in the root directory, in the text editor of your choice.
Here is the code that `react-native-cli` generated:

```
/**
 * Sample React Native App
 * https://github.com/facebook/react-native
 */
'use strict';

var React = require('react-native');
var {
  AppRegistry,
  StyleSheet,
  Text,
  View,
} = React;

var ReactNotes = React.createClass({
  render: function() {
    return (
      <View style={styles.container}>
        <Text style={styles.welcome}>
          Welcome to React Native!
        </Text>
        <Text style={styles.instructions}>
          To get started, edit index.ios.js
        </Text>
        <Text style={styles.instructions}>
          Press Cmd+R to reload,{'\n'}
          Cmd+D or shake for dev menu
        </Text>
      </View>
    );
  }
});

var styles = StyleSheet.create({
  container: {
    flex: 1,
    justifyContent: 'center',
    alignItems: 'center',
    backgroundColor: '#F5FCFF',
  },
```

```
    welcome: {
      fontSize: 20,
      textAlign: 'center',
      margin: 10,
    },
    instructions: {
      textAlign: 'center',
      color: '#333333',
      marginBottom: 5,
    },
});

    AppRegistry.registerComponent('ReactNotes', () => ReactNotes);
```

 Although `react-native-cli` generates the starter template using the ES5 `createClass`, we will be creating our components using ES6 classes.

A lot of things are included in here, but bear with us as we break it down for you. If we take a closer look at the render method, we can see the familiar `View` and `Text` components that we encountered in the previous chapter. Note how the index file is a component itself (`ReactNotes`). Change the value in line 30 to `Welcome to React Notes!`. Save it and then press *Cmd* + *R* from the simulator or, in the top menu, navigate to **Hardware | Shake Gesture** and select **Reload** from the pop-up action sheet. The text on screen re-renders to show the text value we just modified! We are no longer constrained to wait for the Xcode to recompile in order to see our changes as we can reload straight from the simulator. Continue making changes and reload it in the simulator to get a feel for the work flow.

Structuring the application

It's time to add a little interactivity to our application. You can begin by adding a simple button component to the screen that is touchable. In the root directory, create a folder called `App` and another folder inside the `App` folder called `Components`. In the `Components` directory, add a file named `SimpleButton.js`. This will be the directory in which we store and reference the components we create.

 Note that the React Native code created in this chapter will work for both iOS and Android. Simply replace `index.ios.js` with `index.android.js` if you are interested in android only. The screenshots and instructions will be mainly for the iOS simulator.

Creating the SimpleButton component

Let's start by rendering some text to the screen and importing it into our index.ios.js file. In `SimpleButton.js`, add:

```
import React, {
    Text,
    View
} from 'react-native';

export default class SimpleButton extends React.Component {
  render () {
    return (
      <View>
        <Text>Simple Button</Text>
      </View>
    );
  }
}
```

 ES6 de-structuring assignment var `[a, b] = [1, 2];` is used to extract `Text` and `View` from the React Native module.

We are going to include our newly created component in index.ios.js and simplify it to ES6 syntax:

```
import React, {
  AppRegistry,
  StyleSheet,
  View
} from 'react-native';

import SimpleButton from './App/Components/SimpleButton';

class ReactNotes extends React.Component {
  render () {
    return (
      <View style={styles.container}>
        <SimpleButton />
      </View>
    );
  }
}
```

```
var styles = StyleSheet.create({
  container: {
    flex: 1,
    justifyContent: 'center',
    alignItems: 'center',
  }
});
AppRegistry.registerComponent('ReactNotes', () => ReactNotes);
```

The output for the preceding code is:

We're off to a good start; it's time to add some interactivity to our button. In `SimpleButton.js`, add the `TouchableOpacity` component to the destructuring assignment. `TouchableHighlight`, `TouchableOpacity`, and `TouchableWithoutFeedback` are similar components that respond to touches, and it takes an `onPress` prop for a function to react to the touch. Wrap the existing code in the render function with the `TouchableOpacity` component:

```
import React, {
Text,
TouchableOpacity,
View
} from 'react-native';


export default class SimpleButton extends React.Component {
  render () {
    return (
      <TouchableOpacity onPress={() => console.log('Pressed!')}>
        <View>
          <Text>Simple Button</Text>
        </View>
      </TouchableOpacity>
    );
  }
}
```

Go ahead and try tapping (or clicking) on the text now, you should be able to see that the opacity of the text decreases as you press it. But where has our `console.log(...)` output gone? Open the **Developer** menu (**Hardware | Shake Gesture**) and select **Debug** in Chrome. This opens a Chrome Window at `localhost:8081/debugger-ui` for debugging, as shown in the following screenshot:

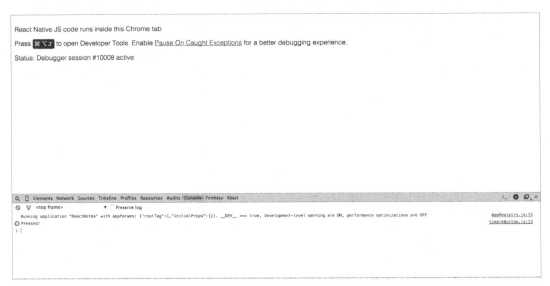

Lo and behold, here is the console log that we specified in our `SimpleButton` component. Behind the scenes, the JavaScript code is being run from inside the Chrome tab and loaded onto the mobile device on startup or reload. From here, you have access to all the Chrome Developer Tools you will normally use, including the addition of break points.

Navigation

Now, its time to make our application more actionable. Let's begin by transforming our `SimpleButton` into a **Create Note** button. When the user clicks on the **Create Note** button, it transitions them to another screen to create notes. To do this, we need our button to be able to accept a function via props from `index.ios.js` to activate the transition. We will add some custom text as well for extra flair:

```
import React, {
Text,
TouchableOpacity,
View
} from 'react-native';
```

```
export default class SimpleButton extends React.Component {
  render () {
    return (
      <TouchableOpacity onPress={this.props.onPress}>
        <View>
          <Text>{this.props.customText || 'Simple Button'}</Text>
        </View>
      </TouchableOpacity>
    );
  }
}

SimpleButton.propTypes = {
  onPress: React.PropTypes.func.isRequired,
  customText: React.PropTypes.string
};
```

Now, we have extended our SimpleButton component to be reusable with minimal changes. We can always pass different functions through the onPress prop and add custom text if we choose. This is all that we need to modify our SimpleButton; now to include the transition functionality to our index.io.js file.

The following image shows the validating props revisited page:

 Remember propTypes from the previous chapter? If we forget to pass the onPress prop, the console will log a warning reminding us to pass it. Note that there is no warning for customText since it was not set to isRequired.

The Navigator component

The **Navigator** component is a reimplementation of the `UINavigationController` provided by React Native to manage various screens. Similar to a stack, you can push, pop, and replace routes onto the Navigator. It is fully customizable on both iOS and Android, which we will cover in the next chapter. Import the Navigator into index.ios.js and replace the contents of the render method with:

```
import React, {
  AppRegistry,
  Navigator,
  StyleSheet,
  View
} from 'react-native';


render () {
  return (
    <Navigator
      initialRoute={{name: 'home'}}
      renderScene={this.renderScene}
    />
  );
}
```

Navigator receives a prop called `initialRoute` that accepts an object to be the first route to be put on the stack. The route object can contain any attribute that you need to pass to the screen components. All we need for now is the name of the screen we want to transition to. Next, we need to create the `function` to pass to the `renderScene` prop. In the `ReactNotes` component, we are going to create a `function` that takes `route` and `navigator` as parameters, as shown:

```
class ReactNotes extends React.Component {
  renderScene (route, navigator) {
    ...
  }
  render () {
    ...
  }
}
```

When we first load our application, the parameter `route` will be the object we pass into `initialRoute`. Using a switch statement and looking at the values of `route.name` allows us to choose the component we want to render:

```
renderScene (route, navigator) {
  switch (route.name) {
    case 'home':
      return (
        <View style={styles.container}>
          <SimpleButton
            onPress={() => console.log('Pressed!')}
            customText='Create Note'
          />
        </View>
      );
    case 'createNote':
  }
}
```

Here, under the `home` case, you can see our slightly modified code from the original `render` method in `ReactNotes`; we have included the `onPress` and `customText` props we created earlier. You can add another component to `App/Componets/` named `NoteScreen.js`; this screen will contain the functionality to create a new note:

```
import React, {
  StyleSheet,
  Text,
  View
} from 'react-native';

export default class NoteScreen extends React.Component {
  render () {
    return (
      <View style={styles.container}>
        <Text>Create Note Screen!</Text>
      </View>
    );
  }
}

var styles = StyleSheet.create({
  container: {
    flex: 1,
    justifyContent: 'center',
    alignItems: 'center',
  }
});
```

For now, we are only going to use this screen when we press the **Create Note** button. In the `onPress` prop arrow function, we are going to push a new route onto the stack using `navigator.push`:

```
import NoteScreen from './App/Components/NoteScreen';

class ReactNotes extends React.Component {
  renderScene (route, navigator) {
    switch (route.name) {
      case 'home':
        return (
          <View style={styles.container}>
            <SimpleButton
              onPress={() => {
                navigator.push({
                  name: 'createNote'
                });
              }}
              customText='Create Note'
            />
          </View>
        );
      case 'createNote':
        return (
          <NoteScreen />
        );
    }
  }
}
```

Note that push also takes a regular JavaScript object, so we need to include the name attribute for our `NoteScreen`; reload the application in the simulator and press on the **Create Note** button. A smooth animated transition between the two screens will occur without adding any extra code.

Navigator.NavigationBar

At this point you must be thinking *A button is OK, but is there a better, more native way to do navigation?* Of course, as a part of the Navigator component, you can pass a `navigationBar` prop to add a persistent top navigation bar across every screen. The `Navigator.NavigationBar` is a subcomponent that accepts an object that defines the left and right buttons, a title, and styles (although we are going to leave it `unstyled` until the next chapter). Modify the `ReactNotes` render function to include the `navigationBar`, as shown:

```
render () {
  return (
    <Navigator
```

```
          initialRoute={{name: 'home'}}
          renderScene={this.renderScene}
          navigationBar={
            <Navigator.NavigationBar
              routeMapper={NavigationBarRouteMapper}
            />
          }
        />
      );
    }
```

The `routeMapper` prop accepts an object containing functions for the `LeftButton`, `RightButton`, and `Title` attributes. Let's insert this object after the imports at the top of `index.ios.js`:

```
var NavigationBarRouteMapper = {
  LeftButton: function(route, navigator, index, navState) {
    ...
  },

  RightButton: function(route, navigator, index, navState) {
    ...
  },

  Title: function(route, navigator, index, navState) {
    ...
  }
};
```

Advancing the flow of our application to the `CreateNote` screen will require displaying a right-hand button in the navigator bar. Luckily, we already have our simple button set up to push the state onto the navigator. In the `RightButton` function, add:

```
var NavigationBarRouteMapper = {
  ...

  RightButton: function(route, navigator, index, navState) {
    switch (route.name) {
      case 'home':
        return (
          <SimpleButton
            onPress={() => {
              navigator.push({
                name: 'createNote'
```

```
            });
          }}
          customText='Create Note'
        />
      );
    default:
      return null;
  }
},


  ...
};
```

Similar to our previous `renderScene` method, we can switch on the value of
`route.name`. The default expression in the `switch` statement is there to ensure that
different screens do not return a button unless we include them. Let's also go ahead
and add a `LeftButton` to the `NavigationBar` when it's on the `NoteScreen` to return
to the home screen.

```
var NavigationBarRouteMapper = {
  LeftButton: function(route, navigator, index, navState) {
    switch (route.name) {
      case 'createNote':
        return (
          <SimpleButton
            onPress={() => navigator.pop()}
            customText='Back'
          />
        );
      default:
        return null;
    }
  },


  ...
};
```

The `navigator.pop()` will remove the route on the top of the stack; thus, returning
us to our original view. Finally, to add a title, we do the exact same thing in the
`Title` attributes function:

```
var NavigationBarRouteMapper = {

  ...

  Title: function(route, navigator, index, navState) {
    switch (route.name) {
```

```
    case 'home':
      return (
        <Text>React Notes</Text>
      );
    case 'createNote':
      return (
        <Text>Create Note</Text>
      );
    }
  }
};
```

Now, let's update the original `renderScene` function to get rid of the button and include the home screen as a component. Create a new component called `HomeScreen`; the contents of this screen won't matter much, as we will come back to it later:

```
import React, {
  StyleSheet,
  Text,
  View
  } from 'react-native';
export default class HomeScreen extends React.Component {
  render () {
    return (
      <View style={styles.container}>
        <Text>Home</Text>
      </View>
    );
  }
}
var styles = StyleSheet.create({
  container: {
    flex: 1,
    justifyContent: 'center',
    alignItems: 'center',
  }
});
```

Then import it into `index.ios.js` or `index.android.js`:

```
import HomeScreen from './App/Components/HomeScreen';
```

. . .

```
class ReactNotes extends React.Component {
  renderScene (route, navigator) {
    switch (route.name) {
      case 'home':
        return (
          <HomeScreen />
        );
      case 'createNote':
        return (
          <NoteScreen />
        );
    }
  }

  ...

}
```

Now, let's see how the navigation bar persists across each route:

That's it! Reload and take a look at how the static navigation bar persists across each route:

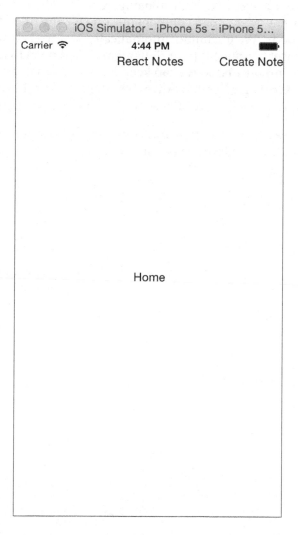

For a more detailed guide on Navigator, check out the React Native documentation at https://facebook.github.io/react-native/docs/navigator.html. We now have the proper infrastructure to go ahead and start adding the create note functionality to our application.

The NoteScreen – first pass

Now that we have a `NoteScreen` and can navigate to it, let's start making it useful. We'll need to add some `TextInput` components, one for the title of the note and one to capture the body. We'll want to automatically set focus on the `TextInput` for the title, so the user can start typing right away. We'll need to listen to events on the `TextInput` components, so we can keep a track of what the user has typed by updating the state. We'd also like to know when the user has finished editing the title of the note, so that we can automatically set focus on the `TextInput` for the body.

First, let's add the `TextInput` component to our list of dependencies and remove the `Text` component since we no longer need it:

```
import React, {
  StyleSheet,
  TextInput,
  View
}from 'react-native';
```

Before we add the `TextInput` components to the `View`, let's get a few style updates out of the way:

```
var styles = StyleSheet.create({
  container: {
    flex: 1,
    justifyContent: 'center',
    alignItems: 'center',
    marginTop: 64
  },
  title: {
    height: 40
  },
  body: {
    flex: 1
  }
});
```

Note that we've added a `marginTop: 64` to the container. This is important because we want to make sure that the `NavigationBar` doesn't accidentally intercept the `onPress` events we want our `TextInput` to receive. We've also added styles for each of the `TextInput`s we're about to add. We'll talk more about styles in detail in *Chapter 4, Working with Styles and Layout*.

Now, in our render function, let's replace the Text component with two Text Input components, such as:

```
render () {
  return (
    <View style={styles.container}>
      <TextInput placeholder="Untitled"
        style={styles.title}/>
      <TextInput multiline={true}
      placeholder="Start typing" style={styles.body}/>
    </View>
  );
}
```

Before we try this out, notice that the Text Input component has a placeholder property that allows us to tell the user what the Text Input is for without having to take up additional screen real estate by labeling our form fields. I've also specified multiline={true} on the second Text Input so the user can add as much text as they want.

Now let's refresh the application in the simulator and you should see something like this:

You should be able to click into `TextInput` and start typing. If you'd like to use the on-screen keyboard available in the simulator, you can press *Cmd+K* / *Ctrl+K*.

Let's improve the user experience a little bit by making the title `TextInput` focus automatically and show the keyboard when the user navigates to the `NoteScreen`:

```
<TextInput
  ref="title"
  autoFocus={true}
  placeholder="Untitled"
 style={styles.title}
/>
```

To be even more user friendly, let's listen for the event that tells us the user has finished editing the title and automatically set focus on the body `TextInput`. To do that we'll need to make a slight change to the body `TextInput` so that we can refer to it in our event handler:

```
<TextInput
  ref="body"
  multiline={true}
  placeholder="Start typing"
  style={styles.body}
/>
```

Notice the `ref="body"`. Any React component can be given a `ref` so that it can be referenced in your `javascript` code. Now, in the title `TextInput`, we can add an `onEndEditing` event handler that sets focus on the `TextInput` body:

```
<TextInput
  autoFocus={true}
  placeholder="Untitled"
  style={styles.title}
  onEndEditing={(text) => {this.refs.body.focus()}}
/>
```

> Avoid using refs to set and get values on your components! That's what `state` is for and we'll learn all about state in *Chapter 5, Displaying and Saving Data*.

Now when you refresh the application in the simulator and navigate to the `NoteScreen`, you will see that the title `TextInput` has focus and you should be able to type something. Press *Enter* and see the focus automatically switch to the body and start typing there as well. If you're not seeing the on-screen keyboard when you try this, press *Cmd + K* / *Ctrl + K* and try again.

Summary

In this chapter, we have created the skeleton of our `ReactNotes` application, walked you through how to create a new project, created `Views` and custom components, navigated between the `HomeScreen` and `NoteScreen`, and debugged your application.

You now have a solid foundation for all of the topics we'll introduce throughout the rest of the module. However, there are two big problems with this application, it's not pretty and it doesn't do anything! In the next two chapters, we'll solve both of those problems and you'll be well on your way to master React Native!

4
Working with Styles and Layout

At this point, you may feel that the application is lacking a certain appeal. The success of any application relies greatly on how the user interface looks. Just like how React Native borrows from React on the web, the same thing goes for styles. In this chapter, you will learn how React Native styles and lays out the components with React CSS.

We will cover the following topics:

- What is React CSS?
- Creating Style Sheets
- Extending the `SimpleButton` to include custom styles
- An introduction to layout with Flexbox
- Styling the `NavigationBar`
- Styling the `NoteScreen`

React CSS

If you have any experience in writing CSS for a browser then you will feel comfortable with the styles in React Native. Although, instead of the browser's implementation of cascading styles, Facebook has developed a subset version of CSS in JavaScript. The benefit of this approach is that the designer can fully utilize features in JavaScript, such as variables and conditionals, which CSS does not support natively.

Style Sheet

Style Sheet is the React Native abstraction to declare styles using object notation. The components can use any style, so if you find that you are not able to get the right look then refer to the React Native documentation on that component in its styles section.

When inserting styles, it is common to include only those styles that you need for that specific component. It is similar to how JSX combines the JavaScript logic and markup into a single component; we are also going to define our styles in the same file.

To create a Style Sheet, use the `Stylesheet.create({..})` method by passing in an object of objects:

```
var styles = StyleSheet.create({
  myStyle: {
    backgroundColor: '#EEEEEE'
    color: 'black'
  }
});
```

This looks similar to CSS but it uses commas instead of semicolons.

Styles are declared to be *inline* on a component using the style prop:

```
// Using StyleSheet
<Component style={styles.myStyle} />
// Object
<Component style={{color: 'white'}} />
```

It is also possible to pass normal JavaScript objects to the style prop. This is generally not recommended, since the Style Sheet ensures that each style is immutable and only created once throughout the lifecycle.

Styling the SimpleButton component

Let's extend our `SimpleButton` component further to accept custom styles for the button background and text. In the `render` method, let's set the `style` attribute of the `View` and `Text` components from the `props`:

```
export default class SimpleButton extends React.Component {
  render () {
    return (
      <TouchableOpacity onPress={this.props.onPress}>
        <View style={this.props.style}>
```

```
            <Text style={this.props.textStyle}>
              {this.props.customText || 'Simple Button'}
            </Text>
          </View>
        </TouchableOpacity>
      );
    }
}


SimpleButton.propTypes = {
    onPress: React.PropTypes.func.isRequired,
    customText: React.PropTypes.string,
    style: View.propTypes.style,
    textStyle: Text.propTypes.style
};
```

Revisiting PropTypes

To validate, the `View` or `Text` styles passed into your component
use `View.propTypes.style` and `Text.propType.style`.

On the `HomeScreen` we are going to style the `simpleButton` component to draw the
user's attention to the `NoteScreen` when there are no notes. We will start by adding
it to the `StyleSheet` and defining some text styles:

```
var styles = StyleSheet.create({
  ...

  simpleButtonText: {
    color: 'white',
    fontWeight: 'bold',
    fontSize: 16
  }
});
```

Here, we want the text on the button to be bold, white in color, and with size
16. To style the button, we need to add another object to the `StyleSheet` called
`simpleButton` and also define a background color; the `simpleButton` code is
as follows:

```
var styles = StyleSheet.create({
  ...

  simpleButton: {
```

```
    backgroundColor: '#5B29C1',
  },
  simpleButtonText: {
    color: 'white',
    fontWeight: 'bold',
    fontSize: 16
  }
});
```

Let's see the output of the preceding command:

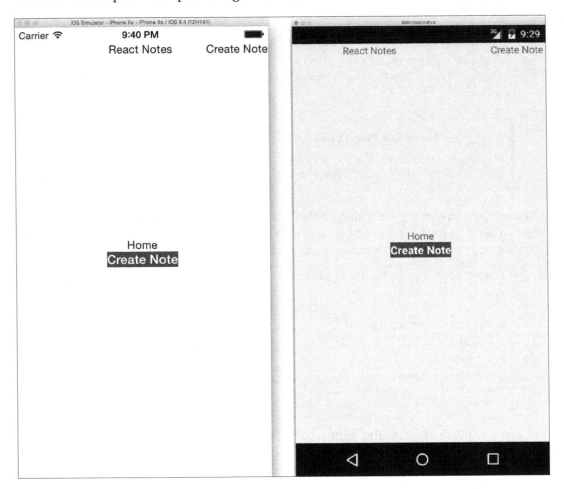

It's not that appealing yet; let's add some padding so that it's easier for the user to press the button:

```
paddingHorizontal: 20,
paddingVertical: 15,
```

paddingVertical is shorthand for paddingTop and paddingBottom. paddingHorizontal is shorthand for paddingLeft and paddingRight.

React CSS does not have a shorthand notion, such as border: 1px solid #000. Instead each item is declared individually:

```
borderColor: '#48209A',
borderWidth: 1,
borderRadius: 4,
```

To add a drop shadow, we define each property similar to borders:

```
shadowColor: 'darkgrey',
    shadowOffset: {
        width: 1,
        height: 1
    },
    shadowOpacity: 0.8,
    shadowRadius: 1,
```

Notice how the shadow offset requires an object with width and height properties. Since we are dealing with JavaScript objects, this is a perfectly acceptable notation. Now, we include the SimpleButton component in our HomeScreen render method:

```
...
import SimpleButton from './SimpleButton';

export default class HomeScreen extends React.Component {
  render () {
    return (
      <View style={styles.container}>
        <Text style={styles.noNotesText}>You haven't created any
notes!</Text>

        <SimpleButton
          onPress={() => this.props.navigator.push({
            name: 'createNote'
          })}
          customText="Create Note"
          style={styles.simpleButton}
          textStyle={styles.simpleButtonText}
        />
      </View>
    );
```

```
      }
    }

    var styles = StyleSheet.create({
      container: {
        flex: 1,
        justifyContent: 'center',
        alignItems: 'center',
      },
      noNotesText: {
        color: '#48209A',
        marginBottom: 10
      },
      simpleButton: {
        backgroundColor: '#5B29C1',
        borderColor: '#48209A',
        borderWidth: 1,
        borderRadius: 4,
        paddingHorizontal: 20,
        paddingVertical: 15,
        shadowColor: 'darkgrey',
        shadowOffset: {
            width: 1,
            height: 1
        },
        shadowOpacity: 0.8,
        shadowRadius: 1,
      },
      simpleButtonText: {
        color: 'white',
        fontWeight: 'bold',
        fontSize: 16
      }
    });
```

Update the renderScene function of ReactNotes in index.ios.js and index.android.js to pass the navigator through the props to the HomeScreen:

```
class ReactNotes extends React.Component {
  renderScene (route, navigator) {
    switch (route.name) {
      case 'home':
        return (
          <HomeScreen navigator={navigator} />
        );
```

```
        case 'createNote':
          return (
            <NoteScreen />
          );
    }
  }


  ...


}
```

Let's see the output of the preceding command:

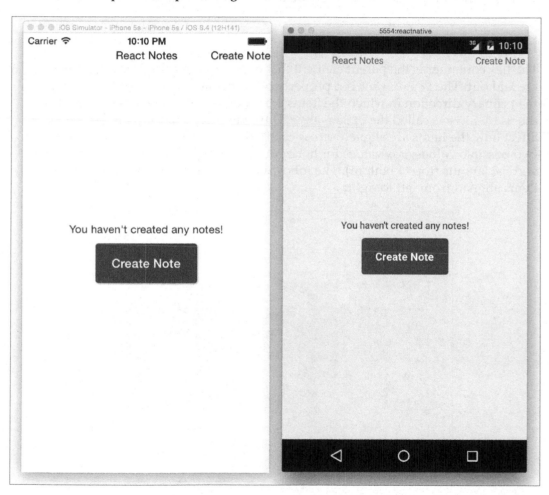

This is not too shabby for a typical call to action button. If you reload this in the simulator and press the button, it will still fade due to the `TouchableOpacity` feedback. For more information on React CSS or to contribute, visit the open source CSS-layout repository at `https://github.com/facebook/css-layout`.

Layout and Flexbox

Since Flexbox is the foundation of React Native's layout, we are going to explore it in depth. If you are already familiar with the intricacies of Flexbox, feel free to jump to the *Styling the NavigationBar component* section. There we will focus more on the styling of the components that we made in the previous chapter.

Flex container

The flex container is the parent element that describes how children or flex items are laid out. The `flexDirection` property of the container specifies the `main-axis`; the primary direction in which the items are rendered. The line perpendicular to the `main-axis` is called the `cross-axis`. Different flex properties on the container affect how the items are aligned across each axis. The `flexDirection` property has two possible values; `row` values for horizontal layouts (left to right) and `column` for vertical layouts (top to bottom). The following figure shows the `flexDirection: row` items aligned from left to right:

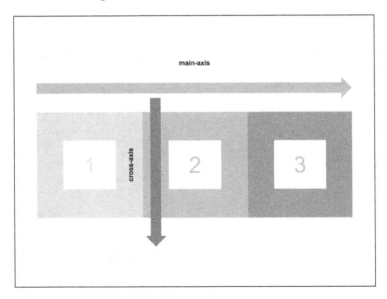

The next figure shows the items laid out from top to bottom when it's set to `flexDirection: column`:

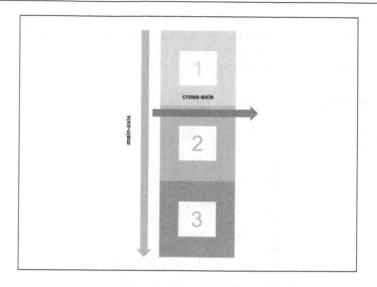

We can move the items in the container along the established `main-axis` with the help of `justifyContent`. The following diagram shows the different options along the `main-axis`:

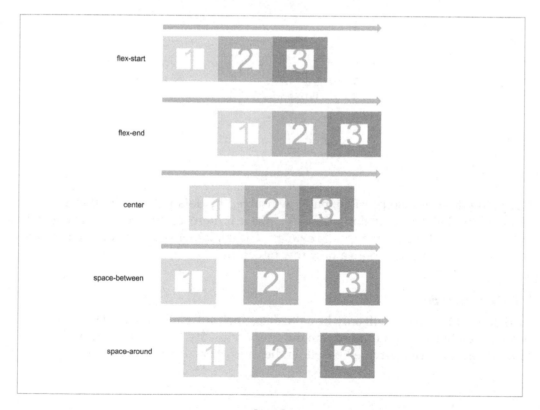

Notice how space-between does not include white space along the left and right edges, whereas space-around does, but it is half the width of the white space included in between the items.

To move items along the cross-axis, we use alignItems:

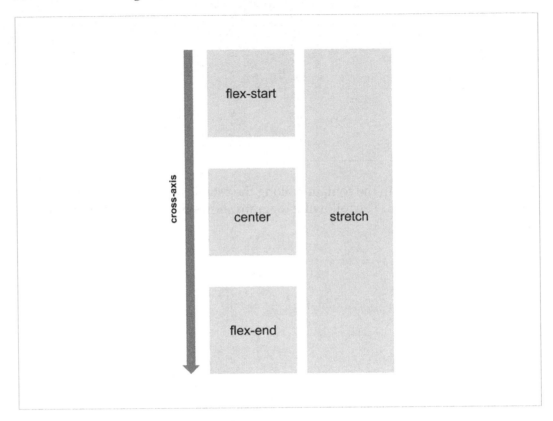

Wrapping items is also possible, but it is disabled by default. Items within a container will all try to fit along the main-axis. If there are too many items or if they are too squeezed, you can apply flexWrap. The container will then calculate if it is necessary to put an item onto a new row or column.

Flex items

By default, flex items will only be as wide as their internal content. The flex property dictates the amount of remaining space the item should take up. The available space is divided based on the ratio of each item's flex value:

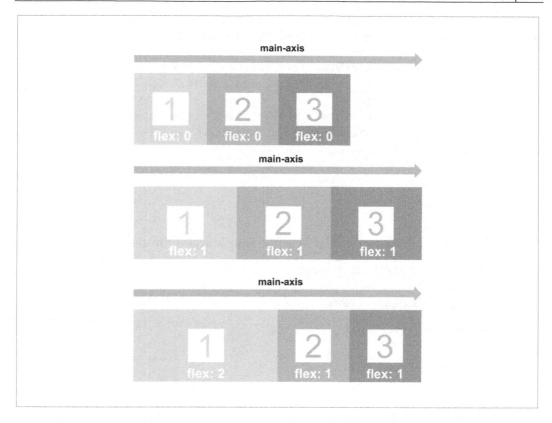

Make a note of how the items in row two are all of the same width, since their `flex` value is 1. The item with `flex` value 2 in row three takes twice as much space as the rest of the items.

Similar to `alignItems`, a `flex` item can align itself along the `cross-axis` with `alignSelf`.

Horizontal and vertical centering

Let's take a look at a quick example of how Flexbox makes layout easier. One of the biggest challenges in CSS is the vertically and horizontally centered elements (take five minutes and attempt to accomplish this in normal CSS). We're going to start by creating our `Center` components and defining a `flex` container with three `flex` items:

```
class Center extends React.Component {
    render () {
        return (
            <View style={styles.container}>
```

```
                <View style={[styles.item, styles.one]}>
                    <Text style={styles.itemText}>1</Text>
                </View>
                <View style={[styles.item, styles.two]}>
                    <Text style={styles.itemText}>2</Text>
                </View>
                <View style={[styles.item, styles.three]}>
                    <Text style={styles.itemText}>3</Text>
                </View>
            </View>
        );
    }
}
```

Initialize a new `StyleSheet` and define some simple styles for the items:

```
var styles = StyleSheet.create({
  item: {
    backgroundColor: '#EEE',
    padding: 25
  },
  one: {
    backgroundColor: 'red'
  },
  two: {
    backgroundColor: 'green'
  },
  three: {
    backgroundColor: 'blue'
  },
  itemText: {
    color: 'white',
    fontSize: 40,
  }
});
```

Now, we want to control where the items are aligned along the main-axis and cross-axis with justifyContent and alignItems. Create a container style and set justifyContent and align items to center:

```
var styles = StyleSheet.create({
  container: {
    flexDirection: 'row',
    alignItems: 'center',
    justifyContent: 'center'
  },

  ...
});
```

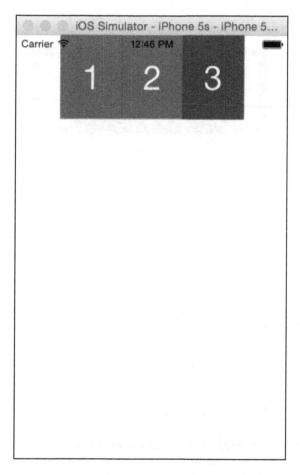

This does not seem like the `behaviour` was specified. The items are aligned along the `centre` of the `main-axis` but not the `cross-axis`. Let's add a border around the container to visualize it:

```
var styles = StyleSheet.create({
  container: {
    borderWidth: 10,
    borderColor: 'purple',
    flexDirection: 'row',
    alignItems: 'center',
    justifyContent: 'center'
  },

  ...
});
```

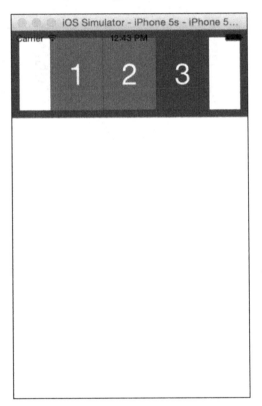

Now we can see that the height of the container does not span the entire screen. Since the default `flexDirection` in the root `View` container is `column`, the content will only span the height of the content. Luckily, we now know the property to take up the remaining space. Adding `flex 1` to our container will have its span in the vertical length of the screen, which gives us the following:

```
var styles = StyleSheet.create({
  container: {
    borderWidth: 10,
    borderColor: 'purple',
    flex: 1,
    flexDirection: 'row',
    alignItems: 'center',
    justifyContent: 'center'
  },

  ...
});
```

This completes our overview of layout with Flexbox! For the entire list of supported Flexbox properties, check out the React Native documentation at `https://facebook.github.io/react-native/docs/flexbox.html#content`.

Absolute positioning

Additionally, React Native gives you the option of positioning the items on your screen. This works the same way as it does in the browser by defining the `top`, `left`, `right`, and `bottom` properties. We recommend that you try to create your layout in Flexbox before resorting to absolute positioning.

Styling the NavigationBar component

It's time to give our `NavigationBar` the iOS and Android style treatment. There is a small difference between the two, except for how the font size and padding are rendered. We will start by giving our `NavigationBar` a background color and a bottom border. Add this to the `StyleSheet` in `index.ios.js` and `index.android.js` and define the `navbar` style:

```
var styles = StyleSheet.create({
    navContainer: {
      flex: 1
    },
    navBar: {
      backgroundColor: '#5B29C1',
      borderBottomColor: '#48209A',
      borderBottomWidth: 1
    }
});
```

Next, update the `Navigator.NavigatorBar` with the style prop:

```
class ReactNotes extends React.Component {
  ...
  render () {
    return (
      <Navigator
        initialRoute={{name: 'home'}}
        renderScene={this.renderScene}
        navigationBar={
          <Navigator.NavigationBar
            routeMapper={NavigationBarRouteMapper}
            style={styles.navBar}
          />
```

```
          }
        />
      );
    }
  }
```

The last things to be updated are our `navbar` title and `SimpleButton` styles. We want the text to be `centered` vertically as well as to give the left-hand and right-hand buttons some padding from the sides of the screen:

```
var styles = StyleSheet.create({
    navBar: {
        backgroundColor: '#5B29C1',
        borderBottomColor: '#48209A',
        borderBottomWidth: 1
    },
    navBarTitleText: {
        color: 'white',
        fontSize: 16,
        fontWeight: '500',
        marginVertical: 9  // iOS
    // marginVertical: 16 // Android
    },
    navBarLeftButton: {
        paddingLeft: 10
    },
    navBarRightButton: {
        paddingRight: 10
    },
    navBarButtonText: {
        color: '#EEE',
        fontSize: 16,
        marginVertical: 10 // iOS
    // marginVertical: 16 // Android
    }
});
```

 As we alluded to earlier, the `marginVertical` for iOS is different than the Android version to produce the same visual result.

Finally, update the NavigationBarRouteMapper to include the styles for the title and buttons:

```
var NavigationBarRouteMapper = {
  LeftButton: function(route, navigator, index, navState) {
    switch (route.name) {
      case 'createNote':
        return (
          <SimpleButton
            onPress={() => navigator.pop()}
            customText='Back'
            style={styles.navBarLeftButton}
            textStyle={styles.navBarButtonText}
          />
        );
      default:
        return null;
    }
  },
  RightButton: function(route, navigator, index, navState) {
    switch (route.name) {
      case 'home':
        return (
          <SimpleButton
            onPress={() => {
              navigator.push({
                name: 'createNote'
              });
            }}
            customText='Create Note'
            style={styles.navBarRightButton}
            textStyle={styles.navBarButtonText}
          />
        );
      default:
        return null;
    }
  },

  Title: function(route, navigator, index, navState) {
    switch (route.name) {
      case 'home':
        return (
```

```
          <Text style={styles.navBarTitleText}>React Notes</Text>
        );
      case 'createNote':
        return (
          <Text style={styles.navBarTitleText}>Create Note</Text>
        );
    }
  }
};
```

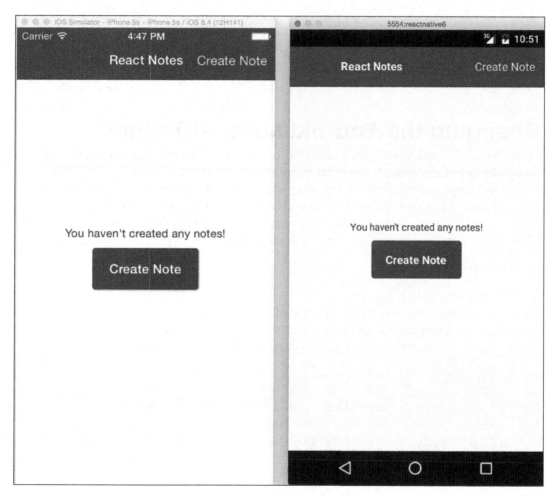

Make a note of how the iOS version, for which we have changed the status bar text to appear white. React Native provides an API to interact with the status bar in iOS. In our `index.ios.js` we can toggle it to white in the `ReactNotes` constructor:

```
class ReactNotes extends React.Component {
  constructor (props) {
    super(props);
    StatusBarIOS.setStyle('light-content');
  }
  ...
}
```

The documentation for `StatusBarIOS` can be found in the React Native documentation at `https://facebook.github.io/react-native/docs/statusbarios.html`.

Changing the Android Material Theme

The color of the status and navigation bar on our Android application appears to be solid black. Currently, there is no support system in React Native to style these from JavaScript like what the `StatusBarIOS` API provides on iOS. We can still use the Material Theme (available in Android 5.0 and above), located in `ReactNotes/android/app/src/6main/res/values/styles.xml`, to apply the colors we want. Change the contents of `styles.xml` to the following:

```
<resources>
    <!-- Base application theme. -->
    <style name="AppTheme"
      parent="Theme.AppCompat.Light.NoActionBar">
        <item name="android:colorPrimaryDark">#48209A</item>
        <item name="android:navigationBarColor">#48209A</item>
    </style>
</resources>
```

The `colorPrimaryDark` refers to the color of the status bar, whereas `navigationBarColor` is the color of the bottom navigation container. When you re-launch the application you should be able to see the status and navigation bars colored correctly.

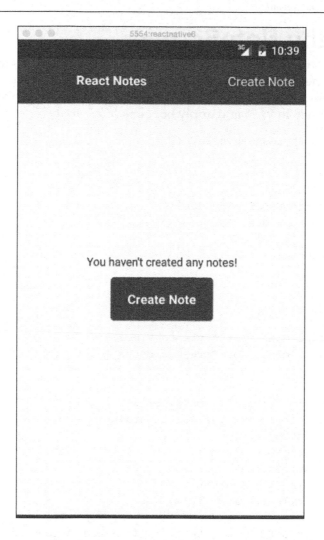

For more information on using the Material Theme, refer to the Android developers documentation at https://developer.android.com/training/material/theme.html.

Styling the NoteScreen

Our `NoteScreen` has two `TextInput`s without any styles. As of right now, it's difficult to see where each input rests on the screen. It is common on iOS and Android to put an underline under each input. To achieve this, we are going to wrap our `TextInput` in `View` and apply `borderBottom` to it:

```
var styles = StyleSheet.create({
  ...

  inputContainer: {
    borderBottomColor: '#9E7CE3',
    borderBottomWidth: 1,
    flexDirection: 'row',
    marginBottom: 10
  }
});
```

Apply the inputContainer style to Views:

```
export default class NoteScreen extends React.Component {
  render () {
    return (
      <View style={styles.container}>
        <View style={styles.inputContainer}>
          <TextInput
            autoFocus={true}
            autoCapitalize="sentences"
            placeholder="Untitled"
            style={styles.title}

            onEndEditing={(text) => {this.refs.body.focus()}}
          />
        </View>
        <View style={styles.inputContainer}>
          <TextInput
            ref="body"
            multiline={true}
            placeholder="Start typing"
            style={styles.body}
```

```
                    textAlignVertical="top"
                    underlineColorAndroid="transparent"
                />
            </View>
        </View>
    );
    }
}
```

The existing title and body styles define the height of each `TextInput`. Since each input will share the `flex` properties and text size, we can define a shared style:

```
var styles = StyleSheet.create({
    ...
    textInput: {
        flex: 1,
        fontSize: 16,
    },

});
```

Then, in each input style we can pass an array to include both styles:

```
class NoteScreen extends React.Component {
    render () {
        return (
            <View style={styles.container}>
                <View style={styles.inputContainer}>
                    <TextInput
                        autoFocus={true}
                        autoCapitalize="sentences"
                        placeholder="Untitled"
                        style={[styles.textInput, styles.title]}
                        onEndEditing={(text) => {this.refs.body.focus()}}
                    />
                </View>
                <View style={styles.inputContainer}>
                    <TextInput
                        ref="body"
                        multiline={true}
                        placeholder="Start typing"
                        style={[styles.textInput, styles.body]}
                    />
```

```
      </View>
    </View>
  );
}
}
```

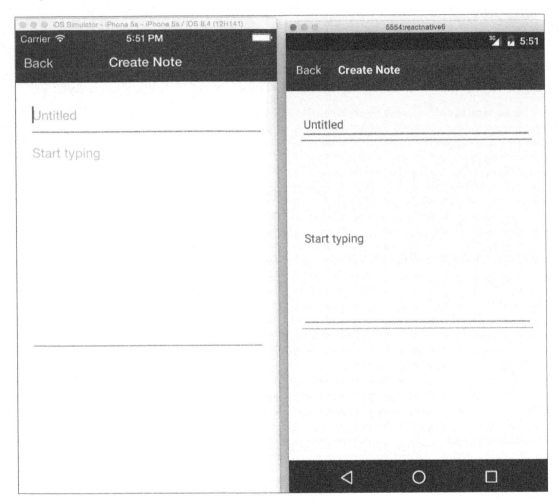

This doesn't look right on Android yet. The TextInputs on Android have a default underline and they center the text vertically on multiline inputs. There are two Android only attributes that can be added to match the look of the iOS application. On each TextInput set the underlineColorAndroid as transparent and textAlignVertical on the body as TextInput:

```
export default class NoteScreen extends React.Component {
  render () {
    return (
      <View style={styles.container}>
        <View style={styles.inputContainer}>
          <TextInput
            autoFocus={true}
            autoCapitalize="sentences"
            placeholder="Untitled"
            style={[styles.textInput, styles.title]}
            onEndEditing={(text) => {this.refs.body.focus()}}
            underlineColorAndroid="transparent"
          />
        </View>
        <View style={styles.inputContainer}>
          <TextInput
            ref="body"
            multiline={true}
            placeholder="Start typing"
            style={[styles.textInput, styles.body]}
            textAlignVertical="top"
            underlineColorAndroid="transparent"
          />
        </View>
```

```
        </View>
      );
    }
  }
```

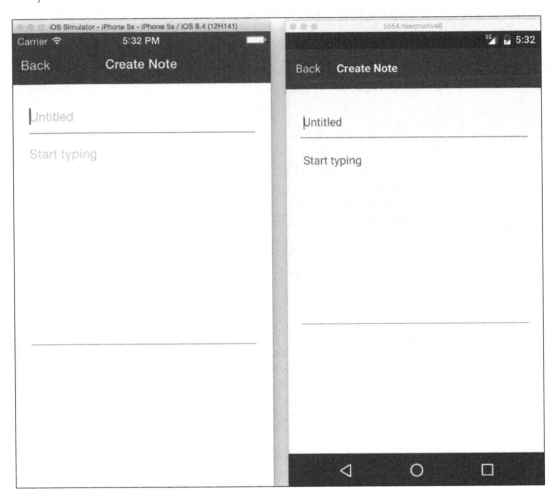

With this we get the same look on both devices! This wraps up the styling of the components we created in the previous chapter. Henceforth, we are going to style as soon as we add new components to our application.

Summary

Styles in React Native are very similar to how CSS works in browser. In this chapter, you learned how to create and manage Style Sheets and add them to your components. If you ever find yourself frustrated with the layout then use the Flexbox section as a guide. Make sure to review where your main-axis and cross-axis are defined, as well as where the flex items are aligned along them. Feel free to go back to our components and play around with any of the styles before continuing with the next chapter.

5
Displaying and Saving Data

Now that we know how to style a React Native application, let's figure out how to actually make it do something. In this chapter, we'll start saving notes to the device, populate a list with the notes we've saved, and select notes from the list to view and edit.

In this chapter, we will cover the following topics:

- Using a `ListView` to display rows of data
- Managing state
- Using props to pass data and callbacks into components
- Using `AsyncStorage` to store data on both iOS and Android devices

Our strategy in this chapter is to first build the basic functionality using dummy data so we can learn some fundamental skills before we learn about saving and loading the data with the `AsyncStorage` API. By the end of the chapter, you will have a fully functional note-taking application!

Lists

The `HomeScreen` of our application is going to display a list of the notes that we have saved. To do this, we will introduce the `ListView` component. Let's start by creating a new file in our `Components` directory called `NoteList` and add the following code:

```
import React, {
  StyleSheet,
  Text,
  View,
  ListView
  } from 'react-native';
```

```
export default class NoteList extends React.Component {

  constructor (props) {
    super(props);
    this.ds = new ListView.DataSource({rowHasChanged: (r1, r2) => r1
!== r2});
  }

  render() {
    return (
      <ListView
        dataSource={
          this.ds.cloneWithRows( [
              {title:"Note 1", body:"Body 1", id:1},
              {title:"Note 2", body:"Body 2", id:2}
            ])
        }
        renderRow={(rowData) => {
            return (
                <Text>{rowData.title}</Text>
            )
          }
        }/>
      )
    }
  }
}
```

The `ListView` component is fairly simple to use. You must provide two pieces of information, the `dataSource` that will provide the data for all of the rows and the `renderRow` function, which is simply a function that takes each row's data (a single note) and returns a React component. In the preceding example, this function returns a `<Text/>` component that displays the title of the note.

We instantiate a `ListView`. The `DataSource` is in the constructor because we only want to create it once. The `DataSource` constructor takes a `params` object to configure the `DataSource`; however, the only required parameter is a `rowHasChanged` function. This function is used by the `DataSource` when it receives new data so that it can efficiently determine which rows need to be re-rendered. If `r1` and `r2` point to the same object, the row hasn't changed.

You'll also notice that we don't pass the `DataSource` reference directly to our `ListView`. Instead we use `cloneWithRows()`, passing it to the `rowData` we want to use. We're hardcoding the row data for now, but by the end of this chapter you will know how to update the `ListView` with new data.

Next, let's add the `NoteList` component to the `HomeScreen` and learn how to respond to touch events on each row. Open the `HomeScreen` component and add the following line to import your new `NoteList` component:

```
import NoteList from './NoteList';
```

Also, let's drop the `NoteList` component into `HomeScreen`'s render method just inside the `View` component, before the `<Text/>` component:

```
render () {
    return (
        <View style={styles.container}>
          <NoteList/>
          <Text style={styles.noNotesText}>You haven't created any
notes!</Text>

          <SimpleButton
            onPress={() => this.props.navigator.push({
              name: 'createNote'
            })}
            customText="Create Note"
            style={styles.simpleButton}
            textStyle={styles.simpleButtonText}
          />
        </View>
    );
}
```

Before we try out our `NoteList`, let's modify our styles to make sure that the list content isn't obscured by the `NavigationBar`:

```
container: {
  flex: 1,
  justifyContent: 'center',
  alignItems: 'center',
  marginTop: 60
}
```

Now, when you reload the application you should see the following screenshot:

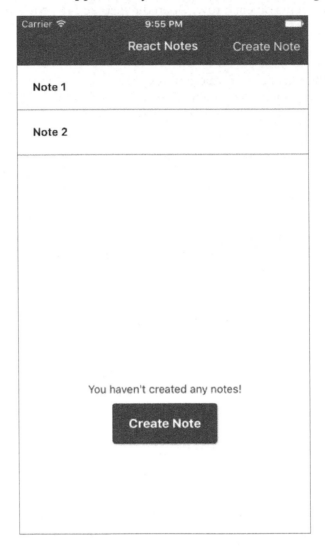

We still have the **You haven't created any notes!** Message at the bottom of the screen, but we'll learn how to take care of that later in the chapter.

Now that we have a list of items, we'd like to be able to respond when the user touches one of the items. To do that, we'll wrap the `<Text/>` component in our `renderRow` function with the `TouchableHighlight` component. First, let's add `TouchableHighlight` to our list of imports:

```
import React, {
  StyleSheet,
```

```
    Text,
    View,
    ListView,
    TouchableHighlight
    } from 'react-native';
```

Then update the `renderRow` function in our `ListView`:

```
renderRow={
  (rowData) => {
    return (
      <TouchableHighlight onPress={() => console.log(rowData)}>
        <Text>{rowData.title}</Text>
      </TouchableHighlight>
    )
  }
}
```

Now, you can reload the application and touch each row to see that the `rowData` has been logged to the console.

Our goal is to be able to touch a row, navigate to the `NoteScreen`, and populate the title and body with the data from the row. Let's add an `_onPress` event handler to our `NoteList` component, as shown:

```
_onPress (rowData) {
  this.props.navigator.push(
    {
      name: 'createNote',
      note: {
        id: rowData.id,
        title: rowData.title,
        body: rowData.body
      }
    });
}
```

And we will call this function from our `TouchableHighlight`, as shown:

```
<TouchableHighlight onPress={() =>
  this._onPress(rowData)}>
  <Text>{rowData.title}</Text>
</TouchableHighlight>
```

Before we try this out, take a look at the `_onPress` handler and notice that we are referring to `this.props.navigator`. This is the navigator that we've been using to go back and forth between the `HomeScreen` and the `NoteScreen`, but what's this props business?

Understanding props

If you take a look at the constructor function of the NoteList, you will notice that it takes an argument called **props**:

```
export default class NoteList extends React.Component {
  constructor (props) {
    super(props);
    this.ds = new ListView.DataSource({rowHasChanged: (r1, r2) =>
      r1 !== r2});
  }
}
```

Props is the mechanism we use to pass data to React components. In our case, we want to pass a navigator reference from the HomeScreen component to the NoteList, so let's make a quick change to our NoteList declaration, as shown:

```
export default class HomeScreen extends React.Component {
  render () {
    return (
      <View style={styles.container}>
        <NoteList navigator={this.props.navigator}/>
        . . .
      </View>
    );
  }
}
```

When you touch a row in the NoteList, you push the note data associated with that row to the navigator, which then triggers renderScene that passes the note to the NoteScreen. So how do we use this note inside the NoteScreen? We learned earlier that props are passed into the component's constructor, but how do we actually get our TextInput components to display the note's title and body? Let's see what happens if we bind the value property of each of our inputs to the passed-in note, as shown:

```
<View style={styles.inputContainer}>
  <TextInput
    autoFocus={true}
    autoCapitalize="sentences"
    placeholder="Untitled"
    style={[styles.textInput, styles.title]}
    onEndEditing={(text) => {this.refs.body.focus()}}
    underlineColorAndroid="transparent"
    value={this.props.note.title}
  />
</View>
<View style={styles.inputContainer}>
```

```
<TextInput
  ref="body"
  multiline={true}
  placeholder="Start typing"
  style={[styles.textInput, styles.body]}
  textAlignVertical="top"
  underlineColorAndroid="transparent"
  value={this.props.note.body}
/>
</View>
```

Now when we reload the application and touch the first note in the list, we will see the following screenshot:

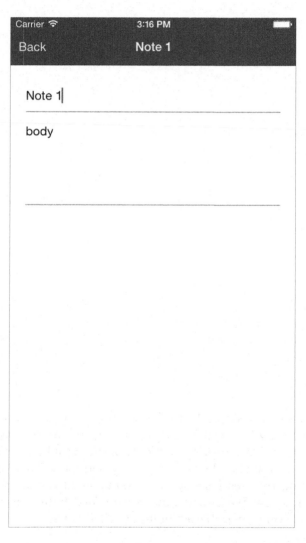

But what happens when you try to edit the title or body? Nothing happens! Before we diagnose what is wrong, let's tap the **Back** button and touch the second note in the NoteList. You will see it displayed, as shown:

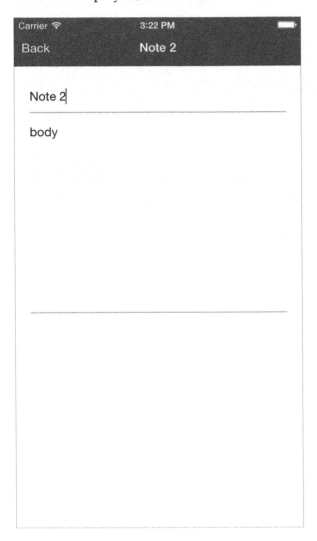

Ok, so our NoteScreen does update, but only when we pass it new props from outside, not when we try to edit the TextInputs. Props can only be passed from the outside of a component. As tempting as it may seem, it's a bad idea to try to modify this.props.note from inside the NoteScreen when the value of each TextInput changes. What we need instead is some way to manage the changes made to the internal state of our NoteScreen when the user makes changes to the TextInputs. For that, each React component has something called **state**.

Using state

React components have a built-in variable called `state` that you can use to keep track of the component's `state`. In the preceding example, we know that we are passing in a note that we want to display, so the initial state of the component is represented by that note. Let's do something totally crazy and modify the `NoteScreen` constructor, as shown:

```
constructor (props) {
  super(props)
  this.state = {note:this.props.note};
}
```

So, `this.state` is an object with title and body properties that are initially set to the title and body of the note we passed. Why the call to *super (props)?* The superclass of our `NoteScreen` is `React.Component`, which takes props as an argument and sets `this.props`. If we omit `super(props)` in `NoteScreen`, then `this.props` will be undefined.

You may have already guessed that we're going to update the `TextInputs` to bind to `this.state.title` and `this.state.body` respectively, but we're also going to listen for `onChangeText` events for each input:

```
<View style={styles.inputContainer}>
  <TextInput
    ref="title"
    autoFocus={true}
    autoCapitalize="sentences"
    placeholder="Untitled"
    style={[styles.textInput, styles.title]}
    onEndEditing={(text) => {this.refs.body.focus()}}
    underlineColorAndroid="transparent"
    value={this.state.note.title}
    onChangeText={(title) => {this.setState({title})}}
  />
</View>
<View style={styles.inputContainer}>
  <TextInput
    ref="body"
    multiline={true}
    placeholder="Start typing"
    style={[styles.textInput, styles.body]}
    textAlignVertical="top"
    underlineColorAndroid="transparent"
    value={this.state.body}
    onChangeText={(body) => {this.setState({body})}}
  />
</View>
```

Note that the `arrow` function that we're using to handle the `onChangeText` event is calling `this.setState(...)` instead of directly setting `this.state.title`. This is an important thing to remember. Anytime you modify state you must use `this.setState()` so that React knows that your component needs to be re-rendered. For performance reasons, calling `setState()` doesn't immediately update `this.state`, so don't let that trip you up!

Reload the application, touch **Note 1** in the list and then change the title to **My note**:

The Text Input attribute now reflects the value of this.state.title on every call to render(), which happens after every call to this.setState({title}). So far so good, but what do you think we will see when we navigate back to the HomeScreen? Tap the **Back** button and take a look — the title of the first note is still **Note 1** instead of **My note**. Now, when you click on **Note 1** to go back to the NoteScreen you'll see that your changes have disappeared. Let's fix this!

We've just identified the need to update our ListView when a note is changed. We know that the internal state of the NoteScreen changes when we type into the TextInput components, but how do we communicate these changes to the rest of the application?

Passing callbacks in props

A common pattern in React is to pass a callback to a component via props. In our case, we want to pass a callback to our NoteScreen so that it can let us know when the note is changed. Let's return to the ReactNotes component in our index.ios.js or index.android.js file and update our renderScene function, as shown:

```
renderScene (route, navigator) {
  switch (route.name) {
    case 'home':
      return (
        <HomeScreen navigator={navigator} />
      );
    case 'createNote':
      return (
        <NoteScreen
          note={route.note}
          onChangeNote={(note) => console.log("note changed",
            note)}/>
      );
  }
}
```

Here, we are defining a prop called onChangeNote and setting its value to an arrow function that will be called when we invoke onChangeNote inside our NoteScreen component. So, somewhere inside our NoteScreen code we're going to add the following line:

```
this.props.onChangeNote(note);
```

Let's revisit the `NoteScreen` and a function to handle the updating of notes:

```
class NoteScreen extends React.Component {
  ...
  updateNote(title, body) {
    var note = Object.assign(this.state.note, {title:title,
body:body});
    this.props.onChangeNote(note);
    this.setState(note);
  }
  ...
}
```

In our title `TextInput`, update the `onChangeText` function, as shown:

```
onChangeText={(title) => this.updateNote(title, this.state.note.body)}
```

And in the body `TextInput`:

```
onChangeText={(body) => this.updateNote(this.state.note.title, body)}
```

Now let's reload our application, touch **Note 1**, and start making changes. If you look at the console you should see each change being logged:

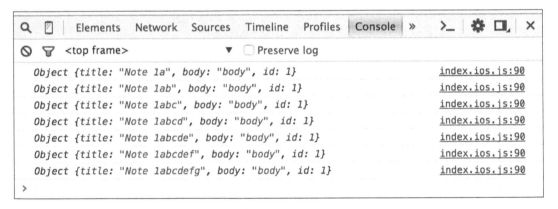

Getting notified of the changes to a note only gets us halfway to our goal to update the `ListView`. Recall that our `NoteList` component's `dataSource` is currently just a hardcoded array of notes:

```
<ListView
    dataSource={
      this.ds.cloneWithRows([
        { title:"Note 1", body:"body", id:1},
        {title:"Note 2", body:"body", id:2}
      ])
```

```
        }
        renderRow={ (rowData) => {
            return (
                <TouchableHighlight onPress={() =>
                    this._onPress(rowData)}>
                    <Text>{rowData.title}</Text>
                </TouchableHighlight>
            )
          }
        }
    />
```

We need to be able to pass in the list of notes to the NoteList component instead of hardcoding them. Now that you're familiar with props, you know that we can pass the list in from the HomeScreen, as shown:

```
export default class HomeScreen extends React.Component {
  render () {
    return (
      <View style={styles.container}>
        <NoteList
          navigator={this.props.navigator}
          notes={ [{title:"Note 1", body:"body", id:1},
            {title:"Note 2", body:"body", id:2}] }
        />
    ...
}
```

Then modify the NoteList component to use this.props.notes in the dataSource:

```
export default class NoteList extends React.Component {
  ...
  render() {
    return (
      <ListView
        dataSource={this.ds.cloneWithRows(this.props.notes)}
        ...
        />
    )
  }
}
```

Let's take our refactoring one step further. We don't really want the HomeScreen to be responsible for managing the state of our list of notes, that's a job for our top-level component, ReactNotes. We can repeat the same trick we just used and replace the hardcoded array of notes in HomeScreen with this.props.notes:

```
export default class HomeScreen extends React.Component {
  render () {
    return (
      <View style={styles.container}>
        <NoteList navigator={this.props.navigator}
          notes={this.props.notes}/>
      ...
      </View>
    );
  }
}
```

In our ReactNotes component, we can pass the notes to the HomeScreen using props:

```
class ReactNotes extends React.Component {
  renderScene (route, navigator) {
    switch (route.name) {
      case 'home':
        return (
          <HomeScreen navigator={navigator}
          notes={[[{title:"Note 1", body:"body", id:1}, {title:"Note
2", body:"body", id:2}]]}/>
          );
      case 'createNote':
        return (
          <NoteScreen note={route.note} onChangeNote={(note) =>
console.log("note changed", note)}/>
          );
    }
  }
  ...
}
```

You may sense that we are getting tantalizingly close to our goal of being able to modify notes and see the changes in the ListView. The source of our notes is now in close proximity to the event handler that knows when the user has modified a note on the NoteScreen. What we're really talking about here is managing the state of our application.

The `ReactNotes` component is the top-level component that is responsible for managing the application state, which consists entirely of notes. So, let's make it official and move the array of notes into the component's initial state:

```
class ReactNotes extends React.Component {
  constructor(props) {
    super(props);
    this.state = {
      notes: [{title: "Note 1", body: "body", id: 1}, {title:
        "Note 2", body: "body", id: 2}]};
  }
  renderScene(route, navigator) {
    switch (route.name) {
      case 'home':
        return (
          <HomeScreen navigator={navigator}
            notes={this.state.notes}/>
        );
      case 'createNote':
        return (
          <NoteScreen note={route.note} onChangeNote={(note) =>
            console.log("note changed", note)}/>
        );
    }
  }


  ...

}
```

Storing notes in an array makes it a little tricky to update a particular note; let's do a quick refactor using an object instead of an array, as shown:

```
class ReactNotes extends React.Component {

  constructor(props) {
    super(props);
    this.state = {
      selectedNote: {title:"", body:""},
      notes: {
        1: {title: "Note 1", body: "body", id: 1},
        2: {title: "Note 2", body: "body", id: 2}
      }
    }
  }
  ...
}
```

Now, `notes` is the object in which the keys correspond to the `ids` of the notes. Since the `NoteList` component is still expecting an array, let's use `underscore.js` to do the conversion:

```
<HomeScreen navigator={navigator} notes={_(this.state.notes).
toArray()} />
```

The `NoteList` should continue to function the way it did earlier; we are just keeping track of our notes a little differently.

Here are the changes that we need to make for the `onChangeNote` handler to actually update a note via state:

```
class ReactNotes extends React.Component {
  ...
  updateNote(note) {
    var newNotes = Object.assign({}, this.state.notes);
    newNotes[note.id] = note;
    this.setState({notes:newNotes});
  }

  renderScene(route, navigator) {
    switch (route.name) {
      case 'createNote':

        return (
          <NoteScreen note={this.state.selectedNote}
onChangeNote={ (note) => this.updateNote(note) }/>
        );
    }
  }
  ...
}
```

Let's walk through the `updateNote` function to understand what's happening. First, we create a copy of `this.state.notes` using `Object.assign()`. Any time you work with nested data in your state object, we recommend making a copy like this to avoid unexpected behavior. React compares the two objects to determine if a component's state has changed and needs to be re-rendered; hence, using a copy like this ensures that the old state and the new state point to different objects. We then put our modified note into `newNotes` using `note.id` as the key. Lastly, we call `setState()` to replace the entire notes object with the new copy.

We've got a few more refactorings to do before we can try out our handiwork. Now that we know how to pass callbacks to our components via props, we can eliminate the need to pass in a navigator to the `HomeScreen` and `NoteList` components, and instead pass in a callback so that the `NoteList` can tell us when the user has selected a note:

```
class ReactNotes extends React.Component {
  renderScene(route, navigator) {
    switch (route.name) {
      case 'home':
        return (<HomeScreen navigator={navigator}
        notes={_(this.state.notes).toArray()}
        onSelectNote={(note) => navigator.push({name:"createNote",
        note: note})}/>);
      case 'createNote':
      return (
          <NoteScreen note={route.note} onChangeNote={(note) =>
          this.updateNote(note)}/>
        );
    }
  }
}
```

This means that we have to update our `HomeScreen` to pass the `onSelectNote` callback into the `NoteList`:

```
export default class HomeScreen extends React.Component {
  render () {
    return (
      <View style={styles.container}>
        <NoteList notes={this.props.notes}
          onSelectNote={this.props.onSelectNote}/>
        <Text style={styles.noNotesText}>You haven't created any
          notes!</Text>
        <SimpleButton
          onPress={() => this.props.navigator.push({
            name: 'createNote'
          })}
          customText="Create Note"
          style={styles.simpleButton}
          textStyle={styles.simpleButtonText}
        />
      </View>
    );
  }
}
```

Also, we'll have to update `NoteList`. We no longer need the `_onPress` handler or a reference to the navigator, we can just invoke the provided callback with `rowData`:

```
export default class NoteList extends React.Component {

  constructor (props) {
    super(props);
    this.ds = new ListView.DataSource({rowHasChanged: (r1, r2) => r1
!== r2});
  }
  render() {
    return (
      <ListView
        dataSource={this.ds.cloneWithRows(this.props.notes)}
        renderRow={(rowData) => {
            return (
          <TouchableHighlight
            onPress={() => this.props.onSelectNote(rowData)}
            style={styles.rowStyle}
            underlayColor="#9E7CE3"
          >
            <Text style={styles.rowText}>{rowData.title}</Text>
          </TouchableHighlight>                    )
            }
        }/>
      )
  }
}

var styles = StyleSheet.create({
  rowStyle: {
    borderBottomColor: '#9E7CE3',
    borderBottomWidth: 1,
    padding: 20,
  },
  rowText: {
    fontWeight: '600'
  }
});
```

You should now be able to reload the application, touch a note, change the title, go back, and see the updated title appear in the NoteList, as shown in the following screenshot:

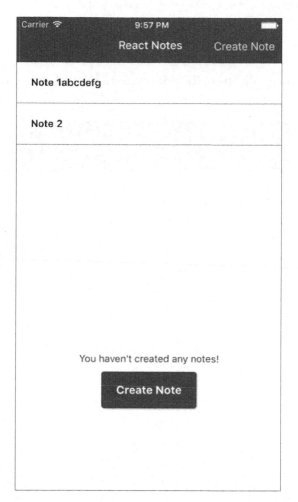

When you select a note and navigate to the NoteScreen, the title that appears in the NavigationBar is still **Create Note**. Let's modify it, so that even if we select an existing note from the list, we use the note's title instead of **Create Note**:

```
Title: function(route, navigator, index, navState) {
  switch (route.name) {
    case 'home':
      return (
        <Text style={styles.navBarTitleText}>React Notes</Text>
      );
```

```
       case 'createNote':
        return (
          <Text style={styles.navBarTitleText}>{route.note ?
            route.note.title : 'Create Note'}</Text>
        );
    }
  }
```

When you reload the application, the `NoteScreen` should reflect the title of the selected note:

Creating new notes

So far, we've been updating existing notes. How do we add new ones? Well, that's actually very easy. We just need to update the **Create Note** button in the `NavigationBar`, as shown:

```
RightButton: function(route, navigator, index, navState) {
  switch (route.name) {
    case 'home':
      return (
        <SimpleButton
          onPress={() => {
            navigator.push({
              name: 'createNote',
              note: {
                id: new Date().getTime(),
                title: '',
                body: ''
              }
            });
          }}
          customText='Create Note'
          style={styles.navBarRightButton}
          textStyle={styles.navBarButtonText}
        />
      );
    default:
      return null;
  }
}
```

As you can see, we're now passing an empty note with a generated id. (A better approach to generate ids will be to use a uuid generator, but we'll leave that as an exercise for the reader!)

That's it! We finally have a full, end-to-end note taking application! However, our notes only exist in memory. We need to be able to save notes to the device, so let's meet our new friend, AsyncStorage.

Using AsyncStorage

React Native provides an abstraction over the native local storage mechanism so that you don't have to worry about the underlying differences between how iOS and Android save data to the device.

It's really simple to use, so let's update our ReactNotes component to use AsyncStorage. First, let's add AsyncStorage to our list of imports:

```
import React, {
  AppRegistry,
  Navigator,
  StyleSheet,
  Text,
  AsyncStorage
} from 'react-native';
```

Next, let's add a saveNotes() function:

```
async saveNotes(notes) {
  try {
    await AsyncStorage.setItem("@ReactNotes:notes",
      JSON.stringify(notes));
  } catch (error) {
    console.log('AsyncStorage error: ' + error.message);
  }
}
```

You may be wondering what the async and await keywords are doing in your JavaScript! These are new keywords in ES7 that simplify working with promises. The AsyncStorage methods are, well, asynchronous and they return promises. Without going into too much detail, the async keyword in front of a function allows us to use the await keyword within the function body. The await keyword will resolve the promise, and if there's a problem, it will throw an error.

Let's modify our updateNote function to call our new saveNotes function:

```
updateNote(note) {
  var newNotes = Object.assign({}, this.state.notes);
  newNotes[note.id] = note;
  this.setState({notes:newNotes});
  this.saveNotes(newNotes);
}
```

We'll also need a function to loadNotes from AsyncStorage:

```
async loadNotes() {
  try {
    var notes = await AsyncStorage.getItem("@ReactNotes:notes");
    if (notes !== null) {
      this.setState({notes:JSON.parse(notes)})
    }
  } catch (error) {
```

```
        console.log('AsyncStorage error: ' + error.message);
      }
   }
```

We want to load our saved notes from the device in our constructor:

```
constructor(props) {
  super(props);
  this.state = {
    notes: {
      1: {title: "Note 1", body: "body", id: 1},
      2: {title: "Note 2", body: "body", id: 2}
    }
  }
  this.loadNotes();
}
```

Reload your application, and save the changes made to a note or create a new note. Then reload the application again. Your changes have been saved! We just have one more job to do, deleting notes!

Deleting notes

The last thing we need to do before we have a fully functional note-taking application is to add a **Delete** button to our `NoteScreen`. To accomplish that, we'll update our `NavigationBarRouteMapper` to add a `RightButton` when the route name is `createNote`:

```
RightButton: function(route, navigator, index, navState) {
  switch (route.name) {
    case 'home':
      return (
        <SimpleButton
          onPress={() => {
            navigator.push({
              name: 'createNote',
              note: {
                id: new Date().getTime(),
                title: '',
                body: '',
                isSaved: false
              }
            });
          }}
          customText='Create Note'
```

```
              style={styles.navBarRightButton}
              textStyle={styles.navBarButtonText}
           />
        );
      case 'createNote':
        if (route.note.isSaved) {
          return (
            <SimpleButton
              onPress={
                () => {
                  navigator.props.onDeleteNote(route.note);
                  navigator.pop();
                }
              }
              customText='Delete'
              style={styles.navBarRightButton}
              textStyle={styles.navBarButtonText}
              />
          );
        } else {
          return null;
        }
      default:
          return null;
    }
  },
```

The first thing to notice is that I've added a condition to check if the note has already been saved (we will need to tweak our `updateNote` function to set this). This is to make sure that the **Delete** button doesn't show up for new notes. The `Create Note` `onPress` handler has been updated to set `isSaved = false` in the empty note that we pass to the `NoteScreen`, when that button is pressed.

Now, let's look at the `onPress` handler for the **Delete** button:

```
              onPress={
                () => {
                  navigator.props.onDeleteNote(route.note);
                  navigator.pop();
                }
              }
```

We've seen `navigator.pop()` before, but we're also invoking a new callback called `onDeleteNote`. We need to pass that callback in through props in our `ReactNotes` render function:

```
render () {
  return (
    <Navigator
      initialRoute={{name: 'home'}}
      renderScene={this.renderScene.bind(this)}
      navigationBar={
        <Navigator.NavigationBar
          routeMapper={NavigationBarRouteMapper}
          style={styles.navBar}
        />
      }
      onDeleteNote={(note) => this.deleteNote(note)}
    />
  );
}
```

Next, we need to modify our `updateNote` function to mark the notes that have been saved:

```
updateNote(note) {
  var newNotes = Object.assign({}, this.state.notes);
  note.isSaved = true;
  newNotes[note.id] = note;
  this.setState({notes:newNotes});
  this.saveNotes(newNotes);
}
```

Just below that, we'll add the `deleteNote` function:

```
deleteNote(note) {
  var newNotes = Object.assign({}, this.state.notes);
  delete newNotes[note.id];
  this.setState({notes:newNotes});
  this.saveNotes(newNotes);
}
```

That's it! Reload the application and create a new note. Notice that there is no **Delete** button in the `NavigationBar`. Press the **Back** button to view the note in the list, then tap that item in the list to view it. You should be able to see the **Delete** button in the top right corner, as shown:

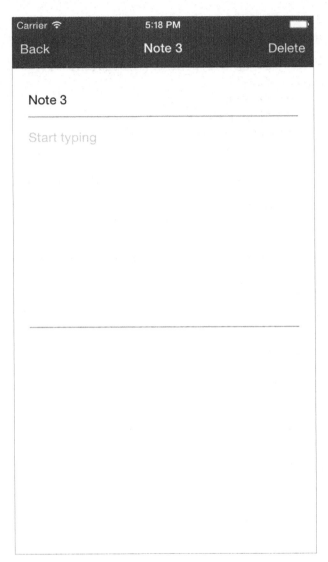

Press the **Delete** button and you will be returned to the `HomeScreen` where the deleted note will disappear from the list!

Summary

In this chapter, we have created a complete note-taking application. You have learned how to use the `ListView` to display data, pass data into components using props, keep track of a component's state, and save data to the device using AsyncStorage. Moreover, you have done did all of this without writing any `platform-specific` code!

6
Working with Geolocation and Maps

So far you've seen that React Native simplifies the creation of native UI components, such as lists, text fields, and buttons, and it gives you simple abstractions, such as AsyncStorage, to work with underlying native APIs. Soon, you'll see that you also have access to advanced components, such as maps using the `MapView` component, and that you can access more advanced native features, such as geolocation using React Native's Geolocation API. We'll demonstrate these capabilities by adding the ability to capture and save current GPS coordinates with each new note. Note that the next two chapters will focus on iOS development, as the feature set for Android is not complete.

In this chapter we will cover the following topics:

- Learning how to get the current geolocation
- Listening for changes to the user's position
- Ensuring that our app requires appropriate permissions
- Saving location data with each note
- Displaying the original locations of all the notes on a `MapView`

Let's get started!

Introducing the Geolocation API

React Native provides an easy-to-use abstraction over the native Geolocation APIs. It follows the **MDN (Mozilla Developer Network)** specification, which recommends the following geolocation interface:

```
navigator.geolocation.getCurrentPosition(success, error, options)
```

This method `asynchronously` asks for the device's current location and will call the `success` callback with a `Position` object if it is successful and the `error` callback if it fails (usually, due to misconfigured permissions in your app or the user explicitly rejecting the request to allow your app to know their location). The `options` argument allows you to request higher position accuracy, define how long you're willing to wait for a response, and specify the maximum age of cached data that you're willing to accept:

```
navigator.geolocation.watchPosition(success, error, options)
```

This function enables you to register a function that will be called each time the position changes. This function returns an integer that represents the `ID` of the callback you registered. This allows you to stop listening for updates by calling the following:

```
navigator.geolocation.clearWatch(id);
```

The location permission in iOS

Before we begin integrating geolocation into our notes, we need to configure a permission to request the user's location. From Xcode, open `info.plist` and make sure that the `NSLocationWhenInUseUsageDescription` key is located in the file (it should be enabled by default):

View controller-based status bar appearance	⬍	Boolean	NO
NSLocationWhenInUseUsageDescription	⬍ ⊕ ⊖	String	⬍ ReactNotes would like to access your location.
▶ App Transport Security Settings	⬍ ⊕ ⊖	Dictionary	(1 item)

Once the application starts up, you should see a permission modal automatically pop up in the center of the screen:

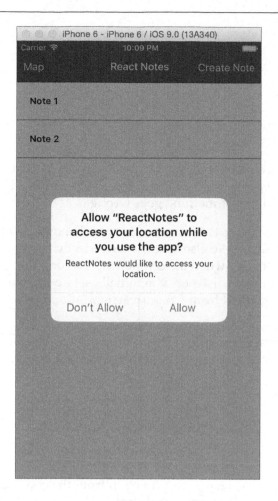

Tagging notes with geolocation

Let's take geolocation for a spin and start capturing the user's location when they save a new note. Since we're going to be using the location data when we save notes, we'll add our code to the `ReactNotes` component in `index.ios.js` or `index.android.js`. Let's begin by adding a function called `trackLocation()`:

```
class ReactNotes extends React.Component {
  trackLocation() {
    navigator.geolocation.getCurrentPosition(
      (initialPosition) => this.setState({initialPosition}),
      (error) => alert(error.message)
    );
```

```
    this.watchID =
      navigator.geolocation.watchPosition((lastPosition) => {
        this.setState({lastPosition});
      });
  }

  ...

}
```

Here we call `getCurrentPosition` and provide a callback that will update the current state with the position information returned from the device. We also provide an error handler if something goes wrong.

Next, we use `watchPosition()` to register an event handler that will be called when the user's position changes. We also save the `watchId` that is returned from this call, so that we can stop listening when the component has been unmounted. It is generally good practice to clear up any listeners you initially set up in your constructor or `componentDidMount` method from the `componentWillUnmount` function:

```
class ReactNotes extends React.Component {
  componentWillUnmount() {
    navigator.geolocation.clearWatch(this.watchID);
  }
  trackLocation() {

    ...

  }
  ...
}
```

Then, we'll call our `trackLocation()` function from the constructor and add some notes with the position data to our initial state:

```
class ReactNotes extends React.Component {
  constructor (props) {
    super(props);
    StatusBarIOS.setStyle('light-content');

    this.state = {
      notes: {
        1: {
          title: "Note 1",
          body: "body",
          id: 1,
          location: {
            coords: {
```

```
            latitude: 33.987,
            longitude: -118.47
          }
        }
      },
      2: {
        title: "Note 2",
        body: "body",
        id: 2,
        location: {
          coords: {
            latitude: 33.986,
            longitude: -118.46
          }
        }
      }
    }
  };

  this.loadNotes();
  this.trackLocation();
}
```

Saving the position data with a note requires a minor adjustment to our
updateNote() function:

```
updateNote(note) {
  var newNotes = Object.assign({}, this.state.notes);

  if (!note.isSaved) {
    note.location = this.state.lastPosition;
  }

  note.isSaved = true;
  newNotes[note.id] = note;
  this.setState({notes:newNotes});
  this.saveNotes(newNotes);
}
```

That's all there is to it! Reload the app, create a new note, and the GPS coordinates
will be stored when the note is saved for the first time. But how can we visualize the
position data associated with each of our notes? Let's make a MapView to display pins
for each note!

The complete documentation of geolocation can be found in the React Native documentation at `https://facebook.github.io/react-native/docs/geolocation.html`.

NoteLocationScreen

Now, since we are capturing the location of the user on note creation, we want to display this information in a useful manner. Location data perfectly matches up with showing the notes on a map UI. This way the user can visually see all of the notes that they have created. We are going to create a new component called `NoteLocationScreen` to house our note locations, but before writing the code for this screen, let's begin by adding the navigation.

On the home screen, we want to have a **Map** button in the `navbar` to transition to the `NoteLocationScreen`. Update the `LeftButton` and `Title` in `NavigationBarRouteMapper` to the following:

```
var NavigationBarRouteMapper = {
  LeftButton: function(route, navigator, index, navState) {
    switch (route.name) {
      case 'home':
        return (
          <SimpleButton
            onPress={() => navigator.push({name:
              'noteLocations'})}
            customText='Map'
            style={styles.navBarLeftButton}
            textStyle={styles.navBarButtonText}
          />
        );
      case 'createNote':
      case 'noteLocations':
        return (
          <SimpleButton
            onPress={() => navigator.pop()}
            customText='Back'
            style={styles.navBarLeftButton}
            textStyle={styles.navBarButtonText}
          />
        );
      default:
        return null;
    }
  },
```

```
...

    Title: function(route, navigator, index, navState) {
      switch (route.name) {
        case 'home':
          return (
            <Text style={styles.navBarTitleText}>React Notes</Text>
          );
        case 'createNote':
          return (
            <Text style={styles.navBarTitleText}>{route.note ?
              route.note.title : 'Create Note'}</Text>
          );
        case 'noteLocations':
          return (
            <Text style={styles.navBarTitleText}>Note
              Locations</Text>
          );
      }
    }
}
```

Here, we are defining a new route called `noteLocations`. Notice that we also want the `back` button to be displayed on the `noteLocation` route, so we include the case along with the `createNote` route.

If you haven't already, add a new `NoteLocationScreen.js` file to `App/Components/` and import it into `ReactNotes`. The last thing we need to do is include it in our `renderScene` function. We are going to pass it in the list of notes and the same `onSelectNote` function to our `NoteLocationScreen`:

```
import NoteLocationScreen from './App/Components/NoteLocationScreen';

...

class ReactNotes extends React.Component {
  ...

  renderScene(route, navigator) {
    switch (route.name) {
      case 'home':
        return (
          <HomeScreen navigator={navigator} notes={_(this.
state.notes).toArray()} onSelectNote={(note) => navigator.
push({name:"createNote", note: note})} />
```

```
          );
       case 'createNote':
         return (
           <NoteScreen note={route.note} onChangeNote={(note) => this.
updateNote(note)} />
         );
       case 'noteLocations':
         return (
           <NoteLocationScreen notes={this.state.notes}
onSelectNote={(note) => navigator.push({name:"createNote", note:
note})} />
         );
     }
   }


   ...


}
```

MapView

MapView is another component provided by React Native to display the map corresponding to each platform: Apple Maps on iOS and Google Maps on Android. You can start by adding the MapView to the NoteLocationScreen:

```
import React, {
  MapView,
  StyleSheet
} from 'react-native';

export default class NoteLocationScreen extends React.Component {
  render () {
    return (
      <MapView
        showsUserLocation={true}
        style={styles.map}
      />
    );
  }
}

var styles = StyleSheet.create({
  map: {
    flex: 1,
```

```
    marginTop: 64
  }
});
```

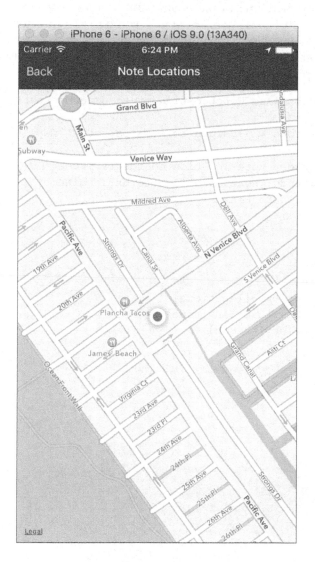

 If the map does not show your location on iOS, you may need
to enable locations in the simulator. Set a custom location by
navigating to **Debug** | **Location** | **Custom Location**.

The `showsUserLocation` function will zoom and display the location of the user on the map; by default, this value is `false`. Next, we want to gather all the notes locations to display them on our map using annotations. The annotation format accepts an object with `longitude`, `latitude`, some `title` information, and `on press` attributes. We will loop through the list of notes passed via props and extract the location data. The list of annotations is then passed to the MapView's `annotations` prop:

```
export default class NoteLocationScreen extends React.Component {
  render () {
    var locations = _.values(this.props.notes).map((note) => {
      return {
        latitude: note.location.coords.latitude,
        longitude: note.location.coords.longitude,
        title: note.title
      };
    });

    return (
      <MapView
        annotations={locations}
        showsUserLocation={true}
        style={styles.map}
      />
    );
  }
}
```

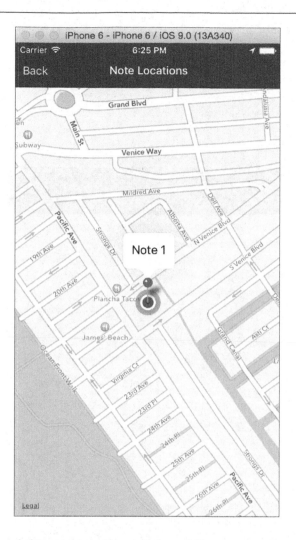

We can also add the ability to view the note by adding a `callout on press` function to the annotations. The `callout on press` method will invoke the `onNoteSelect` function we passed in and transition to the `NoteScreen`. Here we are adding a `left callout`:

```
export default class NoteLocationScreen extends React.Component {
  render () {
    var locations = _.values(this.props.notes).map((note) => {
      return {
        latitude: note.location.coords.latitude,
        longitude: note.location.coords.longitude,
        hasLeftCallout: true,
        onLeftCalloutPress: this.props.onSelectNote.bind(this,
          note),
```

```
            title: note.title
    };
  });

  ...

}
```

Check the React Native documentation for more details on `MapView` at
`https://facebook.github.io/react-native/docs/mapview.html`.

Summary

In this chapter, we explored more of React Native's built-in components and modules to capture the device-specific location data. The Geolocation API provides us the mechanism which hooks into the existing component life cycle to track user location. By incorporating this into our existing saved data, we can use the longitude and latitude values to display a map of where all of our notes were taken.

7
Integrating Native Modules

So far you've seen that React Native contains a large amount of functionality right out of the box. It provides an easy way for you to use a wide variety of native features via JavaScript, but sometimes you may need something that isn't yet covered by the built-in React Native components. Luckily, React Native is fully extensible via Native Modules. Thanks to a very active community, there is a growing list of custom components that are filling in the gaps. In this chapter, we'll use one of those third-party Native Modules to add camera support to our React Notes application.

In this chapter, we'll cover the following topics:

- Installing the custom React Native camera module using `npm`
- Adding a `CameraScreen` and camera component
- Saving captured images to disk
- Displaying the captured images in the `NoteImageScreen`

Adding images to notes

Our note-taking application is shaping up nicely, but a picture is worth a thousand words, so wouldn't it be nice if we could take a photo and store it with a note? Since React Native does not ship with a camera component, we'll need to use a very popular component created by *Lochlan Wansbrough*. The source code can be found at: `https://github.com/lwansbrough/react-native-camera`.

At this point, you are most likely familiar with the addition of new screens to our navigation. Let's quickly write the navigation code for the CameraScreen before we include the Native Module. In the NavigationBarRouteMapper, add the camera route to the LeftButton and Title attributes:

```
var NavigationBarRouteMapper = {
  LeftButton: function(route, navigator, index, navState) {
    switch (route.name) {
      case 'home':
        return (
          <SimpleButton
            onPress={() => navigator.push({name:
              'noteLocations'})}
            customText='Map'
            style={styles.navBarLeftButton}
            textStyle={styles.navBarButtonText}
          />
        );
      case 'createNote':
      case 'noteLocations':
      case 'camera':
        return (
          <SimpleButton
            onPress={() => navigator.pop()}
            customText='Back'
            style={styles.navBarLeftButton}
            textStyle={styles.navBarButtonText}
          />
        );
      default:
        return null;
    }
  },

  ...

  Title: function(route, navigator, index, navState) {
    switch (route.name) {
      case 'home':
        return (
          <Text style={styles.navBarTitleText}>React Notes</Text>
        );
      case 'createNote':
        return (
```

```
          <Text style={styles.navBarTitleText}>{route.note ?
            route.note.title : 'Create Note'}</Text>
        );
      case 'noteLocations':
        return (
          <Text style={styles.navBarTitleText}>
            Note Locations</Text>
        );
      case 'camera':
        return (
          <Text style={styles.navBarTitleText}>Take Picture</Text>
        );
    }
  }
};
```

Then, in the `ReactNotes` component update the `renderScene` method:

```
class ReactNotes extends React.Component {
  ...

  renderScene(route, navigator) {
    switch (route.name) {
      ...

      case 'createNote':
        return (
          <NoteScreen navigator={navigator} note={route.note}
onChangeNote={(note) => this.updateNote(note)} showCameraButton={true}
/>
        );

      case 'camera':
        return (
          <CameraScreen />
        );
    }
  }

  ...

}
```

We pass in another prop called `showCameraButton` to the `NoteScreen`, which we will use later to hide the camera button from the android version.

The same showCameraButton prop, except of value false, should be passed from the renderScene method for the Android version of ReactNotes: showCameraButton={false}.

Installing react-native-camera on iOS

There are three steps to install react-native-camera and to include it in our CameraScreen. From the command line, navigate to the ReactNotes directory and run the following command:

```
npm install react-native-camera@0.3.8 --save
```

If you take a look at the node_modules directory in the ReactNotes project you'll see a new directory named react-native-camera, which contains both the JavaScript and native source code of the module. In the ios subdirectory, you'll notice a file called RCTCamera.xcodeproj, as shown in the following screenshot:

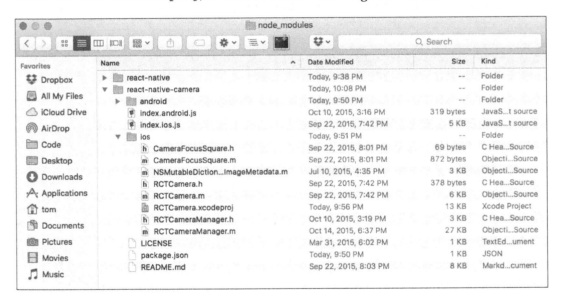

We need to add this file to our Xcode project's library. In the Xcode project navigator, right-click on **Libraries** and choose **Add Files to ReactNotes**:

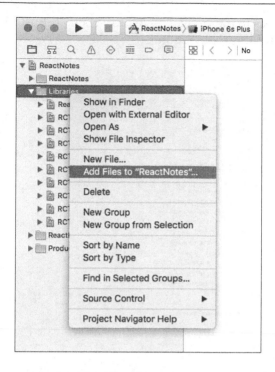

In the Finder window that appears, navigate to **ReactNotes | node_modules | react-native-camera | ios**, select **RCTCamera.xcodeproj** and click **Add**:

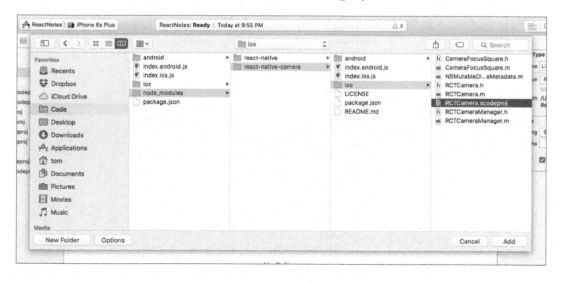

Take a look at the **Libraries** folder in the project navigator and you should see **RCTCamera.xcodeproj** in the list.

Next, select **ReactNotes** in the project navigator, click on **Build Phases** and expand the **Link Binary With Libraries** section:

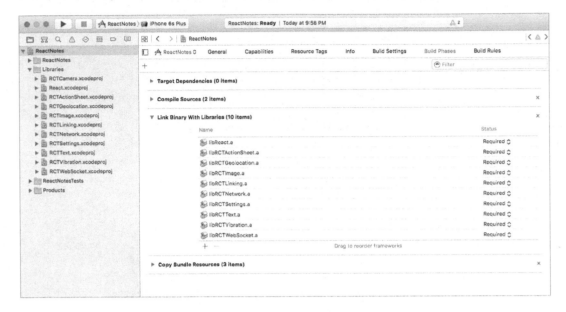

Click the plus sign at the bottom of the **Link Binary with Libraries section**, select **libRCTCamera.a** from the list and click **Add**:

We're now ready to use the camera component in our application.

Searching for Native Modules

A brief note before we start using the camera component is how you can find these modules on your own. The two best places to look for open source Native Modules are either on GitHub (https://github.com) or NPM (https://www.npmjs.com). A search on either of these sites will give you plenty of third-party modules created by the React Native community to use in your projects.

Using the camera component

The hard part is over! Importing the camera module is as simple as including any other React component:

```
import Camera from 'react-native-camera';
```

Using the Camera component is quite simple, as well. Here's the render function of the CameraScreen:

```
render () {
  return (
    <Camera
      captureTarget={Camera.constants.CaptureTarget.disk}
      ref="cam"
      style={styles.container}
    >
      <View style={styles.cameraButtonContainer}>
        <SimpleButton
          onPress={this._takePicture.bind(this)}
          customText="Capture"
          style={styles.cameraButton}
          textStyle={styles.cameraButtonText}
        />
      </View>
    </Camera>
  );
}
```

The Camera module exposes a number of props that you can use to customize its behavior but most of the default values work well for our purpose. However, you'll note that we set the `captureTarget` property to `Camera.constants.CaptureTarget.disk`. This setting will place the saved images into a directory on the device that only our `ReactNotes` application has access to. The default value for the `captureTarget` property is `Camera.constants.CaptureTarget.cameraRoll`, which will put the image in the shared location used by the native camera when you're taking pictures. Although that will normally be acceptable, at the time of this writing there is a bug that prevents ReactNative from loading images from that location.

Take a look at the code listing above. Notice that we've added child components to the camera component. It behaves just like a `View` component; you're now familiar with laying out children using the `Flexbox` attribute. In our example, we've added a `View` and a `SimpleButton` with an `onPress` handler that will capture the image:

```
_takePicture () {
  this.refs.cam.capture((err, data) => {
    if (err) return;
    this.props.onPicture(data);
  });
}
```

Recall that we added `ref="cam"` to the camera component declaration; thus, allowing us to refer to it in our handler. When we call the `capture()` function, we pass in a callback that takes two arguments, `err` (which should be null unless the user doesn't permit `ReactNotes` to use the camera) and data, which will include the full path to the image once it is saved to disk.

In order to save the path to the image along with the note, we'll need to pass the data up using `this.props.onPicture(data)`. We'll need to update our top-level `ReactNotes` component, but before we do that, here's the complete code for the CameraScreen:

```
import React, {
  StyleSheet,
  Text,
  View
} from 'react-native';

import Camera from 'react-native-camera';
import SimpleButton from './SimpleButton';

export default class CameraScreen extends React.Component {
  _takePicture () {
```

```
      this.refs.cam.capture((err, data) => {
        if (err) return;
        this.props.onPicture(data);
      });
    }

    render () {
      return (
        <Camera
          captureTarget={Camera.constants.CaptureTarget.disk}
          ref="cam"
          style={styles.container}
        >
          <View style={styles.cameraButtonContainer}>
            <SimpleButton
              onPress={this._takePicture.bind(this)}
              customText="Capture"
              style={styles.cameraButton}
              textStyle={styles.cameraButtonText}
            />
          </View>
        </Camera>
      );
    }
}

var styles = StyleSheet.create({
  container: {
    flex: 1,
    marginTop: 64
  },
  cameraButtonContainer: {
    position: 'absolute',
    bottom: 20,
    left: 20,
    right: 20
  },
  cameraButton: {
    backgroundColor: '#5B29C1',
    borderRadius: 4,
    paddingHorizontal: 20,
    paddingVertical: 15
  },
```

```
    cameraButtonText: {
      color: 'white',
      textAlign: 'center'
    }
  });
```

Return to `index.ios.js` and add the `onPicture` callback to the `CameraScreen` props:

```
renderScene(route, navigator) {
    switch (route.name) {
      case 'home':
        return (

        ...

      case 'camera':
        return (
          <CameraScreen onPicture={(imagePath) => this.
  saveNoteImage(imagePath, route.note)}/>
          );

      ...
      }
    }
}
```

We're passing in a callback that takes an `imagePath` and then calls `this.saveNoteImage(imagePath, route.note)`. Let's add that function just above `renderScene`:

```
saveNoteImage(imagePath, note) {
  note.imagePath = imagePath;
  this.updateNote(note);
}
```

This function simply takes the `imagePath`, adds it to the note object, and passes the modified note to our `updateNote()` function.

Now you can run the application in the simulator, click the **Take Picture** button and the screen becomes black! Don't worry, there's nothing wrong with your code; the iOS simulator doesn't have access to a camera, so it displays a black screen. However, if you click the **Capture** button, an image will be saved to your file system and when you return to view the image you'll actually see a white screen.

To verify if this works, you can `console.log` the `imagePath`, navigate to the image, modify the image, and then return to the `NoteImageScreen` to see your changes.

Viewing images

With images, it is important that they are getting saved to the `imagePath` attribute correctly, we want to be able to view them again. We will add another screen called `NoteImageScreen` that displays the image captured by the camera component. In the `App/Components/` directory, create the `NoteImageScreen.js` file. Same as before, we are going to include this in the navigation as shown:

```
import NoteImageScreen from './App/Components/NoteImageScreen';

var NavigationBarRouteMapper = {
  LeftButton: function(route, navigator, index, navState) {
    switch (route.name) {

      ...

      case 'createNote':
      case 'noteLocations':
      case 'camera':
      case 'noteImage':
        ...
    }
  },

  ...

  Title: function(route, navigator, index, navState) {
    switch (route.name) {

      ...

      case 'noteImage':
        return (
          <Text style={styles.navBarTitleText}>{`Image: ${route.note.
title}`}</Text>
        );
    }
  }
};

class ReactNotes extends React.Component {

  ...
```

```
renderScene(route, navigator) {
  switch (route.name) {

    ...

    case 'noteImage':
      return (
        <NoteImageScreen note={route.note} />
      );
  }
}


...


}
```

You might notice that in the title code for the `noteImage` route we use another ES6 feature known as string interpolation. This allows us to format a string directly between the back ticks `` `${variable}` `` with the value of a variable, in this case its `route.note.title`.

The image component

The Image component is provided by React Native to display images from various sources, such as the local disk or over a network. To render our image, all we have to do is pass in the `imagePath` from our note to the source prop. In the `ImageNoteScreen` add:

```
import React, {
  Image,
  View,
  StyleSheet
} from 'react-native';

export default class NoteImageScreen extends React.Component {
  render () {
    return (
      <View style={styles.container}>
        <Image
          source={{uri: this.props.note.imagePath}}
          style={styles.image}
        />
      </View>
    );
```

```
    }
  }

  var styles = StyleSheet.create({
    container: {
      flex: 1,
      marginTop: 64
    },
    image: {
      flex: 1
    }
  });
```

Here, we specify an object with an `uri` attribute to pass in the path. You can also use a `url` from the internet to render images this way also:

```
source={{uri: https://example.com/example.png}}
```

To require images locally just specify the path to the image:

```
source={require('./example.png')}
```

For more information on the Image component, see the React Native documentation at `https://facebook.github.io/react-native/docs/image.html`.

Deleting images

In case the user takes the wrong picture, we need a way to be able to remove the image from a note. Similar to the navigation of the `NoteScreen`, we are going to add a `delete` button to the right-hand side. In the `ReactNotes` component, we are going to add the `deleteNoteImage` method to remove the `imagePath` attribute from the note:

```
class ReactNotes extends React.Component {

  ...

  deleteNoteImage (note) {
    note.imagePath = null;
    this.updateNote(note);
  }

  saveNoteImage(imagePath, note) {
    note.imagePath = imagePath;
```

```
        this.updateNote(note);
    }

    ...

}
```

This looks similar to our `saveNoteImage` function, except that we are setting the value to `null`. Next, to add the button, we once again add the `noteImage` attribute to the `RightButton` function in `NavigationBarRouteMapper` and pass the `deleteNoteImage` function to the Navigator component:

```
var NavigationBarRouteMapper = {

    ...

    RightButton: function(route, navigator, index, navState) {
        switch (route.name) {

            ...

            case 'noteImage':
                return (
                    <SimpleButton
                        onPress={() => {
                            navigator.props.onDeleteNoteImage(route.note);
                            navigator.pop();
                        }}
                        customText='Delete'
                        style={styles.navBarRightButton}
                        textStyle={styles.navBarButtonText}
                    />
                );
            default:
                return null;
        }
    },

    ...

}

class ReactNotes extends React.Component {

    ...
```

```
    render () {
     return (
       <Navigator
         initialRoute={{name: 'home'}}
         renderScene={this.renderScene.bind(this)}
         navigationBar={
           <Navigator.NavigationBar
             routeMapper={NavigationBarRouteMapper}
             style={styles.navBar}
           />
         }
         onDeleteNote={(note) => this.deleteNote(note)}
         onDeleteNoteImage={(note) => this.deleteNoteImage(note)}
       />
     );
    }
   }
```

Connecting the final pieces

Now that we have `CameraScreen` and `ImageScreen`, we need to be able to navigate to them via the `NoteScreen`. We are going to add a button that will change the state based on the `imagePath` of the note. If it does not exist, then we want the user to transition to the `CameraScreen` and the `ImageScreen` when it does. Visually we are going to place the button in-line with the title input:

```
import SimpleButton = from './SimpleButton';

export default class NoteScreen extends React.Component {

  ...

  blurInputs () {
    this.refs.body.blur();
    this.refs.title.blur();
  }

  render () {
    var pictureButton = null;
    if (this.props.showCameraButton) {
      pictureButton = (this.state.note.imagePath) ? (
        <SimpleButton
          onPress={() => {
            this.blurInputs();
```

```
                 this.props.navigator.push({
                   name: 'noteImage',
                   note: this.state.note
                 });
               }}
             customText="View Picture"
             style={styles.takePictureButton}
             textStyle={styles.takePictureButtonText}
           />
         ) : (
           <SimpleButton
             onPress={() => {
               this.blurInputs();
               this.props.navigator.push({
                 name: 'camera',
                 note: this.state.note
               });
             }}
             customText="Take Picture"
             style={styles.takePictureButton}
             textStyle={styles.takePictureButtonText}
           />
         );
       }

       return (
         <View style={styles.container}>
           <View style={styles.inputContainer}>
             <TextInput
               ref="title"
               autoFocus={true}
               autoCapitalize="sentences"
               placeholder="Untitled"
               style={[styles.textInput, styles.title]}
               onEndEditing={(text) => {this.refs.body.focus()}}
               underlineColorAndroid="transparent"
               value={this.state.note.title}
               onChangeText={(title) => this.updateNote(title, this.
       state.note.body)}
             />

             {pictureButton}
```

```
        </View>
        . . .

      </View>
    );
  }
}
```

Note that if the `showCameraButton` prop is enabled, we render a different button to indicate the next step to the user based on the existence of the `imagePath`. Each of the corresponding functions on the `SimpleButtons` will push the camera or `noteImage` route onto the navigator stack.

 `blurInputs` is a function that we defined to disable the focus on the `TextInputs` and to hide the keyboard when transitioning to the next screen.

The styles for the button are similar to what we have had before. The main difference is the padding around the text:

```
var styles = StyleSheet.create({

  . . .

  takePictureButton: {
    backgroundColor: '#5B29C1',
    borderColor: '#48209A',
    borderWidth: 1,
    borderRadius: 4,
    paddingHorizontal: 10,
    paddingVertical: 5,
    shadowColor: 'darkgrey',
    shadowOffset: {
        width: 1,
        height: 1
    },
    shadowOpacity: 0.8,
    shadowRadius: 1
  },
  takePictureButtonText: {
    color: 'white'
  }
});
```

We can place the button in the same line as the `TextInput` since the `inputContainer` style we defined earlier has a `flexDirection` of row, as shown:

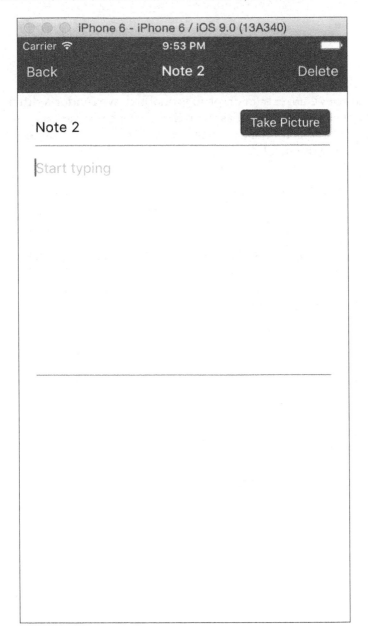

Summary

In this chapter, you learned that even if React Native lacks a feature you need, you'll be able to find a Native Module that suits your needs. In our case, we need camera support for our note taking the application and we showed you how to install a great third-party module via `npm`. We created a new screen for our Camera component and wired it up to our note saving mechanism to store the path of the image that is captured. We then created a `NoteImage` screen to view the captured image and added a way to delete the images we captured.

Facebook exposes native device functionality in exactly the same way that react-native-camera does. If you're curious, you can take a look at the very simple vibration module that ships with React Native: `https://github.com/facebook/react-native/tree/master/Libraries/Vibration`. Even if you do not consider yourself an Objective-C, Swift, or Java programmer, don't be afraid to try creating a Native Module yourself—you might be surprised by how easy it is!

8
Releasing the Application

The first version of our application is complete, which means that we are ready to go through the process of creating the production builds. In this chapter, we will start by showing you how to generate and run the application off of a static JavaScript bundle. Then, in preparation for the App Store, we will use Xcode to build our iOS release. Lastly, for Android we will walk through the set of command-line tools and scripts provided by React Native to build the final APK.

In this chapter, we will cover the following:

- Generating the static bundle for iOS
- Using the `static bundle` in place of `react-native start`
- Building a release in Xcode
- Signing and building the Android release APK

Generating the static bundle in iOS

So far, we have been serving the application's static bundle (where all of our JavaScript code lives) from a node server started by either Xcode or a terminal using `react-native start`. Before we create releases for iOS and Android, we need to generate the static JS bundle that our application will load. We will begin by creating the release in iOS; for Android, skip to the `generating the Android APK` section.

Once again, we are going to use the `react-native-cli` and execute the `bundle` command. The `bundle` command requires three flags: `c`, `platform`, and `bundle-output`. The `entry-file` specifies the path to the root component, the platform is either iOS or Android, and `bundle-output` is the path to place the generated bundle.

From the terminal in the root directory, run `react-native bundle` with an `entry-file` of `index.ios.js`, platform `iOS`, and point the path of the `bundle-output` to `ios/main.jsbundle`:

```
$ react-native bundle --entry-file index.ios.js --platform ios
--bundle-output ios/main.jsbundle
bundle: Created ReactPackager
bundle: Closing client
bundle: start
bundle: finish
bundle: Writing bundle output to: ios/main.jsbundle
bundle: Done writing bundle output
```

Assets destination folder is not set, skipping...

More details about `react-native bundle` for iOS can be found in the React Native documentation at `https://facebook.github.io/react-native/docs/running-on-device-ios.html#using-offline-bundle`.

Testing the static bundle in iOS

First, we need to test that the static bundle can be loaded by our iOS application in the simulator. Open `AppDelegate.m` in Xcode and take a look at the following code and comments:

```
 * Loading JavaScript code - uncomment the one you want.
 *
 * OPTION 1
 * Load from development server. Start the server from the
repository root:
 *
 * $ npm start
 *
 * To run on device, change `localhost` to the IP address of your
computer
 * (you can get this by typing `ifconfig` into the terminal and
selecting the
 * `inet` value under `en0:`) and make sure your computer and iOS
device are
 * on the same Wi-Fi network.
 */

  jsCodeLocation = [NSURL URLWithString:@"http://localhost:8081/index.
ios.bundle?platform=ios&dev=true"];

  /**
   * OPTION 2
```

```
    * Load from pre-bundled file on disk. To re-generate the static
bundle
    * from the root of your project directory, run
    *
    * $ react-native bundle --minify
    *
    * see http://facebook.github.io/react-native/docs/runningondevice.
html
    */


//   jsCodeLocation = [[NSBundle mainBundle] URLForResource:@"main"
withExtension:@"jsbundle"];
```

The various methods of loading the JavaScript bundle are outlined here. We are interested in OPTION 2, loading a pre-bundled file from the disk. Comment out the jsCodeLocation statement from OPTION 1 and uncomment the second in OPTION 2:

```
// jsCodeLocation = [NSURL URLWithString:@"http://localhost:8081/
index.ios.bundle?platform=ios&dev=true"];
...


jsCodeLocation = [[NSBundle mainBundle] URLForResource:@"main"
withExtension:@"jsbundle"];
```

Make sure that no react-native start terminal sessions are running, then build and run the application from Xcode (*Cmd + R*). You should be at the top of the simulator to indicate that it is loading from a pre-bundled file:

Creating an iOS release in Xcode

In order to submit to the AppStore, we need to build our application for distribution. Luckily, the Xcode project we initially created with `react-native init` has some of this preconfigured for us. First, we want to change our **Build Configuration** to **disable** features, such as the developer menu that we get while we are debugging.

Let's configure the iOS release:

1. In Xcode, navigate to **Product | Scheme | Edit Scheme...** and select **Run**, and under the **Info** tab change **Build Configuration** from **Debug** to **Release**:

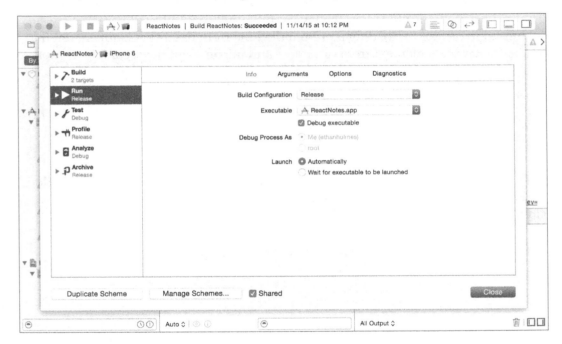

2. Target the **iOS Device** instead of the simulator:

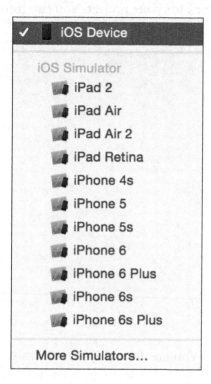

3. Finally, run the build from **Product | Archive**. The **Organizer** window will open a list of archives for your project. You can return to this screen later by selecting **Window | Organizer** from the top menu:

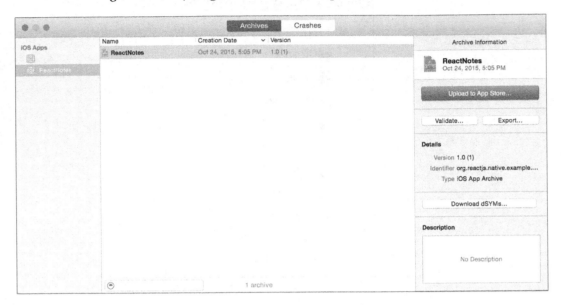

4. In the future, when you create multiple releases, you should increase the version number found in **Targets | ReactNotes | General**. For the purposes of our first release, this can be disregarded:

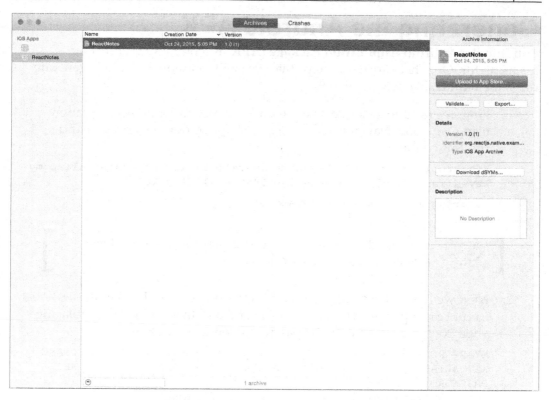

Once your build has been archived, it is ready to be submitted to the
Apple App Store. This module doesn't cover the application to the App
Store but the next steps will be available on the Apple developer website
at `https://developer.apple.com`.

Generating the Android APK

Building the **Android Application Package (APK)** is a bit more cryptic than releasing for iOS. There are a few steps that we need to follow before we generate the static bundle, like we did in iOS:

1. First, we need to generate a key that we can use to sign our application using `keytool`. Navigate to the `android/app` folder in a terminal and run this command:

   ```
   $ keytool -genkey -v -keystore my-release-key.keystore -alias my-key-alias -keyalg RSA -keysize 2048 -validity 10000

   [Storing my-release-key.keystore]
   ```

    Note that this is a private file and should never be shared with anyone. Keep it somewhere safe!

2. Next we have a few configuration files to update. Up a level in the `android/` directory open `gradle.properties` and add these four lines, replacing `YOUR_KEY_PASSWORD` with the password you used for `keytool`:

   ```
   MYAPP_RELEASE_STORE_FILE=my-release-key.keystore MYAPP_RELEASE_
   KEY_ALIAS=my-key-alias MYAPP_RELEASE_STORE_PASSWORD=YOUR_KEY_
   PASSWORD
   MYAPP_RELEASE_KEY_PASSWORD= YOUR_KEY_PASSWORD
   ```

3. Add the following in `android/app/build.gradle`:

   ```
   android {
       ...

       signingConfigs {
           release {
               storeFile file(MYAPP_RELEASE_STORE_FILE)
               storePassword MYAPP_RELEASE_STORE_PASSWORD
               keyAlias MYAPP_RELEASE_KEY_ALIAS
               keyPassword MYAPP_RELEASE_KEY_PASSWORD
           }
       }
       buildTypes {
           release {
               ...
               signingConfig signingConfigs.release
           }
       }
   }
   ```

4. Now, we can generate the static bundle for Android. Create a new directory `android/app/src/main/assets/` and run this modified form of the `react-native bundle` command:

```
react-native bundle --platform android --dev false --entry-file
index.android.js --bundle-output android/app/src/main/assets/
index.android.bundle --assets-dest android/app/src/main/res/
```

This gives the following output:

```
$ react-native bundle --platform android --dev false --entry-file
index.android.js --bundle-output android/app/src/main/assets/
index.android.bundle --assets-dest android/app/src/main/res/

Building package...

transforming [========================================] 100%
326/326

Build complete

Successfully saved bundle to android/app/src/main/assets/index.
android.bundle
```

5. Build the final APK in the `android/` directory using the `gradle` command:

```
./gradlew assembleRelease
```

If you have set up the key signing correctly, you can test your release in the simulator or on a device with the following:

```
./gradlew installRelease
```

6. With this, we have our final release APK (that can be found in `android/app/build/outputs/apk/app-release.apk`). Check out the launch checklist on Android developers for more information on the Play Store submission process at `https://developer.android.com/distribute/tools/launch-checklist.html`.

Summary

In this chapter, you learned how to build a release of our application in preparation for submitting it to the App Store or Google Play Store. iOS had a pre-configuration scheme in Xcode to disable the developer features. We then created an archive by targeting the iOS device. On Android, we created a private release key with **keytool** and built the release APK using the command line and `gradle`. It is important to follow up and test that both of these release builds work before submission, to decrease the likelihood of rejection.

We hope that this module gave you the fundamentals you need to start creating mobile apps with React Native. Although React and React Native are still very early in terms of development, you can expect the core concepts discussed in this module to stay relevant for some time to come. When Android finally reaches feature parity with iOS, the doors will open for a lot more rapid development between the two platforms. Good luck, and we can't wait to see your apps out there on the App and Google Play Stores!

Module 3

Ionic Framework By Example

Build amazing cross-platform mobile apps with Ionic, the HTML5 framework that makes modern mobile application development simple

Module 3

1
First Look at Ionic

Before we begin this module, it is very important that we understand just exactly what we are dealing with. The best way to understand this is by having a short history on mobile development, in general, and understand how tools like Ionic help mobile developers create beautiful mobile apps.

The beginning

The year 2006 saw the beginning of the smartphone era with the launch of the iPhone by Apple. By 2008, Google had launched its answer to Apple's iOS operating system. This new operating system was called **Android**, and by 2010, it was clear that smartphones running iOS and Android dominantly covered the mobile ecosystem. Fast forward to today, the dominance of iOS and Android is not so different even though Windows for mobile by Microsoft has made some gains on the mobile front. It is fair to say that Android, iOS, and Windows make up the majority of the ecosystem with the first two at the forefront by a large margin.

The launch of the smartphone era also gave birth to the concept of mobile applications. Mobile apps are the medium by which we deliver and obtain most of our content on mobile phones. They are great and everyone with a smartphone pretty much has a number of apps downloaded on their devices to perform specific actions or achieve specific goals. This was massive for developers, and the software vendors also provided tools that enabled developers to create their own third-party mobile apps for users. We refer to these applications, built using the tools provided by the software vendors, as **native mobile applications**.

The problem

As great as mobile apps are, there is a small problem with how they are developed. Firstly, for each mobile development platform, the software vendor provides its own unique set of tools to build applications for its platforms. We know these tools as SDKs. The following table shows how each platform differs in terms of tools and SDK options to create native mobile apps for their ecosystems:

Operating system	SDK	Programming language
iOS	iOS SDK	Objective-C/Swift
Android	Android SDK	JAVA
Windows for mobile	Windows SDK	.NET

To make a clear statement, we are not trying to downplay the use of native tools. As noted earlier, native tools are great but come with a great cost and time constraint. Firstly, you are unable to build the same app for different platforms with the same set of tools. For the Android version of your app, you will need a team of skilled android developers. For the iOS version of your app, you will need a team of Objective-C or Swift developers to create the iOS version of the same app. Also, there is no code sharing between these two teams, meaning that a feature developed on one platform will have to be completely developed on the other platform again. This is highly inefficient in terms of development and very time consuming.

Another problem is that because you are hiring two separate teams that are completely independent of one another even though they are both trying to create the same thing, you are left with a growing cost. For example, if you decided you wanted to create a Windows for mobile version of your mobile app, you will need to recruit another team of .NET developers and they will have to build everything present on the other existing platforms from scratch since they cannot reuse any of the already built tools.

For a company like Facebook, which makes revenue in the billions, it might make sense to go down the native path as cost and talent for native development would probably not be a part of their concern. However, for the most part, not everyone building or trying to build a mobile app is a company like Facebook. Most people want to get a simple, great, powerful app out there as quick as possible. Furthermore, some of these people want to use their preexisting skill set to build apps for multiple platforms without having to learn new programming languages.

Before mobile applications, web apps ruled the world for the most part. We had more people developing for the web technologies consisting mostly of HTML, CSS, and JavaScript. One great thing we got used to with the web was that it was platform independent. This meant that as long as you had a browser application on any device, you were able to interact with any web application without any problem.

So when mobile apps came, it was a big change for most web developers because with mobile apps, each platform was self-dependent, and apps made for one platform would not work for another platform.

Apache Cordova

Apache Cordova is a technology that lets any web application be packaged as a native mobile application while also providing access to device features. Thanks to Adobe and the open source community, this technology has seen great growth over the years and more and more apps are being built with Cordova. The apps built with Cordova are commonly referred to as **hybrid applications**. But what is a hybrid app?

A hybrid application in the context of Cordova is actually a web app that lives within the thin container of a native mobile application.

In reality, the only difference between a native mobile app and a web application in terms of what they can do is the fact that the native mobile app has access to the device hardware features.

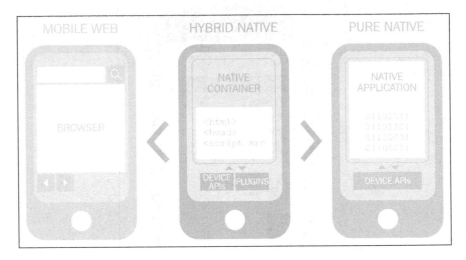

In truth, a hybrid app is actually a native app that serves up a web application on the phone's web view. It behaves and acts like a normal application and has complete device access, thanks to Cordova.

However, the main advantage that Cordova has over native development techniques is that you only have to maintain one code base, and can use that same code base to build applications for multiple platforms. This was and still is the main selling point of Cordova to date, as with this technique you are provided with a big cost and time saving advantage.

Early hybrid apps

When the first few hybrid apps started rolling out, there were a couple of problems that seemed to persist. The first problem was that a lot of people complained that these hybrid applications did not have the same user interface and user experience as native mobile apps. The major reason for this was that when building a native app, all the building blocks are already provided for you. For example, we have things like pre-provided animations, swipe gestures, tabs, and so on. Hybrid apps failed to provide similar features like these because on the web, all we have is HTML, CSS, and JS. There is no pre-provided component for things like animations, gestures, and tabs.

This meant that pretty much anyone trying to build a hybrid app had to build these features from scratch. This was not very good and different people had different implementations of the same features. As a result, a lot of applications that were built by the hybrid way were not so visually appealing. What we needed was a framework that was centrally maintained that provided us with all the tools we needed to build features that native apps had with web technologies.

What is Ionic?

Ionic is a framework that lets you build hybrid mobile applications with web technologies like HTML5, CSS, and JavaScript. But that is not where it stops with Ionic. Ionic provides you with components that you can use to build native-like features for your mobile applications. Think of Ionic as the SDK for making your Hybrid mobile application. Most of the features you have on a native app such as modals, gestures, popups, and many more, are all provided to you by Ionic and can be easily extended for new features or customized to suit your needs.

Ionic itself does not grant you the ability to communicate with device features like GPS and camera; instead, it works side-by-side with Cordova to achieve this. Another great feature of Ionic is how loosely coupled all its components are. You can decide to use only some of Ionic on an already existing hybrid application if you wish to do so.

The Ionic framework is built with AngularJS, which is arguably the most well-tested and widely-used JavaScript framework out there. This feature is particularly powerful as it gives you all the goodness of Angular as part of any Ionic app you develop. In the past, architecting hybrid applications proved to be difficult, but with Angular, we can create our mobile applications using the **Single Page Application** (**SPA**) technique. Angular also makes it really easy to organize your application for the development and working across teams while providing you the possibility of easily adding custom features or libraries.

Short history of Ionic

Before we dive in, first let's revisit what we already know about hybrid applications and how they work. Remember that a hybrid mobile application is simply a web application that runs in a web view, within a thin native wrapper environment.

Also remember that native apps came with already built components that enabled you to create beautiful user interfaces for mobile applications. Since hybrid apps used web technologies, there was no SDK or components provided for creating mobile UIs. The Ionic team saw this problem and created a solution in the form of the Ionic framework. The Ionic framework provides UI components to build beautiful hybrid applications.

Features of Ionic

Ionic provides you with a lot of cool neat features and tricks that help you create beautiful and well functioning hybrid apps in no time. The features of Ionic come under three categories:

- CSS features
- JavaScript features
- Ionic CLI

CSS features

To start off, Ionic comes stock with a great CSS library that provides you with some boilerplate styles. These Ionic CSS styles are generated with **SASS**, a CSS preprocessor for more advanced CSS style manipulation.

Some of the cool CSS features that come built-in with Ionic include:

- Buttons
- Cards
- Header and footers
- Lists
- Forms elements
- Grid system

All these features and more, are already provided for you and are easily customizable. They also have the same look and feel that native equivalents have so you will not have to do any editing to make them look like native components.

JavaScript features

The JavaScript features are at the very heart of the Ionic framework and essential for building Ionic apps. They also consist of other features that let you do things from under the hood like customize your application or even provide you with helper functions you can use to make developing your app more pleasant. A lot of these JavaScript features actually exist as HTML custom elements that make it easy to declaratively use these features.

Some of these features include:

- Modal
- Slide box

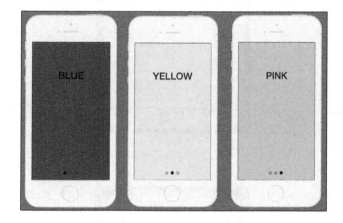

- Action sheet

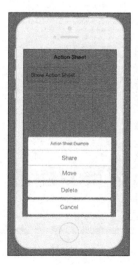

- Side menu

- Tabs

- Complex lists

- Collection repeat

All the JavaScript features of Ionic are built with Angular, and most can be easily plugged in as Angular directives. Each of them also perform different actions that help you achieve specific functions and are all documented in the Ionic website.

The Ionic CLI

This is the final part that makes up the three major arms of the Ionic framework. The Ionic CLI is a very important tool that lets you use the Ionic commands via the command line/terminal. It is also with the Ionic CLI that we get access to some Ionic features that make our app development process more streamlined. It is arguably the most important part of Ionic and it is also the feature you will use to do most actions.

Ionic CLI features let you do the following:

- Create Ionic projects
- Issue Cordova commands
- Development and testing
- Ionic splash/Icon generator

- Ionic labs
- SASS
- Upload app to Ionic view
- Access `Ionic.IO` tools

The Ionic CLI is a very powerful tool and most of the time, it is the tool we will be using throughout this module to perform specific actions. This is why the first thing we are going to do is set up the Ionic CLI.

Setting up Ionic

The following steps will give a brief of how to setup Ionic:

1. **Install NodeJS**: To set up Ionic, the first thing you will need to do is to install NodeJS on your computer so you can have access to **Node Package Manager (NPM)**. If you already have node installed on your computer, you can skip this step and go to step 2. To install NodeJS on your computer, perform the following steps:

    1. Go to `www.nodejs.org` and click on the latest stable version for your computer. That should download the latest version of NodeJS on your computer. Don't worry if you are on Mac, PC, or Linux, the correct one for your operating system will be automatically downloaded.

    2. After the download is finished, install the downloaded software on your computer. You might need to restart your computer if you are running Windows.

    3. Open up the terminal if you are on Mac/Linux or the Windows command line if you are on a Windows machine. Type the command `node -v` and press *Enter*.

    You should see the version number of your current installation of NodeJS. If you do not see a version number, this might mean that you have not correctly installed NodeJS and should try running step 1 again.

2. **Install Ionic CLI**: The next step is to use NPM to install the Ionic CLI.

    1. Open a new terminal (OS X and Linux) or command-line (Windows) window and run the following command: `npm install ionic -g`. If you are on Linux/OS X, you might need to run `sudo npm install ionic -g`. This command will aim to install Ionic globally.

2. After this has finished running, run the command `ionic -v` on your terminal/command line and press *Enter*.

You should see a version number of your Ionic CLI. This means that you have Ionic installed correctly and are good to go. If you are on a Windows machine, you might need to restart your machine to see the version number appear.

If you did not see a version number, then you do not have Ionic installed correctly on your machine and should do step 2 again.

Summary

In this chapter, we started off by getting to know a bit of background about mobile applications in general. We learned how native mobile applications work, how they are built with native SDKs, and how each platform is built with a completely different set of tools without any resource sharing between them all. We then went ahead and discussed briefly about Apache Cordova and how it aimed to solve the problem of cross-platform development.

We then discussed exactly what Ionic means and what problems it aims to solve. We also got to discuss the CSS, JS, and Ionic CLI features of the Ionic framework lightly.

In the next chapter, we will be creating our very first Ionic application with the Ionic CLI, and we will create a nice to-do list style application with some great Ionic features.

2
To-Do List App

In this chapter, we will be diving headfirst into Ionic and will be using a lot of the Ionic CLI tool. We will create our first Ionic application and add some basic Ionic features to our app. We will also get to run our app for the first time using Ionic and will debug our app in Chrome. We will finish this chapter by creating a to-do list application with Ionic. This application will simply let us add items to our app and also provide us a way of deleting these items or marking them as done.

Creating our first application

Creating a new project with Ionic is actually a very pain-free experience with the Ionic CLI. There are different ways to create a new Ionic project but the easiest and more standard technique is to use the Ionic templates. This is by far the easiest way, and it let us use any of the three standard templates provided by Ionic.

These templates include:

- **The blank template**: This creates a new project with some boilerplate code to help you get set up with a blank application
- **The tabs template**: This is the same as the first but instead of a blank application, you get an application with a tabbed design
- **The side menu template**: This creates a new application with a side menu design and some boilerplate

We will be using each of these in this module at some point of time. For now, we are going to start with the first and create a brand new Ionic project using the blank template. Before we move on, let's have a look at the command that the Ionic CLI uses to create a new application:

```
ionic create [Name Of App] [template]
```

The `create` command for the Ionic CLI allows us to provide two parameters, the first being the name we want our app to be called. This first parameter will also be the name given to the folder that gets generated with our files. The second parameter is the template name. As discussed earlier, there are three template styles. You can either pass in blank, tabs, or side menu as a parameter to represent the type of template you want your app to be generated with.

Creating our to-do list app

We are going to create our to-do list application. We are going to use the blank template to do this. We will be calling our app `todo` for the sake of consistency. To create the `todo` app, go ahead and run the following command:

```
ionic start todo blank
```

This command will create a new blank Ionic application called `todo`. When this command has finished running, enter the project of your application via the command line by running the following command:

```
cd todo
```

To further explore our newly created `todo` app, open the `todo` app folder in your favorite IDE.

The Ionic workflow

When you create a new Ionic project, there are a couple of folders and files that come as stock as part of the generated project. Your directory should look similar to what is seen in the following screenshot:

The structure you see is pretty much the same as in every Cordova project, with the exception of a few files and folders. For example, there is a scss folder. This contains a file that lets us customize the look and feel of our application and will be covered in detail in later chapters. There are also the platforms and plugins folder. The platforms folder, in most cases is auto-generated, but we will not be covering them in this module so you can ignore them for the time being.

You will also notice that in your www/lib folder, there is a folder called ionic that contains all the required files to run Ionic. There are css, fonts, js, and scss folder.

- css: This folder contains all the default CSS that come with an Ionic app.
- fonts: Ionic comes with its own font and Icon library called **Ionicons**. This Ionicons library contains hundreds of icons, which are all available for use in your app.

- `js`: This contains all the code for the core Ionic library. Since Ionic is built with Angular, there is a version of Angular here with a bunch of other files that make up the Ionic framework.

- `scss`: This is the folder that contains SASS files that are used to build the beautiful Ionic framework CSS styles. Everything here can be overwritten easily in order to make your app feel a bit more customized and we will discuss how you can do this in *Chapter 7, Customizing the App*.

If you have a look at the root folder, you will see a lot of other files that are generated for you as part of the Ionic workflow. These files are not overly important now, but let's have a look at the more important ones in the following list:

- `bower.json`: This is the file that contains some of the dependencies acquired from the bower package manager. The browser dependencies are resolved in the `lib` folder as specified in the `bowerrc` file. This is a great place to specify other third-party dependencies that your project might need.

- `config.xml`: This is the standard `config` file that comes along with any Phonegap/Cordova project. This is where you request permissions for device features and also specify universal and platform-specific configurations for you app.

- `gulpfile`: Ionic uses the Gulp build tool, and this file contains some code that is provided by Ionic that enables you do some amazing things. We will use some features of this file in *Chapter 7, Customizing the App*, when we do some customization tasks.

- `ionic.project`: This is a file specific for Ionic services. It is the file used by the Ionic CLI and the `ionic.IO` services as a place to specify some of your Ionic-specific configuration. We will use some of the features of this file when we use the Ionic view app in *Chapter 3, Running Ionic Apps*.

- `package.json`: This is a file used by node to specify some node dependencies. When you create a project with the Ionic CLI, Ionic uses both the Node and Bower Package Manager to resolve some of your dependencies. If you require a node module when you are developing Ionic apps, you can specify these dependencies here.

These files are some of the more important files that are by default a part of a project created with the Ionic CLI. At the moment you do not need to worry too much about them, but it's always good to know that they exist and have an idea about what they actually represent.

In-depth look at our project

Before we go ahead and do any development, it is imperative that we understand how to actually add features to our app and where to do this. There are two files in particular that we are going to pay great attention to:

- `index.html`: This file is the entry point of your application in terms of what you actually see. It is a normal HTML page with some boilerplate code based on the blank Ionic template. If you pay close attention, you will see some custom HTML tags such as `<ion-pane>`, `<ion-header>`, and `<ion-content>`. These custom tags are actually Ionic components that have been built with Angular, and for now, you need not worry about what they do as we will be discussing this shortly. A closer look at the `<body>` tag will also reveal the attribute `ng-app=starter`. This is a custom attribute provided by Angular, which we use to provide the name of the main module of an angular application.

- `app.js`: This file lives in the `js` folder, and this is the file that contains the main module of our application. In Angular, modules provide us a way to create isolated chunks of code that our application uses. The main module is the module that actually gets loaded to our application when it starts. Think of the main module as the entry point of our application. If you take a closer look at the `app.js` file, you will see how we create the module and specify its name as starter:

```
angular.module('starter', ['ionic'])

.run(function($ionicPlatform) {
  $ionicPlatform.ready(function() {
    // Hide the accessory bar by default (remove this to
    show the accessory bar above the keyboard
    // for form inputs)
    if(window.cordova && window.cordova.plugins.Keyboard) {
      cordova.plugins.Keyboard
      .hideKeyboardAccessoryBar(true);
    }
    if(window.StatusBar) {
      StatusBar.styleDefault();
    }
  });
})
```

You will also see that it takes a second parameter, an array which contains one string called `ionic`. In Angular, this array is used to provide the names of any module that our application depends on. So, just like we specified the name of our main module, starter to the `ng-app` attribute in the `index.html` file, we specify a list of modules that our main module relies on, in this case, `ionic`.

You would have also noticed a `run` function in the `app.js`. This function is the function that fires as soon as our app is ready and all our dependent Angular modules and factories have loaded. The `run` function is a great place to do little pieces of tidying up that you want done as soon as your application begins.

These two files are the ones you need to worry about as they are the two main files we will be working with in order to build our to-do list application.

Envisioning our app

It is always good to do a small bit of wireframing before you build any application. This enables you to understand how the app will work and how it will probably look just before you actually begin to code the app. The following screenshot is a rough wireframe of what our `todo` app will look like:

Our `todo` application allows a user to simply enter any task they want added to their to-do list. Think of this app as a mini diary where you put in things you want done later. In this section, we will only be building the very basic feature of our `todo` app, and we will only be allowing the user to add new items. In later chapters, as we learn more about Ionic, we will be adding more complex features like using a complex list and also letting the user edit, remove, and even archive to-do list items.

Building our todo app

To get started with building our `todo` app, we will need to further break down what we want to achieve into smaller steps. The first thing we need to do is to create the UI for our application.

Creating the UI

The first thing we are going to do to get started with building our `todo` application is building the user interface. We are going to build the input form and the button that will add the `todo` item currently typed in the input. After we have written the code for this, we will add the markup for the list where we want any entered `todo` item to be displayed. I have already compiled this markup for you in the following code:

```
<div class="list">
    <div class="item item-input-inset">
        <label class="item-input-wrapper">
            <input type="text" placeholder="enter todo item">
        </label>
        <button class="button button-small">
            Add
        </button>
    </div>
</div>
<ul class="list">
    <li class="item">

    </li>
</ul>
```

From the preceding code, you can see the skin of our user interface ready. We have an input that receives what we want entered into our to-do list. We have an HTML unordered list that will be placed where our to-do list items will be situated. You can see some classes on some of our elements. These are actually classes from the auto-generated Ionic CSS styles that come as part of any Ionic project.

The code

Since we have written the user interface for our application, we will also need to write the Angular code to enable it to work. What we need to do is to create an array that will hold the list of `todo` items and also create a function that will add a `todo` item into this list anytime we click the **Add** button we created earlier. We will achieve this all by creating an Angular controller in our main module and insert all this logic into it. I have already written this code and you can copy it and get it into your project from the following:

```
.controller('TodoController', function ($scope) {
  $scope.todos = [];
  $scope.todoModel = {};
  $scope.todoModel.todo = '';
  $scope.addTodo = function () {
    $scope.todos.push($scope.todoModel.todo);
    $scope.todoModel = {
        todo: ''
    };
  };
})
```

From the preceding code, you can see that we have created a controller called the `TodoController`. Within this `TodoController`, we have a `todos` array. This is the array that will hold all our `todo` items. We also have a `todoModel` object that is an empty object that will hold our entered `todo` item. Lastly, we have a function called `addTodo` that adds the current value in our `todoModel` object to our `todos` array and then sets the value of our current `todoModel` object to an empty string so we can type from scratch again.

Wiring things up

Now that we have created our user interface boilerplate code and also written our code for it, it is time to wire the two together and dictate what gets to appear where:

```
<ion-content ng-controller="TodoController">
    <div class="list">
        <div class="item item-input-inset">
            <label class="item-input-wrapper">
                <input type="text" placeholder="enter todo item"
                  ng-model="todoModel.todo">
            </label>
            <button class="button button-small" ng-
              click="addTodo()">
                Add
```

```
            </button>
        </div>
    </div>
    <ul class="list">
        <li class="item" ng-repeat="todo in todos track by
         $index">
            {{todo}}
        </li>
    </ul>
</ion-content>
```

If you have a look at the preceding code, you will see that the UI code now looks a bit different. Firstly, we have associated our `<ion-content>` element with our `TodoController`. This is done in order to create a binding context, meaning any variable within the `TodoController` is now available for data binding to all its descendants. Secondly, you will also notice that our input now has a new `ng-model` attribute that binds to our `todoModel` variable from our `TodoController`. This is binding the value of the input tag at any point in time to the `todoModel` object. Thirdly, we have set an `ng-click` attribute on the **add todo** button to ensure that any time it is clicked, a new `todo` item is added to our array. Finally, we have done an `ng-repeat` within the UL element to specify that we want all children of the `todo` array to be rendered with the LI.

With this, we have successfully completed the `todo` application and all that is left is to see it in action. We will be learning how to run this application we have just built-in different ways in the next chapter, so do follow up to learn how to get your app to run and test it live.

Summary

In this chapter, we got to create our very first Ionic application using the Ionic blank application template. We had a look at what the Ionic workflow looks like and also got to see some of the files that make up the workflow. We then dived in and discussed about how we intended to build our to-do list application. We further went ahead and actually implemented the UI of our to-do list app based on a wireframe. We wrote some Angular code and wired it up to the user interface we created.

In the next chapter, we will learn different ways to run and test our application for the very first time with the Ionic CLI.

3
Running Ionic Apps

In this chapter, we are going to learn how to test and run our Ionic application using various methods. We will start by learning to test our application using the simplest Ionic technique: by serving our app to the Chrome browser using the `ionic serve` command. We will then go ahead and use the Ionic view mobile app for iOS/ Android to see how we can test our application on a mobile device. Lastly, we will learn to run and deploy our Ionic application to a mobile device using the traditional build system of the native SDKs of our respective platforms.

Running our todo app

In the last chapter, we created our first Ionic application using the Ionic blank template. We worked on the application further, and made a to-do list app. We wrote some Angular code and had some initial exposure to some Ionic code. However, we did not get to see our application in action. There are many ways by which we can run an Ionic app, and the first technique we will be learning is the `ionic serve` technique.

The ionic serve technique

The `ionic serve` technique is the simplest way to see your app in action. It requires no extra setup after the Ionic CLI, and only requires you to have a web browser. We are now going to test our `todo` application, which we created in the preceding chapter using the `ionic serve` technique. To test your application with this technique, simply open a new command-line window and follow the following steps.

Browser choice

It is advisable that you use Google Chrome as your default browser. Google Chrome has some very powerful development tools and all exercises in this module expect that you have Google Chrome installed as your default browser. You can download a copy of Google Chrome by visiting this URL: `http://www.google.com/chrome`.

1. From your terminal, navigate to the root directory of your Ionic `todo` application.

2. Run the following command in your command-line window:

```
ionic serve
```

In case you are prompted to select an IP address, you can select any one from the list prompted and press *Enter* to initiate.

If you followed the steps correctly, you should see a browser window come up with your app running in it. You will also notice that the command-line window where you typed the command has some things going on within it.

With this, we have successfully served our application to the browser and can test our Ionic application like any other web application on Chrome. The great thing about this technique is the fact that no extra setup is required, and all you need is just Ionic CLI and the Chrome browser installed on your machine.

Emulating with Chrome

Even though our application is served on the Chrome browser, it is fullscreen and is served like a normal fullscreen web app. This is not ideal for us, as our application is a mobile application. Luckily, Chrome has a neat emulation tool that lets you emulate your application as if it were running on a normal mobile phone.

To use Chrome's emulation feature, follow the following steps.

 These steps assume that you already have your app served on the Chrome browser and you are currently on the tab that it is served on.

1. Click the Chrome menu icon, as shown in the following screenshot:

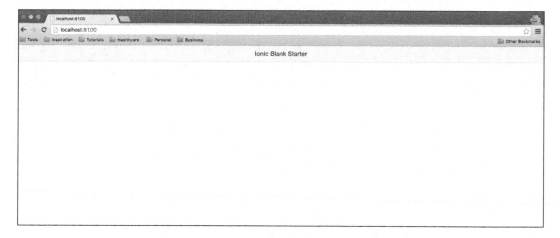

2. Scroll down to the **More Tools** options and select the **Developer Tools** option, as shown in the following screenshot:

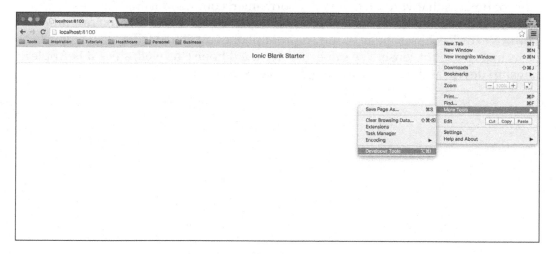

3. Click the **Device Mode** toggle icon, as shown in the following screenshot:

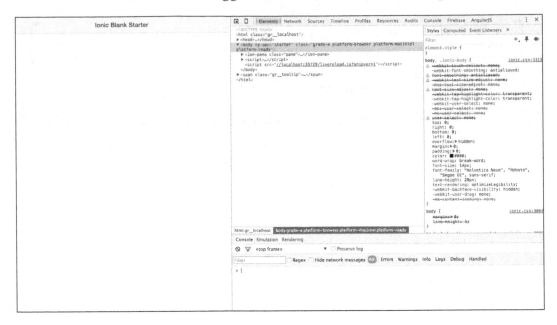

This should bring up the Chrome emulator window with your app running on it. You might need to refresh the page for it to render the app correctly. If you have a look at the window, you will see a dropdown menu on the upper-left corner that has a list of devices that you can emulate. I normally recommend using the Nexus 5 for testing Android and the iPhone 6 for iOS. The reason for this is that the resolution of the Nexus 5 eclipses many of the Android phones available today so using it as a basis makes a lot of sense. The same goes for the iPhone 6 as well; since it is Apple's flagship device at the time of writing, it makes sense to use it for emulation.

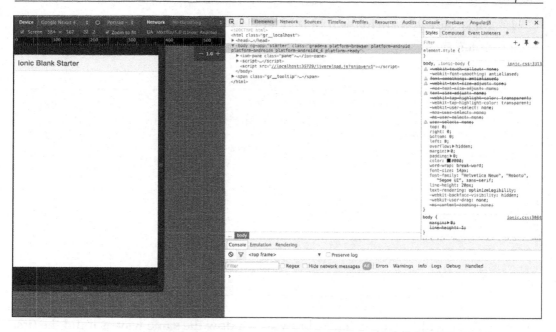

You can fully interact with your app as if it were running in an emulator. You also have the full power of the Chrome developer tools to inspect elements and see how the code of your application is represented. Why don't you have a go with your app and try and add some to-do list items and see them populating.

Ionic serve labs

There is another flavor in the `ionic serve` technique that lets us see our app the way it looks on both iOS and Android simultaneously. This technique is called the Ionic labs technique.

 This technique should only be used to view your app and is not intended to be used for debugging.

To view your app using the Ionic labs technique, simply follow the following steps.

 If you are already viewing your app using the `ionic serve` technique, simply press *Q* to quit the current session or close the command-line window and open a new one.

1. Make sure you are in the root folder of your project.

2. Enter the following command in your terminal:

```
ionic serve --lab
```

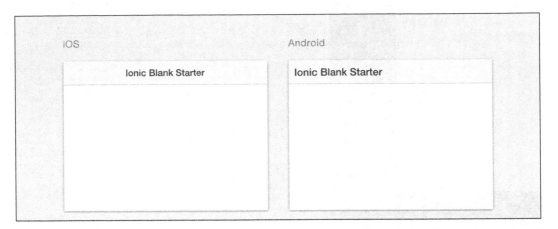

Running this should bring up a new browser window the same way as it did the first time when we ran the `ionic serve` command; only that this time, you will see two emulations for your app, one for iOS and one for Android, as shown in the preceding screenshot. This is a really nice way to see your app running in action on both platforms simultaneously. Ionic has a term called **Continuum** which you will see in action in later chapters. This phenomenon refers to the fact that certain elements look different on different platforms. For example, tabs on iOS are normally placed on the bottom, while on Android, they are traditionally positioned on the top. Ionic offers us these features out of the box with a further way to override these behaviors. The `ionic serve` technique is a great way to see the features like the tab positioned differently on different platforms simultaneously.

The Ionic view

Another technique to view an Ionic app is by using the Ionic view application. The Ionic view app is a mobile application created by Ionic with Ionic framework available on iOS and Android. The application is used to view any Ionic application you are developing and works hand-in-hand with the Ionic IO platform. The Ionic IO platform is a suite of tools that Ionic provides for some extra services like push notifications, analytics, and so on.

Testing todo app with the Ionic view

In order to use the Ionic view app, you must have an iOS or Android device. You must also possess an Ionic IO account. Navigate to `http://apps.ionic.io` to create your Ionic IO account. Go ahead and download the Ionic view app by visiting `http://view.ionic.io` on your mobile device and downloading the correct version for your mobile device.

In order to test our `todo` application, follow the following steps to test it with the Ionic view app:

1. Open a terminal window and navigate to the root folder of your `todo` application from `Chapter 2`.

2. Simply enter the following command on your terminal:

    `ionic upload`

This command will request the e-mail and password details of your Ionic IO account. Enter these details when prompted and if the app uploaded correctly, you should see a message saying `Successfully Uploaded (APP_ID)`, where `APP_ID` is an auto-generated identifier for you app.

Now you are ready to view the app on your mobile device. To do this, simply open your Ionic view app on your phone and login with the same Ionic IO account you uploaded your app to. You should see your application in a similar fashion to the following screenshot:

From here, you simply tap the todo app and a prompt will come up with a number of options. You should select the **download files** option. After this has finished, you can simply click the **View App** option. If you followed the instructions correctly, the todo app should replace your current view and you should see it running within the Ionic view app.

 You can simply tap the screen with three fingers to go back to the Ionic view menu at any time.

The Ionic view is a good way to view your application, and is extremely useful when you want to share progress with your friends, clients, or your boss about an app. It has a feature that lets you share to people's e-mails and you can find these documented in the Ionic official documentation. You can also manage the apps you upload to Ionic view from within the app or online via the Ionic IO website at http://apps.ionic.io.

Device

You can also test your Ionic application by running it on a physical device. To do this, however, you must have the native SDK for each platform installed on your computer. Let's take a brief look at how you can run an Ionic app on your device.

Android

To run an Ionic app on a physical device, first you simply ensure that you have your Android device plugged in via USB. You also need to ensure that you have developer mode enabled in your computer with USB debugging on.

 This step assumes that you have already set up the Android SDK on your computer and you also have Cordova and Ionic set up on your machine.

Ensure that you are in the root folder of your project in a terminal window and run the following command:

```
ionic run android
```

If you have everything set up correctly, this command will build your app and run it on the device plugged into the computer automatically.

iOS

To run an Ionic app on an iOS device, first you need to ensure that you have the `iOS-deploy` package installed.

 You can only deploy your app to an iOS device using a Mac computer. This step also assumes that you have the iOS SDK set up correctly alongside X-Code on your Mac computer.

If you do not have the `iOS-deploy` package installed, you can install it via NPM by running the following command:

```
npm install ios-deploy -g
```

Plug in your device to your Mac computer and ensure that it does not have the lock screen enabled. Simply run the following command to deploy your Ionic app to your device:

```
ionic run ios --device
```

This command should build and run your application automatically on your plugged iOS device.

Summary

In this chapter, we learned the various ways to test and deploy our app. We started off by using the `ionic serve` command to deploy our app to the browser using Chrome. We then had a look at how we can also serve our application using Ionic labs. We then went ahead to use the Ionic view application to see how we can run our app on an iOS and Android device with the Ionic view app installed in it. Lastly, we touched on how we can actually run our Ionic application on a real Android or iOS device.

In the next chapter, we are going to dive into some more complex Ionic controls, and we will get to use Angular's `$http` service to see how we can make Ajax calls and retrieve data within our Ionic application.

4

Ionic Components

In this chapter, we will be learning how to use some more complex Ionic components and controls. We will be creating a more advanced version of our to-do list application we created in *Chapter 2*, *To-Do List App*, using some more advanced built-in Ionic list components. We will call this more advanced to-do list application `Bucket-List` app. The idea behind this application is that it will allow us to enter all the interesting things we want to try in a lifetime. Therefore, we can enter the names of places we want to visit, the names of activities we want to do, and so on.

Creating a new to-do list application

In *Chapter 2*, *To-Do List App*, we created a simple to-do list application with the Ionic blank template. We were able to get this application to work by allowing us to add items into our to-do list application. We will be creating a new to-do list application using the Ionic blank template for us to add our new, more advanced components to our brand new BucketList application. Let's go ahead and create this new blank application by following the following steps. We will be calling our new application `Bucket-List` in order to differentiate it from the one we created in *Chapter 2*, *To-Do List App*.

1. To create the `Bucket-List` app, fire up a terminal window on your computer and navigate to the `Desktop` folder of your computer by running the following command:

   ```
   cd Desktop
   ```

2. After navigating to the `Desktop` folder of your computer, go ahead and run the following command to create the `Bucket-List` application based on the Ionic blank template:

   ```
   ionic start Bucket-List blank
   ```

3. This command will create a new blank Ionic application called `Bucket-List`. When this command has finished running, navigate to the project of your application via the command line by running the following command:

```
cd Bucket-List
```

Now you have successfully completed the process of creating your `Bucket-List` application, and we can start developing the app by adding features to it.

Overview of the Bucket-List app

To understand what we are trying to build, have a closer look at the following screenshot. We aim to achieve a final app that closely resembles what we have in the following screenshot:

Breaking down the app

A good way to build Ionic apps is by building them in bits. For our `Bucket-List` application, we can start by first developing the user interface and then writing the code behind it to enable it to work. Our user interface will contain an input box to enter a new item into our bucket list. Secondly, we have to design the UI for the list of `Bucket-List` items.

Designing the UI

Designing the UI involves two main implementations:

*   Implementing the input box
*   Implementing the `ion-list` element

We will have a look at each.

Implementing the input box

The first thing we are going to implement is an input box. This input box is the form where the users of our app will enter an interesting item they wish to add in the `Bucket-List` application. This will be in the form of an HTML textarea input box with some Ionic CSS styles applied to it in order to give it a more mobile look and feel. There also will be a button next to the input box with the label **ADD**. This button will be what we tap after we have typed some text and want it to appear as a part of our list. Perform the following steps:

1. Open up the `Bucket-List` application you created earlier in your favorite text editor.

2. Now, open the `index.html` file that can be found in the www folder of your project. You will see a screen that closely resembles what we have in the following screenshot:

```html
<!DOCTYPE html>
<html>
  <head>
    <meta charset="utf-8">
    <meta name="viewport" content="initial-scale=1, maximum-scale=1, user-scalable=no, width=device-width">
    <title></title>

    <link href="lib/ionic/css/ionic.css" rel="stylesheet">
    <link href="css/style.css" rel="stylesheet">

    <!-- IF using Sass (run gulp sass first), then uncomment below and remove the CSS includes above
    <link href="css/ionic.app.css" rel="stylesheet">
    -->

    <!-- ionic/angularjs js -->
    <script src="lib/ionic/js/ionic.bundle.js"></script>

    <!-- cordova script (this will be a 404 during development) -->
    <script src="cordova.js"></script>

    <!-- your app's js -->
    <script src="js/app.js"></script>
  </head>
  <body ng-app="starter">

    <ion-pane>
      <ion-header-bar class="bar-stable">
        <h1 class="title">Ionic Blank Starter</h1>
      </ion-header-bar>
      <ion-content>
      </ion-content>
    </ion-pane>
  </body>
</html>
```

You can see that this boilerplate code already contains some code for some custom Ionic elements just like we saw in our first application in *Chapter 2, To-Do List App* all of which are prefixed with ion. Pay close attention to the <ion-content> element! This element is the element that contains the bits and pieces of our application or the content area. It is in between this element that we are going to place all the markup for our Bucket-List application.

Let's start by placing the code for the input box of our application. I have provided the code for our input box in the following code block. You are to place this code within the <ion-content> element in your index.html file:

```
<div class="list">

<div class="item item-input-inset">
<label class="item-input-wrapper">
<input type="text">
</label>
<button class="button button-small">
      Add
</button>
</div>

</div>
```

The preceding code is the HTML code that will display an input box and a button as we described earlier. If you pay close attention to the markup, you will see that some elements contain some classes. These classes are custom Ionic classes that are available as part of the Ionic CSS. The Ionic CSS comes with a lot of nifty classes and features, but for now just be aware of these classes and know that they are part of the Ionic CSS.

If you run your app in the browser using the ionic serve method, you should be able to see something that looks very similar to what I have in the following screenshot. Enter the following command in a terminal window to run your app using the ionic serve method. Make sure you run it from the root folder of your project:

ionic serve

You should be able to see the input box with the button placed on its right-hand side.

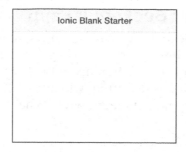

Implementing the ion-list application

The next step of developing our `Bucket-List` application is to implement the `ion-list` application. We are going to use one of the built-in components called `ion-list`. The `ion-list` element is a component for creating and rendering lists. It has a lot of cool features that let us render complex lists that can have side options. Take a look at the following screenshot that shows the mail app from an iOS mobile device showing a list of features that we can implement using `ion-list`:

As seen above, one of the most obvious features we can implement with `ion-list` is the ability to show options when we swipe on a list item. It also has other features like the ability to delete items or rearrange them.

Using ion-list for our Bucket-List app

For our `Bucket-List` application, we will be aiming to use the `<ion-list>` component to render every item we enter through the input box. In addition, we would want to be able to delete each item from the list by simply swiping from the left and thus revealing a delete button, which we can click. The following screenshot gives a sample graphic breakdown of what we aim to achieve and what items are involved:

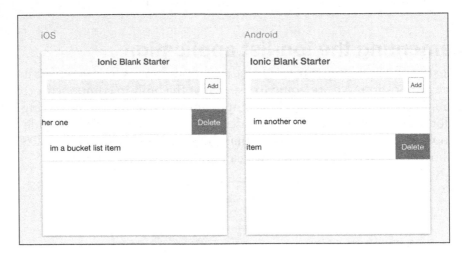

The ion-list component

The first thing we will do is implement the code for our `<ion-list>` component. The following code is the code for `<ion-list>`. You are to copy this code and place it just below the code for the input box you already implemented:

```
<ion-list>

</ion-list>
```

This is the top-level component needed to create our `<ion-list>` component. The `<ion-list>` component has some attributes that let us perform some more complex implementations. We will not be exploring these attributes but it is worth knowing that they do exist.

The next step is to implement the child item for our `<ion-list>` component. Each item in an `<ion-list>` component is called `<ion-item>`.

ion-item

As briefly noted in the previous subsection about the `<ion-list>`component, each item in an `<ion-list>` is called an `<ion-item>`. Within an `<ion-item>`, we will put the code for what we want each list item to render. It is also the `<ion-item>` where we will use Angular's `ng-repeat` feature. For our application, we simply want to render the name of each `Bucket-List` item. This means that we can think of every `Bucket-List` item as an `<ion-item>`.

For now, we are just going to have some dummy text in our implementation showing how a `Bucket-List` item will prospectively look. The following block of code is the implementation of our `<ion-item>` representing a `Bucket-List` item in our app:

```
<ion-item>
<h2>Bucket List Item</h2>
</ion-item>
```

This is a sample representation of our `<ion-item>`. If you still have your app running in the browser via the `ionic serve` technique, you should be able to see the `<ion-item>` rendered just like in the following screenshot:

Now, with that implementation completed, there is one more thing we need to do in order to finish the implementation of the user interface of our `Bucket-List` app. The one thing remaining is the delete feature. Remember from our initial implementation plan that we want the user to be able to swipe each item in our list and have a **Delete** button revealed. Luckily for us, the `<ion-item>` component has a neat feature for this called the `<ion-option>`.

ion-option-button

The `<ion-option-button>` component lives within an `<ion-item>` component as its child. Its sole purpose is to allow us to define buttons that we can reveal when the user of our app swipes from the right of each `<ion-item>`component just like in the original sample screenshot of our implementations. To get this implementation underway, copy the following code and paste it just before the closing tag of your `<ion-item>` component markup:

```
<ion-option-button class="button-assertive">
    Delete
</ion-option-button>
```

If you have a look at the preceding code, you can see that`<ion-option-button>` has a class attribute of `button-assertive`. This is also another Ionic class that is used to define a red button by default on Ionic buttons. Ionic has some built-in classes to easily add colors to elements. We will be discussing this later on in this module but for now just be aware of this feature.

By now, your final code for your`<ion-item>`component should look something similar to what I have in the following code block:

```
<ion-item>

<h2>Bucket List Item</h2>

<ion-option-button class="button-assertive">
        Delete
</ion-option-button>

</ion-item>
```

Your final code for your `<ion-content>` component should closely resemble what we have in the following code block:

```
<ion-content>
<div class="list">
<div class="item item-input-inset">
<label class="item-input-wrapper">
<input type="text">
</label>
<button class="button button-small">
                Add
</button>
</div>
```

```
    </div>

    <ion-list>
    <ion-item>

    <h2>Bucket List Item</h2>

    <ion-option-button class="button-assertive">
                Delete
    </ion-option-button>

    </ion-item>
    </ion-list>

    </ion-content>
```

With this, we have completed the implementation of the user interface of our
`Bucket-List` application using the `<ion-list>` component. Provided you still have
your app running in the browser via the `ionic serve` technique, go and try to swipe
the sample list item in your app from the left-hand side. You should be able to see a
Delete button when you do this. See the following screenshot for guidance:

With this step completed, we are finished with the user interface of our application
completely. Now, it is time we start to wire up the app by focusing on the Angular
code that we will be writing to ensure our application works the way we want it to.

Writing the Angular code for our Bucket-List app

Before we begin, let's recap what behavior we want to implement in order for our application to work the way we want it to.

Coding our input box

The first thing we want is to be able to enter some text into our input box later. After we enter the text, we want to click the **Add** button and have this text entered into an array that holds all out Bucket-List items. To begin this first, we create our Angular controller that will hold all the logic for our app.

Creating the controller

Open to the app.js file of your application in your favorite IDE. This file can be found in the js folder, which is found in the www folder of your app.

```
www/js/app.js
```

There should already be a folder called starter with code similar to that which I have in the following code block:

```
angular.module('starter', ['ionic'])

.run(function($ionicPlatform) {
  $ionicPlatform.ready(function() {
    // Hide the accessory bar by default (remove this to show the
    accessory bar above the keyboard
    // for form inputs)
if(window.cordova&&window.cordova.plugins.Keyboard) {
cordova.plugins.Keyboard.hideKeyboardAccessoryBar(true);
    }
    if(window.StatusBar) {
StatusBar.styleDefault();
    }
  });
})
```

To begin, we will first start by creating a controller called `BucketListController` just after where we declared our module. If you have done this correctly, you should have code that closely resembles the following:

```
angular.module('starter', ['ionic'])

    .controller('BucketListController', function ($scope) {

    })

.run(function($ionicPlatform) {
    $ionicPlatform.ready(function() {
        // Hide the accessory bar by default (remove this to show
        the accessory bar above the keyboard
        // for form inputs)
if(window.cordova&&window.cordova.plugins.Keyboard) {
cordova.plugins.Keyboard.hideKeyboardAccessoryBar(true);
        }
        if(window.StatusBar) {
StatusBar.styleDefault();
        }
    });
})
```

With this done, we have now completed the process of creating our controller called `BucketLisController`. This controller is where all the logic for our app will live.

Creating the input box model

We are going to need to create a model that will be bound to our input box. This model will be in the form of an object, and it will hold the data that will be represented by the text we enter in our input box. We will call this model `bucketListItem`. To create this model, simply enter the following code within `BucketListController` that you just created in the previous step:

```
$scope.bucketListItem = {
title : ''
};
```

The preceding code is initializing the model for our `bucketListItem` model. This model has a property called `title` that will hold the text of what we type in the input box at every point in time.

Creating an array for the Bucket-List items

The aim of our app is to have a list of the `Bucket-List` items. These items, as we enter them in our input box, will need to be stored in an array. We are going to create this array, and we will simply call it `bucketListItems`. This array is what we will use in Angular's `ng-repeat` attribute to iterate and render in our view. To create this array for our `Bucket-List` items, simply attach an array called `bucketListItems` to the `$scope` variable of your controller. The following code illustrates this step:

```
$scope.bucketListItems = [];
```

Implementing code for the Add button

The final step to ensure that we are able to add items to our Bucket-List app with the input is by writing the code in the form of a function for the **Add** button. This button is responsible for two things. Firstly, it will ensure that the current text in our input box is added as an entry to the output box array of the `Bucket-List` items. Secondly, it will also clear up the model to ensure that after we click the button, the input box is cleared up for the next item.

The following code represents the implementation for our **Add** button:

```
$scope.addBucketListItem = function () {
    //Add Current Bucket List Item To The Front Of Our Bucket List
    Items Array
    $scope.bucketListItems.unshift($scope.bucketListItem);
    //Clear Current Bucket List For Next Entry
    $scope.bucketListItem = {
        title: ''
    };
};
```

From the preceding code you can see that we have created a function called `addBucketListItem`, and attached it to the `$scope` variable of our controller so it is available to our view. Within our function, we first add the current value of the `bucketListItem` variable to our `bucketListItems` array. Secondly, we clear up the `bucketListItem` variable to ensure it is cleared for the next entry.

Now, you can go ahead and implement the preceding code within your controller.

Implementing the Delete button

The last piece of our code is to implement the **Delete** button of our `<ion-option-button>`. Remember that we want this button to be able to delete the item which it belongs to. The following code shows the implementation of the **Delete** button:

```
$scope.deleteBucketListItem = function (index) {
$scope.bucketListItems.splice(index, 1);
};
```

The preceding code simply shows how we have created a function called `deleteBucketListItem`. This function takes in the index of the current item to be deleted as a parameter. It then uses this index to remove the corresponding element that is placed in that index from the `bucketListItems` array, which holds all our `Bucket-List` items.

With that complete, we have pretty much finished the code aspect of our application. Your final controller should look similar to what I have in the following code block:

```
controller('BucketListController', function ($scope) {
    $scope.bucketListItem = {
      title : ''
    };

    $scope.bucketListItems = [];

    $scope.addBucketListItem = function () {
      //Add Current Bucket List Item To The Front Of Our Bucket
      List Items Array
      $scope.bucketListItems.unshift($scope.bucketListItem);
      //Clear Current Bucket List For Next Entry
      $scope.bucketListItem = {
        title: ''
      };
    };

    $scope.deleteBucketListItem = function (index) {
      $scope.bucketListItems.splice(index, 1);
    };

  })
```

Now, before we go ahead and test your application, we have one last step to complete. We need to wire up all the code we have just created with the UI we implemented earlier so that they can work together.

Wire it all up

With our controller ready, now we have to go ahead and wire all the code to the UI so that they can work together in harmony.

Binding the controller

The first thing we need to do is to wire up the controller we created. The simple and easiest way to do this is by simply using Angular's `ng-controller` attribute directive to specify our controller. In our case, we will be wiring the controller on `<ion-content>` of our app. Once again, open up the `index.html` file of your application. Find the opening `<ion-content>` tag of the page and specify an `ng-controller` attribute with the name of your controller.

Your code should closely resemble the following code:

```
<ion-content ng-controller="BucketListController">
```

This code is simply telling Angular that we wish to use `BucketListController` within the scope of this `<ion-content>` element. This means that all the methods and properties scoped within this controller are now available to the `<ion-content>` element and all its descendant elements.

Binding the input box model

The next step is to ensure that the `bucketListItem` variable we created in our controller is data bound to our input box in the view. Angular also has a simple but great attribute directive for this called `ng-model`. We simply provide `ng-model` with a value that matches an object or variable that we want to data bind to. In our case, we want to data bind to the title property of our `bucketListItem` variable from our controller. Again, I have provided the following code for your convenience:

```
<input type="text" ng-model="bucketListItem.title">
```

The preceding piece of code we just added tells Angular to bind this variable to this input box. Therefore, anytime the value of the input changes from the view, we have the same value in our controller and vice versa.

Wiring up the Add button

The **Add** button is next in line for our implementation. For this button, we simply need to tell it to run our `addBucketListItem` function every time it is clicked. Once again, Angular has a helper directive for this called the `ng-click` directive. The `ng-click` directive is like the classic Java `onClick` event listener and you provide it with a function that you want to run every time the wired element is clicked. The following code demonstrates how we can wire up our **Add** button with the `ng-click` directive:

```
<button class="button button-small" ng-
click="addBucketListItem()">
    Add
</button>
```

The preceding code implementation simply ensures that when the **Add** button is clicked, the addBucketListener function will run with its expected behavior.

Binding ion-item

The last part of our wiring up will be to wire our bucketListItems array to our Ion-Item elements, and also bind the ion-option-button element to our deleteBucketListItem() function.

Using ng-repeat to render the list

Right now we have a sample implementation that has one hardcoded ion-item. However, we will want a more dynamic solution where we automatically render the items within the bucketListItems array each as an ion-item. For this implementation, we are going to use one of the most important Angular features in the form of ng-repeat. The ng-repeat angular directive lets us dynamically repeat an array.

Right now, you have a code that looks similar to the following:

```
<ion-item>

<h2>Bucket List Item</h2>

<ion-option-button class="button-assertive">
        Delete
</ion-option-button>

</ion-item>
```

We are going to change this implementation to use the ng-repeat directive of Angular. The following code shows you how this is achieved:

```
<ion-item ng-repeat="item in bucketListItems">

<h2>{{item.title}}</h2>

<ion-option-button class="button-assertive">
        Delete
</ion-option-button>

</ion-item>
```

The preceding code now uses Angular's `ng-repeat` attribute. This code tells Angular to repeat the `bucketListItems` array and also binds the title of each item to an HTML `<h2>` element.

Wiring up the ion-option-button element

The `ion-option-button` element is still untouched and will do nothing if we don't tell it to do so. All we need to do for this element is to provide it with a function we want to be executed when it is clicked, like we did with the **Add** button. For this, we will be using the `ng-click` directive again, but this time, we will point it to the `deleteBucketListItem()` function from our controller. The following code shows just how we can achieve that:

```
<ion-option-button class="button-assertive" ng-
click="deleteBucketListItem($index)">
    Delete
</ion-option-button>
```

From the preceding code, you will notice one alien thing, `$index` being specifically passed as a parameter for our `deleteBucketListItem` function. This variable is a magic variable that the `ng-repeat` directive of Angular exposes to us. It represents the index of the current element being rendered by `ng-repeat`. With this index, we can learn what particular element should be deleted from our array of bucket list items, and delete the correct one.

The final `<ion-content>` in your `index.html` file should closely resemble what I have in the following code block:

```
<ion-content ng-controller="BucketListController">

<div class="list">
<div class="item item-input-inset">
<label class="item-input-wrapper">
<input type="text" ng-model="bucketListItem.title">
</label>
<button class="button button-small" ng-
click="addBucketListItem()">
                Add
</button>
</div>
</div>

<ion-list>

<ion-item ng-repeat="item in bucketListItems">
```

```
<h2>{{item.title}}</h2>

<ion-option-button class="button-assertive" ng-
click="deleteBucketListItem($index)">
            Delete
</ion-option-button>

</ion-item>

</ion-list>

</ion-content>
```

Testing our Bucket-List app

We have completed the implementation of our application, and now it is time
for us to see it in action. Ensure you have your app running in the browser via
the `ionic serve` technique, and test it. Try entering some things into your
`Bucket-List` app such as skydiving, jet-skiing, and so on. You should see that
every time you enter an item and click **Add**, the item will appear in the list and
the input box will clear up ready for your next input. Also, make sure you test the
delete option by swiping an item from the left to reveal the **Delete** button, and
clicking it to see the item disappear.

Summary

In this chapter, we focused on creating our `Bucket-List` application from scratch
using the Ionic blank template. We also learned to use the `<ion-list>` component
of Ionic and its child elements. We wrote some Angular code to wire everything up
and got it running. The `<ion-list>` component is a very powerful component, and
although the task of this chapter might appear a bit more complex that the previous
ones, there are still some more powerful features that the `<ion-list>` component
lets us do. For more information about `<ion-list>`, visit the official documentation
of `<ion-list>` from the provided links in the appendix of this module to learn even
more complex features.

In the next chapter, we will be learning some very exciting stuff about creating side
menu applications with Ionic. We will also build ourselves a tourist application and
work with the AJAX calls for the very first time using Angular's `$HTTP` service.

5
The London Tourist App

In the previous chapter, we created an application called the Bucket-List application that enabled us to create a list of interesting things we wanted to do in our lifetime. In this chapter, we will create a new application called "The London Tourist" application. It is an application that will display a list of top tourist attractions in the city of London in England. We will build this application with a new type of Ionic template called the side menu template. We will also be using the Angular $http service to query our data via Ajax.

Introduction to the London Tourist App

London is the largest city in England and it is a city that is well known to attract tourists around the world. The city is very urban but it has many historical and non-historical tourist attractions. With this large number of attractions, it can be difficult to pick out the best places to go. This is the entire idea behind the London Tourist App as it will provide users with five handpicked destinations that tourists visiting London can actually visit. These destinations will be stored in a JSON file in our project that we will be querying via AJAX and populating.

Creating the London Tourist app

To begin the process of creating our app, we are going to start by creating a brand new Ionic application. So far in this module, we have learned to create a new Ionic application using the blank template. For the application we are about to build, we are going to use a new type of Ionic template to create the application. We are going to be using the side menu template to create our London Tourist app.

The side menu app design

You might not be familiar with what the side menu template looks like. In fact, the side menu design for mobile applications is very common in mobile app development. It involves having the ability to slide from the left or right edges of a mobile application to reveal more options, normally more menu options:

The side menu design technique is one that is used in a lot of contexts, both on mobile and on the web. Normally, you will see an icon positioned either on the far upper-right or upper-left, indicating that you can swipe or click that icon to reveal the extra menu options. This icon is normally referred to as the hamburger menu icon.

The Ionic framework actually comes built-in with a side menu template that automatically creates a side menu application for us with some useful boilerplate code. We will be using this template to create our London Tourist Application.

Using the Ionic side menu template

To begin developing our London Tourist Application, we will begin by using the Ionic CLI to create the app. You can do this by running the following command from a terminal window:

 We will shorten the name of our app from London Tourist App to LTA to make it easier to type.

```
ionic start LTA sidemenu
```

This command will create a new Ionic application called LTA using the default Ionic side menu template.

Seeing the LTA side menu app in action

As soon as your LTA app is created, you can simply change your directory into the app from the terminal and run it on your computer using the `ionic serve` technique. You can do this by running the following commands:

- Change directory to app:

  ```
  cd LTA
  ```

- Run using the `ionic serve` technique:

  ```
  ionic serve
  ```

 Remember to use Chrome and emulate to a device of your choice with the Chrome emulation tools as taught in previous chapters.

You should see a screen that looks something like the following screenshot:

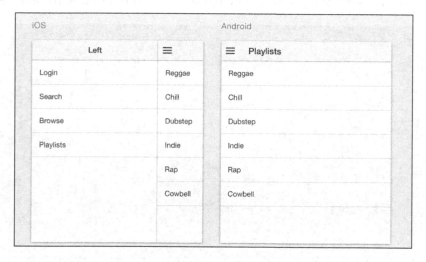

As you can see from the preceding screenshot, the side menu app we have just created contains some pre-rendered content.

Exploring the LTA side menu app's code

Now, we are going to have a look at the code of the LTA app based on the side menu template:

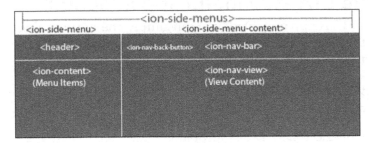

Now, I will require you to fire up the LTA project you have just created in your favorite IDE. The first thing you will notice is the folder structure that you are already used to from previous chapters.

The index.html file

Now, focus on the www folder and open the index.html file. A look through this file should show you something similar to what we have in the following screenshot:

```html
<!DOCTYPE html>
<html>
  <head>
    <meta charset="utf-8">
    <meta name="viewport" content="initial-scale=1, maximum-scale=1, user-scalable=no, width=device-width">
    <title></title>

    <link href="lib/ionic/css/ionic.css" rel="stylesheet">
    <link href="css/style.css" rel="stylesheet">

    <!-- IF using Sass (run gulp sass first), then uncomment below and remove the CSS includes above
    <link href="css/ionic.app.css" rel="stylesheet">
    -->

    <!-- ionic/angularjs js -->
    <script src="lib/ionic/js/ionic.bundle.js"></script>

    <!-- cordova script (this will be a 404 during development) -->
    <script src="cordova.js"></script>

    <!-- your app's js -->
    <script src="js/app.js"></script>
    <script src="js/controllers.js"></script>
  </head>

  <body ng-app="starter">
    <ion-nav-view></ion-nav-view>
  </body>
</html>
```

> To get to this file from the root folder, navigate to www/index.html.

A look at this file will show you some things we have seen from previous projects in this module. For example, you can see some CSS and JS references to the Ionic `styles` and `script` files respectively. You will also see from the `body` tag that a generated Angular module called `starter` is being instantiated using the `ng-app` attribute.

Pay close attention to the `<ion-nav-view>` tags within the `<body>` tags. This is an Ionic element that is used to specify the view to which the entire app is injected into. It is similar to the `ng-view` feature of Angular but has more powerful features. It also automatically handles navigation for us within our Ionic app. You need not pay a great deal of attention to this part of the code anymore but just have it at the back of your mind that `<ion-nav-view>` is where all content gets injected in, and acts like a wrapper for our app's content.

The menu.html file

The next file we are going to explore is the `menu.html` file. This file is probably the most important file at this moment as it contains most of the generated code for the side menu parts of our app. To have a look at this file, navigate to the `menu.html` file which can be found by navigating into the folder called `templates` under the `www` folder. Here is the path: `www/templates/menu.html`.

If you have successfully done this, you should see a file that closely resembles what we have in the following screenshot:

The <ion-side-menus>element

The first thing you should pay attention to is the `<ion-side-menus>` element. Think of this element as a container for any side menu application. It allows us to specify what the main content area will be via the `<ion-side-menu-content>` element and also allows us to specify the side menus via the `<ion-side-menu>` elements. There can be more than one side menu specified within the `<ion-side-menus>` elements and we have the ability to specify whether the menu is placed on the left, right, or even both. There are a lot of cool and powerful controls that the `<ion-side-menus>` elements let us utilize to control its containing items. For now, we will focus on trying to learn more about the child elements that are needed to work with the `<ion-side-menus>` elements. These are the `<ion-side-menu-content>`and`<ion-side-menu>` elements.

The <ion-side-menu-content>element

This element is what houses the main content area or the visible part of the app:

In the preceding screenshot, which is a view of our LTA app, the part you see is a representative of`<ion-side-menu-content>`. Let's have a closer look at the code of `< ion-side-menu-content>` to see how it actually works in detail:

```
<ion-side-menu-content>
  <ion-nav-bar class="bar-stable">
    <ion-nav-back-button>
    </ion-nav-back-button>

    <ion-nav-buttons side="left">
      <button class="button button-icon button-clear ion-navicon" menu-toggle="left">
      </button>
    </ion-nav-buttons>
  </ion-nav-bar>
  <ion-nav-view name="menuContent"></ion-nav-view>
</ion-side-menu-content>
```

Within `<ion-side-menu-content>`, you can see two direct child elements.

Firstly, you can see the `<ion-nav-bar>` element which is used to build the navigation buttons of the main content area with the`<ion-nav-buttons>` element as its child element. For example, within these`<ion-nav-buttons>` elements, you can see a navigation button on line 8-9, which has a `menu-toggle` attribute of value `left`. This is simply saying that when this button is tapped, the left-sided side menu should be triggered. Remember that there can be up to two side menus with one being on the left and one being on the right in a side menu app.

The second direct child element is the`<ion-nav-view>` element on line 12 from the preceding screenshot. We talked about this same element earlier when we had a look at the `index.html` file. This element is a placeholder for where the actual content is injected. This particular `<ion-nav-view>` element has a `name` attribute with the value of `menuContent`. This attribute is important as it is used like a value to uniquely identify`<ion-nav-view>`.

With all that said, we have now lightly touched on the `<ion-side-menu-content>` element and its main functions. Always think of this element as the element that houses the main content area of your side menu application.

The `<ion-side-menu>`element

The `<ion-side-menu>` element is an element that we use to specify the side menu of our app. Just like the `<ion-side-menu-content>` element, it lives as a direct child of the `<ion-side-menus>` element. There can be up to two`<ion-side-menu>` elements within the`<ion-side-menus>` element, with only one being on each side. Let's have a closer look at the code of`<ion-side-menu>` of our LTA application.

```
<ion-side-menu side="left">
  <ion-header-bar class="bar-stable">
    <h1 class="title">Left</h1>
  </ion-header-bar>
  <ion-content>
    <ion-list>
      <ion-item menu-close ng-click="login()">
        Login
      </ion-item>
      <ion-item menu-close href="#/app/search">
        Search
      </ion-item>
      <ion-item menu-close href="#/app/browse">
        Browse
      </ion-item>
      <ion-item menu-close href="#/app/playlists">
        Playlists
      </ion-item>
    </ion-list>
  </ion-content>
</ion-side-menu>
```

The preceding screenshot is from our `menu.html` file, and it showcases the code of `<ionic-side-menu>` from our LTA application. If you look at it closely, you will notice that opening tag of our `<ion-side-menu>` element has a `side` attribute with value `left`. This is basically saying that we want this particular side menu to be on the left-hand side. Remember that we can have up to two side menus in our app, and one can be positioned on the left and another on the right, but two side menus cannot be positioned on the same side. We can also see that this `<ion-side-menu>` has two direct child elements. These child elements are `<ion-header-bar>` and `<ion-content>`. `<ion-header-bar>` is an element used to construct the header of a side menu. If you have a look at the following screenshot of our side menu, you should see a representation of it:

From the preceding screenshot, you can see the header with the title LEFT as reflected in the code as an `<h1>` element.

The second child element we can see from the code is the `<ion-content>` element. Think of this element as what houses the content area below the header of the side menu. Basically, this is anything below the header. `<ion-content>` could contain any HTML code we want but in this case, it contains `<ion-list>` which is something that we used to build our Bucket-List application from *Chapter 4, Ionic Components*. You can also see a reflection of this code on the screenshot from when we ran our application.

With that said, you can see that we have successfully had a brief look at what the `<ion-side-menu>` element entails and how the side menu template of Ionic functions. The next step is for us to actually go ahead and build our LTA application in full scale now.

Developing the LTA application

We are now equipped with the know-how on how to code our LTA side menu based application. Remember that the idea behind our application is to have some of our favorite tourist destinations listed in our app. In a normal scenario, we would query this data from a real API. But for the sake of simplicity, we will mimic this API request by making a request to a local JSON file that would act like a real database with the information we need.

The local JSON database

As discussed earlier, we are going to create a JSON file that will act like a real-life API containing our destinations. This local file will contain five top tourist destinations in London. The first thing we will need to do is to create this file.

Creating the local JSON database file

If you do not have your LTA application open, make sure you open it in your favorite IDE. Now, go ahead and create a new JSON file called sites.json within the www folder of your project. Make sure you name the file as the .json extension in order for it to be parsed as a JSON file. Your directory structure should look similar to what is shown in the following screenshot:

With that done, you have successfully created your local JSON file representing your database for your tourist sites.

Populating the JSON file

Now we are going to populate the JSON file with some data. This data will be the data of five top tourist attractions in the city of London. The following is a JSON array that represents the content of our local JSON database. You should copy all the content of the following piece of code into your `sites.json` file:

```
[
  {
"id":"1",
"name":"London Eye",
"description":"Shows you a great view of the city"
  },
  {
"id":"2",
"name":"The Shard",
"description":"Highest building in London"
  },
  {
"id":"3",
"name":"Oxford Circus",
"description":"The place to shop in London"
  },
  {
"id":"4",
"name":"Buckingham Palace",
"description":"The Queen lives here"
  }
]
```

The preceding piece of code is a JSON array that represents four top destinations in London as JSON objects. Each object representing a site has three properties. These properties are:

- **ID**: A unique identifier for the site.
- **Name**: The name of the Tourist site.
- **Description**: Some small information about the site.

By now, we have successfully completed the creation of our JSON local database. The next step is to see how we can actually render these items and query the database.

Designing the view

We have created our app and we have the data for the application. Before we query data, we first need to design how the data will look when rendered. For this very task, we will call on an old friend of ours in the face of `<ion-list>`. We will use `<ion-list>` to render a list of tourist attractions from our JSON database.

Currently if we run our application, the first page we see is the playlist application, as shown in the following screenshot:

This is because by default the page is specified in the app.js file by Angular as the root page of our app. We will keep things simple and change the contents of this playlist page and design the view of our LTA application on it. From your LTA project folder, navigate into the www folder and look into the templates folder. Within the templates folder, there is a playlists.html file. This is the file that contains the code for our playlist page shown in the preceding screenshot. Open this file and you should see some code that closely resembles what we have in the following screenshot:

```
<ion-view view-title="Playlists">
  <ion-content>
    <ion-list>
      <ion-item ng-repeat="playlist in playlists" href="#/app/playlists/{{playlist.id}}">
        {{playlist.title}}
      </ion-item>
    </ion-list>
  </ion-content>
</ion-view>
```

The playlists.html file from the root folder of your LTA project will have a path www/templates/playlists.html.

The first thing we will want to do here is to change the name of the title of our view. Currently, the view as seen from the screenshots previously, has a title `Playlists`. This is specified by the `view-title` attribute of the opening`<ion-view>` element. This `view-title` attribute currently has a value `Playlists`. Change this to `London Sites`. This is to ensure that the title reflects the mission of our app, which is to show the top London tourist sites.

The second thing we need to do is to edit the code for`<ion-list>`. Replace the `<ion-list>` code with the one provided in the following code block:

```
<ion-list>
<ion-item ng-repeat="site in sites">
        {{site.name}}
</ion-item>
</ion-list>
```

If you have done this correctly, your code should now closely resemble what we have in the following screenshot:

With this done, we have now completed the process of designing our UI. The next step is to go ahead and wire up our data to our view.

Wiring up the data

Earlier, we created a `sites.json` file that represented our database. We will be making a real Ajax call to this file in order to retrieve its data and serve it within our app. The thing we need to do to achieve this is firstly to write the code to retrieve the data.

Retrieving the data with the $http service

To retrieve the data, we will need to make an Ajax call to the `sites.json` file. For this, Angular has a great service called the `$http` service. This is a service that provides us with functionality to make Ajax calls to local and remote resources via Ajax. To begin using the `$http` service to write our code, we first need to go to the controller associated with our view. By default, when you create an Ionic app based on the side menu template, there is a controller attached to the views. To find out which controller is attached to our `playlist.html` file, we need to look at the `app.js` file of our app to discover this.

You can find the `app.js` file by navigating to the www folder of your project and looking into the `js` folder within it. You should see the `app.js` file. Open it. After you open this `app.js` file, look thorough the part where you have code that looks closely to what we have in the following screenshot:

```
.state('app.playlists', {
  url: '/playlists',
  views: {
    'menuContent': {
      templateUrl: 'templates/playlists.html',
      controller: 'PlaylistsCtrl'
    }
  }
})
```

The code from the preceding screenshot represents the state definition of the `playlist.html` file. Pay close attention to the part of the code from the preceding screenshot where the controller is defined and you will see that the controller specified there is called `PlaylistsCtrl`. This is the name of the Angular controller that our `playlist.html` file is wired with.

The next step is to go to this `PlaylistsCtrl` controller and write the code to retrieve our data. By default, the controllers are contained in the `controller.js` file that can be found in the same `js` folder as our `app.js` file.

Open the `controller.js` file and look for a stub of code that closely resembles what I have in the following screenshot:

```
.controller('PlaylistsCtrl', function($scope) {
    $scope.playlists = [
        { title: 'Reggae', id: 1 },
        { title: 'Chill', id: 2 },
        { title: 'Dubstep', id: 3 },
        { title: 'Indie', id: 4 },
        { title: 'Rap', id: 5 },
        { title: 'Cowbell', id: 6 }
    ];
})
```

The preceding code block represents the controller definition of `PlaylistsCtrl`. The first thing we need to do is to clear all the code within the controller. Basically, we need to delete all the code found within the controller. If you have done this correctly, your controller should now look similar to what we have in the following screenshot:

```
.controller('PlaylistsCtrl', function($scope) {

})
```

With that done, we can now begin to create the code to query our local JSON database with the angular `$http` service. The first thing we need to do to achieve this is to first add the dependency of our `$http` service to our controller. This step is very important as if we do not add this dependency correctly, our app will not load. To do this, simply add `$http` as the second parameter in the anonymous function part of your controller definition. If you have done this correctly, you should see something similar to what I have in the following screenshot:

```
44    .controller('PlaylistsCtrl', function($scope, $http) {
45
46    })
```

With that done, we can now go ahead and start writing the code to grab our data from our local database. To start this process, simply write the following code into your controller:

```
$scope.sites = [];
$http.get('/sites.json')
.then(function (response) {
    $scope.sites = response.data;
});
```

If you have done this correctly, your code should look very close to what we have in the following screenshot:

```
.controller('PlaylistsCtrl', function($scope, $http) {
    $scope.sites = [];
    $http.get('/sites.json')
        .then(function (response) {
            $scope.sites = response.data;
        });
})
```

At this point, I will explain what this block of code is doing. We start by simply initializing the variable sites as an array to the $scope. It is a good practice to always initialize your Angular $scope variables before using them. The next thing we try to do is make an Ajax get request using the shorthand $http.get() method. This $http.get method returns a promise so we handle this promise by using the .then() method of promise handling of Angular. In the promise handler function, you can see that we start by setting the data property of the response from the promise (response.data). This data property of the promise response (response.data) is the property that holds any data returned which in our case is the data from our sites.json file.

One thing that might be a bit confusing is the fact that, for the first parameter of the $http.get() function, which takes the URL of the API or the file we want to consume, we have provided the following relative path '/sites.json'. You might be wondering why we have not correctly given a path relative to the controller.js file. This is because when working with Angular, all paths are referenced from the root index.html file. In our case, the sites.json and index.html files are in the same directory under the www directory, which is why we do not have the path '../sites.json', and instead have the path '/sites.json'.

With all this done, we have completed the process of creating our LTA application. All that is left now is to run the application. Go ahead and run this application using the ionic serve technique learned from *Chapter 1, First Look at Ionic*. Make sure you run this command from the root directory of your LTA app project.

If you have done this correctly, you should see a list of our tourist destinations as shown in the following screenshot:

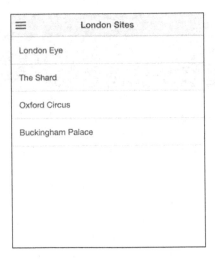

Summary

In this chapter, we learned how to create an Ionic application based on the side menu template. We used this knowledge to create our London Tourist Application. We also had a look at the code that makes up an Ionic side menu template and learned about the building block elements of a side menu application. We rounded up by querying some data via Ajax using the Angular $http service and rendered our tourist destinations.

In the next chapter, we will extend our existing application and use some more complex Ionic components to do some really cool stuff.

Advanced Ionic Components

6

In this chapter, we will extend the application we created in *Chapter 5, The London Tourist App*. We are going to learn how to add some more complex features like the Ionic Popover and the Ionic Modal components to our current application. At the end of this chapter, we will have a popover menu and a modal window as part of our application.

The Ionic Popover

The Ionic Popover component allows us to add a popover menu to our application. A popover menu is a contextual menu that is used to provide a hidden menu or extra menu options. It is normally used when we have limited space and want to present a list of options. Instead of cramming our limited available space, we create some sort of button so that, when clicked, the popover menu can pop up and show these menu items.

The following screenshot shows a good description of what a popover does in reality:

Implementing the popover

We are going to implement our popover in our already existing application. The first thing you should do is open your application, as you have left the London Tourist Application in the previous chapter. What we will be aiming to do is create a popover that has three extra options as a list. These three options are **About**, **Help** and **Logout**. These three options will not perform any action as we will only be placing them for the sake of example. The following screenshots show a sample of what we will be aiming to achieve.

- For iOS:

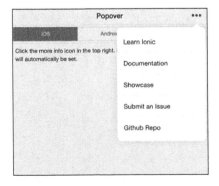

- For Android:

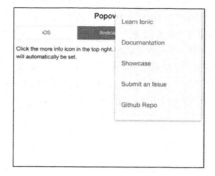

To begin implementing our popover, open the `playlists.html` file of your LTA application project. Remember that this `playlists.html` file can be found by navigating to the `www` folder and looking into the `templates` folder within it. Here is the path: `www/templates/playlists.html`.

Now, you should have a file that closely resembles the following code:

```
<ion-view view-title="London Sites">
  <ion-content>
    <ion-list>
      <ion-item ng-repeat="site in sites">
        {{site.name}}
      </ion-item>
    </ion-list>
  </ion-content>
</ion-view>
```

Adding the menu button

The first thing we are going to do is add the menu button that we want to trigger for our popover. This menu will display the popover when tapped. The following code block represents the code for button icon of our popover:

```
<ion-nav-buttons side="right">
    <button class="button button-clear icon ion-more"></button>
</ion-nav-buttons>
```

You are to replicate the preceding code just after the opening `<ion-view>` tag of your `playlists.html` page. The preceding code is using the `<ion-nav-buttons>` element to specify that we want to place a navigation button in our header. This element also has a `side` attribute with the value `right`. This `side` attribute is there to tell the `<ion-nav-buttons>` element which side of the page title to position itself. Within the `<ion-nav-buttons>` element is a simple button with some ionic styles that ensure that the button has an icon (`ion-more`) as our popover icon. If you have followed all the steps and replicated the code block correctly, your code should closely resemble the following code block:

```
<ion-view view-title="London Sites">

  <ion-nav-buttons side="right">
    <button class="button button-clear icon ion-more"></button>
  </ion-nav-buttons>

  <ion-content>
    <ion-list>
      <ion-item ng-repeat="site in sites">
        {{site.name}}
      </ion-item>
    </ion-list>
  </ion-content>
</ion-view>
```

At the moment, it is probably a good idea to test our application and see how our icon button looks. Fire up your application on a Chrome browser using the `Ionic serve` technique as we have done in the past. Your screen should look close to what we have in the following screenshot.

 If your title is centered to the left when using an Android emulator on Chrome, this is perfectly normal. The iOS equivalent will be centered.

Coding the popover

The next step is to write the actual logic for our popover menu. The first thing we need to do is go into our `controller.js` file. This file can be found by looking in the following path from the root of your project:

```
www/js/controller.js
```

Within the `controller.js` file, locate the `PlaylistsCtrl` controller. It is within this controller that we will be implementing our popover, as it is the controller associated with our `playlists.html`.

Adding the $ionicPopover service

In order to use the Ionic Popover, Ionic has a special service called `$ionicPopover` that makes this very easy. Add `$ionicPopover` as a dependency by specifying it as a parameter on your `PlaylistsCtrl` controller. If you have done this correctly, your `PlaylistsCtrl` controller should now look similar to the following code:

```
.controller('PlaylistsCtrl', function($scope, $http,
$ionicPopover) {
    $scope.sites = [];
    $http.get('/sites.json')
        .then(function (response) {
          $scope.sites = response.data;
        });
})
```

Finishing the popover code

The next step is to write the actual code to create the popover using the `$ionicPopover` service, as shown in the following code:

```
$ionicPopover.fromTemplateUrl('templates/popover.html', {
    scope: $scope
}).then(function(popover) {
    $scope.popover = popover;
});

$scope.openPopover = function($event) {
    $scope.popover.show($event);
};
```

The preceding code block uses the `$ionicPopover` service to instantiate a new popover. We also use the `.fromTemplateUrl` function of `$ionicPopover` to create the popover. This function allows us to pass a URL for a file that contains the HTML for our popover. The `.fromTemplateUrl` function also returns a promise which returns the instance of a popover created. We then bind this popover instance to our scope so that it is available for use in our view. There is, however, one small part that we have not done. We passed in a file path `templates/popover.html` as the file which contains the code for our popover. However, this `popover.html` file does not currently exist so we need to create it.

Creating the popover.html file

To create our `popover.html` file, create a new file called `popover.html` under the `templates` folder. This `templates` folder can be found under the www folder located in the root directory of your project. Here is the path: www/templates/popover.html.

Now that we have created this file, the next step is to populate this file. Remember that what we are trying to achieve is to have a list of menu items in `popover.html`. We want these three options to be **About**, **Help**, and **Logout** to mimic a fake set of popover options.

To start creating the content of our popover, replicate the following code block into your `popover.html`:

```
<ion-popover-view>
    <ion-content>
        <div class="list">
        <b class="item" href="#">
            About
        </b>
        <b class="item" href="#">
```

```
        Help
    </b>
    <b class="item" href="#">
        Logout
    </b>
    </div>
    </ion-content>
</ion-popover-view>
```

If you have done this, you have completed implementing the template of your popover. Now, let's understand what the HTML code we just implemented on our `popover.html` file does. The `<ion-popover-view>` element is an element that is essential for indicating that this particular view is a popover. It also contains an `<ion-content>` element which is a container for all the visible parts of our view, or popover in this case. We then put a `div` tag with a class `list` which is one of the Ionic's built-in classes. Within this `div`, there are three HTML bold tags that represent our three fake options. That is all we need to complete the implementation for our template. The final step is to wire our popover to ensure it works as it should.

Wiring up the popover

This is the final step to get our popover to work. Remember that we created a function on our `PlayListsCtrl` controller called `openPopover()` which takes in a `$event` parameter. This function will initiate the popover when executed. We will also have to pass the `$event` parameter, which is a reserved parameter that represents an event sent from the view.

To put this into action, we will first need to wire this `openPopover()` function to be executed when the popover icon we created earlier is clicked. This popover button is in our `playlists.html` file from earlier steps. Your current `playlists.html` file should look close to what we have in the following code block:

```
<ion-view view-title="London Sites">

  <ion-nav-buttons side="right">
    <button class="button button-clear icon ion-more"></button>
  </ion-nav-buttons>

  <ion-content>
    <ion-list>
      <ion-item ng-repeat="site in sites">
        {{site.name}}
      </ion-item>
    </ion-list>
  </ion-content>
</ion-view>
```

What we need to do is add an Ionic tap event on the popover icon button that we created. We can do this with the Ionic provided attribute directive called `on-tap`. This `on-tap` attribute directive takes in a function which we want to be executed when the containing element is tapped. In our case, we want this function to be the `openPopover` function. Right now our popover Icon button code looks as follows:

```
<ion-nav-buttons side="right">
    <button class="button button-clear icon ion-more"></button>
</ion-nav-buttons>
```

Now, the code for the `on-tap` ionic attribute directive for `<button>` will look as follows:

```
on-tap="openPopover($event)"
```

You can see `$event` being passed as a parameter. Remember that this is very important and must be passed exactly as that. The final code for your `playlists.html` will look like the following code block:

```
<ion-view view-title="London Sites">

  <ion-nav-buttons side="right">
    <button class="button button-clear icon ion-more" on-
      tap="openPopover($event)"></button>
  </ion-nav-buttons>

  <ion-content>
    <ion-list>
      <ion-item ng-repeat="site in sites">
        {{site.name}}
      </ion-item>
    </ion-list>
  </ion-content>
</ion-view>
```

With that done, we have completely finished the implementation of our popover. Now, we can run it in our browser using the `ionic serve` technique to see what it looks like.

If you correctly ran your app using the `ionic serve` technique, you should see something that looks like the following screenshot when you click the popover icon button. The view will be different depending on whether you are testing with an Android or iOS emulator setting:

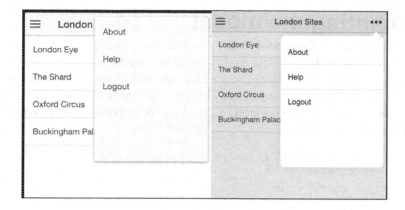

The popover is a great contextual menu tool for fitting extra menu options. It also has an automatic way of displaying a different version depending on what mobile operating system it is being displayed on. Now that we have learned how to use the Ionic Popover, let's learn to use the Ionic Modal.

The Ionic Modal

The Ionic Modal is a component feature that Ionic provides and is used to create a modal window in our application. A modal window is a view that pops up on an existing page without losing the context of your current action. As soon as it is dismissed, the previous view state is restored. It is a great tool for collecting extra information or displaying something on the screen without losing track of our current state.

Creating the modal

Ionic exposes the modal functionality via a service called the $ionicModal service. This service provides us a way of creating a modal in our application. Before we begin implementing our modal, let's understand what we aim to do with the modal feature in our application.

We will still be using our LTA application and adding a modal. We want this modal to mimic a sample **About** page of our application which will have some small details about the app. Remember that we already have a button from the popover we created earlier which has a text labeled as **About**. We will wire this popover item to simply open the modal when tapped.

Implementing the modal

To begin implementing the modal, open your `controller.js` file and locate the `PlaylistsCtrl` controller. The first thing to do is add a dependency to the `$ionicModal` service on the `PlaylistsCtrl` controller. This is done by adding `$ionicModal` as a parameter for the `PlaylistsCtrl` controller function definition. Doing this correctly should make your `PlaylistsCtrl` controller look like what we have in the following code block:

```
.controller('PlaylistsCtrl', function($scope, $http,
$ionicPopover, $ionicModal) {
    $scope.sites = [];
    $http.get('/sites.json')
        .then(function (response) {
          $scope.sites = response.data;
        });

    $ionicPopover.fromTemplateUrl('templates/popover.html', {
      scope: $scope
    }).then(function(popover) {
      $scope.popover = popover;
    });

    $scope.openPopover = function($event) {
      $scope.popover.show($event);
    };
})
```

The next thing we are going to do is write the code for our modal in our `PlaylistsCtrl` controller. The following code represents the code for our modal:

```
$ionicModal.fromTemplateUrl('templates/modal.html', {
        scope: $scope
    }).then(function(modal) {
        $scope.modal = modal;
    });
    $scope.openModal = function() {
        $scope.modal.show();
    };
    $scope.closeModal = function() {
        $scope.modal.hide();
    };
```

Replicate the preceding code into your `PlaylistsCtrl` controller. If you have done this correctly, your code block for the `PlaylistsCtrl` controller should look like the following:

```
.controller('PlaylistsCtrl', function($scope, $http,
$ionicPopover, $ionicModal) {
    $ionicModal.fromTemplateUrl('templates/modal.html', {
        scope: $scope
    }).then(function(modal) {
        $scope.modal = modal;
    });

    $scope.openModal = function() {
        $scope.modal.show();
    };

    $scope.closeModal = function() {
        $scope.modal.hide();
    };

    $scope.sites = [];
    $http.get('/sites.json')
      .then(function (response) {
        $scope.sites = response.data;
      });

    $ionicPopover.fromTemplateUrl('templates/popover.html', {
    scope: $scope
    }).then(function(popover) {
    $scope.popover = popover;
    });

    $scope.openPopover = function($event) {
    $scope.popover.show($event);
    };
})
```

Now, let's understand what the code for the modal is doing. We used the `$ionicModal` service to create a modal via its `.fromTemplateUrl()` method. This method takes two parameters; the first being the path to an HTML file containing the modal, and the second being an `options` object. This `options` object lets us customize the modal and even provides us with ways to customize things like what animation to use. For now, we only specify the scope the modal should use, which in this case is the scope of our controller.

The .fromTemplateUrl method returns a promise with the created modal, which we set to our $scope. The following code is a reflection of the modal creation:

```
$ionicModal.fromTemplateUrl('templates/modal.html', {
        scope: $scope
    }).then(function(modal) {
        $scope.modal = modal;
    });
```

We also have two functions that we created. These functions are .openModal() and .closeModal(). The openModal() function is bound to the $scope, and all it does is use the created modal's .show() method. The .closeModal() function does the opposite by implementing the .hide() method of the created modal. One thing we have not done yet is create the HTML template we passed, which is the modal.html in this case.

Creating the modal.html file

Navigate to your templates folder and create a new HTML file called modal. html. The following code represents the template file for our modal, and you are to replicate this code into your modal.html file:

```
<ion-modal-view>
    <ion-header-bar class="bar bar-header bar-positive">
        <h1 class="title">About The App</h1>
        <button class="button button-clear button-primary" on-
            tap="closeModal()">Cancel</button>
    </ion-header-bar>

    <ion-content class="padding">
        The LTA app is part of the Ionic By Example book written
        by Sani Yusuf.
    </ion-content>
</ion-modal-view>
```

If you look at this code closely, you can see an <ion-modal-view> element as the root element of the code. This <ion-modal-view> element is the root element of any modal template. We can also see that we have an <ion-header-bar> element and this element has a <h1> element used to declare the title of the modal header. There is also a <button> element that has an on-tap attribute that is directed to a closeModal() function which we created earlier.

There is also an <ion-content> element which is used to contain the visible main body of the modal. There is some dummy text to mimic the **About** page of the LTA app, but feel free to add some of your own HTML text. The last step we need to do is wire our popover button to open our modal.

Wiring up the modal

To wire up our modal, remember that we want our **About** popover menu item to open the modal when tapped. To begin, first open the popover.html file of your project. What you have currently is as follows:

```
<ion-popover-view>
    <ion-content>
      <div class="list">
        <b class="item">
            About
        </b>
        <b class="item">
            Help
        </b>
        <b class="item">
            Logout
        </b>
      </div>
    </ion-content>
</ion-popover-view>
```

All we need to do is use the Ionic on-tap attribute on the About entry to reference the openModal() function. Doing this correctly will make our popover code look like the following:

```
<ion-popover-view>
    <ion-content>
        <div class="list">
        <b class="item" on-tap="openModal()">
            About
        </b>
        <b class="item">
            Help
        </b>
        <b class="item">
            Logout
        </b>
    </div>
    </ion-content>
</ion-popover-view>
```

With this done, we have completed the implementation of our modal window. The next thing to do is to go ahead and test this. To do this, run your application using the `Ionic serve` technique. When your app is up and running in the browser, tap the popover icon and the **About** option. This should bring up a modal window like the one shown in the following screenshot:

Summary

In this chapter, we used two very important features of Ionic and learned to create a popover and modal. We still used our LTA application from the previous chapter. The Ionic Popover is a great feature which is used to add extra menu items or provide contextual menu options. We also learned about the Ionic Modal, which is used to provide a view over another view of the app while maintaining the context.

In the next chapter, we will learn to use some of the customization techniques of Ionic, along with how to customize our Ionic app.

7
Customizing the App

In the previous chapter, we dug deeply into some more advanced features of Ionic like the popover and the modal features. In this chapter, we will be focusing on customizing an Ionic application. The Ionic SDK comes by default with some great tools that make it easy to customize your application to fit the design guides of your brand. This is thanks to its built-in integration of Gulp for your build process needs and SCSS for CSS preprocessing.

Ionic also has a special Angular provider called `$ionicConfigProvider`. This provider can be used to do a lot of configuration and customization like specifying what type of animations your application should use or even more advanced stuff like specifying how many cache items you want in your cache. The `$ionicConfigProvider` also lets you specify these configurations on a global level, or on a platform-by-platform basis.

Customizing the look and feel of your app

When you created an Ionic application using one of the Ionic templates, you would have noticed by now that it comes with some built-in default CSS styles. Many times you will want to know how you can add your own colors and styles while keeping some of the built-in Ionic styles.

Ionic styles with SASS

This is well thought out by the Ionic team and for this reason, they actually created all their CSS styles using SCSS. SCSS is an independent technology based on SASS that lets you write CSS in an object-oriented way which then gets compiled into CSS. SCSS is a really cool way to write CSS rules as it allows us to create variables and use them to create our style sheet. If you are completely new to SCSS and you want to see some brief information about SCSS, feel free to visit http://sass-lang.com.

Now, let's have a look at the folder structure of an Ionic project once more with customization of our styles with SCSS in mind.

Ionic SCSS overview

To have an overview of the SCSS structure of Ionic, we are going to create a brand new application using the Ionic blank template. We are going to call this application custom-app. The following is the command to create this new application. Fire up a terminal window on your computer and CD into a directory of your choice and run the following command:

```
ionic start custom-app blank
```

After you have created your new custom-app application, open this new project in your favorite IDE to have an overview of the folder structure. You should see something close to what we have in the following screenshot:

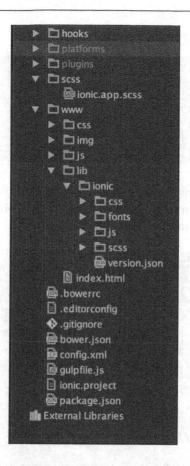

There are two folders that you should pay close attention to. The first folder is the scss folder found in the root directory of the project. This folder has a file called ionic.app.scss within it; we will take a look at this in more detail. The following is a screenshot of what this folder looks like:

The second folder is also titled scss, but this folder can be found by navigating to the following path from the root folder www/lib/ionic/scss.

The following screenshot shows this folder:

Now, if you look even further within this second `scss` folder, you should see something that closely resembles what we have in the following screenshot with a number of SCSS files within the `scss` folder:

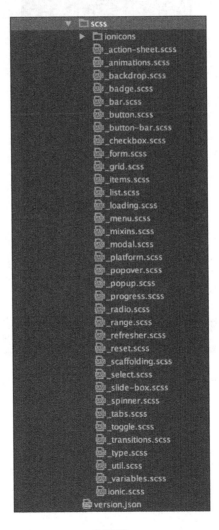

This scss folder contains a numerous amount of files and you might be wondering what these files are for. As a part of this module, you do not need to understand the entire process of what these files are doing, but you need to know that they are the files that contain the SCSS code for every Ionic element. The entire Ionic CSS style sheet is generated by compiling these SCSS files. It is possible to go into these files to make changes to any SCSS file, but this is probably not a good idea, as you will risk breaking any dependencies in the SCSS code. For this reason, Ionic provides a much simpler way to do this thanks to ionic.app.scss that we briefly looked at earlier and will be looking at closely now.

The ionic.app.scss file

The ionic.app.scss file can be found within a directory called scss in the project root directory, as shown in the following screenshot:

This file is the most important file for customizing the styles of your Ionic app. Think of this file as an interface for overriding any SCSS style contained in any of the SCSS files we noted in the www/lib/ionic/scss path. If you look at this ionic.app.scss file currently, it should look like what we have in the following code:

```
/*
To customize the look and feel of Ionic, you can override the
variables in ionic's _variables.scss file.

For example, you might change some of the default colors:

$light:                    #fff !default;
$stable:                   #f8f8f8 !default;
$positive:                 #387ef5 !default;
$calm:                     #11c1f3 !default;
$balanced:                 #33cd5f !default;
$energized:                #ffc900 !default;
$assertive:                #ef473a !default;
$royal:                    #886aea !default;
$dark:                     #444 !default;
*/

// The path for our ionicon's font files, relative to the built CSS in
www/css
```

```
$ionicons-font-path: "../lib/ionic/fonts" !default;


// Include all of Ionic
@import "www/lib/ionic/scss/ionic";
```

From the preceding code, you can even see some comments that tell you how to use the file to override your SCSS styles. Now, before we start learning how to actually override these files, first let's learn how to set up our SCSS for our project.

Setting up SCSS

Before we set up the SCSS, we will first have a brief look at how our CSS is currently integrated. When you create a new Ionic project, the project uses styles from two sources by default.

The first source is the `ionic.css` file which can be found in the path `lib/ionic/css/ionic.css`. This file contains already compiled CSS code for all the Ionic default styles. It is simply a CSS compilation of all the SCSS files found in the `www/lib/ionic/scss/ionic` directory relative to the root directory of your project.

The second source is the `style.css` file found in the `css/style.css` path relative to the root directory of your project. This file is normally empty at the time you create your project and is a place where you can enter your own custom styles in CSS, if you do not want to use SCSS. A look at the `index.html` file as shown in the following screenshot shows how these two files are referenced as CSS style sheets by default:

```
<!DOCTYPE html>
<html>
  <head>
    <meta charset="utf-8">
    <meta name="viewport" content="initial-scale=1, maximum-scale=1, user-scalable=no, width=device-width">
    <title></title>

    <link href="lib/ionic/css/ionic.css" rel="stylesheet">
    <link href="css/style.css" rel="stylesheet">

    <!-- IF using Sass (run gulp sass first), then uncomment below and remove the CSS includes above
    <link href="css/ionic.app.css" rel="stylesheet">
    -->

    <!-- ionic/angularjs js -->
    <script src="lib/ionic/js/ionic.bundle.js"></script>

    <!-- cordova script (this will be a 404 during development) -->
    <script src="cordova.js"></script>

    <!-- your app's js -->
    <script src="js/app.js"></script>
  </head>
  <body ng-app="starter">

    <ion-pane>
      <ion-header-bar class="bar-stable">
        <h1 class="title">Ionic Blank Starter</h1>
      </ion-header-bar>
      <ion-content>
      </ion-content>
    </ion-pane>
  </body>
</html>
```

With this explained, we will go ahead and start setting up SCSS on our Ionic application.

Setting up SCSS can be quite challenging traditionally but Ionic comes built-in with some tools that make it easy. To begin the process of setting up the SCSS of your project, fire up a terminal window and simply navigate into your project's root directory by running the `cd custom-app` command.

The next step is to install `bower` on your computer if you do not already have this installed. You can do so by running the following command:

```
npm install bower -g
```

> You might need to prefix the `sudo` command if you are on a Linux or Mac computer. This will be `sudo npm install bower -g`.

After this, the final step to get SCSS setup is by running the following command:

```
ionic setup sass
```

This command will do all the necessary things behind the scenes that are needed to enable your project to work with SCSS. After this command is complete, you will notice a new folder called the `node-modules` folder in the root of your project. This is completely normal and is the folder that contains the packages necessary for your project to work with SCSS.

By now, we have successfully set up SCSS for our project. The first thing you should look at is your `index.html` file. Your `index.html` should resemble the following code block:

```
<!DOCTYPE html>
<html>
  <head>
    <meta charset="utf-8">
    <meta name="viewport" content="initial-scale=1, maximum-
      scale=1, user-scalable=no, width=device-width">
    <title></title>


    <!-- compiled css output -->
    <link href="css/ionic.app.css" rel="stylesheet">

    <!-- ionic/angularjs js -->
    <script src="lib/ionic/js/ionic.bundle.js"></script>
```

```
   <!-- cordova script (this will be a 404 during development)
   -->
   <script src="cordova.js"></script>

   <!-- your app's js -->
   <script src="js/app.js"></script>
 </head>
 <body ng-app="starter">

   <ion-pane>
     <ion-header-bar class="bar-stable">
       <h1 class="title">Ionic Blank Starter</h1>
     </ion-header-bar>
     <ion-content>
     </ion-content>
   </ion-pane>
 </body>
</html>
```

The first thing you will notice in the header is that the reference to CSS files have changed in comparison to what we briefly discussed earlier. Now, you have only one CSS reference in the <head> part of index.html pointing to css/ionic.app. css. You might be wondering how this happened. Well, basically when you set up SCSS like we have done in this chapter so far, Ionic automatically sets up the SCSS to compile all the SCSS and output them into ionic.app.css.

If you navigate to the www/css path, you will see that we have three files as opposed to one as we saw earlier. You will see an ionic.app.css file and an ionic.app. min.css file. These two files are the same with ionic.app.min.css being a minified version of the ionic.app.css. They are the output of all the SCSS files that we checked out earlier compiled into one file. There are a lot more things that happen behind the scenes to ensure that this SCSS compilation happens, but for the sake of simplicity we won't be going deep into that in this module.

Customizing the SCSS

To begin customizing our app, the first thing you want to do is to run your application using the `ionic serve` technique learned from previous chapters in this module, using the following command:

```
ionic serve
```

This should bring up your application running in the browser and you should see something that closely resembles what we have in the following screenshot:

 Make sure you don't close your terminal or terminate the serve session from here on, in order to follow the instructions that come soon.

Now to explain what we will try to do, first let's have a look at the code for the head of this app. The code block is the code for our app and you can find this in the `index.html` file in the www folder of your project:

```
<!DOCTYPE html>
<html>
  <head>
    <meta charset="utf-8">
    <meta name="viewport" content="initial-scale=1, maximum-
      scale=1, user-scalable=no, width=device-width">
    <title></title>


    <!-- compiled css output -->
    <link href="css/ionic.app.css" rel="stylesheet">

    <!-- ionic/angularjs js -->
    <script src="lib/ionic/js/ionic.bundle.js"></script>
```

```
      <!-- cordova script (this will be a 404 during development)
      -->
      <script src="cordova.js"></script>

      <!-- your app's js -->
      <script src="js/app.js"></script>
    </head>
    <body ng-app="starter">

      <ion-pane>
        <ion-header-bar class="bar-stable">
          <h1 class="title">Ionic Blank Starter</h1>
        </ion-header-bar>
        <ion-content>
        </ion-content>
      </ion-pane>
    </body>
  </html>
```

Pay close attention to the piece of code that represents the main view part of the
preceding code block which is also represented in the following code block:

```
    <ion-pane>
      <ion-header-bar class="bar-stable">
        <h1 class="title">Ionic Blank Starter</h1>
      </ion-header-bar>
      <ion-content>
      </ion-content>
    </ion-pane>
```

If you look at the opening `<ion-header>` tag, you will see that it has a class called
`bar-stable`. This is an in-built class that Ionic comes with which gives the header a
sort of light gray color, as seen from the screenshot we visited earlier.

Let's say we want to customize this header to fit our brand color and let's say, for
example, that our brand color and this brand happens to be my favorite accent of red
which has the hex code of `#D71300`.

Now, you might be tempted to go into the `ionic.app.css` file to look for every
occurrence of this in our CSS style sheet and change it. But remember that this
`ionic.app.css` is generated based on our SCSS files. Ionic gives us a great way to
override default styles with SCSS thanks to the `ionic.app.scss` file which can be
found in the `scss` directory. We looked at this file earlier and we are going to look
at it again:

```
    /*
    To customize the look and feel of Ionic, you can override the
    variables in ionic's _variables.scss file.
```

For example, you might change some of the default colors:

```
$light:                         #fff !default;
$stable:                        #f8f8f8 !default;
$positive:                      #387ef5 !default;
$calm:                          #11c1f3 !default;
$balanced:                      #33cd5f !default;
$energized:                     #ffc900 !default;
$assertive:                     #ef473a !default;
$royal:                         #886aea !default;
$dark:                          #444 !default;
*/

// The path for our ionicons font files, relative to the built CSS
in www/css
$ionicons-font-path: "../lib/ionic/fonts" !default;

// Include all of Ionic
@import "www/lib/ionic/scss/ionic";
```

The preceding code block resembles what you currently have in your `ionic.app.scss` file. To override the color of the header, we will override the current color of the `$stable` variable of our SCSS.

The code for this is as follows:

```
$stable: #D71300;
```

You are supposed to replicate the preceding code anywhere but just before the last line of the following code block:

```
@import "www/lib/ionic/scss/ionic";
```

Now, your final code should resemble the following:

```
/*
To customize the look and feel of Ionic, you can override the
variables in ionic's _variables.scss file.

For example, you might change some of the default colors:

$light:                         #fff !default;
$stable:                        #f8f8f8 !default;
$positive:                      #387ef5 !default;
$calm:                          #11c1f3 !default;
$balanced:                      #33cd5f !default;
$energized:                     #ffc900 !default;
```

```
$assertive:                  #ef473a !default;
$royal:                      #886aea !default;
$dark:                       #444 !default;
*/

$stable: #D71300;

// The path for our ionicons font files, relative to the built CSS
in www/css
$ionicons-font-path: "../lib/ionic/fonts" !default;

// Include all of Ionic
@import "www/lib/ionic/scss/ionic";
```

Once this is done, save the `ionic.app.scss` file. By doing this, you have completed
the process of overriding the app, and your header should now be red. Go back to
your application on the browser or run your app with the `ionic serve` technique if
you don't have it running and you should see something that looks similar to what
we have in the following screenshot:

You can see that header now takes the color of the hex code we provided in the
`ionic.app.scss` file. We can override any default file with this file. All you need to
do is have a glance through the `lib/ionic/scss` folder, identify the SCSS rule you
want to override, and override in `ionic.app.scss`.

With this done, we have completed the process of learning how to override and set
up SCSS of our Ionic app. The next step is to learn about `$ionicConfigProvider`.

$ionicConfigProvider

$ionicConfigProvider is a provider that Ionic exposes and which allows us to do some very powerful configurations. We will not be writing any code for this as it is an advanced feature but you should be well aware of its existence.

Some of the features that $ionicConfigProvider lets you do, include the following:

- Specify the transition type for your app
- Set the maximum cache
- Disable/enable animations
- Enable/enable native scrolling
- Specify tabs positions

These and many more are some of the features that $ionicConfigProvider lets you fiddle with. Remember that this feature is a fairly advanced feature and it is very likely possible to completely design your app without it. Most apps most likely do not use its features but if you find yourself ever needing to use it, you can visit the official documentation for $ionicConfigProvider to see its full potential at http://ionicframework.com/docs/api/provider/$ionicConfigProvider/.

Summary

In this chapter, we learned how to customize our application by setting up SCSS for our Ionic app. We also had a brief look at $ionicConfigProvider and saw some of its wonderful features. In the next chapter, we will get to learn how to create a new type of Ionic app based on the tabs template.

Building a Simple Social App

In this chapter, we are going to focus on learning how to create an Ionic application that has tabs using the Ionic tabs template. We will also have a look at some of the things that make up the tabs template and learn how to add features into it.

The Ionic tabs application

Tabs are a very common menu system in mobile apps. They provide users with a simple yet effective way to create independent views in an app that sort of act like apps within an app.

The preceding screenshot is a view of a sample Ionic tabs application. One great feature that a tabbed menu system provides is the ability to maintain the independent context within each individual tab menu. No matter where you are in the application, you always have the option of switching to another tab at any point. Navigation history is another feature that the tabs menu provides. You are able to navigate to different views within each tab, and you do not lose this navigation history when you switch back and forth between any tab menu. Now that we have some clarity about what the tabs application entails, let's go ahead and create a brand new tab application and look in detail at how it operates.

Creating an Ionic tabs application

Creating an Ionic tabs application is not too different from creating the side menu and blank Ionic applications as we have done in the previous chapters of this module. We are going to create a new Ionic tabs application, and we will call this application tabs-app. To create this new application, fire up a terminal window and run the following command:

```
ionic start tabs-app tabs
```

Using the preceding command, you will create your tabs-app ionic application successfully. The next thing we are going to do is to have an overview of the application we just created. To do this, simply open the tabs-app project in your favorite IDE. You should have a projects folder structure that looks similar to what I have in the following screenshot:

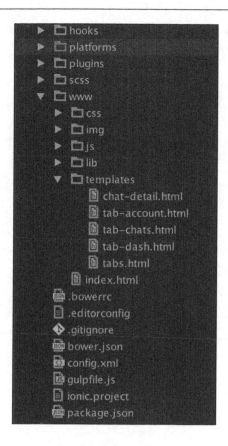

Running the tabs-app application

Now that we have created our app, let's go ahead and see it in action. To do this, fire up a terminal window on your computer and run your application using the `ionic serve` technique.

> Make sure you are within your project's folder by running `cd tabs-app`. To run your app using the `ionic serve` technique, run the `ionic serve` command on your terminal.

You should see an application with three tabs that looks similar to what we have in the following screenshots.

- For iOS:

- For Android:

Overview of the tabs-app application

To begin to understand the life cycle of our `tabs-app` Ionic tabs application, we first need to have a look at the entry module of our application. Our entry module is normally specified within the `index.html` file of our app via the `ng-app` directive.

 The `index.html` file is located in the www directory of your application.

A look through your `index.html` will reveal a file that closely resembles what we have in the following screenshot:

```html
<!DOCTYPE html>
<html>
  <head>
    <meta charset="utf-8">
    <meta name="viewport" content="initial-scale=1, maximum-scale=1, user-scalable=no, width=device-width">
    <title></title>

    <link href="lib/ionic/css/ionic.css" rel="stylesheet">
    <link href="css/style.css" rel="stylesheet">

    <!-- If using Sass (run gulp sass first), then uncomment below and remove the CSS includes above
    <link href="css/ionic.app.css" rel="stylesheet">
    -->

    <!-- ionic/angularjs js -->
    <script src="lib/ionic/js/ionic.bundle.js"></script>

    <!-- cordova script (this will be a 404 during development) -->
    <script src="cordova.js"></script>

    <!-- your app's js -->
    <script src="js/app.js"></script>
    <script src="js/controllers.js"></script>
    <script src="js/services.js"></script>
  </head>
  <body ng-app="starter">
    <!--
      The nav bar that will be updated as we navigate between views.
    -->
    <ion-nav-bar class="bar-stable">
      <ion-nav-back-button>
      </ion-nav-back-button>
    </ion-nav-bar>
    <!--
      The views will be rendered in the <ion-nav-view> directive below
      Templates are in the /templates folder (but you could also
      have templates inline in this html file if you'd like).
    -->
    <ion-nav-view></ion-nav-view>
  </body>
</html>
```

You will see an Angular module called `starter` specified as on the opening `<body>` tag of our page via the `ng-app` directive. This can be seen highlighted in the preceding screenshot. This `starter` module is normally located in our `app.js` file, and we are going to have a look at it to understand the module even more deeply.

 The `app.js` file is located in the `www/js` path of you project.

Open your `app.js` file and pay close attention to the `.config()` function where your routes are configured. Pay close attention to the first route definition of a route called `tab`. This route definition is represented in the following screenshot:

```
.config(function($stateProvider, $urlRouterProvider) {

  // Ionic uses AngularUI Router which uses the concept of states
  // Learn more here: https://github.com/angular-ui/ui-router
  // Set up the various states which the app can be in.
  // Each state's controller can be found in controllers.js
  $stateProvider

  // setup an abstract state for the tabs directive
  .state('tab', {
    url: '/tab',
    abstract: true,
    templateUrl: 'templates/tabs.html'
  })
```

This `tab` state is an abstract state. An **abstract state** in Angular is a state that you cannot directly navigate to but which can contain child states that can be navigated to. This is a great way to create some sort of hierarchy for your states.

Based on the state definition of the tabs as highlighted in the preceding screenshot, you can see that it references `templateUrl` to the `tabs.html` file contained in the `templates/template.html` directory. To understand how Ionic works with tabs, let's explore the `tabs.html` file.

Overview of the tabs.html file

When you open your `tabs.html` file, you will see something that closely resembles what I have in the following screenshot:

```
<ion-tabs class="tabs-icon-top tabs-color-active-positive">

  <!-- Dashboard Tab -->
  <ion-tab title="Status" icon-off="ion-ios-pulse" icon-on="ion-ios-pulse-strong" href="#/tab/dash">
    <ion-nav-view name="tab-dash"></ion-nav-view>
  </ion-tab>

  <!-- Chats Tab -->
  <ion-tab title="Chats" icon-off="ion-ios-chatboxes-outline" icon-on="ion-ios-chatboxes" href="#/tab/chats">
    <ion-nav-view name="tab-chats"></ion-nav-view>
  </ion-tab>

  <!-- Account Tab -->
  <ion-tab title="Account" icon-off="ion-ios-gear-outline" icon-on="ion-ios-gear" href="#/tab/account">
    <ion-nav-view name="tab-account"></ion-nav-view>
  </ion-tab>


</ion-tabs>
```

You will clearly see that the entire markup is wrapped within the `<ion-tabs>` element. This `<ion-tabs>` element is the root element that acts like a container for the tabs that you declare in your Ionic tabs application. You can see that the opening `<ion-tabs>` tag also has a `class` attribute with some built-in Ionic CSS classes provided. This is because the `<ion-tabs>` element is just like every other element and is submissive to some CSS styling.

The <ion-tab> element

Within the `<ion-tabs>` element, you will see three distinct `<ion-tab>` elements. The `<ion-tab>` element is the element used to create a tab and must be a child element of the `<ion-tabs>` element. You will see that each `<ion-tab>` element has some attributes. The `title` attribute is used to specify the title that that particular tab will display. The `icon-on` and `icon-off` are attributes that are used to define what icons get displayed when the tab is in focus and out of focus. Lastly, the `href` attribute is used to provide the path of the route that should be navigated to when that particular tab is selected.

> There are a lot more attributes that are available for different customizations and actions for `<ion-tab>`, and these are all available and duly documented on the official Ionic documentation page.

Within each `<ion-tab>` element, you will find an `<ion-nav-view>` declaration. The `<ion-nav-view>` is an element used to refer to an Angular view. If you pay close attention, you will see that the `<ion-nav-view>` elements have a `name` attribute, which has values. This `name` attribute is used to specify the name of a particular view that is defined in our `app.js` file. If you have another short look at the `app.js` file, as we did previously in this chapter, you will see that some of the states have views defined. A clear demonstration of this is shown in the following screenshot of the `tab.dash` state:

```
.state('tab.dash', {
  url: '/dash',
  views: {
    'tab-dash': {
      templateUrl: 'templates/tab-dash.html',
      controller: 'DashCtrl'
    }
  }
})
```

You can see that there is a `tab-dash` view named within the views object, and this `tab-dash` view has a `templateUrl` definition as well as a `controller` definition similar to a normal state definition. This is how Ionic provides a hierarchy that enables each tab to have a separate `<ion-nav-view>`, where its view is placed. To get an even better understanding of how this tab system works, we will be adding another tab to our application.

Adding tabs to the tabs-app application

We will add one new tab which will contain a feature that will let users post messages like a message board and see that it appears similar to a Facebook wall or a Twitter wall. We will be calling this new tab the `wall` tab. To add this new tab, the first thing we need to do is to add the route for our new tab.

Adding the state for the new tab

To add the state for our new tab, we need to define this tab in our `app.js` file where all our default tab routes are defined. Within the `.config()` function found in your `app.js` file, place the following block of code just after the state definition of the tab abstract state:

```
.state('tab.wall', {
    url: '/wall',
    views: {
      'tab-wall': {
        templateUrl: 'templates/tab-wall.html',
        controller: 'WallController'
      }
    }
})
```

If you have done this correctly, parts of the `.config()` function of your `app.js` file should look something like this:

```
.config(function($stateProvider, $urlRouterProvider) {

    $stateProvider

    // setup an abstract state for the tabs directive
    .state('tab', {
      url: '/tab',
      abstract: true,
      templateUrl: 'templates/tabs.html'
    })

    .state('tab.wall', {
      url: '/wall',
      views: {
        'tab-wall': {
          templateUrl: 'templates/tab-wall.html',
          controller: 'WallController'
        }
      }
    })
    // Each tab has its own nav history stack:

    .state('tab.dash', {
      url: '/dash',
      views: {
        'tab-dash': {
          templateUrl: 'templates/tab-dash.html',
          controller: 'DashCtrl'
        }
      }
    })
```

Let's try to understand what we have just done here. We have created a new state called `tab.wall`, which has a route `/tab`. This means that we are able to navigate to this `tab.wall` state or `/tab` route as part of our Angular application. We have also created a new view called `tab-wall`, and later in this chapter, we will use this `tab-wall` view to reference it as where we want the content of our newly created tab to be displayed.

If you take a closer look at our new state definition, you will see that we referenced a `templateUrl` to a file with the path `templates/tab-wall.html` and a controller, `WallController`, both of which we have not yet created. We will need to create this `tab-wall.html` file and also create the `WallController` controller.

Creating the tab-wall.html file

To create the `tab-wall.html` file correctly, we need to make sure that we create it within the `templates` directory in order for it to match the `templates/tab-wall.html` directory which we passed when declaring our state definition.

Create a file called `tab-wall.html` within your `templates` folder. If you have done this correctly, your `templates` directory should look something like very similar to what we have in the following screenshot:

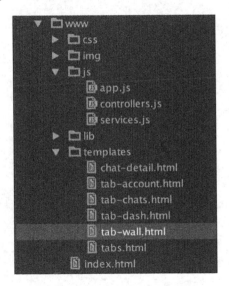

The next step is to actually populate the newly created `tab-wall.html` file. Place the code as shown in the following code block into your `tab-wall.html` file:

```
<ion-view view-title="Wall">
  <ion-content class="padding">

    <div class="list">
      <div class="item item-input-inset">
```

```
      <label class="item-input-wrapper">
        <input type="text" placeholder="enter your message">
      </label>
      <button class="button button-small">
        Post
      </button>
    </div>
  </div>

  <div class="card">
    <div class="item item-text-wrap">
      This Is A Sample Message Post
    </div>
  </div>

  </ion-content>
</ion-view>
```

If you have correctly done this, your `tab-wall.html` should look something like the following screenshot:

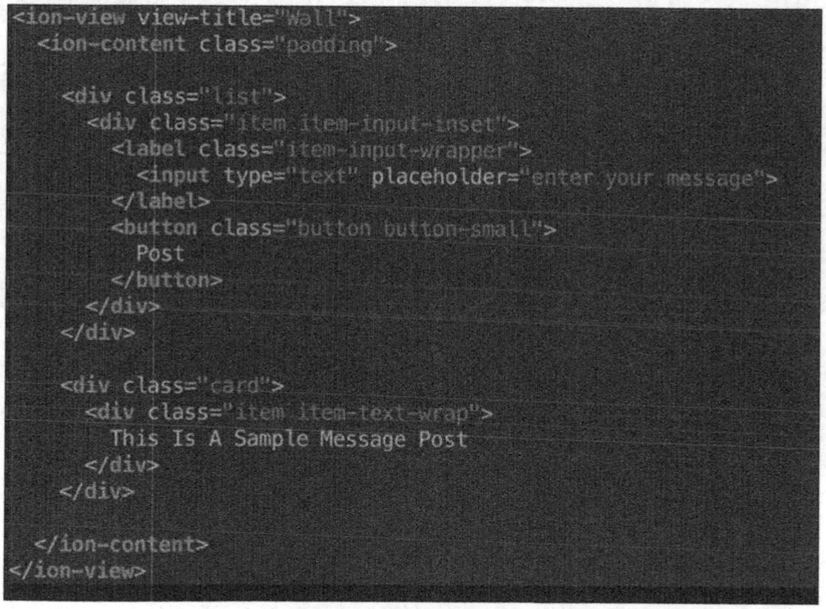

This next step is to create the controller we defined in our state definition.

Creating the WallController controller

To create the `WallController` controller, first we need to open the `controller.js` file. This file can be found within the same folder as our `app.js` file, that is, the JS folder. Your `controller.js` file should closely resemble what we have in the following screenshot:

```javascript
angular.module('starter.controllers', [])

.controller('DashCtrl', function($scope) {})

.controller('ChatsCtrl', function($scope, Chats) {
  // With the new view caching in Ionic, Controllers are only called
  // when they are recreated or on app start, instead of every page change.
  // To listen for when this page is active (for example, to refresh data),
  // listen for the $ionicView.enter event:
  //
  //$scope.$on('$ionicView.enter', function(e) {
  //});

  $scope.chats = Chats.all();
  $scope.remove = function(chat) {
    Chats.remove(chat);
  };
})

.controller('ChatDetailCtrl', function($scope, $stateParams, Chats) {
  $scope.chat = Chats.get($stateParams.chatId);
})

.controller('AccountCtrl', function($scope) {
  $scope.settings = {
    enableFriends: true
  };
});
```

To create the `WallController` file, simply place the code found in the following code block just after the first line where you can find the line of code, `angular.module('starter.controllers', [])`:

```javascript
.controller('WallController', function($scope) {

})
```

If you have correctly replicated this code, your `controller.js` file should closely resemble to the following screenshot:

```javascript
angular.module('starter.controllers', [])

.controller('WallController', function($scope) {

})

.controller('DashCtrl', function($scope) {})

.controller('ChatsCtrl', function($scope, Chats) {
  // With the new view caching in Ionic, Controllers are only called
  // when they are recreated or on app start, instead of every page change.
  // To listen for when this page is active (for example, to refresh data),
  // listen for the $ionicView.enter event:
  //
  //$scope.$on('$ionicView.enter', function(e) {
  //});

  $scope.chats = Chats.all();
  $scope.remove = function(chat) {
    Chats.remove(chat);
  };
})

.controller('ChatDetailCtrl', function($scope, $stateParams, Chats) {
  $scope.chat = Chats.get($stateParams.chatId);
})

.controller('AccountCtrl', function($scope) {
  $scope.settings = {
    enableFriends: true
  };
});
```

By doing this, we have successfully created the `WallController` controller. However, we still have one last step to complete the implementation of our new tab. We need to actually create the tab itself using the `<ion-tab>` element.

Creating the tab

To create our tab, we need to revisit the `tabs.html` file. Within the file, locate the opening `<ion-tabs>` tag and place the code mentioned in the following code block just after that:

```
<!-- Wall Tab -->
  <ion-tab title="Wall" icon-off="ion-ios-compose-outline" icon-
  on="ion-ios-compose" href="#/tab/wall">
    <ion-nav-view name="tab-wall"></ion-nav-view>
  </ion-tab>
```

If you have done this correctly, your `tabs.html` file should look like what is shown in the following screenshot:

By doing this, we have successfully created a new tab in our application. Let's recap what we did to achieve this feat. First, we created a new state definition for our tab and referenced it a controller and template file. We then went ahead to create the tab itself using the `<ion-tab>` element, as in the preceding screenshot.

If you look at the preceding screenshot and pay close attention to `<ion-tab>` that we just replicated from the code block, you will see that its `<ion-nav-view>` child element has a `name` attribute with the value `tab-wall`. This is simply referencing the view we defined while defining our `tab.wall` state in our `app.js` file. These steps complete our tabs implementation.

Now, the next step is to go on and run our app and see it in action. To do this, simply run your application using the `ionic serve` technique.

 To run your app using the `ionic serve` technique, simply run `ionic serve` from the root directory of your `tab-app` application.

If you have done this correctly, you should see something that closely resembles what we have in the following screenshots.

- For iOS:

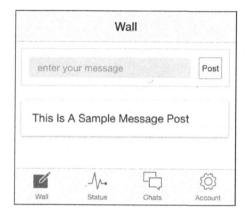

- For Android:

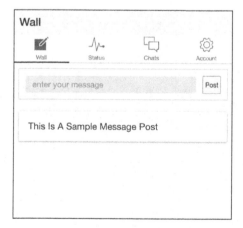

Summary

In this chapter, we learned about the Ionic tabs application template. We also created a tabs application called `tabs-app` and even got as far as adding a new tab of our own. In the next chapter, we will be using this same application to learn how to use Firebase to add backend services to our application.

Connecting to Firebase

9

In this chapter, we are going to focus solely on learning how to use Firebase to integrate a backend with our Ionic application. Firebase is a real-time data store technology that uses JSON-style database structure to let you store your data in the cloud. We will also be using the `tabs-app` app that we created in *Chapter 8, Building a Simple Social App,* to learn to integrate Firebase into our application.

Extending our tabs-app Ionic app

In *Chapter 8, Building a Simple Social App,* we created `tabs-app`. If you recall correctly, we added a new tab called `walls`.

The basic idea we had for the `wall` tab we added was that it would be like a message board where a user could type a post and then tap the button labeled **Post** to see it on the message board, as shown in the following screenshot:

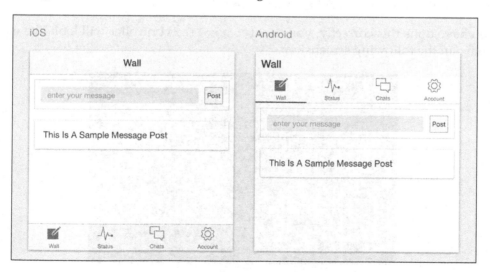

The first thing we need to do is to implement our mechanism to allow users to post, as this does not currently work in our `tab-app` application.

Implementing the post wall feature

To recap what we want from our `wall` tab, we want to be able to enter message in the message box, as seen in the preceding screenshot, and have the message appear like the sample message post. To begin, we start by implementing the code for adding a post in our controller.

This code is provided in the following code block:

```
$scope.post = {
    message : ''
};

$scope.posts = [];

$scope.addPost = function () {
  $scope.posts.unshift($scope.post);

  $scope.post = {
    message: ''
  };
};
```

You will need to replicate the code provided in the preceding block within your `WallController` controller. This `WallController` controller can be found within the `controller.js` file of your `tabs-app` application. The `WallController` controller can be found in the path `www/js/controller.js`.

If you have done this correctly, your `WallController` controller will look like what we have in the following screenshot:

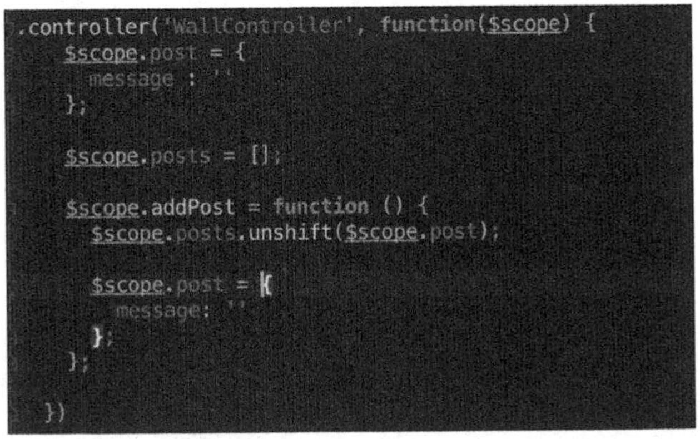

Let's understand what this code is doing. We are simply attaching a post object to the controller. We are also declaring a posts array where all our posts will be stored.

Lastly, we have a function called addPost() which will add a new post to the posts array every time it is fired.

The next step is to wire this controller into the view of our Wall tab. The markup for this view is located in the tab-wall.html file. Now, this file looks like what we have in the following screenshot:

```html
<ion-view view-title="Wall">
  <ion-content class="padding">

    <div class="list">
      <div class="item item-input-inset">
        <label class="item-input-wrapper">
          <input type="text" placeholder="enter your message">
        </label>
        <button class="button button-small">
          Post
        </button>
      </div>
    </div>

    <div class="card">
      <div class="item item-text-wrap">
        This Is A Sample Message Post
      </div>
    </div>

  </ion-content>
</ion-view>
```

You will need to completely replace the markup found within `<ion-content>` with the markup provided in the following code block:

```html
<div class="list">
    <div class="item item-input-inset">
      <label class="item-input-wrapper">
        <input type="text" placeholder="enter your message"
        ng-model="post.message">
      </label>
      <button class="button button-small" on-tap="addPost()">
        Post
      </button>
    </div>
</div>

<div class="card" ng-repeat="post in posts">
  <div class="item item-text-wrap">
```

```
        {{post.message}}
    </div>
</div>
```

If you have done this correctly, your `tab-wall.html` file will have a markup that looks like the following screenshot:

```
<ion-view view-title="Wall">
  <ion-content class="padding">

    <div class="list">
      <div class="item item-input-inset">
        <label class="item-input-wrapper">
          <input type="text" placeholder="enter your message" ng-model="post.message">
        </label>
        <button class="button button-small" on-tap="addPost()">
          Post
        </button>
      </div>
    </div>

    <div class="card" ng-repeat="post in posts">
      <div class="item item-text-wrap">
        {{post.message}}
      </div>
    </div>

  </ion-content>
</ion-view>
```

By doing this, we have completed the process of implementing and wiring our wall post feature on the `Wall` tab. The next step is to test it using the `ionic serve` technique. Go ahead and run your app using the `ionic serve` technique and you should see your app running in the browser.

If you try to add a message in the text box found in the `Wall` tab and click the **Post** button, you will see a message appear, like what we have in the following screenshot:

The backend challenge

The one problem or challenge we have with our current application is that it does not persist. By this, we mean that once we refresh the browser, all our data is gone and we have to start again. How cool would it be if we could enter a post and when we revisited our app, we could carry on from where we left off just like every other message board in other applications? Well, we can achieve this thanks to a great technology called Firebase. The first thing we will do is try to understand Firebase and what exactly it is.

Firebase

Before we begin this chapter, it is very important that we understand the technology we are going to be using to integrate our backend. The technology in question is called Firebase. Firebase is a technology that lets us store real-time data. Unlike traditional backend databases where you need a server running, you do not need to have a hosted server with Firebase.

All you need to get going with Firebase is an active Google account and you are good to go. Let's set up a new Firebase account.

If you do not have a Google account, you can create one by visiting http://www.gmail.com.

Setting up a new Firebase account

The first thing you need to do to set up your Firebase account is go to the Firebase website, which is http://www.firebase.com.

You should see a screen that looks like what we have in the following screenshot:

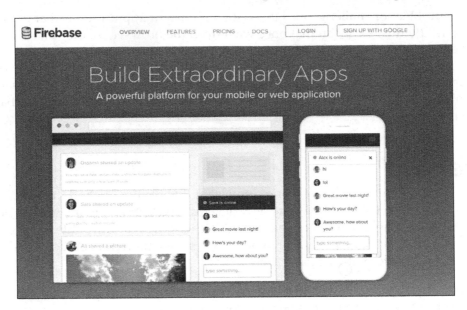

Once this is done, you should see a button labeled **Sign Up With Google** on the top right-hand corner.

When you click this button, you should see a Gmail window asking you to select or log in to a Google account. After you select the Google account you want to use, you should be redirected to your brand new Firebase account. The window you will be redirected to should look like what we have in the following screenshot:

All the examples we have here are based on our sample account. You should not use the URLs from the preceding screenshot but instead use the ones you see in your own window. If you do not, your sample will not work.

You will see that there is a Firebase app created for you called **MY FIRST APP**. When using Firebase, for each app we create we also create an app for it on our Firebase dashboard. This is because Firebase uses a distinct URL to provide you access to the data of each unique application you create. So, think of this **MY FIRST APP** Firebase app as a database.

Now, let's take a closer look at **MY FIRST APP**:

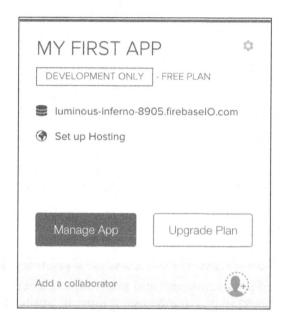

You should see something very similar to the preceding screenshot. You can access the URL for your Firebase database by clicking on the post fixed with the `.firebaseIO.com` URL. Remember that the URL you see on the screenshots will be different from the ones you see on your dashboard, and you are to use the ones on your dashboard.

You can see that the URL we have here for demonstration is `luminous-inferno-8905.firebaseIO.com`.

Click the URL you have on your dashboard and that should take you to your
Firebase database, which should look similar to the following screenshot:

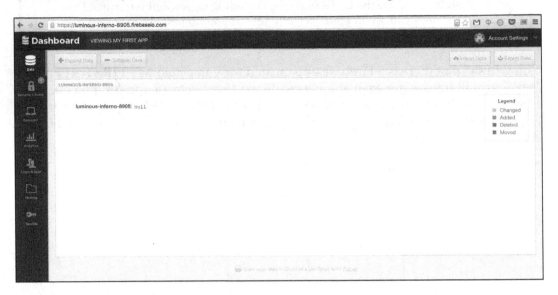

Just to clarify once again, Firebase uses URLs to access databases. What you see in
the preceding screenshot is the dashboard for your database. You can also see the
same database URL in the browser's address bar. Firebase uses JSON-style data
structure, so basically what we send to it is JSON, and what we store is JSON too.

When we add data to our database, we will be able to see it in this dashboard.

Integrate Firebase into tabs-app application

Now that we have our Firebase account and know how to get the URL of our
Firebase database, the next step is to integrate it into our application.

Adding Firebase and Angular-Fire scripts

The first thing we need to do is to add the scripts we will need. We will need two
scripts. The first is the Firebase library. The second script is the Angular-Fire library.
Angular-Fire is an Angular library that makes working with Firebase in an AngularJS
application much simpler.

The simplest way is to use the hosted library references. To add this to our app, open your `index.html` file and add the following script references within `<head>` of your application:

```
<!-- Firebase -->
<script src="https://cdn.firebase.com/js/client/2.2.4/firebase.js"></script>
<!-- AngularFire -->
<script
src="https://cdn.firebase.com/libs/angularfire/1.1.3/
angularfire.min.js"></script>
```

If you have done this correctly, the `head` part of your `index.html` should look like the following screenshot:

```
<head>
    <meta charset="utf-8">
    <meta name="viewport" content="initial-scale=1, maximum-scale=1, user-scalable=no, width=device-width">
    <title></title>

    <link href="lib/ionic/css/ionic.css" rel="stylesheet">
    <link href="css/style.css" rel="stylesheet">

    <!-- IF using Sass (run gulp sass first), then uncomment below and remove the CSS includes above
    <link href="css/ionic.app.css" rel="stylesheet">
    -->

    <!-- Firebase -->
    <script src="https://cdn.firebase.com/js/client/2.2.4/firebase.js"></script>
    <!-- AngularFire -->
    <script src="https://cdn.firebase.com/libs/angularfire/1.1.3/angularfire.min.js"></script>
    <!-- ionic/angularjs js -->
    <script src="lib/ionic/js/ionic.bundle.js"></script>

    <!-- cordova script (this will be a 404 during development) -->
    <script src="cordova.js"></script>

    <!-- your app's js -->
    <script src="js/app.js"></script>
    <script src="js/controllers.js"></script>
    <script src="js/services.js"></script>
</head>
```

 Make sure your references are below the Ionic bundle as seen in the preceding screenshot. This is very important or else your app will not work properly.

The next step is to reference your Angular-Fire module. This step will ensure that we can use Angular-Fire within our application. The name of this module is `firebase`. This will be added to the root module of your application, called `starter` in your `app.js` file.

Currently, this module's declaration looks something like what we have in the following screenshot:

```
angular.module('starter', ['ionic', 'starter.controllers', 'starter.services'])
```

You will need to add the `firebase` module as a dependent module. Doing this will make the module declaration to look something like what we have in the following screenshot:

```
angular.module('starter', ['ionic', 'starter.controllers', 'starter.services', 'firebase'])
```

You can see that the `firebase` module is now added to the module declaration as a dependency. By doing this, we have successfully integrated Firebase into the skin of our app. The next step is to actually implement it to save our data.

Implementing Firebase to our app

To implement Firebase in our app, we will need to do some work within our `WallController` controller. The first thing we need to code for is the ability to pull items from the database. The second thing we need to code for is the ability to add items to the database.

Pulling from database

The first thing we need to do is to add the `$firebaseArray` service dependency into our `WallController` controller. This service is part of the Angular-Fire library and makes it easy for us to work with arrays in Firebase.

Adding the service dependency correctly should make your `WallController` controller definition look like what we have in the following screenshot:

```
.controller('WallController', function($scope, $firebaseArray) {
```

The next step is to actually write code to pull the data from the database. Replicate the code provided in the following code block in your `WallController` controller:

```
var postsDatabaseRef = new Firebase("https://<YOUR-
FIREBASE-APP>.firebaseio.com").child('posts');
var postsData = $firebaseArray(postsDatabaseRef);
```

This piece of code creates a new Firebase reference at first. We passed in the URL of the Firebase database that we created earlier. Make sure you change the placeholder text (YOUR-FIREBASE-APP) to reflect the URL of your Firebase database.

After this, we used the $firebase service that we added earlier to create a path called postData. The last step we need to do is to allow our app to load data from this postData path and use it. To do this, we need to edit the code of our WallController slightly. Currently, our WallController controller's code looks like what we have in the following screenshot:

```
.controller('WallController', function($scope, $firebaseArray) {
    var postsDatabaseRef = new Firebase("https://<YOUR-FIREBASE-APP>.firebaseio.com");
    var postsData = $firebaseArray(postsDatabaseRef).child('posts');

    $scope.post = {
        message : ''
    };

    $scope.posts = [];

    $scope.addPost = function () {
        $scope.posts.unshift($scope.post);

        $scope.post = {
            message: ''
        };
    };
})
```

Pay close attention to the piece of code highlighted in the preceding screenshot. We need to edit this piece of code such that instead of equating to an empty array, it should equate to our postData variable. Doing this correctly should make us end up with a WallController controller that looks like the following screenshot:

```
.controller('WallController', function($scope, $firebaseArray) {
    var postsDatabaseRef = new Firebase("https://<YOUR-FIREBASE-APP>.firebaseio.com");
    var postsData = $firebaseArray(postsDatabaseRef).child('posts');

    $scope.post = {
        message : ''
    };

    $scope.posts = postsData;

    $scope.addPost = function () {
        $scope.posts.unshift($scope.post);

        $scope.post = {
            message: ''
        };
    };
})
```

By doing this, we have implemented the first part; our Firebase implementation and our app now loads data from our database. The next step is to implement the code to add our posts to our database.

Adding to database

Adding to the database is actually pretty easy. All we need to do is slightly edit our `addPost()` function. Currently, our `addPost()` function looks like what we have in the following screenshot:

```
$scope.addPost = function () {
    $scope.posts.unshift($scope.post);

    $scope.post = {
        message: ''
    };
};
```

To make our data persist in our database, we only need to replace the code highlighted in the preceding screenshot with the following code block:

```
$scope.posts.$add($scope.post);
```

Now, your `addPost()` function should look like what we have in the following screenshot:

```
$scope.addPost = function () {
    $scope.posts.$add($scope.post);

    $scope.post = {
        message: ''
    };
};
```

All we did was just change the `unshift()` method to the `$add()` method. The `$add()` method is a method from Firebase that adds items to a Firebase database. At this point, we have completed the implementation of our backend. As easy as that was, we have a working database in just a few short steps and can now test this live. Your final `WallController` controller should look like the following code block:

```
.controller('WallController', function($scope, $firebaseArray) {
    var postsDatabaseRef = new Firebase("https://<YOUR-FIREBASE-
    APP>.firebaseio.com").child('posts');
    var postsData = $firebaseArray(postsDatabaseRef);

    $scope.post = {
```

```
      message : ''
   };

   $scope.posts = postsData;

   $scope.addPost = function () {
     $scope.posts.$add($scope.post);

     $scope.post = {
       message: ''
     };
   };

 })
```

To test your application, simply run your app using the `ionic serve` technique. When you do this, you should be able to enter messages in your application, and even after you refresh your browser, the data that you have already posted will still exist. Also, if you have a look at the Firebase dashboard for your database, you will see that the data you entered in the app is present there.

Summary

In this chapter, we learned some really cool ways of using Firebase to easily add a backend to our Ionic app. We only touched upon what Firebase lets us do, and you can look at the Firebase documentation available at `https://www.firebase.com/docs/` to see the full features of Firebase.

At this point, we have almost come to the end of our module. The next chapter will be the final one, and it is one you should definitely read. It contains some very useful information on how to harness skills learned in this module to get even better at using Ionic.

10
Roundup

In this chapter, we are going to have an overview of the important things that we haven't covered yet about Ionic and which you might find very useful. You will also learn some useful tips about Ionic and discover some great tips about how to make even better use of Ionic to develop great apps.

Uncovered features of Ionic

Although we covered many great topics in this module, there are a lot of great features that we did not cover as they were beyond the scope of this module. We mostly focused on the core features of Ionic, such as how to get Ionic set up. We then learned to create Ionic apps using the blank, side menu, and tabs templates. We also learned to test our Ionic application using the Chrome browser via the `ionic serve` technique.

In this section of the module, I will name a couple of things that will be useful for you to get to grips with in order to become better at Ionic.

Appcamp.IO

`Appcamp.IO` is a free website created by some of the Ionic staff. It is a place where you can go and learn some tips and tricks that will sharpen your Ionic development skills.

The content on `Appcamp.IO` is great for beginners, and it is in some ways in line with the philosophy of this module.

The Ionic documentation

The Ionic documentation page is pretty much the Bible for everything on Ionic. Ionic is very well documented and any feature you want to use is provided there with the sample code and how to use it. You can access the Ionic documentation at `http://www.ionicframework.com/docs`:

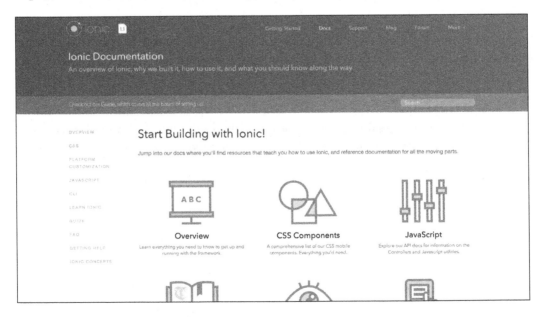

The Ionic creator

This is the drag-and-drop tool built by Ionic for people who want to design their first app or people with limited coding skills. Its greatest feature is that anything you design by dragging and dropping Ionic elements can be tested in the browser, and the code can be extracted as a ready-to-go application. This is great news for designers who don't know how to code as they can quickly use the visual drag-and-drop features of the Ionic creator to design their apps and pass on the code to seasoned developers. You can visit the Ionic creator website at `https://creator.ionic.io`.

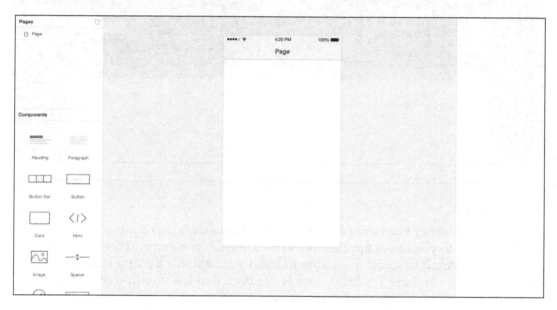

The Ionic code pen

Sometimes, even after you have visited the documentation for some component of Ionic, you will still want to see a real code sample. Or maybe you want to try to reproduce a bug to show others. This is where the Ionic code pen site shines. It is a place where you can find some really great implementations of different features with the code available for you to learn from. It is also the best way to showcase a bug to people who can see it and help you resolve any issues.

You can visit the Ionic code pen website at `http://codepen.io/ionic`.

Ionic.IO

The Ionic.IO platform is a complete suite of premium tools that enable you to add great services to your Ionic application. With Ionic.IO, you can add things like **Push Notification**, **Analytics**, and the ability to build your app for the app store in the cloud. There is also Ionic deploy, which is a feature that lets you update your app live without resubmitting it to the app store.

At the time of writing this module, the Ionic.IO tools were all in beta, and although they were free at the time of writing, Ionic has announced that they will be paid services in future. This is something that you should closely follow as you might find yourself needing to use some of the services provided by the Ionic.IO platform.

You can visit the Ionic.IO platform at `http://www.ionic.io`.

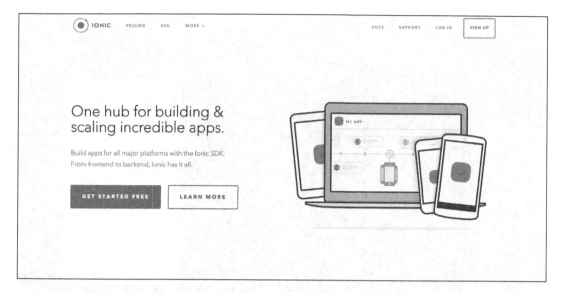

The Ionic playground

The Ionic playground is a very new and useful tool to quickly bootstrap an idea. It is a great way to simply spin off code and have it show you the results right there in the browser. I personally see this tool as very useful in the educational world as it makes it easy to create Ionic applications with only a browser.

If you find yourself needing to showcase/demo something quickly without any setup, and have a computer close-by, then make sure you give the Ionic playground a try.

You can visit the Ionic playground at `http://play.ionic.io/`.

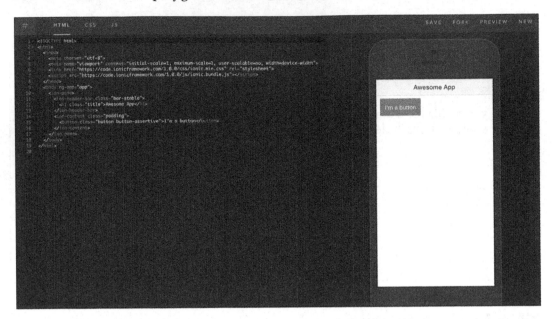

The Ionic community

One of the chief reasons Ionic is very successful is the fact that it has a strong active community. From social media and meetup groups to open source activists, Ionic has a wide range of support from people around the world. This means that if you do run into problems of any sort, you are never too far from help. With that in mind, here are some great links to community elements that you might want to keep an eye on:

- **The Ionic forum**: The Ionic forum really is a great place to voice your troubles or find solutions to shared problems. There are multiple active members and users who also get motivational badges for contributing to the forum by commenting and helping others find solutions. You can access this forum at `http://forum.ionicframework.com`.

- **The Ionic Slack channel**: This channel has over 4000 people active on it 24/7 and in multiple countries. It is a great place to meet people, find work, look for help, employ someone, or just simply express yourself. To join the Ionic Slack channel, simply request an invitation for free at `http://ionicworldwide.herokuapp.com`.

- **Twitter**: Twitter is the most vibrant social medium when it comes to finding the latest and greatest thing about Ionic. If you use Twitter, you can follow `@ionicframework` for more information and updates.

- **The Ionic blog**: Ionic writes blog posts very actively about various topics relating to using Ionic. Some of these posts could be about critical updates, inspirational stories, or even announcements of new products or features. You can find the Ionic blog at `http://blog.ionic.io`.

- **Ionic meetup groups**: Around the world, there are hundreds of meetup groups autonomously hosting events and meetups. This is a community effort by local people to grow Ionic awareness in their locality, and you are almost guaranteed to have one in your nearby city. If you do not have one, feel free to start your own local meetup. You can find a list of all meetups at `http://blog.ionic.io/ionic-worldwide`.

The community around Ionic is pretty much the main reason why it grew so rapidly, and you should be sure to trust the community for any needs. As a note, make sure to use the skills you have learned from this module to really strive and improve your Ionic skills and build some great mobile applications. Remember that nothing is too simple to be great and nothing is too great to be too difficult to build.

Useful resources

The following are some useful links to some sites and resources that will aid you further in your quest to learn more about Ionic:

- **The Ionic framework**: `http://www.ionicframework.com`
- **The Ionic GitHub**: `http://www.github.com/driftyco/ionic`
- **AngularJS**: `http://www.angularjs.org`
- **Ionic stack overflow**: `http://stackoverflow.com/questions/tagged/ionic-framework`
- **Firebase**: `http://www.firebase.com`
- **NodeJS**: `http://www.nodejs.org`
- **Bower**: `http://www.bower.io`
- **Gulp**: `http://www.gulpjs.com`
- **Cordova**: `https://cordova.apache.org`
- **Ionic market**: `https://market.ionic.io`
- **ngCordova**: `http://ngcordova.com`
- **Ionic jobs**: `http://jobs.ionic.io`
- **Ionic showcase**: `http://showcase.ionicframework.com`
- **Ionic lab**: `http://lab.ionic.io`

Summary

This chapter was a roundup of Ionic and all its features. I hope you will now know how to build rich features for your mobile applications and have them possess native-like features with the help of Ionic.

Bibliography

This Learning Path is a blend of content, all packaged up keeping your journey in mind. It includes content from the following Packt products:

- *JavaScript Mobile Application Development, Hazem Saleh*
- *Getting Started with React Native, Ethan Holmes and Tom Bray*
- *Ionic Framework By Example, Sani Yusuf*

Index

H

handlePlayError(error) method 155
handlePlaySuccess() method 155
handleRecordError(error) method 154
handleRecordSuccess(filePath) method 154
handleRecordSuccess function 45
heading object
    headingAccuracy attribute 111
    magneticHeading attribute 111
    timestamp attribute 111
    trueHeading attribute 111
hooks directory, Sound Recorder 30
HTML page, accelerometer plugin 91
hybrid applications
    about 449, 450
    issues 450, 451
hybrid mobile application
    comparing, with mobile web and native
        mobile applications 5-7
HyperText Markup Language (HTML) 3

I

Image Component 426, 427
images
    deleting 427
    viewing 425, 426
InAppBrowser API 21
InAppBrowserManager
    about 145
    closeWindow(windowRef) method 146
    openWindow(url) method 145
    window.open() method 146
InAppBrowser plugin, Cordova Exhibition
    app
    about 141
    API 144
    demo 142
    HTML page 143
    view controller 143, 144
index.html file, weather application 229
index.html page, www directory 30, 31
initialize() method 31
initPage() method 154
input box, Bucket-List app
    array, creating for Bucket-List items 490

code, implementing for Add button 490
controller, creating 488, 489
Delete button, implementing 491
model, creating 489
text, entering into 488
Integrated Development
    Environment (IDE) 7
Ionic
    about 451
    features 452, 571
    history 451
    jobs, URL 578
    lab,URL 578
    resources 577
    setting up 456, 457
    showcase, URL 578
    stack overflow, URL 577
Ionic application
    blank template 459
    creating 459, 460
    customizing 527
    side menu template 459
    tabs template 459
    to-do list app, creating 460
ionic.app.scss file 531, 532
Ionic CLI
    about 455, 456
    features 455
    installing 456, 457
Ionic community
    about 576
    Ionic blog 577
    Ionic forum 576
    meetup groups 577
    Twitter 576
Ionic creator
    about 573
    URL 573
ionic folder, Ionic workflow
    css folder 461
    fonts folder 461
    js folder 462
    scss folder 462
Ionic forum
    URL 576
Ionic framework
    URL 577

navigator.camera.getPicture() function
  cameraError parameter 101
  cameraOptions parameter 101
  cameraSuccess parameter 101
navigator.camera.getPicture() method
  captureSuccess parameter 271
  capturingCallback.captureError
    parameter 271
navigator.camera object
  navigator.camera.cleanup(cameraSuccess,
    cameraError) method 104
Navigator component 332-334
navigator.contacts.find() method
  about 123
  contactError parameter 123
  contactFields parameter 123
  contactFindOptions parameter 123
  contactSuccess parameter 123
navigator.geolocation.getCurrentPosition()
  method
  about 134
  geolocationError parameter 134
  geolocationOptions parameter 134
  geolocationSuccess parameter 134
navigator.globalization.getLocaleName()
  method
  about 140
  errorCallback parameter 140
  successCallback parameter 140
navigator.globalization method
  reference link 141
Navigator.NavigationBar 334-339
ngCordova
  URL 578
Node.js
  installing 456
  URL 456, 577
Node.js v4+ 320
node package manager (npm)
  about 26
  URL 421
Node Version Manager (NVM)
  URL 245
NoteList component 375
NoteLocationScreen 406, 407

notes
  creating 393
  deleting 395-398
  images, adding 415, 417
NoteScreen
  about 340-342
  CameraScreen and ImageScreen,
    navigating via 429-432
  styling 366-370
Notification API 21
NotificationManager
  about 171
  beep(times) method 172
  showAlert() method 171
  showConfirm() method 171
  showPrompt() method 172
  vibrate(milliseconds) method 172
notification plugin
  about 165
  API 170
  demo 166
  HTML page 167
  view controller 167-169

O

onDeviceReady() method 32
OpenWeatherMap
  URL 236
openWindow(url) method
  about 145
  options parameter 145
  target parameter 145
  url parameter 145
options attributes, captureAudio() method
  duration 161
  limit 161

P

PhantomJS
  URL 253
platforms directory, Sound Recorder 29
playground, Ionic
  about 575
  URL 575

Thank you for buying

Mobile Application Development: JavaScript Frameworks

About Packt Publishing

Packt, pronounced 'packed', published its first book, *Mastering phpMyAdmin for Effective MySQL Management*, in April 2004, and subsequently continued to specialize in publishing highly focused books on specific technologies and solutions.

Our books and publications share the experiences of your fellow IT professionals in adapting and customizing today's systems, applications, and frameworks. Our solution-based books give you the knowledge and power to customize the software and technologies you're using to get the job done. Packt books are more specific and less general than the IT books you have seen in the past. Our unique business model allows us to bring you more focused information, giving you more of what you need to know, and less of what you don't.

Packt is a modern yet unique publishing company that focuses on producing quality, cutting-edge books for communities of developers, administrators, and newbies alike. For more information, please visit our website at www.packtpub.com.

Writing for Packt

We welcome all inquiries from people who are interested in authoring. Book proposals should be sent to author@packtpub.com. If your book idea is still at an early stage and you would like to discuss it first before writing a formal book proposal, then please contact us; one of our commissioning editors will get in touch with you.

We're not just looking for published authors; if you have strong technical skills but no writing experience, our experienced editors can help you develop a writing career, or simply get some additional reward for your expertise.

Please check www.PacktPub.com for information on our titles

CPSIA information can be obtained
at www.ICGtesting.com
Printed in the USA
LVOW04s2045301117
558160LV00004B/314/P